D1475728

working WORDS

A BUSINESS-BASED READER

WENDY WILSON

Fanshawe College

THOMSON

NELSON

Australia   Canada   Mexico   Singapore   Spain   United Kingdom   United States

Working Words: A Business-Based Reader
First Edition
Wendy Wilson

Editorial Director and Publisher:
Evelyn Veitch

Acquisitions Editor:
Anne Williams

Marketing Manager:
Cara Yarzab

Developmental Editor:
Klaus Unger

Production Editor:
Carrie Withers

Senior Production Coordinator:
Hedy Sellers

Copy Editor and Proofreader:
Nick Gamble

Creative Director:
Angela Cluer

Interior Design:
Allan Moon

Interior Design Modifications:
Peter Papayanakis

Cover Design:
Ken Phipps

Cover Image:
©Jon Feingersh/ Corbis/ Magma

Compositor:
Doris Chan

Printer:
Transcontinental

COPYRIGHT © 2003 by Nelson Thomson Learning, a division of Thomson Canada Limited. Nelson Thomson Learning is a registered trademark used herein under license.

Printed and bound in Canada
1 2 3 4 05 04 03 02

For more information contact Nelson,1120 Birchmount Road, Scarborough, Ontario, M1K 5G4.
Or you can visit our internet site at
http//www.nelson.com

ALL RIGHTS RESERVED. No part of this work covered by the copyright hereon may be reproduced, transcribed, or used in any form or by any means—graphic, electronic, or mechanical, including photocopying, recording, taping, web distribution or information storage or retrieval systems—without the written permission of the publisher.

For permission to use material from this text or product, contact us by
Tel 1-100-730-2214
Fax 1-800-730-2215
www.thomsonrights.com

Every effort has been made to trace ownership of all copyrighted material and to secure permission from copyright holders. In the event of any question arising as to the use of any material, we will be pleased to make the necessary corrections in future printings.

National Library of Canada Cataloguing in Publication Data

Wilson, Wendy, 1946-
    Working words: a business-based reader/Wendy Wilson— 1st ed.

ISBN 0-17-622445-9

1. Business Writing.
2. Journalism, Commercial.
3. Readers—Business.
4. Readers—Canada— Economic Conditions I. Title.

HF5718.3.W54   2002
808'.06607   C2002-903428-0

CONTENTS

Part One: On Writing

Part Two: The Readings

Part Three: Research and Documentation

PREFACE

Almost all of the forty-two articles in this reader were written by Canadians and published in Canadian newspapers or magazines. Of the three exceptions, one—"The Tyranny of the Brands" by Naomi Klein—was written by a Canadian and was used because it gives a taste of her best-selling book *No Logo*. The second exception—"Distilled Wisdom: Buddy Can You Paradigm?" by Brian Dumayne—was chosen because it is such an excellent summary of the trends in business management theories of the last fifty years and saved me from filling the management section with dry articles on the topic. Finally, the third exception, Bruce Sterling's "Will Cybercriminals Run the World," was selected simply because I liked it. Sterling's only connection to Canada is the fact that he has written a book with Canadian William Gibson.

Although the book is aimed primarily at business students taking English courses at college, it will interest many other students. Readings include such student-friendly topics as the operation of a sports franchise, the story of a student attempt to start a union at a fast-food chain, the purchasing power of teenagers, and the setting up of a gambling casino in South America. Other readings cover such important issues as business ethics, corporate social responsibility, globalization, the fair trade movement, free trade, native fishing rights, corporate branding and business and the environment.

Each article is followed by a section that clarifies potentially unfamiliar words or terms used by the writer. My personal favourite discovery was the original meaning of "basket case." Did you know that this expression was used in the First World War to describe a soldier who had had all his limbs blown off? Now, it's a popular name for gift-basket stores and flower shops.

Suggestions for discussion and written assignments are covered in the "Talking Points" section; a "Writing that Works" section indicates effective writing techniques; and a "Web Research" section gives the addresses of useful Web sites.

Space limitations meant that clarification of every slightly unusual word was not possible. For the same reason, there are fewer assignments than most English teachers would like. However, both these issues are addressed in the Instructor's Manual, available separately from the publisher.

Note

Web links have an annoying habit of disappearing just when you need them. To help combat this problem, I have created a Web site at *www.workingwords.ca* where I will update links from the text and add new links as I find them. Students and teachers are welcome to contact me through this Web site with suggestions.

Acknowledgements

Faculty from several colleges reviewed the text of this reader as I worked on it. I would like to thank Janet M. Bargh, Denise Blay, Paul Burkhart, Jana Davis, Barry McKinnon, Marion Ross and Mark Rust for their invaluable feedback. I incorporated many of their suggestions and cut any readings that were universally disliked. In addition to the reviewers, I would like to thank very much my good friend Susan Braley for her support and enthusiasm throughout the project. You helped make it a reality, Susan. Acquisitions Editor Anne Williams and Developmental Editor Klaus Unger were a pleasure to work with, as were Carrie Withers, the Production Editor, and Nick Gamble, the Copy Editor. Thanks to Natalie Barrington for all her hard work in obtaining permissions from the various writers.

Part One: On Writing

STRUCTURAL TECHNIQUES

Written work must have a structure that allows the reader to follow where the writer is heading. There are many ways to structure a piece of work, some of which are more appropriate to particular types of writing than to others. For example, process and instructional writing have certain structural requirements, as does writing that uses comparison, classification cause and effect to get its message across. Although these various rhetorical strategies cannot be covered in detail here, we present some pointers to help you as you write various kinds of essays and reports.

Thesis Statement

A thesis statement announces the writer's position on an issue and limits the topic to be discussed. A good, detailed thesis statement can outline the entire essay or article, or it can point to the direction of the entire work. Often, a thesis statement is introduced with a lead-in story or example, or is followed by a blueprint or map of the essay. Below are three examples seen in this reader.

Detailed Thesis Statement

This thesis statement gives an overview of the entire article.

> Organizations and individual managers at all levels must understand the natural emotional response to downsizing and learn to manage this response in order to realize the operational and technical goals of the downsizing effort. (From "How to Build a Resilient Organization")

Thesis Statement with Expert Opinion

The thesis of this article is the opinion of the expert quoted in the introduction, rather than the opinion of the writer. In this excerpt and the one that follows, the thesis statement is italicized. You may want, in a similar way, to quote directly or indirectly from one of your secondary sources in the introduction to your essay.

Takeo Kanade is fun to be with. Pleasant, bright—very bright, in fact—Kanade speaks with a playful enthusiasm, smiling or chuckling often when making a particularly fantastic point about his work in robotics, and the future. A self-described optimist, Kanade is the internationally respected director of The Robotics Institute at Carnegie Mellon University in Pittsburgh. And like many in his field, Kanade is convinced that *rapid advances in computing power mean today's children will live to see machines that are smarter than they are.*

Such a machine may be a humanoid robot, or it may take on a form more suited to its task. Kanade is confident that, whatever it looks like, scientists' creations will in effect outdo human evolution within a generation. (From "Robot Renaissance")

Thesis Statement with Example

Many of the articles in this reader are based on one example. In the paragraphs below, the writer herself serves as an example and a blueprint of what the article contains.

Sometimes, you forget to breathe. It might happen on the day you skip lunch to make a meeting so you can finish work in time to collect the children from swimming, buy groceries, cook and eat, and wave to your partner or babysitter coming in the door as you rush out to a parent–teacher meeting. It could even be in bed, late that night, as your drift into blessed sleep is interrupted by thoughts about the messy house, and how you avoided your boss for fear she'd ask for overtime, and how long it's been since you visited your parents, and how you skipped the kids' bedtime story because the laundry needed doing.

If this describes me, a full-time writer striving to match up the puzzle pieces of work and family, it seems to apply equally to the 1,237 readers who responded to *Chatelaine*'s survey on the work-family crunch last August. Your responses—and several hundred appended stories scrawled on hospital notepads, computer paper from home businesses and scrap paper at the family cottage—painted a vivid picture of how *Canadians with double (and sometimes triple) duties struggle to care for their children and parents, pay their bills, nurture their careers, and do it all, somehow, even if it means sacrificing necessities like sleep.* (From "The Work–Family Crunch")

Classification and Division

The classification method breaks the main topic into parts or subtopics. If you use classification you must cover, or at least mention, all the subtopics, so that that your reader is aware of all the different aspects of the topic. Think of a pie chart. It may consist of larger and smaller segments, but taken together they form a complete circle or pie. In the case of an essay or article structured by the classification method, the reader must see the whole pie in his or her mind's eye, even if only the larger pieces are discussed. Sometimes the smaller pieces of the pie—such as the "third argument" in the article quoted below—are also mentioned.

> There are really two main arguments. In the first place, we don't really know what we're doing when we modify plants, and once they are out in the world, they can't be recalled. Their genetically modified pollen will have spread, they will have contaminated their non-engineered cousins, and the novel genes will have jumped to closely related species. Whether all this is immediately harmful, or not, isn't the issue. There may be unintended effects, perhaps decades down the road, and it will be too late to do anything about it....
>
> The second argument is more political: The modified plants are being made by giant multinational corporations whose goal is to dominate agriculture worldwide and turn farmers into peons dependent on the company....
>
> A third argument—one that's not emphasized very much, but which underlies the whole debate—is what you might call the theocratic view: that God (or Nature) created species to be separate. (From "Food Fright")

Comparison and Contrast

Students write more compare-and-contrast essays and reports than any other type. The main thing to remember is that there should always be a good reason for making the comparison or contrast.

> Will opposition in Canada continue to grow? Unlike the British, we tend to trust our government regulators to make sure foods are safe (see below), and our farmers not to poison us. "It comes down to consumer confidence," says Doug Powell, an assistant professor of plant agriculture at the University of Guelph, Ont. In Britain, he says, the public has been rocked by food scandal after food scandal, including the infamous Mad Cow debacle. Britain has also seen regular outbreaks of bacterial infections, such as so-called hamburger disease— abdominal pain, diarrhea, vomiting and fever. "They just have problems with food," Powell says. (From "Food Fright")

In this example, the author contrasts Canada with Britain to undercut the argument that Canada is likely to have a problem with genetically modified foods. This rhetorical device appeals to our emotions, particularly Canadians' sense of pride in our national identity as reasonable people.

> Still, more women than men will relate to Adamo's management style. That's because women and men have distinct styles when it comes to managing their staff and their businesses. (From "Ms. Versus Mr.")

As the title indicates, this article is a direct comparison of male and female styles of management. Note that it concentrates on female management style and how it differs from male management style. Comparison essays should focus on either the differences or the similarities, whichever are the more unusual or notable.

Instruction and Process

Instructional writing is one of the most common types of writing in the workplace: it is found, among many other contexts, in software and procedure manuals, forms and memos. Instructions are usually written in the second person using an implied "you." More than any other type of writing, instructional writing must be clear and easy to follow. Process writing is similar, but differs in that it details how something *works*, rather than how something *is done*. Process writing should also be very clear, but does require such a step-by-step approach as instructional writing. Both forms use analogies, parallel structure and description.

> Where does their money come from? Studies show that while the popularity of after-school jobs is important, it is not the source of the vast majority of kids' cash. A recent report by the Canadian Council on Social Development showed the youth labour market is actually at its lowest point in 25 years—fewer than half of 15-to-19-year-old students worked in 1997, down from two-thirds in 1989. The big money instead comes from family sources. Foot calls teens "six-pocket kids" who get money from mom, dad, grandparents and often step-parents. (From "How Teens Got the Power")

The style of development of this article is made clear in the title. The article discusses economic power and explains why teenagers have more money in their pockets these days. Notice that this passage also uses the question-and-answer format, and defines the term "six-pocket kids," an intriguing idea.

Competing to win in the global economy will require an ability to attract, retain, motivate and develop high-potential employees of both genders from a variety of cultural and ethnic backgrounds. The challenge facing today's corporate leaders is to foster an organizational culture that values differences and maximizes the potential of all employees. In other words, leaders must learn to manage diversity. (From "Building a Business Case for Diversity")

This article, which is the best example of a process essay in this book, discusses how to manage diversity, as well as why diversity is necessary in today's business world.

Cause and Effect

Cause-and-effect discussions are often the most difficult to write and the most interesting to read. It may be a challenge to persuade your readers that your point of view is the correct one, since the topics under discussion are often contentious. In this kind of discussion, you are either writing about a result or effect and speculating on the cause, or writing about changes (causes) and speculating where they will lead (effects). Cause-and-effect writing typically makes use of persuasive techniques such as description and appeals to the emotions. It is also somewhat speculative.

In some ways, of course, depopulation will be a boon. In overcrowded Japan, "low population density means more space—more available land, greenery, and housing," Makoto Atoh, deputy director-general of the National Institute of Population and Social Security Research, noted recently. "These benefits might even create a spiritually affluent society." (From "The Lonely Planet")

This article, by John Ibbitson, speculates about the possible results of a declining world population. The article's success rests on the author first showing that the population is in fact expected to decline. Without first making sure that the reader can believe that premise, the speculation would be pointless. To set up his premise, the author uses expert opinion and statistics.

This shift to branding explains many of the most fundamental economic and cultural shifts of the past decade. Power, for a brand-driven company, is attained not by collecting assets per se, but by projecting one's brand idea on to as many surfaces of the culture as possible: the wall of a college, a billboard the size of a skyscraper, an ad campaign that waxes philosophic about the humane future of our global village. Where a previous generation of corporate giants used drills, hammers and cranes to build their empires, these companies need an endless parade of new ideas for brand extensions, continuously rejuvenated imagery for marketing and, most of all, fresh new spaces to disseminate their brand's idea of itself. (From "The Tyranny of the Brands")

This article, by Naomi Klein, discusses the growth of branding and speculates about what has caused that shift—mostly corporate greed, she argues.

Definition

Some articles set out to define or redefine a term. For example, "Samaritan Inc." defines corporate social responsibility. Others, such as "Bad Bosses and How to Handle Them," combine definition with classification to define types of bad boss.

> Poon Tip is not alone. Doing the right thing is top of mind for many business-people today. The buzzword is "corporate social responsibility," a grassroots movement that believes values, ethics and community well-being should be part of everyday business. (From "Samaritan Inc.")

> What makes for a bad boss? Some are just plain nasty, but often, a bad boss is all in the eye of the beholder. One person's boss from hell may be another person's pinup. If you need regular direction, for example, you will be miserable with a hands-off, absentee manager, but if you have strong needs for autonomy you will flourish under the same regime. (From "Bad Bosses and How to Handle Them")

Narrative

You have probably listened to friends tell long, boring and seemingly pointless stories, and seen other people yawn as you talked about a dream you had or a concert you attended. Narrative, or storytelling, is one of the most difficult types of communication. Good narrative is specific and concrete, showing rather than telling. Most importantly, good narrative has a point.

> Spraying icy mist over the wakes of their high-powered outboard motor boats, the hunters sped toward a small, rocky group of islets called the Harbour Islands, less than a hour from town. Here, where 19th-century British and American bowhead whalers once sought protection from the boat-crushing ice, the hunters, clad in orange survival suits, reassembled to finalize their strategy. After a brief meeting, they dispersed again, using satellite-fed global

positioning system receivers to pinpoint their location and high-frequency radios to communicate with each other. (From "Licence to Whale")

The contradictions are what makes this piece of narrative so effective. Inuit hunters wear "orange survival suits" and use "satellite-fed global positioning system receivers" and drive "high-powered outboard motor boats," while they pursue the ancient hunting traditions of their ancestors. Thus, with a few descriptive points, the writer underlines his ambivalence about native whaling rights.

In the Inter-Continental's sleek dining room—dominated by a huge window that overlooks a palm-fringed azure pool and a cage full of riotously colored parrots—they are poring over last-minute logistics. Deferential waiters glide through the room, their jet-black hair slicked back, delivering platters of seafood and fruit. The casino opening, trumpeted in an April press release, is weeks behind schedule. But that's the least of Thunderbird's worries. The company has been awaiting a final permit from Venezuela's newly formed casino commission, which has been mired in internal politicking. And Thunderbird must open this casino—and fast—because it's in serious need of revenue. The company's operations in Panama and Guatemala are generating some cash—US$16 million in 2000 and almost US$4 million in the first quarter of this year. But it's not enough to cover costs. (From "The Big Bet")

The setting adds telling details to this narrative. The "sleek dining room," the gliding "deferential waiters" with "slicked back" hair shows—rather than tells—that this is a big-money setting. Casinos and fast cash: the reader understands that the writer is telling him it's all a little bit shady.

Top-Down Style

Generally, business writing is done in a top-down or bottom-line-first style. Business writers do not leave their readers in suspense about what they intend to say. They say it, they expand on it, then sometimes they say it again. The top-down style is sometimes called the deductive style—the style you have probably been taught throughout your high-school and college career in the form of the five-paragraph essay with thesis and three main points. Articles in this reader tend not to follow that format. Often, the thesis and main points are covered in a single paragraph, as in the example below, or sometimes more.

Forward-thinking Canadian organizations have recognized that competing successfully in the new global marketplace requires more than the latest technology, most efficient production processes, or most innovative products. Canadian organizations' competitive strength is increasingly contingent on human resources. Competing to win in the global economy will require an ability to attract, retain, motivate and develop high- potential employees of both genders from a variety of cultural and ethnic backgrounds. The challenge facing today's corporate leaders is to foster an organizational culture that values differences and maximizes the potential of all employees. In other words, leaders must learn to manage diversity. (From "Building a Business Case for Diversity")

Problem/Solution

A way of approaching an essay or report that is different from the top-down or deductive style is the problem/solution or inductive style. Many articles in this reader use the problem/solution style, stating the problem, giving examples, and concluding with the specific changes the writer wants to see made.

Long after the dead have been buried in Walkerton, Ont., rural Canadians who rely on groundwater will continue to feel and smell the impact of a largely unreported revolution: the growth of factory farms. This new industry, or what governments call "intensive livestock operations," has unsettled farm communities from New Brunswick to Alberta. Unlike the family enterprises of old, which proudly cared for 20 pigs or 60 cattle, these new facilities operate on an entirely different and largely unregulated scale. (Introduction to "When Water Kills")

Critics agree there are some obvious reforms. Provincial governments should cap livestock density in many regions, while many rural Canadians want to see animal factories regulated and taxed for what they are: industries. Canada also needs laws that recognize that E. coli 0157 and other pathogens have forever changed the nature of manure. Many experts also recommend that animal waste should be properly treated before the dung ever leaves the barn. Most producers support higher standards for the simple reason that disasters like Walkerton aren't good for business. Last but not least, Schindler, Canada's top water scientist, would also like to see federal funding for freshwater research restored (it is now, he says, at an all-time low) and comprehensive management plans for the nation's watersheds. "Walkerton," Schindler concludes, "should be a wake-up call—for the entire nation." (Conclusion to "When Water Kills")

Persuasion

It is always important to pay attention to your reader, but especially so in persuasive writing. Persuasion is used to win the reader over to your way of thinking. Therefore, you must seek to answer any questions the reader might have, and acknowledge the reader's potentially differing point of view. Persuasion is most likely to work when supported by facts from neutral or authoritative sources. Emotional arguments can be used, but carefully. Don't assume that what triggers your emotions will necessarily trigger your reader's emotions in the same way.

> That famous national reticence could be killing us. Once-proud Canadian brands such as Admiral and Massey Ferguson are defunct or shadows of their former selves. Just six years after venturing north, Wal-Mart has become our largest department-store chain, eclipsing such established rivals as Eatons, The Bay and Zellers. It will happen again and again. With the growth of world trade, the rise of the Internet and the globalization of brands, Canadian companies that aren't up to speed in marketing should prepare to be crushed. (From "Why Canadians Can't Market")

> Let's face it, the world thinks the only buzz that comes from Canada is lumberjacks firing up their chainsaws. In its annual survey of international executives, Chicago-based A.T. Kearney Inc. recently found Canada was 12th as an investment choice in the global marketplace. Who's ahead of us? Poland, with a paltry $4,014 (U.S.) GDP per capita. (From "Canada Isn't Working")

Both the articles excerpted above are filled with examples and statistics. The writer of "Canada Isn't Working" also uses numerous personal anecdotes to support his point, which work because they are amusing.

STYLISTIC TECHNIQUES

As the previous section demonstrates, a good structure helps the reader to follow a discussion. Equally important, good style makes the reading experience more pleasant and may add clarity and enhance understanding. Below are some stylistic techniques evident in the readings.

Attention-Grabbing Titles

Most of the articles in this reader were initially chosen because of their titles. Simply put, the titles caught my interest. Many of them manage to imply much in a few words. For example, "Arch Enemy," the title of an article about young people who attempt to start a union at MacDonald's, uses a common phrase meaning an extreme enemy, while simultaneously alluding to the golden arches symbol that represents the company. Many titles contain puns or plays on words: "When Pros Become Cons" and "The Game of the Name" are two examples. Then there are the titles that allude to literary works or media productions: "What's in a Name?" comes from Shakespeare's *Romeo and Juliet*, while "Licence to Whale" is reminiscent (probably deliberately) of the James Bond movie *Licence to Kill*. And of course, "One Nation under Molson" is a reference to "One nation under God," a line from the American Declaration of Independence, implying a certain level of patriotism in the television commercial.

Introductions

After the title, the next thing that grabs the reader's attention is an effective opening statement. Journalists use a number of strategies to catch readers' attention, and these methods can also work well for student writers—provided the essay or report moves quickly to a thesis statement. Here are some examples of attention-grabbing introductions.

1. Anecdote

Nothing gets the reader's attention faster than an anecdote or story. Writers typically use this technique to personalize an issue.

> Bruce Poon Tip built his business on a foundation of environmental, ethical and social responsibility. Since 1990 his Toronto company, G.A.P Adventures Inc.. has been specializing in ecologically minded tours, providing travellers with unique, authentic cultural experiences. G.A.P's guiding principle of sustainability dictates that tours are kept to small groups of 12 and visitors stay in guest houses or private homes instead of hotels, thereby interfering with the environment as little as possible. Respect for the local people and the environment, says Poon Tip, is the sine qua non of the company's philosophy. "Being responsible is at the top of our agenda," he says. "We are constantly

evaluating ourselves so that we can be as responsible as we can be. The mentality is, we can always do better." (From "Samaritan Inc.")

This opening introduces the company around which the article is built. It sets the parameters of the story, telling us the article is going to be about ethics and social responsibility, as well as the environment, from a business point of view.

2. Definition

Unusual or unfamiliar terms must be defined for your reader. An opening that includes a definition can signpost the purpose of the entire article.

They have never known a world without personal computers at their fingertips. They were surfing the Internet before they'd lost all their baby teeth. They are the first Web generation, young teenagers who use the global network as unconsciously as you or I would flip a light switch. (From "Web Spawn: The Keystroke Kids")

In the jargon of the diamond trade they are known as "conflict" or sometimes "blood" gems. No one knows exactly how many of the 860 million diamonds cut every year may fall into the category; perhaps four percent of total world production, perhaps as much as 10 percent. But there are plenty of people, like Canada's Ian Smillie, who are acutely aware that the diamonds that are being mined and sold illegally are fuelling ferocious civil wars in African trouble spots from Sierra Leone to Angola. (From "Diamonds and Blood")

3. Example

If the topic under discussion is something that is happening in many places or to many people, a single good example can make the issue concrete and understandable for the reader.

A grade-six class settles down to a math lesson on simplifying fractions. Students open their textbooks and read: "The best selling packaged cookie in the world is the Oreo cookie. The diameter of an Oreo cookie is 1.75 inches. Express the diameter of the Oreo cookie as a fraction in simplest form." (From "Today's Lesson Brought to You By...")

Baher Abdulhai is on the fast track—in fact, he's creating it. The Cairo-born civil engineer is one of the world's top experts in a field known as intelligent transportation systems, which aims to improve urban and highway traffic flows by networking cameras, computers and electronic message boards placed along the way. Abdulhai was on a team at the University of California at Irvine that developed an ITS network that's now being set up on California's jammed highways. In the ever more congested world of the future, ITS will be an invaluable tool for urban planners, traffic cops and busy commuters. "It's a multibillion-dollar business that's very popular in the States, Europe and Japan," says Abdulhai, "and now it's catching up in Canada, Australia and Asia." (From "Opening Our Eyes to Immigration")

This second example illustrates the kind of talent Canada has gathered through immigration. The article then goes on to show how important immigration is to Canada's economic future.

4. Scenario

A report on, for example, an environmental problem can get the reader's attention by describing a worst-case scenario. Bruce Sterling uses this technique in his article on cybercrime, partly to indicate the unlikelihood of the idea, and partly because he is such an engaging writer that he can pull in the reader with a movie-style scenario. The scenario in the second example speculates about the future. (Unfortunately, the effect of the scenario is diminished for today's reader by the prediction later in the article that machines more intelligent than man would emerge in the early twenty-first century. The article was written in the twentieth century.)

Picture this scene from the near future: organized crime gets hold of encryption technology so powerful even IRS supercomputers can't crack it. An underground electronic economy emerges, invisible to U.S. tax code. The Federal Government, unable to replenish its coffers, let alone fund a standing army, shrinks until it wields about as much power as a local zoning board. Militias and gangs take over, setting up checkpoints at state borders and demanding tribute of all who pass. (From "Will Cybercriminals Run the World?")

Imagine a world of lonely children. They are lonely because there are so few of them. They long for brothers or sisters, cousins, classmates, friends. They share the world with old, tired people, who are dying slowly, selfishly.

The old people are lonely too, and they are poor. Because there are so few young people, pension funds are drying up, jobs are going begging for want of workers, knowledge is stagnating for want of innovative young minds, economies are shrinking for want of consumers. (From "The Lonely Planet")

5. Startling Fact, Statistic or Story

Readers sometimes need to be shocked into reading a story.

> At a few minutes past five on a brilliant August afternoon in 1996, a bowhead whale was breathing its last in the waters of Repulse Bay, a remote, ice-freckled firth straddling the Arctic Circle. (From "Licence to Whale")

This introduction works on a number of levels. It reads like the opening line of a good murder mystery, and, like a good mystery, starts *in medias res* (in the middle of the story). The passage is descriptive and grabs the reader's attention because it is shocking. Read the rest of the opening (on page 117) and see if you can remain unaffected by it.

> On a sunny morning last May, a senior partner in a large construction firm left his office in the suburbs of Toronto. The partner—let's call him John—got into his car, fired up the engine and headed out on some errands. At first, he did nothing out of the ordinary—an appointment with an insurance company, a couple of meetings with clients. Business as usual.
>
> Then John took a detour and went downtown. Way downtown, ending up in the gritty, concrete wasteland where Dundas and Sherbourne streets meet. There, he spotted a woman (later described by a witness as a "crack whore") hanging around on the corner. John flagged her down, and she got into his car. The two of them then drove to a secluded industrial park near Toronto's lakeshore, where she serviced him in the comfort of his car. (From "He Likes to Watch")

6. Question

Questions asked in the introduction are an easy and effective way to start an essay. If you ask a question you should answer it—unless you are striving for rhetorical effect.

> Canada's Armed Forces want women to feel welcome—in the trenches and in the top ranks. So why do so many female soldiers complain of harassment and humiliation? (From "Battle Wary")
>
> If you were to turn to Diversa for help, what exactly would this company do for you? Perhaps you'd expect it to deliver a wide variety of groceries to your doorstep, or to train dim executives to be more sensitive to their ethnic employees. (From "The Game of the Name")

Conclusions

A good conclusion leaves the reader thinking about the topic, possibly even wanting to read more. The conclusion to a piece of writing can invite further discussion, make a prediction about the future or make suggestions for change. Sometimes, it merely summarizes the discussion.

1. Inviting Further Discussion

The Rant, he declares, is "a spurious attempt to establish something that Canadians have been trying to establish for the last 100 years: a national identity. A country that is always seeking to establish its identity has none." (From "One Nation Under Molson")

2. Pointing to the Future

Monsanto Canada president Ray Mowling said the lawsuit is aimed at creating a "level playing field for the farmers who have signed agreements." It's also aimed at protecting Monsanto's intellectual property, of course, in the same way that software companies prosecute alleged pirates.

The agreement is a new form of control on seeds, and one that farmers appear to be accepting: Mowling says about 20,000 Canadian farmers signed the agreements in order to grow the company's plants in 1999.

But if Schmeiser wins, it could make enforcing the more difficult, since transgressors could argue they were the innocent recipients of drifting seed. (From "Food Fright")

Will there be anyone to teach them when they hit campus in 15 years or so, just as the boomer bulge finally goes bust? Immigration Minister Caplan is confident there will be. "Immigration built this country," she says, "and there are still a lot of smart, talented people who want to come here to keep building it." They will be needed more than ever. (From "Opening Our Eyes to Immigration")

3. Summary

In the end, finding a balance between the two management styles may be the key to success. "Women have the emotional sensitivity, but sometimes we apologize too much," says Denise Meehan. "You have to have a balance empathy plus the ability to put your foot down. Men are going to have to be more like women, and women can learn a few things from men." (From "Ms. Versus Mr.")

4. Suggestion

And contrary to conventional wisdom, now is the time to spend even more money, not less, on professional development and training. "People who feel that their employer has invested in them have a feeling of being valued; these are the ones more likely to stay," she says. "The attitude of an employer should be: 'You may not stay with us forever, but while you are here, we want it to be a good experience for both of us.'" (From "Win the Loyalty Game")

5. List of Suggestions

Wondering how your company can incorporate some CSR-inspired principles? Canadian Business for Social Responsibility suggests some easy steps to help you get started:

- Donate 1% of pre-tax profits to your community
- Give priority to local suppliers and employees
- Develop an employee volunteer program
- Ensure that employees and suppliers are fairly and promptly paid
- Promote from within and institute fair performance packages… (From "Samaritan, Inc.")

Headings

Essays, as well as reports, can benefit from headings. Headings help to guide the reader through a discussion or process and also act as markers for quick review. Notice how the headings in "Building a Business Case for Diversity" (listed below) lead the reader from problem (the changing mosaic) to solution (the need for diversity) to the process (initial environment, plans, leadership in following plans, monitoring progress) and, finally, to a forward-looking conclusion.

> Canada's Changing Mosaic
>
> The Business Case for Diversity
>
> Creating an Environment for Success
>
> Putting Plans into Action
>
> The Leadership Imperative
>
> Monitoring Progress, Measuring Results
>
> Looking Ahead

Parallel Structure

Parallelism is a grammatical concept, but it also works well as a way of emphasizing a point—or even adding a humorous punch line. Often a list in parallel form builds towards the end, as in the second example below. The parallel, or repeated, terms are italicized in the examples.

> *Few* of the conversations *are* particularly gripping or deep; *few are* even grammatical. (From "'Hey. Wassup?' 'Nothin'")

> They use similar methods to *hide money*, *move money*, even *raise money*. (From "Follow The Money")

Analogy

Although analogy is considered a literary technique it is used frequently in business writing, especially in technical writing. Manual writers are fond of using analogy to explain how something works, though unfortunately they sometimes just confuse the reader more. The advantage of a well-thought-out analogy is that it clarifies and often personalizes a process or description for a reader.

> A 25,000-head feedlot produces in excess of 50,000 tonnes of dung—more fecal matter than 250,000 Calgarians excrete over a year. It, too, is just spread on land bases often too small to absorb all nutrients. Alberta's livestock industry may hold a national manure record: dung heaps equivalent to the waste of 48 million Canadians. (From "When Water Kills")

> Catalyst's decision to work closely with business is, well, pardon the sexual innuendo, like getting into bed with the enemy. (From "Ms. Versus Mr.")

Definition

As we noted earlier, definitions can be used in introductions. They may also be used throughout essays and reports. In fact, unusual or unfamiliar terms must always be defined. Sometimes a definition can shape the entire article (see page 11).

> GMOs—dubbed "frankenfoods" by the always-colourful British press—are living things that have been genetically altered in some way. (From "Food Fright")

> Back in 1980, Sandy Cotton, then a lieutenant-colonel, wrote a PhD thesis that identified a critical group of men within combat ranks as what he called

"beleaguered warriors." They were tough guys who were resistant to change and imbued with a "masculine warrior mind-set." Among other things, they would tend to believe their job was to protect women, not march into battle with them. ("From Battle Wary")

Examples

Examples come in two styles: first, in the form of descriptions of particular situations; second, in the form of lists. The use of examples can be a good way to build a case.

> It also doesn't help, in the eyes of critics, that Monsanto has been aggressively protecting its engineered crops, by requiring farmers to sign an agreement that they won't save seed from year to year and threatening them with legal action if they do. In the first case to make it to court anywhere, Saskatchewan farmer Percy Schmeiser is being sued for growing Monsanto's canola without a licence; his defence is that modified seed blew onto his land and took root. (From "Food Fright")

> Teens have more money in their pockets than ever before, and their influence is everywhere—in music stores with CDs by bands ranging from The Moffatts and Britney Spears to Korn and The Offspring; in clothing stores with labels such as JNCO and Snug; on TV with programs such as *Dawson's Creek* and *Felicity*; and in movies such as *Cruel Intentions* and *Varsity Blues*. (From "How Teens Got the Power")

Question and Answer

A question-and-answer format can be useful to articulate the important questions a reader might have. The key, as we noted in the section on opening an essay or article with a question, is that if you ask a question you should answer it.

> What proportion of Canada's crops are genetically modified? Are foods made from those crops safe? Good questions. The answers are: a) lots, and b) probably. (From "Food Fright")

> Is health being compromised? In a study published last year, Health Canada mapped cattle densities and the incidence of Escherichia coli 0157 infections in rural Ontario, only to discover that six rural Ontario counties with the highest number of cattle—and Walkerton is located smack dab in the middle of them—routinely registered the highest rates of E. coli 0157 infection between 1990 and 1995. (From "When Water Kills")

Description

Descriptive writing is something we associate mostly with fiction, but it can also be an effective technique of persuasion. A good description can help the reader to empathize with one of sides in an argument.

> Nightfall came with a flourish of pastels in the western sky. We again set up camp, fishing for arctic char in the chilly evening, drinking coffee, and scanning the rocky hillsides for caribou. Radio communications with the other hunters were regular; there was as much talk of seals and caribou as there was of bowheads. The hunt was being billed as a turning point in the history of the Inuit, but all the hype seemed far from the hunters' minds. (From "Licence to Whale")

Notice in the description of the Inuit whale hunt, how both sides of the story are represented: the ancient fishing and hunting activities of the Inuit, and the modern world to which they now belong, with radio communications and cups of coffee.

Figures of Speech

Figures of speech are devices that are intended to intensify meaning., Metaphors and similes are figures of speech that are based on comparison—implied in the case of a metaphor, and direct in the case of a simile. Sometimes metaphors and similes use personification, giving human characteristics to something that is not human—though this is not a technique you would expect to find in business writing. Hyperbole, or exaggeration for effect, is another figure of speech. If you use hyperbole, make sure it is to good effect and not just plain exaggeration.

1. Metaphor

Metaphors may be sustained, running through an entire paragraph or longer, as in the first example below, or may be one-time affairs. In the second example, the procedure is described as having teeth, meaning it is effective. The industry, which is able to "change gears," is represented as being like an efficient machine.

> In 1997, then-California-governor Pete Wilson *unleashed a legal battle* against the Indian casinos, arguing that they had to share their revenues with the

state. The tribes *counterattacked*, maintaining they should be subject to federal, not state, law. As the legal *battle raged*, the statehouse in Sacramento applied pressure to gaming suppliers to stop outfitting the casinos so California could force the natives into signing a revenue-sharing contract that would formalize its Indian gaming industry. (From "The Big Bet")

To *give the procedure teeth*, a new body, provisionally entitled the International Diamond Council, will be established to ensure that no diamonds from illegitimate sources are traded. And . "I've never seen an industry *change gears* so fast," noted Smillie, formerly executive director of the Canadian University Service Overseas and now a private international aid consultant based in Ottawa. (From "Diamonds and Blood")

These companies are forever *on the prowl* for new and creative ways to build and strengthen their brand images. (From "The Tyranny of the Brands")

"On the prowl" suggests that the company is like a predatory animal, which is exactly the author's point.

2. Simile

A simile is essentially a metaphor that is spelled out to make it obvious; the comparison is not implied but is stated, using either *like* or *as*.

He was trotted out before the media like a child forced to play the piano at his parents' dinner party. (From "Canada Isn't Working")

But with loan interest being sucked out of company coffers as fast as coins into a slot machine…. (From "The Big Bet")

3. Hyperbole

Hyperbole is exaggeration for effect. The key word to remember here is "effect." Don't simply lie. In the following example the exaggeration is used for ironic effect.

In 1984 a grumpy old woman named Clara Peller held up a hamburger and demanded, "Where's the beef?", thereby changing the course of American history. (From "One Nation Under Molson")

ACKNOWLEDGING SOURCES WITHIN THE TEXT

Any kind of writing that involves research must be documented. For students, this means that every quotation from a primary or secondary source and every idea that is not considered to be in the common realm, or common knowledge, must be documented—both in the text and in a list of works cited or references at the end of the work.

Journalists do not include in-text references and lists of works cited with their articles. However, they almost always acknowledge their sources in writing, in the text. Most of the articles in this book are based on research. While journalists may do some secondary research (at the library, in databases, or on the Internet), they more often do primary research. which includes talking to experts Secondary research often makes use of studies, which may present their conclusions as findings of fact or as statistics. Student writers can learn from the way journalists, in effect, document their sources by mentioning them within the text.

Below are some examples of how journalists use expert opinion and studies.

Expert Opinion

Journalists develop articles by reading studies and by conducting primary research, such as interviewing experts. When quoting experts they name the expert and give his or her qualifications, including profession or business; sometimes they add the expert's geographical location because it can indicate a bias or a particular point of view. Experts fall into two categories: those with relevant educational qualifications, and those with first-hand experience.

1. Expert by qualification:

"Most people think Canada and they think tree. Not very sexy, I'm afraid," says Jay Jaffe of Washington, D.C.–based Jaffe Associates, a business development consultancy. Jaffe has been involved in repackaging the images of major Bay Street law firms—companies that continue to lose their talent to the U.S. brain drain. (From "Canada Isn't Working")

Alan Middleton, a marketing professor at York University's Schulich School of Business, says you can only charge so much for tickets before you drive away the very people you need to support you. (From "How the Game Is Played")

2. Expert by experience:

> At a lunch last year, John Kenneth Galbraith—who became an American citizen in 1937—remarked that one old frustration to him about Canada was that our traditional style of nationalism prevented us from looking and learning much beyond our borders. But that's changing, he thought. (From "A New Kind of Patriotism")

Try naming your sources in the text rather than just in parentheses after a quotation. An essay or report has more authority if the reader knows why a source is being quoted. See "Documenting Sources" (page 379) for more suggestions on how to document experts within the text.

Statistics and Studies

Statistics and studies can contribute persuasive detail to business writing. However, vague references to "a study" or to undocumented statistics can be counterproductive to an argument, especially if the argument seems intuitively flawed to a reader.

Notice how writers in this reader note the source of studies and statistics:

> But who can fault investors for misunderstanding Canada? Even Canadians are caught in the past. A recent Ekos study found that 46% of Canadians still think that our No. 1 export is wood pulp products. Actually, it's only about 5% of total exports. (From "Canada Isn't Working")

> Still, more women than men will relate to Adamo's management style. That's because women and men have distinct styles when it comes to managing their staff and their businesses. According to research done by the Ottawa-based Centre for Excellence for Women's Advancement and The National Foundation for Women Business owners in the U.S., men are more likely to think in hierarchical terms and focus on establishing rules and procedures, while women business owners tend to emphasize creative thinking. (From "Ms. Versus Mr.")

> Canada's recent spurt of economic growth has created a dearth of skilled workers in high technology, medical sciences, nursing, teaching and computer programming. A survey by the Canadian Federation of Independent Business put the national shortage of such people between 250,000 and 300,000 in small and medium-size businesses alone. (From "Opening Our Eyes to Immigration")

TYPES OF WRITTEN WORK

All writing should be clear, correct and concise. However, certain specific rules apply for some types of writing. Generally, business writing should not include anecdotes, or such techniques as metaphor or simile,. However, it may include techniques such as lists, question and answer, and parallel structure. Business writing usually takes a top-down, conclusions-first approach. The exception to this rule is persuasive writing, of the kind you might see in advertising copy or proposal writing.

Essays

Once you leave university or college you will probably never write another essay for the rest of your life. However, postsecondary education is more than just learning to do a job; it is also about learning to think and to express yourself. Essay writing is a tool that helps you to acquire those important skills. When you write an essay you must organize your thoughts, marshal evidence, and communicate clearly and effectively.

All the techniques listed below can be used when you write an essay. The standard essay begins with an attention-grabbing introduction followed by a thesis statement and a summary or blueprint of the essay. The essay is developed with material secondary sources, such as articles, books and reference sources. Sometimes, students use primary sources such as personal interviews or first-person accounts. Whatever sources are used, they must be acknowledged, and this is where the importance of the journalistic style becomes clear. Journalists always acknowledge their sources within the actual text.

An excellent resource for essay writing can be found at Princeton University's Writing Center at *http://web.princeton.edu/sites/writing/ Writing_Center/WCWritingRes.htm.* Another source is the Paradigm Online Writing Assistant at *www.powa.org/.*

Reports

Report writing is often a major concern of business students. And, unlike with essays, you may find yourself writing reports after you have graduated. Reports should be written in a to-the-point, clear, concise style, with the conclusion presented first. They will likely include reference to secondary sources, so note how the authors of the articles in this reader use these sources. Also note such techniques as lists and parallel structure.

The best place to read up on report writing is at Purdue University's Online Writing Lab (OWL) at *http://owl.english. purdue.edu.* Check the site's "Handouts" section for information on report writing. Another site that Purdue recommends is David A. McMurrey's Online Technical Writing Textbook at *www.io.com/ ~hcexres/tcm1603/acchtml/acctoc.html.*

Letters and Memos

Letters and memos—particularly the latter—are increasingly being replaced by e-mail. The important difference between letters and memos used to be that letters were for external communications, while memos were restricted to internal communication. Perhaps because of this change, good Web sites for letter and memo writing are hard to come by. The Purdue site has good information on content, but is lacking on format. The Online Technical Writing Textbook mentioned above has sections on business letters, complaint and adjustment letters and letters of application. Another excellent letter-writing resource can be found at Wendy's World (*www.wendy.com*), a site that is not connected to the author of this text.

Shorter reports are often formatted in letter or memo style. Informal reports make use of such structural methods as comparison and contrast, process (instruction) and classification. Definitions of terms are also an important component of any kind of report.

Manuals

Manuals are written in second-person direct address (that is, they tell the reader—"you"—what to do), and include a strong visual compo-nent. Read the section on instructional writing (page 4) for help in writing a manual. Consider such techniques as analogy, parallel struc-ture and question and answer. Good Web sites for help with manual writing include The Technical Communicators' Resource Site at *www.techcommunicators.com* and Gary Conroy's Technical Writing page at *www.gary-conroy.com.*

E-mail

Generally agreed rules for e-mail use have evolved over the past decade. A Web search for "netiquette" (as Internet etiquette has become known) will find you a list of these rules. They include avoiding the use of all capital letters in e-mail because this practice often makes the reader feel that he or she is being shouted at. In my experience, the number one e-mail rule is: Write an effective subject line. With so much junk mail clogging our mailboxes, a poor subject line can lead to premature deletion of your message. As well, if you are constantly exchanging e-mails with colleagues, you should create a new subject each time and not just hit the reply button. Otherwise it may become difficult to track down important information at a later date.

As a student, you may be used to using those little characters called emoticons, and colloquial abbreviations such as *LOL* ("lying on the floor laughing"). These are inappropriate for business email. You may also have an account with a Web-based e-mail provider such as Hotmail, where you call yourself *hotbabe* or *studlyone*. Now is the time to get a new e-mail address.

For more information, check The Beginner's Guide to Effective Email at *www.webfoot.com/advice/email.top.html*.

Web Pages

One Web page that discusses writing for the Web notes that "75% of users scan the page instead of reading word for word," and that reading from a Web page is slower than reading from a paper page of an equivalent size. This site suggests that the word count on a Web page should be 50% of the paper equivalent. It also suggests that key words be highlighted and that conclusions should go first. In other words, the rules for Web writing are similar to those for business writing. For more details, see the Sun Microsystems Web site at *www.sun.com/980713/webwriting*.

Summaries and Abstracts

A summary is an abstract, and an abstract is a summary, at least if dictionaries are to be believed. However, if you are asked to hand in one or the other, you must be sure you understand what is being requested of you. Below are brief descriptions of two types of summaries or abstracts you might be asked to submit, with examples of each. To help you understand the difference, each example is based on the same article, "The Lonely Planet" by John Ibbitson.

Descriptive Abstract or Summary

A descriptive abstract or summary is the kind of thing you might find on the Web site of a library or an on-line bookstore. It will read as if it was written by someone other than the author of the article or book itself. Your job in writing a descriptive abstract is to encourage the reader to look at the article, not to save him or her the bother of reading it. Follow these general rules when writing a descriptive summary:

1. Begin with a summary sentence that covers "who, what, where, when and why." Include publication details if required by the assignment.
2. Keep it short—under 100 words, or less than half a page.
3. Write in the present tense.
4. Use bullet points in the central part of the paragraph if the original article divides neatly into three or four categories or themes.
5. Cover the pertinent information either in descending order of importance or from general to somewhat specific (however, keep in mind the next rule).
6. Omit specific details such as statistics, expert opinion or examples.
7. Write in your own words. If you include a few words from the original, place them in quotation marks followed by a page number.

Example

In his article "The Lonely Planet," published in the Globe and Mail on March 2, 2002, John Ibbitson notes that the population explosion that we once thought was the destiny of the planet is now expected to peak in the mid-twenty-first century, and then begin to decline, bringing with it social, economic and political changes. Ibbitson shows that, contrary to our commonly held beliefs, signs of a population decline are starting to appear in the developing world as well as the developed world, with countries like India and China beginning to see major drops in birth rates. Ibbitson speculates on several possible reasons for the decline, concluding that we may not be able to guess how the world might change as a result of this "baby bust" (C4) and the subsequent greying of the population.

Informative Abstract, Abstract or Executive Summary

What is called variously an informative abstract, an executive summary or simply an abstract is the piece of writing that goes at the front of a report, and communicates the contents of that report to the reader. It is usually written by the same person who wrote the report, and is aimed at what writing teachers kindly call "the busy reader" who may not have time to read the entire report. Follow these guidelines when creating an informative abstract or executive summary:

1. Explain what the report contains, including the purpose, the scope, the methods, the results, the conclusions and the recommendations.
2. Start with the main point of the article or report and highlight the important points.
3. Keep it short—about 10% of the original report or less. The article used as an example has about 3,400 words, so a summary should have about 340 words or less. In other words, the summary should be about a page long, and should include three or four paragraphs.
4. Use language aimed at a general rather than an expert reader. As noted above, an informative abstract is often aimed at a busy reader such as a manager who will rely on the professional expertise of the writer to make a decision. This reader may never read the entire report.
5. Although you can't be accused of plagiarizing your own work, you should avoid simply transferring the introduction of the report to the abstract. Apart from anything else, doing so will make it boring for the reader.
6. Use bullets only if the abstract is written at a somewhat informal level. Don't reduce the entire contents to bullet points.
7. Use the same chronology as the report.

To read some excellent examples of executive summaries, look at the CPRN (Canadian Policy Research Networks) Web site. There are many publications available and each has an executive summary.

Example

The population of the world is no longer expanding rapidly, and will probably begin to decline within the next fifty to one hundred years.

Western countries have already stopped producing enough children to sustain their populations and the developing world shows signs of following the same trend. The decline in numbers, coupled with the aging population, may become the major issue of the twenty-first century.

The reason for the population decline is partly that many countries have been successful in encouraging their citizens to have fewer children. Other reasons for the drop include the empowerment of women; the movement of people away from farms, where children are needed as workers, to cities, where they are not; and the lower mortality rates experienced as medical science advances.

The decline in population will change the way many of us live. Racial tensions may increase as immigration is used as a method to boost populations, and there may be pressure to open the gates wider in some countries. Another problem is that declining birth rates will result in aging populations with fewer workers supporting pension structures, and labour shortages rather than unemployment becoming the norm.

A solution to global population shrinkage will require creative thinking and unprecedented changes that we cannot currently predict. These changes may be drastic, such as a change in our views on nationalism, and may even have religious or ideological roots. Whatever happens, it is clear that the story of the twenty-first century is the baby bust, just as the story of the twentieth century was the baby boom. For those still alive at the end of this century, there will be more room than there is now.

WORKING ON YOUR WRITING

Many writing teachers like to teach how *not* to write before they teach how to write. I prefer to start on a more positive note. However, sooner or later you are going to have to find out what it is you are doing wrong. This reader lacks the space to cover all the potential problems. You might like to check out Jack Lynch's Guide to Grammar and Style at *www.andromeda.rutgers.edu/~jlynch/Writing*. Lynch was one of the first people to post this kind of information on the Internet. You can also check out his section entitled "Getting an A on an English Paper."

The Importance of Editing Your Work

Very few people spend time editing their writing, but editing is key to creating a readable and understandable piece. Students often ask, "Does this sound good?", meaning "Are you impressed? Have I fooled you into thinking I know what I'm talking about?" The question they should really be asking is, "Am I conveying my meaning to you, my reader?"

In his essay "Politics and the English Language," George Orwell wrote:

> A scrupulous writer, in every sentence that he writes, will ask himself at least four questions, thus:
>
> 1. What am I trying to say?
> 2. What words will express it?
> 3. What image or idiom will make it clearer?
> 4. Is this image fresh enough to have an effect?
>
> And he will probably ask himself two more:
>
> 1. Could I put it more shortly?
> 2. Have I said anything that is avoidably ugly?

The full text of this very interesting article is widely available on the Internet.

Six Questions To Ask Yourself About Your Writing

Orwell's six questions will serve a student writer well. Below are the six questions in an expanded form, with some suggestions on how to fix the problems.

1. *What am I trying to say?* Do I have a thesis? Have I divided my work into parts so that I can talk about one area at a time? Does my work include all the necessary details? Have I used sufficient sources (library and Internet research, interviews, examples, studies, etc.) to make my point clear?

   Suggestion:

   Try telling someone else, in one sentence, what it is you are trying to prove. Then explain to that person the types of detail you will use to expand on that one sentence.

2. *What words will express it?* Is my writing concrete and specific? Do I use vague generalities, or are the situations I discuss specific?

Suggestion:

Look for words and situations that you can't visualize and replace them with words and situations that you can easily picture in your mind's eye.

3. *What image or idiom will make it clearer?* Have I used analogies, similes, metaphors and description to make my writing clearer and to make it relate to the reader's understanding?

Suggestion:

Apply the stylistic techniques discussed above (see page 9).

4. *Is this image fresh enough to have an effect?* Have I avoided using clichés and trite, overused expressions?

Suggestion:

If you like the sound of a phrase because you have heard someone else say it, chop it from your writing and say it your own way. Most people are unaware that many of the everyday expressions they use originally came from somewhere specific. Have you ever used any of these common expressions?

- refuse to budge an inch
- tower of strength
- foregone conclusion
- seen better days
- haven't slept a wink
- tongue-tied
- vanished into thin air.

All of these were originally written by William Shakespeare. They are still being used because they are useful. In fact, even after four hundred years they sound fresh enough that they still don't really qualify as clichés. However, many much-used phrases become worn out, probably because they weren't coined by such a master. How many times can you hear someone say "Wassup?" before you tire of it? Try to be original.

5. *Could I put it more shortly?* Have I completely eliminated wordiness and repetition?

Suggestion:

Go though your work and cut every word or phrase you can. This may be hard when you have been given a word count you are expected to reach. Start to think of the word count as the maximum number of words you can use, not the minimum.

6. *Have I said anything that is avoidably ugly?* If I read aloud, does the writing "sound" good. Does it flow? Have I avoided strings of Latinate verbs and nouns that are difficult to decode?

Suggestion:
Read what you have written. If your essay is difficult to read aloud, or if you find yourself "spitting" as you read, rewrite. Spitting indicates that you have used to many long, Latinate words.

Recognizing Flawed Logic

Several Web sites exist to educate you on the types of problems you can get into with logical fallacies. Some good ones include:

Stephen's Guide to Logical Fallacies at *www.datanation.com/fallacies/index.htm*

St. Cloud State University's Literacy Education Online (LEO): Logical Fallacies at *http://leo.stcloudstate.edu/acadwrite/logic.html*

A Handbook of Logical Fallacies at *www.cas.mcmaster.ca/~stpp3ao3/doc/handbook-of-fallacies.html.*

Avoiding Clichéd, Repetitive, Wordy Writing

Rewriting is much more important than writing. You should spend at least as much time rewriting as you do writing, and probably more. Clichés, repetition and wordiness are three things you can include in a first draft and eliminate later. Many Web sites will show you more specifically what needs to be eliminated from your writing. The one with the best links is the University of California at Berkeley's Student Learning Center page at *http://slc.berkeley.edu/nns/l2writing/gramstyle/style.htm.* And then, of course, there is always Purdue's OWL.

Part Two: The Readings

TOPIC 1

CREATING A CORPORATE BRAND

INTRODUCTION

The concept of branding—creating an image to identify a product—belongs primarily to the latter part of the twentieth century, especially when the image is built through the association of, say, athletes like Michael Jordan or, more recently, Tiger Woods, with sports brand Nike. In propaganda terminology, this relationship between product and athlete is called "transference." However, transference as a method of branding a product is not new.

An 1899 a magazine advertisement trumpeted the virtues of Pears Soap by showing Admiral Dewey, an American hero of the Spanish–American War, washing his hands with the soap. The text of the advertisement notes: "The first step towards lightening the white man's burden is through teaching the virtues of cleanliness." The ad continues: "Pears Soap is a potent factor in brightening the dark corners of the earth as civilization advances, while amongst the cultured of all nations it holds the highest place—it is the ideal toilet soap."* Thus, as in our time, a hero was used to confer on a product an intrinsic value that simply did not exist. Of course, the Pears ad seems amazingly racist to us now, and it is interesting to note that the premier brand hero of our time is a black athlete.

---

* The phrase "The white man's burden" refers to a poem of that name by the British poet Rudyard Kipling. You can look at a Web site that discusses this and other advertisements at www.boondocksnet.com/kipling/pears.html. The site also reproduces the actual advertisement.

Transference is one important part of branding. Another is repetition. Biologist Richard Dawkins, in his book *The Selfish Gene,* refers to these two elements when he talks of "memes." A meme is "the tune you can't get out of your head, the phrase you keep using in your conversation … ideas which have passed from somewhere *out there* into your head and into your consciousness." The New Hacker's Dictionary, which is available on several Web sites, compares a meme to a virus. When a company like McDonald's can make you think of a hamburger when you see golden arches, then a meme has been successfully implanted. Incidentally, the quotation above is taken from the on-line, peer-reviewed journal First Monday (*www.firstmonday.org*), a site well worth checking out.

The first article in this section, "The Game of the Name," discusses the etymology, or word origins, of brand names. Transference is a two-way street. That is, a corporation can transfer ideas to its name, but the name may also work as a description of what a company does. Other articles discuss specific Canadian brands, including the Toronto Maple Leafs and Molson.

The section concludes with an article by Naomi Klein, author of the book *No Logo.* Klein, who takes on corporate brand tyranny, has become the antiglobalization voice of her generation. In "The Tyranny of the Brands," she writes, "That shift [in corporate priorities] centres on the idea of corporate branding and the quest to build the most powerful brand image. It will, I believe, be one of the issues that shapes the first decade of the 21st century." Which brings us back to Nike and, of course, Tiger Woods. Read what Klein has to say about those two in her book.

The Game of the Name
by Elizabeth Renzetti

ROB Magazine, August 31, 2001

If you were to turn to Diversa for help, what exactly would this company do for you? Perhaps you'd expect it to deliver a wide variety of groceries to your doorstep, or to train dim executives to be more sensitive to their ethnic employees.

Well, my friend, you'd be wrong. Diversa is the company formerly known as Recombinant BioCatalysis, a biotech outfit that performs highly specialized tricks with enzymes. "The old name sounded like they were replicants from outer space," says Nan Budinger, head of San Francisco's Metaphor Name Consultants, which created the new moniker.

"Clients usually come to us when they're stuck," says Budinger, who founded Metaphor eight years ago, when naming was largely the purview of nervous new parents, not specialized branding companies. All right, so Recombinant BioCatalysis isn't a name you'd find in a sonnet, but at least it screams biotechnology. What does Diversa say? "It's a good example of a coined name that has a lot of inherent meaning," Budinger says. "As soon as you see it, you think, 'Uh huh, that comes from the idea of diversity.'"

And so Diversa Corp. takes its place in the corporate lexicon, standing next to Clarica and Accenture, Agilent and Avilent and Aviant, and all the other puzzling new company names that have rapidly become the Dylan and Tyler of the business playground.

It used to be, if a company wanted a new name, it went for something that telegraphed its intentions to the world. But Scient and Viant, what do they do? (They're internet consulting rivals, struggling ones.)

"Ninety per cent of the names you see now are stupid," says Chris Yaneff, an Ontario-based consultant responsible for Brewer's Retail's transformation into The Beer Store. "The name has to relate to the business you're in." Today, names of no clear logic litter the landscape like so many spilled Scrabble tiles.

Why do companies assume new identities, and so readily? (Some 2,976 U.S. companies changed their names last year, triple the number from eight years before.) It usually occurs after a merger or acquisition, to signal a new direction to Bay Street or Wall Street or because the old name carried the stench of scandal, failure, or just stale air. In 1991, Kentucky Fried Chicken changed its name to KFC in a valiant attempt to make people forget its poultry products are coated in fat.

Other companies may want to compete globally. Consider American Building. Great name, right? Virile, muscular, and there's no doubt about how it makes its money. Still, in 1999, the Alabama-based construction company hired Naseem Javed of ABC Namebank to help ease its expansion into Asia. Javed came up with Magnatrax, a name he viewed as powerful and, more importantly, one that had not been trademarked globally.

Javed, like many of his colleagues, is cagey about the methodology used to develop a new name; this skill is, after all, the equivalent of his company's secret sauce. "I sit with the CEO and in one meeting in one day I solve a global problem," says the man the American design magazine *I.D.* called "the granddaddy of naming."

Javed says, "What we don't do is the norm of holding focus groups where you hold hands and come up with 300 names. We don't brainstorm or computer-generate lists of 7,000 names."

What he's mocking here are the companies that do believe in the transformative power of the morpheme, the linguistic building blocks that convey negative or positive images. For example, suffixes such as "izon," "pro" or "vant" are considered forward-looking. Indeed, some companies such as Metaphor firmly believe that morphemes, successfully hitched together, lead to powerful new words. Others, like San Francisco's A Hundred Monkeys, spurn "ideophonemes" in favour of cheeky names such as Cruel World (a career-placement service) and Left Field (an advertising agency).

A sophisticated linguistic analysis can still lead to a Herbert of a name, so let's spare a moment of pity for the companies whose new identities have sent up hoots of derision. Perhaps you saw the ads imploring people to banish from their memories the stodgy label Mutual Life Assurance Co. and replace it with the glistening but identity-challenged Clarica Life. Chris Yaneff calls the new name "terrible. It sounds like a hairspray." Shed a tear for the British Post Office, which was clobbered when it became Consignia in January. "I hope the new name will be consignia'd to the dustbin," wrote one correspondent to a British newspaper.

Early this year, Canadian Occidental Petroleum, with the help of two identity specialist firms, changed its name to Nexen Inc., despite the fact that there were already a handful of global companies with that name, and the domain name *http://www.nexen.com* was already taken. "Nexen is a classic case of stupidity" on the consultants' part, says Javed. The cost of its baptism? Reportedly $8 million (U.S.).

And then there is the corporate metamorphosis that raised eyebrows around the world. "I'm sitting there watching the SuperBowl, and I saw an ad for Accenture," says John Hulland, a visiting associate professor of marketing at the Wharton School of Business in Philadelphia. "I thought, what the blazes is that?"

Of course, Accenture was the name chosen, after painstaking deliberation, by Andersen Consulting when it was divorced from its corporate spouse, the accounting firm Arthur Andersen. The company called in the world's largest naming firm, San Francisco–based Landor Associates, and perused some 5,500 possible new names. In the end, the winning entry came from a manager in Andersen's Oslo office. His prize? A trip to the company's golf tournament in Australia. Cost to Accenture? A reported $100 million (including the printing of 6.5 million new business cards).

As that case suggests, the coinage itself is not expensive, so to speak. Chris Yaneff charges $25,000 to $75,000 for a job, and Javed $100,000. The larger U.S. naming companies charge substantially more, it's true, but the real bills are in marketing. Given the average total tab, Yaneff is convinced that many companies leap before they look. "The Harvard Business School is telling everyone to change their name. You get these MBAs who come in and want to change the name, change the product, change the ad manager and change the agency before they sit down and see what's wrong."

Naseem Javed remembers that when he launched his company 21 years ago, before he had developed names like Telus and Celestica, people would look at his card and say, "ABC Namebank? What do you mean, you come up with names for companies?" Now, thanks in part to the corporate baby boom of the digital age, naming firms are flourishing. "And contrary to the myth," Javed adds, "there's no shortage of names out there. Any impression that all good names are taken up is just a whitewash from the [ad] agencies."

Metaphor's Nan Budinger disagrees. Names such as Apple are gorgeous and dramatic, she says, but just try finding ones that aren't taken. She insists, "it's become particularly important to hire a consultant to help you. The issues are more difficult now than ever before."

Naming is an increasingly complicated field pitted with legal land mines. The law varies across the globe, so a company (or its naming agency) must conduct exhaustive searches to make sure the name, logo or internet domain isn't taken already.

The toughening of trademark law means that a company has to be more careful about choosing a name that sounds like another's (in other words, a company is not allowed to "dilute" another's brand by calling its software Whindows). Also, there now exist "intent to use" provisions, which allow a name to be registered six months before a company plans to use it.

After a name is finally settled upon, Budinger tells her clients the really good news: The work has just begun. A name is only as valuable as the effort the company puts into implanting it in the mind of the public and investors. "A new name won't save a bad company," she says, "and it can only make a good one better."

Clarifications

Bay Street, Wall Street: These two streets represent the financial districts of Toronto and New York.

A Hundred Monkeys: This company (which you can find on-line at *www.ahundredmonkeys.com*) apparently selected its name based on the fable of the monkeys who sit at typewriters, eventually randomly typing the complete works of Shakespeare. The story seems to have originated at a famous 1860 debate at the Oxford Union between Bishop Samuel Wilberforce and evolutionist Thomas Huxley. Huxley, in trying to mathematically prove that life could have started randomly, is said to have (rhetorically) asked Wilberforce to give him six monkeys that would live forever, six typewriters that would never wear out and an unlimited supply of paper and ink. He argued that given an infinite amount of time, these monkeys would eventually type all the books in the British Library, including the Bible and the works of Shakespeare. The fable itself was visually referenced in Molson's "typing monkeys" ad campaign.

The accounting firm Arthur Anderson: This international accounting firm attained notoriety during the collapse of U.S. energy giant Enron in early 2002 as the accountants who allegedly shredded thousands of incriminating documents for Enron.

Talking Points

In groups, make up a product and use the suggestions on the Name Stormers Web site (*www.namestormers.com*) to create a product name. How does the name you chose relate to the product? Test the product name on other members of the class. What kind of product do they think it might be?

Here are some names of companies listed on the Toronto Stock Exchange. What do you think they produce? What impression does the name of each company give?

- Silent Witness
- Burnt Sand
- BCE Emergis
- Intrinsyc
- Global Crossing.

What kind of product is the popular BlackBerry? Does the name have any connection to the product?

Web Research

Brand name consultants include Metaphor Name Consultants (*www.metaphorname.com*), ABC Namebank (*www.abcnamebank.com*) and NameLab (*www.NameLab.com*).

The Name Stormers Naming Guide gives useful tips on how to select a product or brand name, or a domain name. Use the hints to create a brand name, then go to *www.register.com* to check if the domain name is already taken. Note that you can check a domain name under many extensions—in addition to the original *.com*, *.net* and *.org*, you can now use *.info*, *.ws* ("website") and *.tv*. Depending on the product, these newer extensions or primary level domains may be more appropriate than the popular *.com*.

Companies specializing in corporate names and trademarks include NUANS (*www.incorporate-it.ca/nuans.htm*) and Arvic (*www.arvic.com*).

Research word meanings at Wilton's Words and Phrase Origins (*www.wordorigins.org*) and The Word Detective (*www.worddetective.com*).

Writing That Works

Introduction—opposite opinion: Student writing guides often mention this style of introduction, but it has not proven to be a common style among the articles in this book. However, this article does have such an opening: "Perhaps you'd expect it to deliver a wide variety of groceries to your doorstep, or to train dim executives to be more sensitive to their ethnic employees. Well, my friend, you'd be wrong." The style of introduction, of course, has a lot to do with the topic of the article. Naming companies is not always about finding a name that describes them.

Analogy: The author compares company names to children's names: "…all the other puzzling new company names that have rapidly become the Dylan and Tyler of the business playground." By comparing company names to children's names at this point, the author is picking up on an analogy from the previous paragraph about "nervous new parents." However, she is also comparing the unusualness of the names—the two boys' names she picks are examples of modern name types, both being, originally, surnames.

How the Game Is Played

by Andy Holloway

Canadian Business, April 2, 2001

The morning radio DJs in Toronto were having a field day. The NHL deadline for the final trades of the season had come and gone, and the Toronto Maple Leafs, fresh off a not-so-successful Western Canada road trip, had bombed yet again. Earlier, the team had failed to acquire Eric Lindros from the Philadelphia Flyers, disappointing fans hungry for a superstar. The best the club could do in its season trading finale was snag run-of-the-mill defenceman Aki Berg, who couldn't even crack the line-up of the lacklustre Los Angeles Kings on a regular basis. The broadcasters couldn't resist. Repeatedly, they poked fun at the Finnish-born player's name, at the trade, and at the Leafs themselves. "Make a space on the shelf for the Stanley Cup," cackled one. "Aki Berg's coming to town!"

Leaf fans love to hate their team—especially when it isn't doing so well. Who can forget the scene at Maple Leaf Gardens just a few years ago when the stands were filled with Torontonians sporting paper bags over their heads in mock shame induced by a losing streak? Leaf fans may weep for the Blue and White when the club is underperforming. But they shouldn't shed a single tear for the owners of privately held Maple Leaf Sports & Entertainment Ltd. (MLSE). No matter how the Leafs perform on the ice, their home games are almost always standing room only at Toronto's Air Canada Centre (ACC). Through their first

31 home games this so-so season, the Leafs, on average, drew 19,239 fans—people who paid from $20 all the way up to $325 a pop—even though seating capacity is just 19,200. The storied weakness of Toronto ticket buyers for the team, win or lose, isn't the only reason its owners are the envy of the Canadian pro-sports business, however. Ticket sales are by far the largest component of MLSE revenue, but that merely pays for players' salaries "almost on a dollar-for-dollar basis," says Richard Peddie, the company's president and CEO. Nor is it because Peddie's business includes ownership of the National Basketball Association's Toronto Raptors or the ACC arena—modern successor to the Gardens—where both teams play. The profits roll in because those combined assets enable MLSE to create such secondary revenue streams as advertising sponsorships, corporate partnerships and broadcast rights—not to mention the retailing of souvenir merchandise, concessions and renting out its arena for other events.

Sure, the Leafs may be unspectacular on the ice this year, but there's plenty in their owner's cash drawer. The hockey club is spending upward of US$43 million on players' salaries, according to the NHL Players Association, the fifth-highest payroll in the 30-team NHL (behind the New York Rangers, Detroit, Colorado and St. Louis). But despite that statistic, in the standing that counts most with fans, the Leafs sat a decidedly mediocre 15th in mid-March. So, while the team lost out in the trading-deadline frenzy, it wasn't because ownership was pinching pennies. In fact, during the three years that Peddie has been in charge, the MLSE board has approved every single increase in players' salaries. It even agreed to take on Lindros—along with his potential $9-million salary and much-concussed head—before that deal collapsed under the egos involved.

Peddie openly acknowledges that it would be tough not to make money on the Maple Leafs, a cultural icon that will celebrate its 75th anniversary in 2002. But he's being a tad modest about his personal marketing skills—and the additional profits he's managed to squeeze for MLSE. In fact, it's his track record that may have inspired media conglomerates BCE Inc. and Rogers Communications Inc. (the owner of *Canadian Business*) to sniff around MLSE. Both are hungry for content and potential corporate synergies. MLSE, its assets valued at more than $1 billion, is 51% owned by Maple Leaf Gardens Holdings Ltd., whose majority shareholder is former grocery magnate Steve Stavro. He is joined by minority partners Larry Tanenbaum and TD Capital. The rest is held by the powerful Ontario Teachers' Pension Plan Board.

Regardless of the company's ownership, the future of the Leafs and Raptors—and any successful sports property—depends less on ticket sales and more on how executives play their brands into non-sporting arenas. That's more critical now than ever, as teams in all sports approach limits on how much they can suck out of ticket buyers' pockets to pay skyrocketing salaries. Major league baseball may have already reached that point, notes Pete McAskile, CEO of Second Dimension International Ltd., a Toronto based sports marketing company. "I truly believe there are going to be some shutdowns in baseball next year," he predicts. "They can't keep going this way, because teams can't keep losing $40 million a year. Your franchise isn't worth that much."

It wasn't too long ago that the Toronto Blue Jays (now owned by Rogers) were selling out on a regular basis. Today, tickets are available for every game. That lesson is not lost on Peddie. "The Blue Jays in 1990 probably made $19 million in EBITDA [earnings before interest, taxes, depreciation and amortization]," he says. "This year they could lose $45 million to $50 million. We can't afford that. We built the ACC with our own money; I have to pay that off. We've got debts. I've got a bank syndication that I manage along with my CFO. We have covenants. People think this is sitting at games and talking about trading for Eric Lindros, but that's a small part of the job. It's a business job."

While Peddie agrees that making money with the Leafs may be a no-brainer, he quotes Miami Heat coach Pat Riley's warning that "complacency is the success disease." Not only are his Leafs and Raptors competing for dollars against other sports teams in and around the city, they also have to contend with other forms of entertainment and recreation—the hot World Wrestling Federation, the Playdium videogame complex, movies, theatre and extreme sports—as well as all the entertainment that can now be brought into the home. Peddie estimates people spend up to 10% of their disposable income on sports and entertainment—and he wants as much of that as possible.

But there are limits. Alan Middleton, a marketing professor at York University's Schulich School of Business, says you can only charge so much for tickets before you drive away the very people you need to support you. Corporate Toronto may be prepared to shell out big bucks to attend professional sporting events, but eventually that will hit a ceiling. "We've gone through this typically Canadian whining about, 'Oh, we're going to lose all our hockey teams. Winnipeg's gone.

Quebec City's gone,'" says Middleton. "One of the ways around it is to create powerful community relationships so that you touch on other revenue sources."

Middleton, for one, expects Peddie to lead the charge as the sports business increasingly becomes a licensing business. "He, more than anybody else, gets this," Middleton says. But how far you can extend a brand depends on how willing the market is to receive it—and whether the quality of the offshoots is the same or higher than that of the originating source. Middleton says the food service industry is a good illustration of branding gone awry. "You've got the Rainforest Cafe, Planet Hollywood and all these theme restaurants, but where they've all gone wrong is they are using the brand power of Hollywood or the brand power of ecology to attract people into an entertainment medium, but they failed to deliver a quality menu when you walked into the door." How far sports teams can extend their brand into the community is something Peddie is about to find out—especially as he adds two television stations to the MLSE empire, and looks at the possibility of a wireless service to increase his company's value.

Although the Leafs are the more traditionally popular part of MLSE, if truth be told Peddie is more in his element on the Raptors side of operations. When he agreed to take over MLSE as president and CEO in 1998 after the Leafs acquired the Raptors and the $265-million Air Canada Centre, he requested to stay on as president of the basketball club. Peddie is so protective of his Raptors that when Vancouver Grizzlies executive Dick Versace suggested Toronto's NBA franchise would soon be extinct, he called the league asking that Versace apologize. The Raptors, Peddie emphasizes, have already met their ticket sales projections for the season, which almost covers the team's approximately US$37-million payroll. "We're having an outstanding year right across the board," he boasts.

Peddie watches every Raptors home game, whereas he attends only half of the Leafs Toronto appearances, and often leaves midway through the game. He's not just keeping his eye on the players, however—although he did provide a running commentary during a recent game against the rival New York Knicks. He also scours the arena for the faces of corporate sponsors, takes an avid interest in the time-out entertainment and watches how his employees are behaving. Every conceivable non-seating space in the ACC has been exploited for advertising and entertainment. "We assault your senses for two hours and nine minutes," Peddie says of a Raptors game. You can take a businessman to the game, but you can't take the game out of the businessman. "Sports is a business, and it's a high-stakes, sophisticated business," Peddie declares. "And I believe it should be run as a business."

It's a challenge that is a dream come true for Peddie. While studying commerce at the University of Windsor in the late 1960s, the then-20-year-old wrote in his journal, "I want to be involved in the NBA." Not being tall of stature or filled with talent (although he claims to have a 60% free-throw percentage, something Shaquille O'Neal can only dream of), management was the clear option. He started in sales and marketing with Colgate Palmolive in 1970 and moved to General Foods three years later as a brand manager. In 1983, Peddie became president of Hostess Snack Foods, a subsidiary of General Foods, and two years later he took over as president and CEO of Pillsbury Canada Ltd., where he received the Donald B. McCaskill Award for Marketing Excellence in Canada.

While at Pillsbury in 1988, Peddie refined his original vision. Now he was saying, "I want to bring the NBA to Toronto." A year later, he took over as president and CEO of the Stadium Corp. of Ontario (better known as SkyDome), believing that such experience would bring him closer to the teams. Sure enough, he started working with and learning from Blue Jays president Paul Beeston, and met and turned down jobs from football's Toronto Argonauts. It wasn't until 1993 that Peddie got his first shot at the NBA as part of the Palestra Group, a consortium of businessmen headed up by Larry Tanenbaum seeking an NBA franchise for Toronto. They lost out to another group led by John Bitove and Allan Slaight, who launched the Raptors in 1995. Peddie took over Labatt Communications Inc., the then parent company of The Sports Network, Discovery Channel and Dome Productions. In November 1996, Slaight called Peddie and said, "Richard, you're the only guy in the country who has general manager, packaged goods and facility and broadcast experience. Come run the Raptors for me." Two years later, Peddie was managing MLSE—and very much a public figure.

Even though MLSE is prominent in the public eye, its success depends more on traditional business practices than you might think. Peddie has a hands-on management style that starts with meeting every new employee. The company uses a "Create Champions" presentation designed to show how important each member of the team is. It may sound hokey, but how many CEOs meet or try to understand what it's like to be at the bottom of the corporate ladder? Peddie says he wants to know what everybody involved with MLSE thinks, from season ticket holders and the fan on the street to the company's 51 corporate partners and 343 full-time employees. (MLSE also employs 1,800 part-timers.)

Peddie's other obsession is the customer. "We think service sells and service resells," he says. MLSE has 30 employees in ticket sales and service alone, but service in the sports world means going a little beyond the norm. After all, if people are going to shell out up to $12,000 for a season ticket, they're going to expect something extra. MLSE used to spend a few thousand dollars sending out Xeroxed invoices, but for its 2000–2001 campaign, season ticket holders received packages that reflect team identities. The Leafs one, including tickets, pin and information, was packed in a maple wood box, while Raptor fans received their goodies in a brushed metal container. "One's more traditional but contemporary," Peddie says. "One's very urbane and hip." Total cost of these "works of art": more than $200,000. The tickets themselves were also redesigned. Leaf tickets feature stories and pictures sent in by fans, illustrating the team's long history; Raptor tickets have pictures of Toronto.

As many differences as there are between how the two clubs are presented, it's surprising how much Peddie has used them in tandem. MLSE has one human resources department, one marketing unit, and one call centre team of seven (who will field 75,000 calls this year). More importantly, Peddie forced corporate sponsors to buy into both teams, thus ensuring the Raptors would enjoy the same revenue advantages the Leafs have over their competitors. Leveraging one team off the other has helped the Raptors enjoy success while the Vancouver Grizzlies, who don't have such a relationship, have suffered. "If you split off the Raptors here, they would have a tougher time," Peddie admits. "I think they'd have a very tough time."

In addition to making his teams profitable, Peddie has turned the Raptors—which three years ago managed a woeful 16 wins in 82 games—into a viable and successful franchise. The team posted 20 sellouts in its first 32 home games this season and will likely make the playoffs for the second straight year. The Grizzlies, meanwhile, are rumored to be shambling off to a US city, tails tucked between legs, shot down by annual losses of US$40 million.

Where others have failed, Peddie has been able to capitalize on his experience: 19 years in the packaged-goods industry, five in facility management and three in broadcasting. He is keenly aware of the importance of his brand and the need to keep fans happy. Teams that don't, often end up having to leave town. "If we don't deliver, our teams suck, our ushers are surly, the place is dirty or the food's cold," he says. "The fans won't be there."

The public's interest in sports makes the business unlike any other. Let's face it, no one would take it personally if the Pillsbury Doughboy cooked himself or Snap, Crackle and Pop were lost at sea in a fight with Captain Crunch. Sports teams belong to the fans. And "they're right here," says Peddie, holding his hand two inches from his face. "The fan at Pillsbury was an 800-number away or a letter away. Here, the fans are sitting behind me, and they may be booing the team."

As much as a sports team depends on public trust, however, it's largely a private industry. There are few publicly owned teams and even fewer publicly traded ones (the Leafs once traded on the TSE, but went private following legal battles after boss Harold Ballard's death). "From the numbers I've seen, public ownership has not worked," Peddie says. "You get a lot of fans buying the stock so it ends up being very thinly traded, and people don't know how to react because predictable quarterly earnings don't happen in sports." Fans are also fickle, reacting to fortunes on the floor, field or ice. Stock prices of Boston Celtics LP (NYSE: BOS), for example, were flat during the summer months when the team wasn't playing, became more active at the start of the season and lost 20% when the Celtics sank into a prolonged slump at the end of 2000. Since then, the team has rebounded, and so too has its stock. British soccer's Manchester United PLC (London: MNU) has seen its stock price cut in half during the past 12 months even though the team continues its winning ways. Baseball's Cleveland Indians tried public ownership in 1998, but went private again when owner Richard Jacobs sold to Ohio lawyer Lawrence Dolan.

Peddie says he "can't imagine" going public. He says it is a tricky enough balancing act trying to run a profitable business while managing pressure to win from the general public, let alone from stockholders. Shareholders generally want loyal fans to drive revenue, but fans want winners. "New Yorkers are not inherently loyal fans to their baseball teams, but they are loyal fans to their winning baseball teams, which is why the Yankees are worth so much more than the Mets," Middleton says. The more owners spend to win, however, the less they use athletes and coaches from the local community—and the less the team connects with its fan base. It can be a catch-22. "The clubs that don't have powerful community links and that have average records are the ones that are hardest to brand, but it's not impossible," Middleton says.

The Leafs don't have that problem, but the Raptors, like almost every other NHL and NBA team in Canada, do. "The name of the game is you've got to be out there with your brand, you've got to be front and centre," says Ron Bremner, president and CEO of the NHL's Flames, which last April outlined a four-goal strategy to keep the team in Calgary. That included increasing season ticket sales to 14,000 from 9,000, making better use of the team logo and sports properties, attracting new sponsors, getting more money from existing suite holders and advertisers, and negotiating a better arena deal. "You need to keep looking for new revenue sources or new ways to build or extend your brand," adds Bremner. "It's as simple as that. Whether you're in the high-tech business, the sports business or running a corner store, there is a lot of pressure on the bottom line."

Sold-out arenas are only the beginning. Fifteen months ago, Peddie gathered together his management team to explore ways to continue increasing shareholder value even though there were no more tickets to sell and sponsorship inventory had disappeared. Not surprisingly, new media was the target. MLSE decided to relaunch its Web sites, adding more news and information, and to look at creating its own television stations. "We needed a closer connection with our fans," Peddie says. "How do we give them an insider look? Build a better relationship with our fans."

One step toward that goal came when MLSE was awarded licences for two digital TV specialty stations. With cable or satellite carriers still to be lined up, the plan is to inaugurate a Leafs station next fall and a Raptors channel to follow. Because broadcast rights to live games are currently under contract to several channels, the new digital stations initially would show only practices, profiles and educational segments. But possession of the TV licences sets up the prospect of nasty battles for rights to the games when present contracts expire during the next three years. MLSE could carry the games on its own outlets if it doesn't like the offers it receives. It already produces and airs Raptors games and receives the ad revenue. Why buy broadcast rights if you can own the team outright and keep all the revenue for yourself?

All these ideas are designed to keep the buzz about the teams going and promote the Leafs and Raptors brands, even though the arena may be long sold out. "Ten years from now, I want to be retired, come to the occasional game, look around and see that it's still sold out."

Five Ways To Play at the Office: How Corporate Canada Can Copy the Winning Ways of Sports Franchises

Richard Peddie, president and CEO of Maple Leafs Sports Entertainment Ltd., says there are a number of things in the sports world that corporate Canada can emulate. Below are five of them:

1. Reward MVP's. Let your employees know when they are doing a good job and reward them. During events, Peddie and other senior managers hand out "good job" cards that employees can redeem for prizes. A handshake is great, but something tangible is better.

2. Reach for the top. Think about how you can safely and profitably extend your brand. Peddie likes to tell the story about how Colgate Palmolive bombed when it came out with a dishwasher detergent under the Ajax name. Consumers linked Ajax, unfortunately, with harsh—not a good adjective for an everyday cleaner. Be consistent with your brand and reinforce its message with any new product you bring out. "Everything we do on this is consistent," says Peddie. "It reinforces the brand. It's not diluting it at all."

3. Have the best practices. What innovative things are other companies in your sector doing? What about other sectors? Steal the good idea and make it part of your practice. MLSE swiped a money-maker from the San Diego Padres whereby a company sponsors a season. TD Waterhouse ponied up the necessary dollars to sponsor the current seasons of both the Leafs and the Raptors. "I think we have swiped just about every good idea from the other sports teams, and we're now reaching out for good ideas from other companies," Peddie says.

4. Sink those free throws. There may not be anything like free publicity, but it pays to build goodwill with the media. "Many presidents in other sectors are intimidated by the media," Peddie says. "You can't expect to just talk to the media in good times." Return calls promptly

whether the news is good or bad. You won't get a break, but you might get some respect, Peddie advises.

5. Get in the game. While it's true that fans are more involved in sports than most other businesses, that doesn't mean that corporate management doesn't have to get involved in the fray. Spend time in your store or wherever your consumers gather, sit in on group focus sessions, take an hour-long shift on your consumer response line and talk to the people.

Clarifications

Cultural icon: The word *icon* comes from the Greek *eikono,* meaning image. The *American Heritage Dictionary* at *www.Bartleby.com* says that an icon is "a representation or picture of a sacred or sanctified Christian personage, traditionally used and venerated in the Eastern Church" and also "an important and enduring image." Of course, in recent years, *icon* has also come to be used to refer to the little picture one clicks on in a software program. For example, to print a document you may have to click on an icon of a printer. We might say that the Toronto Maple Leafs hockey team, as a cultural icon, is a little picture representing Canadian culture.

Corporate synergies: Synergy refers to a process through which two things interacting create something that is greater than the sum of their parts. The expression "corporate synergies" means that one brand has an effect on another. This process is also referred to as co-branding.

Talking Points

Fantasy sports exercise: Try managing a team of your own. Sporting News has a free fantasy games site (*http://fantasygames. sportingnews.com/crs*) that allows you to recruit and manage a team. Your class should divide into groups and manage one team each over a period of days or weeks. Report back to the class at the end of an agreed period or at regular intervals.

Richard Peddie is described in this article as an ideal CEO who has achieved success where others have not. How much does the identity of the CEO have an effect on a company? Which CEOs of Canadian companies do you know? Does a charismatic CEO add to the corporate brand, and can the close identification of the CEO with the brand sometimes have a negative effect? Think of Jean Monty of BCE and John Roth of Nortel.

Some examples of successful co-branding include Volkswagen of America and Trek Bicycle Corp; Philips Electronics and Levi Strauss, who teamed up to put electronic gadgets into a jeans jacket; and American Airlines and Citibank, who jointly offer a credit card. What other companies have been successful with co-branding? Which companies can you think of that might be successful if they were to combine in this way? For example, who would you like to see co-branded with the Montreal Canadiens, Tim Horton's, Nortel, or Air Canada?

Web Research

Playdium video game complexes are limited to large Canadian cities. However, you can read about them, as well as play some on-line games, at *www.playdium.com*.

A recent business best-seller, *Good to Great* by James C. Collins, claims that a charismatic leader is not necessary for a company to succeed. Read about what he thinks a company needs to succeed, and which eleven companies have moved "from good to great," on the Web site of business magazine *Fast Company* (*www.fastcompany.com*). How does MLSE fit the pattern of these companies?

The writer talks about the "brand power of Hollywood." As discussed in the opening to this section, this kind of brand power is what is known as "transference," a propaganda technique. To read about transference and other propaganda techniques, go to *www.about.com* and search for "propaganda techniques."

Writing That Works

Process and instruction: The article begins by describing the success of MLSE and Richard Peddie, leading in to an overview of how he became successful. A sidebar to the article lists five ways that "corporate Canada can copy the winning ways of sports franchises." The article is structured somewhat like a business report, with discussion and recommendations. Also, most of the paragraphs are constructed in a topic sentence/details format. Starting at the paragraph that begins "Regardless of the company's ownership," skim through the article reading only the first sentence of each paragraph. You will probably find that the article makes sense even read in that way. Good business writing mostly follows the same format, with the bottom line always coming first.

Sidebars/appendices: Articles in magazines and newspapers often include "sidebars"—additional information set off from the article in some way. "Five Ways To Play at the Office" is one such sidebar. In a report, such information is sometimes placed in an appendix. The information in this particular sidebar would be appropriate for the Recommendations section of a report.

One Nation Under Molson
by Kevin Michael Grace

Report/Newsmagazine (Alberta Edition), May 22, 2000

In 1984 a grumpy old woman named Clara Peller held up a hamburger and demanded, "Where's the beef?", thereby changing the course of American history. Walter Mondale took up Clara's cry to crush democratic upstart Gary Hart before winning only his home state of Minnesota in the 1984 U.S. presidential election. In 2000 a passionate young man named Joe clenched his fist and declared, "I am Canadian!", thereby, according to some, changing the course of Canadian history. Sheila Copps has taken up Joe's cry, unmindful of Mr. Mondale's sad end. Meanwhile, Molson will sell a lot of beer and Canadians will grow weary of an increasingly tiresome catchphrase.

The Molson Canadian television spot "The Rant" is already the most famous ad in Canadian history. It has dominated the newspapers for weeks and is the biggest Canadian story abroad since Lucien Bouchard's bout with flesh-eating disease. It has been parodied innumerable times by columnists both friendly and hostile.

The Rant is a celebration of Canadian identity, but curiously its stirring soundtrack is Sir Edward Elgar's Pomp and Circumstance March No. 1, that great anthem of British imperialism. Beginning quietly and concluding in an almost hysterical peroration before a giant flag, Joe proclaims, "I am not a lumberjack or a fur trader. I don't live in an igloo or eat blubber or own a dog sled. And I don't know Jimmy,

Sally or Susie from Canada, although I'm certain they're really, really nice. I have a prime minister, not a president. I speak English and French, not American, and I pronounce it 'about,' not 'aboot.' I can proudly sew my country's flag on my backpack. I believe in peacekeeping, not policing; diversity, not assimilation, and that the beaver is a truly proud and noble animal. A toque is a hat. A chesterfield is a couch, and it's pronounced 'zed,' not 'zee'—'zed!' Canada is the second-largest land mass, the first nation of hockey and the best part of North America. My name is Joe and I am Canadian!"

Molson's chauvinism is calculated. Its "I am Canadian" campaign began two years ago when it paid $1 billion to buy out its Australian partner, Foster Brewing. Early ads in Molson's campaign were nostalgic (a maple tree at dusk), surreal (monkeys flailing at typewriters) and subversive (profane parodies of the Canadian Heritage Moments series). A spokesman commented at the time, "When you pick up a beer, why not pick up a beer with a Canadian soul?" As opposed to one with a foreign soul, like Molson's only serious rival, Labatt, which is owned by Interbrew of Belgium.

Andrea Southcott, managing director of Bryant, Fulton & Shee, says that patriotic marketing is a risky strategy in Canada, where patriotism itself is controversial. Her company has exploited regional patriotism in its popular "The beer round here" spots for B.C.'s Kokanee beer, but these ads are soft sell. Yet she concludes of The Rant's hard sell, "It's been proved not to be risky because it's been such a hit. It's right for the brand." It took a relatively long time for Americans to grow sick of Wendy's "Where's the beef" campaign. Ms. Southcott warns, "Advertising cycles are much shorter now, and there is a much faster burnout rate than before." She admits that a backlash against The Rant is possible, especially if it is hijacked by politicians.

Heritage Minister Copps has never hesitated before rushing in where angels fear to tread. She appropriated The Rant in Boston last week at a panel of the International Press Institute's World Congress in Boston. Afterwards, she told the *St. Catharines Standard*, "I think the message of Joe Canadian is there are a lot of things that make us unique as a country, and it's important that we try hard to preserve them."

But Allen Buchanan, philosophy professor at the University of Arizona, argues The Rant "sells Canada short" because it defines Canadian patriotism as anti-Americanism. Prof. Buchanan, who has written and lectured on Quebec separatism, acknowledges that

America's ignorance of Canada is "shameful." He adds, "Americans think of Canada as being pretty much like us, but second-class and distinctive only in cartoonish ways." And a campaign that emphasizes such stereotypically Canadian particularities as the toque, the beaver and "Zed," might actually increase American disdain.

Hoover Institution scholar and Washington Times columnist Arnold Beichman, who lives half the year in B.C.'s Okanagan, is more dismissive. The Rant, he declares, is "a spurious attempt to establish something that Canadians have been trying to establish for the last 100 years: a national identity. A country that is always seeking to establish its identity has none."

Clarifications

Chauvinism: You may be used to thinking of chauvinism as relating to the way men act towards women. However, the word was derived from the name of Nicolas Chauvin, a soldier under Napoleon who admired him passionately. Chauvinism took on a negative connotation and came to mean a person who was overly passionate and aggressively nationalistic about his or her own country. Early feminists co-opted the word to indicate narrow-minded men, who became "male chauvinists" in the early 1960s.

Walter Mondale and Gary Hart: Wonder who these politicians are, and what happened to them? Walter Mondale was the forty-second vice-president of the United States and, as the article above notes, he crushed "the Democratic upstart Gary Hart" to win the Democratic party nomination for president in 1984. (However, he lost the race for president to Ronald Reagan.) Hart tried again in 1987, this time crushing himself when a young woman named Donna Rice was seen leaving his Washington townhouse; later, photographs surfaced of her sitting on his lap aboard the appropriately named yacht *Monkey Business*. He is now a lawyer who writes thrillers under the name of John Blackthorn. Walter Mondale became the ambassador to Japan under President Clinton.

Foster Brewing: At one time, the Australian company Foster Brewing owned 40 per cent of Molson. Molson came up with the "I am Canadian" campaign after it bought out its Australian partner. In a similar appeal to patriotism, Foster used to advertise itself as "Foster's, Australian for beer."

Talking Points

After the attack on the World Trade Center on September 11, 2001, the Ad Council of America, whose mandate is to create public service announcements that "stimulate action," came out with their "I am an American" campaign designed to bring Americans together—and to encourage them to drop the hyphen (as in "I am an African-American," or "I am an Italian-American"). You can check the Council's Web site at *www.adcouncil.org*. If the details of this campaign are still available, you might contrast it to Molson's "I am Canadian" campaign, keeping in mind, of course, the different functions of the two campaigns.

Catchphrases like "Where's the beef?" come and go. You can check on some of them on the Chicago *Daily Herald*'s Web site at *www.dailyherald.com/special/crossingcenturies/2a/3rest.asp*. Discuss current catchphrases. Which ones come to mind, and where did they come from? The *Daily Herald* lists catchphrases that date back to the beginning of the twentieth century. Where might these earlier catch-phrases have come from?

You might have been surprised to discover that Labatt was owned by a Belgian consortium. Other companies that seem quintessentially Canadian are also foreign-owned. For example, Tim Horton's is now owned by Wendy's, the American hamburger chain. How does this affect the way you feel about such companies? Is patriotism part of the appeal of a company like Tim Horton's?

Web Research

The Molson Web site at *www.molson.com* says: "If you've ever sewn a Canadian flag on your backpack, you belong in here. Check out *IAM.ca* and discover what's so great about this big ol' country. Stay connected with the Canadian music scene, get essential info on hockey, events, and more. See what promos we've got going on and stay in touch with other Canadians. For everything Canadian get to *IAM.ca*." Click the "I am Canadian" link and you are presented with a second choice: "I am of legal drinking age." If you're not, you aren't supposed to go in. Wonder how that would sound in a rant!

While you are checking out Canadian institutions, go to the Tim Horton's Web site and have a virtual cup of coffee: *www.timhortons.com.*

Advertising Age's on-line review of ads at *www.adreview.com* comments on and analyzes recent print and television commercials, and allows you to vote for your favourites.

Writing That Works

Hyperbole: As the introduction to the article above notes, Clara Peller did demand to know where the beef was. However, to say that she changed the course of history is exaggeration for effect.

Comparison: Has Joe, like Clara, changed the course of history? Probably not, but the comparison emphasizes the importance of the ad to the author of the article.

Expert opinion: "But Allen Buchanan, philosophy professor at the University of Arizona, argues The Rant 'sells Canada short' because it defines Canadian patriotism as anti-Americanism. Prof. Buchanan, who has written and lectured on Quebec separatism, acknowledges that America's ignorance of Canada is 'shameful.'"

Conclusion—further discussion: The last statement in the article is provocative and demands further discussion: "A country that is always seeking to establish its identity has none."

The Tyranny of the Brands
by Naomi Klein

New Statesman, 24 January, 2000

What are we to make of the extraordinary scenes in Seattle that brought the 20th century to a close? A *New York Times* reporter observed that this vibrant mass movement opposed to unregulated globalisation had materialised "seemingly overnight." On television, the reliable experts who explain everything couldn't sort out whether the protesters were right-wing nationalists or Marxist globalists. Even the American left seemed surprised to learn that, contrary to previous reports, it did, in fact, still exist.

Despite the seemingly unconnected causes that converged in Seattle that week, there was a common target: the multinational corporation in general and McDonald's, The Gap, Microsoft and Starbucks in particular. And what has given the movement against them a new energy and a new urgency is a profound shift in corporate priorities. That shift centres on the idea of corporate branding and the quest to build the most powerful brand image. It will, I believe, be one of the issues that shapes the first decade of the 21st century.

Branding seems like a fairly innocuous idea. It is slapping a logo on a product and saying it's the best. And when brands first emerged, that was all it was. At the start of the industrial revolution, the market was flooded with nearly identical mass-produced products. Along came Aunt Jemima and Quaker Oats with their happy comforting logos to say: our mass-produced product is of the highest quality.

But the role of branding has been changing, particularly in the past fifteen years: rather than serving as a guarantee of value on a product, the brand itself has increasingly become the product, a free-standing idea pasted on to innumerable surfaces. The actual product bearing the brand-name has become a medium, like radio or a billboard, to transmit the real message. The message is: It's Nike. It's Disney. It's Microsoft. It's Diesel. It's Caterpillar. The late graphic designer, Tibor Kalman, said that a brand used to be a mark of quality; now, it is "a stylistic badge of courage."

This shift in the role of the brand is related to a new corporate consensus, which emerged in the late 1980s. It held that corporations were too bloated: they were oversized, they owned too much, they employed too many people, they were weighed down with too many things. Where once the primary concern of every corporation was the production of goods, now production itself—running one's own factories, being responsible for tens of thousands of full-time, permanent employees—began to seem like a clunky liability.

The Nikes and Microsofts, and later the Tommy Hilfigers and Intels, made the bold claim that production was only an incidental part of their operations. What these companies produced primarily were not things, they said, but ideas and images for their brands, and their real work lay not in manufacturing, but in building up their brands. Savvy ad agencies began to think of themselves as brand factories, hammering out what is of true value: the idea, the lifestyle, the attitude. Out of this heady time, we learnt that Nike was about "Sport," not shoes; Microsoft about "Communications," not software; Starbucks about "Community," not coffee; Virgin about a "Fun-loving Attitude," not an airline, a record label, a cola, a bridal gown line, a train—or any of the other brand extensions the company has launched. My favourite is Diesel, whose chief executive says he has "created a movement," not a line of clothes.

The formula for these brand-driven companies is pretty much the same: get rid of your unionised factories in the west and buy your products from Asian or Central American contractors and sub-contractors. Then, take the money you save and spend it on branding—on advertising, superstores, sponsorships. Based on the overwhelming success of this formula, virtue in the corporate world has become a sort of race towards weightlessness: the companies which own the least, keep the fewest employees on the payroll and produce the coolest ideas (as opposed to products) win the race.

I have come to think of such companies as transcendent brands because their goal is to escape almost all that is earthbound and to become pure idea, like a spirit ascending. This is a goal that is available not only to companies, but also to people. We have human brands as well as company brands and they, too, are cutting ties with what might be broadly described as "doing things." Bill Gates has quit as chief executive of Microsoft so that he can tend to his true mission: being Bill Gates. Michael Jordan has stopped playing basketball and has become a pure brand-identity machine. And not only does he now have his own "Jordan" superstores, he is the first celebrity endorser to get other celebrities endorsing his label. Michael Jordan is no longer an athlete, he is an attitude.

It wasn't until the Internet stock explosion that the extent of this shift became apparent. It marks the complete triumph of branding: the ascent of companies, most of which have yet to make a profit, that exist almost purely as ideas of themselves, leaving, no real-world trace at all. What they are selling to Wall Street is unadulterated brand.

This shift to branding explains many of the most fundamental economic and cultural shifts of the past decade. Power, for a brand-driven company, is attained not by collecting assets per se, but by pro-jecting one's brand idea on to as many surfaces of the culture as possible: the wall of a college, a billboard the size of a skyscraper, an ad campaign that waxes philosophic about the humane future of our global village. Where a previous generation of corporate giants used drills, hammers and cranes to build their empires, these companies need an endless parade of new ideas for brand extensions, continuously rejuvenated imagery for marketing and, most of all, fresh new spaces to disseminate their brand's idea of itself.

In this way, these corporate phantoms become real. If we think of a brand-driven company as an ever-expanding balloon, then public space, new political ideas and avant-garde imagery are the gases that inflate it: it needs to consume cultural space in order to stave off its own deflation. This is a major change. Marketing, in the classic sense, is about association: beautiful girl drinks soda, uses shampoo, drives car; soda/shampoo/car become associated with our aspiration to be beautiful like her.

Branding mania has changed all that: association is no longer good enough. The goal now is for the brands to animate their marketing identities, to become real-world, living manifestations of their myths. Brands are about "meaning," not product attributes. So companies provide their consumers with opportunities not merely to shop but to experience fully the meaning of their brand. The brand-name superstore, for instance, stands as a full expression of the brand's lifestyle in miniature. Many of these stores are so palatial, so interactive, so hi-tech that they lose money hand over fist. But that doesn't mean they aren't working. Their real goal, since they are never the company's only source of sales, is to act as a 3D manifestation of the brand, so grand that their rather mundane products will carry that grandeur with them like a homing device. But this is only the beginning. Nike, which used just to sponsor athletes, has taken to buying sporting events outright. Disney, which through its movies and theme parks has sold a bygone version of small-town America, now owns and operates its very own small town, Celebration Florida.

In these branded creations, we see the building blocks of a fully privatised social and cultural infrastructure. These companies are stretching the fabric of their brands in so many directions that they are transformed into tent-like enclosures large enough to house any number of core activities, from shopping to entertainment to holidays. This is the true meaning of a lifestyle brand: living your life inside a brand. Brand-based companies are no longer satisfied with having a fling with their consumers, they want to move in together.

These companies are forever on the prowl for new and creative ways to build and strengthen their brand images. This thirsty quest for meaning and virgin space takes its toll on public institutions such as schools, where, in North America, corporate interests are transforming education, seeking not only to advertise in cafeterias and washrooms but to make brands the uncritical subjects of study. Maths textbooks urge students to calculate the circumference of an Oreo cookie, Channel One broadcasts Burger King ads into 12,000 US schools and a student from Georgia was suspended last year for wearing a Pepsi T-shirt on his school's official "Coke Day."

Another effect is to restrict choice. Brands, at the core, are selfish creatures, driven by the need to eliminate competitors and create self-enclosed branded systems. So Reebok, once it lands a deal to sponsor campus athletics, wants to exclude not only competing brands but also, as was the case at the University of Wisconsin, all disparaging remarks made about Reebok by officials of the university. Such "non-disparagement" clauses are standard in campus sponsorship deals. Disney, after it bought ABC, decided that it would rather ABC News no longer covered Disney's scandals, and focused instead on promoting its movies in various feats of "synergy." We can look forward to more of the same, no doubt, from this month's merger of AOL and Time Warner.

There is another, more tangible, effect of the shift from products to brands: the devaluation of production itself. The belief that economic success lies in branding—production is a distant second—is changing the face of global employment. Building a superbrand is extraordinarily costly. A brand needs constant managing, tending, replenishing, stretching. The necessity for lavish spending on marketing creates intense resistance to investment in production facilities and labour. Companies that were traditionally satisfied with a 100 per cent mark-up from the cost of factory production to the retail price have spent the decade scouring the globe for factories that can make their products so inexpensively that the mark-up is closer to 400 per cent.

That's where the developing world's "free-trade zones" (free, that is, of taxes and wage or other labour regulations) come in. In Indonesia, China, Mexico, Vietnam, the Philippines and elsewhere, the export-processing zones (as these areas are also called) are emerging as leading producers of garments, toys, shoes, electronics and cars. There are almost 1,000 zones around the world, spread through 70 countries and employing approximately 27 million workers.

Inside the gates of the zones, workers assemble the finished products of our branded world: Nike running shoes, Gap pyjamas, IBM computer screens, Old Navy jeans, or VW Bugs. Yet the zones appear to be the only places left on earth where the superbrands actually keep a low profile. Indeed, they are positively demure. Their names and logos aren't splashed on the facades of the factories. In fact, where a particular branded product is made is often kept secret. And unlike in the brand-segregated superstores, competing labels are often produced side by side in the same factories; glued by the same workers, stitched and soldered on the same machines.

Regardless of where the zones are located, the hours will be long—14-hour days in Sri Lanka, 12 in Indonesia, 16 in southern China, 12 in the Philippines. The workers are mostly young women; the management, military-style; the wages, sub-subsistence; the work, low-skill and tedious. The factories are owned by contractors or subcontractors from Korea, Taiwan or Hong Kong; the contractors meet orders for companies based in the US, Britain, Japan, Germany and Canada.

These pockets of pure industry are cloaked in a haze of transience: the contracts come and go with little notice (in Guatemala the factories are called "swallows" because they might take flight at any time); the workers are predominantly migrants, far from home with little connection to the place in which they find themselves; the work itself is short-term, often not renewed. Many factory workers in the Philippines are hired through an employment agency inside the zone walls which collects their cheques and takes a cut—a temp agency for factory workers, in other words. We tend to think that globalisation moves jobs from one country to another. But in a brand-based economy, the value of the work itself moves to a drastically degraded rung of the corporate hierarchy. What is being abandoned in the relentless quest to reduce the costs of production is the Fordist principle: that labour not only creates products but, by paying workers a decent wage, creates the consumer market for that product and others like it. In Indonesia, the young women factory workers making Nike shoes and Gap jeans live a notch above famine victims and landless peasants. And though it may seem indecent to compare them with the relatively privileged retail workers in the western shopping malls, the same pattern is at work. In developed countries, too, jobs are increasingly temporary, part-time, contract based. Just as factory jobs that once supported families in the west have been reconfigured in the developing world as jobs for teenagers, so have the brand-name clothing companies and restaurant chains—Wal-Mart, Starbucks, The

Gap—pioneered the idea that fast-food and retail-sector jobs are disposable and unfit for adults.

And so we are left with an odd duality: brands have never been more omnipresent in our lives, nor have they ever generated as much wealth. All around us we see these new branded creations replacing our cultural institutions and our public spaces. And yet, at the same time, these same companies are oddly absent from our lives in the most immediate of ways: as steady employers. Multinationals that once identified strongly with their role as engines of job growth—and used it as leverage to extract all kinds of government support—now prefer to identify themselves as engines of "economic growth."

The extent of this shift cannot be overstated. Among the total number of working-age adults in the USA, Canada and the UK, those with full-time, permanent jobs working for someone other than themselves are in the minority. Temps, part-timers, the unemployed and those who have opted out of the labour force entirely—some because they don't want to work but many more because they have given up looking for jobs—now make up more than half of the working-age population.

We know that this formula reaps record profits in the short term. It may, however, prove to be a strategic miscalculation. When corporations are perceived as functioning vehicles of wealth distribution—trickling down jobs and tax revenue—they get deep civic loyalty in return. In exchange for steady pay cheques and stable communities, citizens attach themselves to the priorities and fortunes of the local corporate sector and don't ask too many questions about, say, water pollution. In other words, dependable job creation served as a kind of corporate suit of armour, shielding companies from the wrath that might otherwise have been directed their way. Only now, without realising it, brand-driven multinationals have gradually been shedding that armour: first came their inability to respect public space, next came their betrayal of the central promise of the information age—the promise of increased choice—and, finally, they severed the bond between employer and employee. They may be big, they may be rich, but suddenly there is nothing to protect them from public rage.

And that is the true significance of Seattle. All around us we are witnessing the early expressions of this anger, of the first, often crudely constructed lines of defence against the rule of the brands. We have, for example, the growth of "culture-jamming" which adapts a corporation's own advertising to send a message starkly at odds with the one that was intended. So, for example, Apple Computer's "Think Different" campaign acquires a photograph of Stalin with the slogan "Think Really Different." The process forces the company to foot the bill for its own subversion, either literally, because the company is the one that bought the billboard being altered, or figuratively, because whenever anyone messes with a logo, they are tapping into the vast resources spent to make that logo meaningful.

I've never been thoroughly convinced by the powers of culture-jamming: in a war fought strictly with images, surely the one with the most images will win? But the principles of culture-jamming—using the power of brand-names against themselves in a kind of brand boomerang—are being imported to much more direct and immediate political struggles. People are beginning to fight the big global economic battles by focusing on one or two brand-name corporations and turning them into large-scale political metaphors. They are having more luck with this strategy than they had with decades of fighting these battles on a policy level with governments.

Think of the campaigns that trace the journeys of brand-name goods back to their unbranded points of origin: Nike sneakers back to the sweatshops of Vietnam; Starbucks lattes back to the sun scorched coffee fields of Guatemala and now East Timor; and virtually every ingredient of a McDonald's hamburger dissected into its bio-engineered beginnings.

There is a clear difference between these campaigns and the corporate boycotts of the past, whether against Nestle for its baby formula, or against Union Carbide for its infamous toxic accident in Bhopal, India. In those cases, activists had targeted a specific corporation engaged in an anomalously harmful practice. Today's anti-corporate campaigns simply piggyback on the high profile of their brand name targets as a tactical means of highlighting difficult, even arcane issues. The companies being targeted—Disney, Mattel, The Gap and so on—may not always be the worst offenders, but they do tend to be the ones who flash their logos in bright lights on the global marquee. It may seem unfair to single such companies out for their "success," as some have argued, but it is precisely this success which is becoming an odd sort of liability.

Take McDonald's. In opening more than 23,000 outlets world-wide, the company has done more than spread the gospel of fast, uniform food. It has also, inadvertently, become equated in the public imagination with the "McJob," "McDonaldisation" and "McWorld." So when activists build a movement around McDonald's, as they did around the McLibel Trial, they are not really going after a fast-food chain, but harnessing the branding might behind the chain as a way to crack open a discussion on the otherwise impenetrable global economy: about labour, the environment and cultural imperialism.

Many superbrands are feeling the backlash. With typical understatement, Shell Oil's chief executive, Mark Moody, states: "Previously, if you went to your golf club or church and said, 'I work for Shell,' you'd get a warm glow. In some parts of the world, that has changed a bit." That change flowed directly from the anticorporate campaign launched against Shell after the hanging of the Nigerian author and activist Ken Saro-Wiwa, who was fighting to get Shell to clean up the environmental devastation left behind when it pumped oil out of the Niger Delta. Had the campaigners focused on the dictatorship alone, the death of the activist could well have been yet another anonymous atrocity in Africa. But because they dared to name names—to name Shell as the economic interest behind the violence—it became an instantly globalised campaign, with protests at petrol stations around the world. The brand was the campaign's best asset. Something similar happened in the campaign against the brutal regime in Burma; almost all the major brand-name companies have now pulled out. The campaign against Monsanto—which has abandoned its plans for "terminator" seeds, genetically altered so as to yield only one crop—worked because the pressure was put on the heavily branded supermarkets and packaged food companies.

At the heart of this shift in focus is the recognition that corporations are much more than purveyors of the products we all want; they are also the most powerful political forces of our time, the driving forces behind bodies such as the World Trade Organisation. By now, we've all heard the statistics: how corporations such as Shell and Wal-Mart bask in budgets bigger than the gross domestic products of most nations; how, of the top 100 economies, 51 are multinationals and only 49 are countries. So, although the media often describe campaigns like the one against Nike as "consumer boycotts," that tells only part of the story. It is more accurate to describe them as political campaigns that use consumer goods as readily accessible targets, as public-relations levers and as popular education tools.

I doubt this current surge of anti-corporate activism would have been possible without the mania for branding. Branding, as we have seen, has taken a fairly straightforward relationship between buyer and seller and through the quest to turn brands into media providers, art producers, town squares and social philosophers transformed it into something much more intimate. But the more successful this project is, the more vulnerable these companies become to the brand boomerang. If brands are indeed intimately entangled with our culture and identity, then, when they do wrong, their crimes are not easily dismissed as another corporation trying to make a buck. Instead, many of the people who inhabit these branded worlds feel complicit in their wrongs, both guilty and connected. And this connection is a volatile one, akin to the relationship of fan and celebrity: emotionally intense but shallow enough to turn on a dime.

Branding, as I have stated, is a balloon economy: it inflates with astonishing rapidity but it is full of hot air. It shouldn't be surprising that this formula has bred armies of pin-wielding critics, anxious to pop the corporate balloon and watch it fail to the ground.

Behind the protests outside Nike Town, behind the pie in Bill Gates's face, behind the shattering of a McDonald's window in Paris, behind the protests in Seattle, there is something too visceral for most conventional measures to track—a bad mood rising. And the corporate hijacking of political power is as responsible for this mood as the brands' cultural looting of public and mental spaces.

All around the world, activists are making liberal use of the tool that has so thoroughly captured the imagination of the corporate world: branding. Brand image, the source of so much corporate wealth, is also, it turns out, the corporate Achilles' heel.

Clarifications

Internet stock explosion: Times change. The Internet stock explosion Klein wrote about in January 2000 was about to become the dot-com bubble, followed by the burst of the dot-com bubble. The best way to find out about the current state of affairs of this phenomenon is to search on *Google.com* for "dot-com bubble." You never know—by the time this book goes to press, things may have changed again.

Bad mood rising: A nice turn of phrase that owes something to Creedence Clearwater Revival's song *Bad Moon Rising*. For the record, the lyrics of that song include: "I see a bad moon rising, I see trouble on the way, I see earthquakes and lightnin', I see bad times today." Presumably, Naomi Klein had more than just the title in mind when she wrote that phrase.

Fordist principle: A reference to Henry Ford, the car manufacturer, who was famous for, among other things, saying that consumers could have cars any colour they wanted, as long as the colour was black.

Ken Saro-Wiwa was executed by a Nigerian military dictatorship for his writings and protests. You can read more about him on the Mosop Canada home page at *www.mosopcanada.org/text/ken.html*. His son Ken Wiwa wrote the book *In the Shadow of a Saint,* a memoir of his father's life. Ken Wiwa was a journalist for *The Guardian* in Britain, and now lives and writes in Canada.

Talking Points

Read each side of the sweatshop argument and discuss your findings. The arguments of the "anti" forces are found on the Corporate Watch Web site at *www.corpwatch.org* and the Oxfam site at *www.caa. org.au/campaigns*, while the Global Alliance site at *www. theglobalalliance.org* offers a view that Nike endorses. Sites that let Nike off the hook are hard to come by, but Co-op America's Sweatshop (*www.coopamerica.org/sweatshops/ssshoes.htm*) gives a balanced view on the running shoe issue. Discussions on this issue may become heated. Make sure your arguments are informed by reading what each side has to say.

To what extent should an athlete or movie star maintain a squeaky clean image for the sake of a sponsor? Does that celebrity become part of the brand in everything he or she does? If you wore a uniform at high school, you represented your school even when off the premises. You were the brand image of your school. Was it important that you behaved well while dressed in the uniform?

In October 2001, writer Jonathan Franzen, whose book *The Corrections* had been selected by Oprah Winfrey for her book club, made some disparaging remarks about "Oprah books." Oprah then declined to do her usual interview with him on her show, although she did allow him to stay on her book club list, and to leave her logo on the book cover. In effect, Franzen was objecting to his book being categorized as "brand Oprah." What effect does the Oprah brand have on readers in your class? Does it have the same effect on your teacher?

Web Research

The best examples of culture jamming are at found at Adbusters (*www.adbusters.org*). You might also like to go to CMM (Critical Mess Media) at *www.rootmedia.org/~messmedia/messhome.htm*.

The Onion, an on-line journal that bills itself as "America's finest news source," deals with counter-culture issues and anti-corporate ideas at *www.theonion.com*.

Writing That Works

Introduction—question: "What are we to make of the extraordinary scenes in Seattle that brought the 20th century to a close?" The article is an answer to that question, telling us what we are to make of the scenes.

Definition: "Branding seems like a fairly innocuous idea. It is slapping a logo on a product and saying it's the best. And when brands first emerged, that was all it was. At the start of the industrial revolution, the market was flooded with nearly identical mass-produced products. Along came Aunt Jemima and Quaker Oats with their happy comforting logos to say: our mass-produced product is of the highest quality." Naomi Klein tends not to use secondary sources. Her ideas are original and so are her definitions.

Metaphor: The language is often highly metaphorical: "their goal is to escape almost all that is earthbound and to become pure idea, like a spirit ascending"; "he can tend to his true mission."

Comparison: "Where a previous generation of corporate giants used drills, hammers and cranes to build their empires, these companies need an endless parade of new ideas for brand extensions, continuously rejuvenated imagery for marketing and, most of all, fresh new spaces to disseminate their brand's idea of itself."

Conclusion—summary: "All around the world, activists are making liberal use of the tool that has so thoroughly captured the imagination of the corporate world: branding. Brand image, the source of so much corporate wealth, is also, it turns out, the corporate Achilles' heel."

TOPIC *2*

BRANDING AND REBRANDING CANADA

INTRODUCTION

Although you may be familiar with the concept of branding from a marketing class, you may not have thought of branding a country until you read about it in the previous section. However, many of the articles in this section talk about the image of Canada as a "brand." In his article "Canada Isn't Working," Milo Cernetig observes that "Canada has for too long branded itself as the land of vacations, of beavers and nice folks." Sonia Arrison agrees, noting in "Trying to Package a Unique Canadian Identity" that "Canadian humility gets in the way. Canadians just cannot say, 'We're the best!'" She notes further that Canadians tend to identify themselves as non-American: "They are aggressive; so we are passive. They are a cultural melting pot; so we are a multicultural mosaic. They are rude; so we are polite. You get the picture. Basically, we have branded ourselves as 'Canada: not American.'"

Our lack of strong identity or brand may stem from our proximity to the United States. Former prime minister Pierre Trudeau once famously said that being next door to the United States was "like sleeping with an elephant: no matter how friendly and even-tempered the beast, one is affected by every twitch and grunt."

The articles in this section all look at the problem of Canadian identity from the business perspective of either selling Canada as a brand or, in the case of "Why Canadians Can't Market," aggressively selling our brands overseas. The crux of the problem is best expressed by International Trade Minister Pierre Pettigrew, who said:

> I am struck by how other nations view Canada. We are still seen as a nice country, with Mounties, maple syrup and hockey. We are not yet recognized as an economy fired by information technology, fuelled by telecommunications and fortified by the fifth-largest aerospace industry in the world. This outdated view of Canada has to change, because investment dollars will flow to where they produce the greatest return. We simply cannot afford to forgo opportunities based on false impressions.

Definitions of Brand

Brand is a word with a variety of meanings, as this extract from the *Columbia Encyclopedia* shows:

Noun: 1a. *A trademark or distinctive name identifying a product or a manufacturer.* **b.** *A product line so identified: a popular brand of soap.* **c.** *A distinctive category; a particular kind: a brand of comedy that I do not care for.* **2.** *A mark indicating identity or ownership, burned on the hide of an animal with a hot iron.* **3.** *A mark burned into the flesh of criminals.* **4.** *A mark of disgrace or notoriety; a stigma. See synonyms at stain* **5.** *A branding iron.* **6.** *A piece of burning or charred wood.* **7.** *A sword: "So flashed and fell the brand Excalibur" (Tennyson).*

(The Columbia Encyclopedia, Sixth Edition. 2001.)

Trying to Package a Unique Canadian Identity

by Sonia Arrison

Toronto Star, May 24, 1999

Canadians think of themselves as polite, peace loving, and more deferential to government than our neighbors south of the border. In general, some would say that we're a pretty nice bunch of people. Why we hold these beliefs has been the subject of much debate. One new theory that came to my attention recently as I attended the Canada

Conference in celebration of Newfoundland's 50th Canadian anniversary, is the idea that Canadians believe certain things about Canada because that's how Canada has been "branded."

Branding is a fancy term employed by marketers to mean "image." Don Watt, president of Watt Industries and inventor of the immensely successful President's Choice brand of groceries, gave a presentation at the conference. He explained how it was possible to turn the profits of a business around by re-branding their products or image. To him, branding equals trust. For instance, some people buy only Crest toothpaste or Tide detergent because they trust the brand. They trust that the product sold inside the brand packaging will be what they have come to expect, and in this case what they are expecting is good quality toothpaste and detergent. This same principle, Mr. Watt noted, could be applied to a province such as Newfoundland.

On their 50th anniversary in union with Canada, Newfoundlanders looked back at their triumphs and failures with the hope that this examination will bring ideas of how to get more of the former and less of the latter. But what strategies could work?

What Newfoundland might need, Watt proposed, is a brand. This is not to imply that Newfoundland is void of beauty or interest without corporate marketers to help it. What Watts was implying is that Newfoundland is not as well known to others, both inside and outside Canada, as it should be.

The idea of provincial branding is not new. Other provinces have done it before, some more successfully than others. Remember the 80's slogan "Supernatural: British Columbia," or consider Alberta's brand "the Alberta Advantage." Now contemplate, what do people imagine when they think of BC—yes, that's right: nature, the ocean, the mountains. And Alberta? Tax advantages, and low housing prices. What these provinces did was identify and highlight some of their true strengths. Ontario is attempting this process as I write. The new slogan is "Ontario, open for business." Whether this will be a successful brand or not will depend on how truthful it is as well as on whether a province "open for business" is valued by both those inside and outside the province. The success of a brand depends on how real the image portrayed is, and whether or not that image is desirable to those it is trying to attract.

As for Newfoundland, it is a beautiful place filled with colourful people. The landscape is breathtaking. The rock formations and icebergs are awe inspiring, and Newfoundland can boast that the area of Gros Morne, a UNESCO world heritage site "offers mountains twenty times older than the Rockies and glacially-carved inland fjords." Many of Canada's best comedians and artists are from or live in Newfoundland. Mary Walsh and Rick Mercer of *This Hour Has 22 Minutes* as well as painters Mary and Christopher Pratt are but a few of the examples. Perhaps these truths are something for the Rock to build on.

In any event, I would go farther than Watt did in his presentation and argue that what Canada needs is a new brand. Canadians have spent more time than any other nation I can think of discussing their identity. We can't seem to agree on who we are collectively, or where we see ourselves in the future.

Scholars spend inordinate amounts of time pondering the identity issue, and politicians have racked their brains trying to reach elusive consensus and keep the country together. Perhaps the problem needs to be looked at from a new perspective. Could it be that Canadians don't like their current brand? Or, is it possible that the Canada brand is not based in truth? Maybe it's both.

Scott Reid, an astute observer of Canadian politics, recently noted that one of the flaws of our current Canadian identity is that "Canadians insist on defining themselves in opposition to the Americans."

The U.S. was founded on individualistic principles; so we were founded on public institutions. They are aggressive; so we are passive. They are a cultural melting pot; so we are a multicultural mosaic. They are rude; so we are polite. You get the picture. Basically, we have branded ourselves as "Canada: not American."

This brand has not been immensely successful for Canadians. It relies not on the realities of Canadians, but on the image of Americans. When we look at ourselves in the mirror, the product does not match up with the packaging.

It is clear, then, that a new brand is needed, as the old does not ring true. Canadians need to look in the mirror, forget about the experts and their "analyses" of Canadian identity, and forge ahead with the qualities of Canada that are attractive. A country with a strong liberal democratic tradition, enterprising people, and an abundance of natural resources has more to offer than being "non-American." Oh, and the services of a good marketer would probably be helpful too.

Clarifications

Multicultural mosaics and melting pots: These metaphors refer, respectively, to the way Canada and the United States identify themselves as multicultural countries. In Canada we prefer to see many small groups creating one large picture, rather like a mosaic or tiled image. By contrast, Americans see themselves as mixing and blending different cultures into one homogeneous whole. You can read about culture, identity and values from a Canadian viewpoint on the Media Awareness network at *www.media-awareness.ca*.

UNESCO: United Nations Educational, Scientific, and Cultural Organization. Check the Web page at *www.unesco.org*.

Talking Points

Rick Mercer (the Newfoundland-born comedian mentioned in the article) interviewed Americans about Canada in a feature on *This Hour Has 22 Minutes* titled "Talking to Americans." It aimed to show how little the average American knows about Canada. Mercer achieved fifteen minutes of fame in the U.S. media when he cornered then–presidential hopeful George W. Bush and told him that Canadian Prime Minister "Jean Poutine" had endorsed Bush as the candidate to "take the world into the twenty-first century." Is it true that Americans know less about us than we know about them? Are we equally as guilty of ignorance about the United States? Was Mercer fair? After the terrorist attacks on the World Trade Center, Mercer declined his nomination for a Gemini Award, saying "While I am honoured that the program has received these nominations, I feel that this is not a time to be making light of the differences between two nations, but rather a time to offer our unconditional support to our neighbours, friends and relatives to the south." (*TV Guide*). Do you think the emotion he expressed was a temporary one, or did September 11 change our relationship with the U.S. permanently?

Without reference to the United States, what do you think it is that makes a Canadian? Create a list.

Sonia Arrison mentions slogans for two provinces. Does your province have a slogan? How many people in your class know what it is? Could you come up with a better one? How about a slogan for

Canada? The Symbols of Canada Web page mentioned below may help prompt some ideas.

Arrison's thesis is that "a new brand is needed, as the old does not ring true." What is the effect of putting this thesis at the end of the essay rather than at the beginning?

Web Research

Canada has ten provinces and three territories. Links to each of the thirteen governments can be found on the Government of Canada Web site at *www.canada.gc.ca/othergov/prov_e.html.*

The federal Government has a Symbols of Canada Web page at *www.pch.gc.ca/progs/cpsc-ccsp/sc-cs/index_e.cfm*

Find links to Business Statistics and Analyses at the Government of Canada's Business Gateway at *www.businessgateway.ca.*

Check the government's Web page on multiculturalism on the Canadian Heritage Web site: *www.pch.gc.ca.*

Go to the Government of Canada Web site at *www.gc.ca* and click on the "Non-Canadians" link. Then click on "Canadian Identity" for several useful links.

Writing That Works

Introduction—definition: The opening defines a Canadian, or at least what most of us think is a Canadian. The image, the article explains, is actually a brand. Other definitions are used throughout: "Branding is a fancy term employed by marketers to mean 'image'"; "Canadians insist on defining themselves in opposition to Americans."

Inductive pattern: Try to find a thesis statement in the first few paragraphs of this article. There isn't one. Why not? Because it has been placed at the end: "It is clear, then, that a new brand is needed." Inductive structure moves from the general to the specific. The argument is built with examples, specifically from Newfoundland, British Columbia and Alberta.

Question and answer: "But what strategies would work? What Newfoundland might need, Watt proposed, is a brand."

Canada Isn't Working

by Milo Cernetig

ROB Magazine, May 2001

The subtropical afternoon sun beats down on Shenzhen City, a proletarian hive of grim, no-name factories on the Communist side of the Hong Kong border, where China's poor come to earn a couple of dollars a day. A willowy peasant named Wang Bo happens to stroll out of a noodle shop, and bump into a foreigner.

"American?" he asks, as he saunters over for a chat and maybe to bum a cigarette.

He sticks a bony finger in the factory smog, and then, though he speaks not a word of real English, begins rattling away in a global lingo known even to Chinese peasantry: "Boeing. Microsoft. Coca-Cola. General Motors. IBM...Dou hao, dou hao." All good, all good.

I'm Canadian, I protest, interrupting his stream of brand-name consciousness. Know any Canadian companies? Old Wang's finger comes down, his 50-something brow furrows and he falls silent. He reverts to his thick Mandarin: "Truly, I can't think of a single thing from Canada," he confesses, trailing off with "dui bu qi, dui bu qi," I'm sorry, I'm sorry, and he wanders away.

Several minutes pass and he's back.

"I now remember something."

"Oh, what's that?" I ask.

"Seal oil!" he pronounces, with a discreet wave toward his crotch. "I am using your seal oil for my health! It is really very good."

Great, eh?

The UN rated Canada No. 1 in livability, despite our high taxes and long, cold winters, and our Maple Leaf is instantly recognizable—the favourite flag to put on a knapsack in a war zone. And yet, and yet...

After my encounter with old Wang, I began to try the same test in other countries: Name something, anything, from Canada. In England, a pub owner professed that Canadians supply the world with "wheat, ice skates and hockey sticks, and piss-poor beer but not much else." In North Vietnam, a former Communist official, now making a fortune exporting antiques to New York, said Canada provides his country with development aid and food. But it is Finland and Vietnam's former enemy, the U.S., where the country finds its mobile phones and telecommunications networks.

"Does Canada have such technology?" he asked. "I've never thought this."

And who can blame him? Even Americans still see Canadians as hewers of wood and drawers of water. When shares in Nortel Networks melted down, Americans I met expressed astonishment that the company wasn't American.

"I didn't know you Canadians did high tech on a kind of scale that mattered," said Sammy Meecher, a businessman waiting for a flight to L.A. in a Hong Kong airport lounge. "What other companies do you have like that?"

A Filipina student named Joan Sanchez, working her way through a business degree, added: "I know you have lots of trees and gold and snow, but I don't know really what you make. Is it anything important?" And then the inevitable: "Anyway, isn't Canada just really part of the United States?"

Let's face it, the world thinks the only buzz that comes from Canada is lumberjacks firing up their chainsaws. In its annual survey of international executives, Chicago-based A.T. Kearney Inc. recently found Canada was 12th as an investment choice in the global marketplace. Who's ahead of us? Poland, with a paltry $4,014 (U.S.) GDP per capita.

But who can fault investors for misunderstanding Canada? Even Canadians are caught in the past: A recent Ekos Research Associates study found that 46% of Canadians still think our No. 1 export is wood pulp products. Actually, it's only about 5% of total exports.

Fortunately, the sad state of our national image is finally becoming apparent to politicians. Last fall, then-industry minister (now Foreign Affairs Minister) John Manley acknowledged that the image of Canadians as a "fun-loving people who produce beer and hockey players" is hurting chances of building a high-tech economy.

In an address to a business forum in Banff, International Trade Minister Pierre Pettigrew had this to say: "I am struck by how other nations view Canada. We are still seen as a nice country, with Mounties, maple syrup and hockey. We are not yet recognized as an economy fired by information technology, fuelled by telecommunications and fortified by the fifth-largest aerospace industry in the world. This outdated view of Canada has to change, because investment dollars will flow to where they produce the greatest return. We simply cannot afford to forgo opportunities based on false impressions."

But is Ottawa up to the job of giving us a makeover? Don't count on it.

You smell it the instant you walk into the China World Hotel: the aroma of thousands of freshly made photocopies, $5.1 billion worth of deals newly minted in Beijing. (Or is that $1.4 billion? About $3.7 billion were Memorandums of Understanding. Who knows what becomes of them after they hit the news headlines?) The papers fill four tables in the small conference room.

In February, Jean Chrétien's spin doctors buzzed around this place, pushing the Ottawa press corps to report on just how much business the PM had sealed during his recent visit to China. "It's an amazing number," gushed one of the dark-suited minions charged with putting Jean Chrétien in the headlines. "We've scored big this time. Really big."

It was all part of the strange, uniquely Canadian phenomenon known as Team Canada, the Prime Minister's idea of how to go about branding us overseas. Think of it as an all-star hockey game, with Chrétien as centre, and 600 business and government delegates skating around him. On first blush, the idea doesn't seem all that bad. Come to a country with your best companies and then push through deals, which the Prime Minister certainly did, from selling Bombardier jets to landing contracts with small companies to sell Canadian fish.

The thing is, it doesn't work. And the strategy, about the only strategy the Liberal government offers to put Canada on the map overseas, breaks every modern rule in building a national brand. For one thing, the PM's outings—which cost the taxpayers $5 to $10 million each time—are too few and far between. Chrétien's first Team Canada visit to China was in 1994, and the latest this past February (though a smaller delegation did land on Chinese soil in 1998). The trips help Canada make a big splash—for a day or two. But the fascination ends as soon as the politicians go home. Canadian companies now rarely make the business headlines in China, where total trade amounts to $360 billion (U.S.) a year.

Worse, the Team Canada trips abroad are abysmally short on focus. Hundreds of businesses have come to China with Chrétien, but only a handful snagged any real publicity that might help them crack into the marketplace. Even though the corporate bigwigs spend about $10,000 each to be in the PM's company, they are definitely second-stringers. The attention always swirls around Chrétien.

With a few exceptions. On the last Team Canada trip, it was 12-year-old Keith Peiris, a part-time web-page designer, who took the lion's share of publicity for his London, Ont., startup, Cyberteks

Design. He was trotted out before the media like a child forced to play the piano at his parents' dinner party. Here was Canada's high-tech representative: a preteen Peiris wearing a tiny pinstripe suit.

"I thought it was amusing," said a U.S. investment banker. "But it didn't tell us much about Canada's business strengths."

Sitting in his corner office overlooking Beijing's business district, John Gruetzner shakes his head ruefully when he ponders Team Canada's impact. "The first trip in 1994 was an excellent idea," says Gruetzner, the Toronto native who heads Intercedent Ltd., a consulting firm in Beijing. Sure, he concedes, "the first Team Canada mission worked. It gave Canadians a sense of unity, it helped the business community realize that they could—and should—compete on the international stage."

But John Gruetzner says it's now a self-defeating exercise. "You don't repeat your wedding reception every four years. People won't keep coming to it." Plus, he adds, there's a strategic flaw. "Look, Team Canada subordinates Canadian companies and products under a generic banner. It's the wrong way to go about branding. Think of a big company like Procter & Gamble. P&G doesn't care if you know who P&G is. They brand their products. We should be doing the same: brand our 200 most successful Canadian companies abroad and not the Prime Minister. It's confusing to international consumers."

The numbers prove it. We are failing to build a presence in China, a market Chrétien has identified as crucial to Canada's economic growth. According to the Department of Foreign Affairs and International Trade, our trade deficit with China has soared to $7.5 billion and total trade is only $15 billion, falling below the $20 billion Chrétien predicted when launching his first Team Canada mission.

What's more, we've made some embarrassing missteps. Consider Chrétien's 1998 trip to China, in which he appeared at a photo op with some of China's most senior leaders. The event aimed to promote the Beijing Toronto International Hospital, a proposed private health-care facility targeted to expats and China's rich. It never opened. Few in China wanted to pay the $10,000 (U.S.) membership fee. And it left the Chinese a tad confused about what Canada stood for. If Canada was a leader in providing universal health care, why was its Prime Minister promoting health care for profit overseas, using a model that wouldn't be allowed in his own country?

On the same 1998 trip, Chrétien chose to make fast food a trademark of Canadian entrepreneurialism. Inside a grimy Beijing bus station, he and several image-makers posed for pictures with Anne Chong Hill, a business woman whom the Liberals later appointed to the Canadian Agri-Food Council. Chong Hill had big plans to put "Annie's" fast-food kiosks, each emblazoned with the Maple Leaf, in bus terminals around the Chinese capital. The PM trumpeted Annie's as a symbol of Canadian dynamism, predicting the franchise would soon challenge McDonald's for a slice of China's multibillion-dollar a year fast-food market.

Mistake. The Beijing Bus and Trolley Co. Ltd., Annie's Chinese partner, did not secure the necessary permits and capital. Annie's $682,245 in investment was written off.

"Oh yes, we remember your leader here," recalls Fu Guowei, a station ticket-taker. "He said Canada makes better French fries than Americans? But we cannot find those Canadian French fries he talked about."

Bland and invisible. That's how Paul Temporal describes our country. The soft-spoken Brit, a branding consultant based in Singapore, has conceived image campaigns for international corporations such as Intel, Motorola and Marks & Spencer. "You know, Canada really has no profile on the global stage," he says, trying to be encouraging. "But that's actually a positive thing. You have no real negative attributes to overcome, which is important when you try to create a brand, believe me."

Temporal should know. He was hired for a campaign to spice up Britain's image in Asia—a precursor to Tony Blair's "Cool Britannia"—hard going in a continent where there are still lingering resentments of Britain's colonial policies. "Some countries have a lot of negative baggage to overcome," he continues. "Canada doesn't. That's a big advantage. The problem is that nobody really knows much about the country. Nortel is the classic example. Nobody sees it as a Canadian company. You've got to fix that."

The only solution is to kick-start a national branding strategy. Temporal, the author of *Branding in Asia*, urges a program that creates a national task force, then takes two or three months to study exactly what we should tell the world about the Canadian economy. The job isn't hard, since Canada already has a brand symbol: the Maple Leaf. "Canadians just need to decide what to build into it." That means promoting the more exciting companies. Pick passenger jets over potash—and suffer the hurt feelings of the people of Saskatchewan. And if you send trade delegations, make sure the companies involved represent a united front—projecting an image Ottawa has agreed upon.

Temporal also prescribes a multimillion-dollar, international ad campaign launched by the government to run over an 18-month to five-year period. "Canada has no time to waste. This is a crowded market and other countries have a lead." Specifically, Singapore, Taiwan and Ireland are rapidly building up their own national brands to take a bigger share of high-tech trade.

Ireland has even re-engineered its entire tax structure to attract high-tech investment and workers. Despite early setbacks—remember John DeLorean wanting to produce cars in Northern Ireland?—the country has done away with its "paddy Irish" past. You won't hear Irish fiddles or see tipsy leprechauns on much of Ireland's overseas advertising today. Instead: images of high-tech software plants and new yuppies, smiling over pints of Guinness as they think about their red-hot real estate.

Ultimately, rebranding Canada comes down to one unassailable difficulty: The United States is right next door. The world's largest cultural and economic engine will almost always overshadow us. Canada's most innovative products and companies are too often regarded as American. We have few flagship consumer goods, certainly nothing like what an IKEA is to Sweden, or Armani and Ferrari represent to Italy.

"Most people think Canada and they think tree. Not very sexy, I'm afraid," says Jay Jaffe of Washington, D.C.–based Jaffe Associates, a business-development consultancy. Jaffe has been involved in repackaging the images of major Bay Street law firms—companies that continue to lose their talent to the U.S. brain drain.

The issue, he says, is that Canada's image hasn't changed in decades. "Canada has for too long branded itself as the land of vacations, of beavers and nice folks," says Jaffe. "I think there's a psychological problem. It's a country where you are always looking for consensus, to be pleasant. The problem is that when you always look for that agreement, you are left with no direction—and this creates a fuzzy national brand that is empty of meaning. Let me tell you what we Americans think. We liked to watch Pierre Trudeau. We thought of him as your JFK, there was spark to him and he added spark to Canada. But the sparks have gone."

The key to changing that is to make the world believe that Canadians can be aggressive: "Let people know the beaver has fangs," says Jaffe. "Cover your Maple Leaf in computer chips."

As for Team Canada missions, Jaffe dismisses them as passé. "That's the old way of doing things, like a Chamber of Commerce meeting. You need to get out of the suits and ties—it's a new world."

For instance, we should get behind a high-tech product, like the BlackBerry by Waterloo's Research In Motion, and use it to represent a more tech-savvy Canada. "It's a fabulous product the world loves, but almost nobody realizes it's from Canada," says Jaffe. Take this product, or a basket of Canadian gadgets and then promote them as Canadian originals. Better yet, pay Mike Myers an endorsement deal to hold the product as part of a national ad campaign. Much of the world thinks he's American too.

Ambassador Leonard Edwards sits on the porch of the official residence behind the Canadian Embassy in Tokyo, looking reflectively at the Japanese garden that stretches before him. Edwards gets the point of rebranding. He says that in 1998, within weeks of taking up post as Canada's man in the world's No. 2 economy, he sensed Canada was losing out in the branding wars.

Speaking in a voice just audible above the garden's burbling water wheel, Edwards explains that his first move was to set up a branding committee inside the embassy and then commission a survey of attitudes toward Canada. "We needed to know exactly what the Japanese thought about us."

It wasn't pretty. The survey of 150 Japanese, picked to represent a demographic slice of the country, painted Canada as a friendly but stodgy country that few thought capable of surprise. Ninety-five per cent of respondents knew Anne of Green Gables was a Canadian creation. But only 3% thought of Canada as a source of high technology. The greatest blow, however, was that the Japanese, ardent consumers of digital technology and perhaps the world's greatest assimilators of Western popular culture, saw us as dull. Only 9% of the Japanese actually deemed Canada "a country with lively and exciting cities."

The survey, Edwards explains, shows a need for a fusion of business and culture to reinvigorate our brand. This spring, the embassy has launched "Think Canada 2001," a PR campaign to barrage the Japanese with Canadiana. It features a visit by Margaret Atwood, performances by Cirque du Soleil, foreign-policy conferences on Canada's views on geopolitics and social policy, as well as a "high-tech caravan" rolling out with Canadian executives in biotech, infotech, health care, transportation and aerospace. Anne of Green Gables is definitely not invited.

It's only a first, small step, says Edwards. And it's still too early to see if the Think Canada campaign will be able to turn around perceptions in Japan. And then there's the unspoken fear back home. Established companies which still play a major role in the economy and in campaign financing aren't happy to hear politicians talk about an exercise that spends millions promoting new industries. "It's a balancing act, but it has to be done," admits Edwards, gazing up at the embassy's canopy of trees. "Part of a search for a brand means finding champions. In a global world, the big players have no difficulty being identified. Smaller countries need branding. We have to get the Japanese to think Canadian. We still want them to think Canadian when they buy agricultural products. But we also want them to think Canadian when they are buying software."

Among politicians and bureaucrats, Edwards is a pioneer. There's still no clear rebranding plan from Ottawa. But he insists that branding has become a hot topic in the backrooms. And he'll keep it that way. Edwards is expected to return to Ottawa this summer as a senior mandarin, perhaps the Deputy Minister of Trade. That would make him a key architect in a national rebranding strategy. "It's something we can't be left behind on," he vows.

In some ways, it's no surprise that Canada has allowed its brand to wilt. After all, we haven't had to advertise ourselves in order to prosper. A decade of unprecedented growth in the U.S. economy spilled over the border. Canada's economy not only grew but actually transformed itself. At the start of the 1990s, exports accounted for about 25% of our GDP. Today, according to the Foreign Affairs Department, it's more than 45%.

But now, we are ever more reliant on the U.S. economy, with a staggering $92-billion trade surplus that keeps the Canadian economy's pistons pumping. So what? Well, if the U.S. economy cools down, Canada may get pneumonia. And politicians in Washington, now watching American companies lay off tens of thousands, won't stay quiet forever about that surplus.

International diversification is essential. But the latest trade stats from Foreign Affairs show that 87% of Canada's international trade is now with the United States. Meanwhile, trade with China has shrunk to about 0.9% of Canada's total exports—down from 1.2% at the start of the '90s. In Canada, China sees a marginal player, a client state of the U.S.

Consider this scene near Beijing's Tiananmen Square last February. The Canadian flags flap in the cold Gobi Desert wind blowing down the Boulevard of Eternal Peace, put up by Chinese officials to greet Jean Chrétien. Suddenly, the official limo flies by, with the PM's massive delegation in tow, their sedans sporting the Maple Leaf.

"Why are all these Canadian people here?" asked Jenny Li, recognizing our flag.

"It's our Prime Minister," I promptly answer. "He wants to sell things to China. Planes. Other things."

"Oh, Canada sells Boeing jets?"

"Actually we have a company that makes our own—it's called Bombardier."

"That is good," she says, offering a surprised smile. "But it will be hard for your leadership. We buy such things from America. Or from England and France. They make very good planes, you know."

Clarifications

Mandarin: As used in this article a mandarin is a high government official, more specifically a bureaucrat. Check an on-line dictionary (available at *www.bartleby.com*) to see what the original meaning of the word was. Why is it especially appropriate in this article? While there, you may also want to check on the meaning of the word *proletariat*, also used in this article.

Minion: A subservient, sycophantic follower. Mr. Burns's assistant Smithers on *The Simpsons* is the archetypal minion.

Cool Britannia: A phrase used to describe Britain's new business image. The phrase is a play on title of the patriotic British song "Rule Britannia." See a more complete explanation at World Wide Words: Investigating International English from a British Viewpoint (*www.worldwidewords.org/turnsofphrase/tp-cool.htm*).

Flagship: The most important of a related group of things. In this article the term refers to the chief business in a group of businesses. Of course, the the word originates from the ship in a fleet that bears the commander's flag.

Trudeaumania: As a young Canadian you may find it hard to understand what would make your parents view a forty-something politician as a sixties version of Brad Pitt. A paragraph from an obituary on the American news channel CNN best captures the spirit of Trudeau: "A sharp, energetic figure, he wore sandals to Parliament, dated celebrities such as singer Barbra Streisand and actress Margo Kidder, flashed an obscene gesture to protesters and once did a pirouette behind the back of Britain's Queen Elizabeth." Read the complete obituary at *www.cnn.com*. Search for "Pierre Trudeau."

Talking Points

The article suggests that Canada could create a new brand image by having an actor like Mike Myers use a product like the BlackBerry (see the BlackBerry Web site at *www.rim.com*). What other combinations of actors or celebrities and companies could you suggest?

Are there students in the class who have been in Canada for a year or less? Find out what their image of Canada was before they came here. Did they have preconceptions about the weather, the people, the businesses they would find in Canada? Did they think our police officers all wore red jackets and Stetsons? That we all mushed across frozen wastelands behind teams of huskies? Or was their image more up to date than mine was when I came to Canada in 1973 with those ideas firmly in mind!

In his book and on his Web site, Paul Temporal, an expert mentioned in the article above, writes about the branding problems of the All Blacks, the New Zealand national rugby team. Temporal reports that the team "was viewed as cold, remote, stern, unforgiving, and reticent. People perceived the team to be arrogant and full of themselves, and their behavior on and off the field tended to reinforce this unfavourable perception." (Read the case study at *www.brandingasia. com/cases/cases.htm*). The team has made a concerted effort to establish a new brand, focusing on professionalism and consistency. In groups, take one of Canada's professional sports teams and discuss the image or brand of that team. Is there anything the team could change about its image? How could the team work on creating a new image? Do Canadian teams in leagues dominated by American teams (the National Hockey League, for example) have to distinguish themselves as Canadian? Report to the class on your findings.

International Trade Minister Pierre Pettigrew is quoted in the article as saying, "I am struck by how other nations view Canada. We are still seen as a nice country, with Mounties, maple syrup and hockey. We are not yet recognized as an economy fired by information technology, fuelled by telecommunications and fortified by the fifth-largest aerospace industry in the world." Which Canadian companies are associated with these forward-looking industries he mentions?

Web Research

The Team Canada Web site is at *www.tcm-mec.gc.ca.*

Read Paul Temporal's Asia Branding Tips at *www.brandingasia.com* to help you understand what a country needs to do to improve its "brand."

Sports in Canada is concerned with branding the image of sports. See the Web site at *www.sportmatters.ca.*

Writing That Works

Introduction—anecdote: Like many of the articles in this book, the introduction here is an anecdote with literary overtones. The anecdote, or story, is a microcosmic version of what the article is about: People in other countries don't know about Canada and therefore it is difficult for us to sell out products overseas.

Examples: The argument is built with examples the writer gathered through asking people in other countries about what they knew about Canada. "In England, a pub owner professed that Canadians supply the world with 'wheat, ice skates and hockey sticks, and piss poor beer'"; "I know you have lots of trees and gold and snow, but I really don't know what you make."

Metaphor: "Jean Chretien's spin doctors buzzed around this place." The spin doctors are likened to flies or mosquitoes—something annoying, anyway.

Expert opinion: "Bland and invisible. That's how Paul Temporal describes our country. The soft-spoken Brit, a branding consultant based in Singapore...."

Studies and statistics: "In its annual survey of international executives, Chicago-based A.T. Kearney Inc. recently found Canada was 12th as an investment choice in the global marketplace. Who's ahead of us? Poland, with a paltry $4,014 (U.S.) GDP per capita."

Why Canadians Can't Market

by Hilary Davidson, with additional material by Susanne Baillie and Kali Pearson

Profit: The Magazine for Canadian Entrepreneurs, April 1, 2001

Canadians are world-renowned engineers, hockey players, peace-keepers and comedians. But try to name a successful Canadian marketer, and the talent pool seems to run dry. "We're probably the world's worst marketers," says new-economy entrepreneur Ken Nickerson, former general manager of Microsoft Canada.

There's no lack of remarkable Canadian innovations to trumpet: think frozen foods, the pacemaker and even the zipper. But for many reasons, Canadians seem uncomfortable promoting themselves and their brands. "We could find a cure for the common cold," says Nickerson, "and we would go, 'Uh, we've got this pill and, uh, you know, we hate to interrupt you, but...'"

That famous national reticence could be killing us. Once-proud Canadian brands such as Admiral and Massey Ferguson are defunct or shadows of their former selves. Just six years after venturing north, Wal-Mart has become our largest department-store chain, eclipsing such established rivals as Eatons, The Bay and Zellers. It will happen again and again. With the growth of world trade, the rise of the Internet and the globalization of brands, Canadian companies that aren't up to speed in marketing should prepare to be crushed.

The experts agree that our dismal marks in marketing stem from an inability to grapple with a gamut of disciplines starting with branding.

"Marketing is often misunderstood," says Brett Marchand, the former vice-president of marketing for Molson who was behind the "My name is Joe, and I am Canadian" phenomenon. "People focus on advertising... [but] marketing is about positioning your company, about creating a brand character." It's building an identity around your product—and your company. It includes the total sales and support environment: packaging, public relations, customer service, merchandising, market research and advertising.

Marchand, who worked in Philadelphia for branding wizards Campbell Soup Co. for five years, sees big differences between the approaches to marketing in Canada and the U.S. South of the border, companies create what he calls a "brand-positioning statement," which details a brand's character. The brand identity of the Pillsbury Doughboy even specifies what the character can or can't do (e.g., he's always friendly, never says a harsh word to anyone). But in Canada, says Marchand, companies "hire an agency and want an ad. They don't discuss brand creation."

It's not only our companies that can't turn strong products and services into great brands. Canada as a whole, with all its natural and human sources, can't seem to get the message across that it's a good place to do business. In a recent survey by A.T. Kearney Inc., the world's top executives were asked to list their picks for foreign direct investment. Canada ranked No. 12—after Spain, India and Poland. Twelfth! Why does a tiny country like Ireland sit higher on that list? The poll credits the Celtic Tiger's powerful marketing and sales. Even the brand "Celtic Tiger" was the result of a concerted marketing campaign that Canadians have yet to equal.

Lousy marketing stifling our businesses—and our country. It's time we got serious about selling.

WHY WE STINK

How did we get here? Many reasons. "Our economy is resource-driven," says Evan Chrapko, high-tech entrepreneur and currently the CEO of A-LIVE Holdings II Inc. in Toronto. "There's just not a hell of a lot of selling with a commodity. But once you add value to those resources, we're at a loss about how to go about selling."

Our branch-plant economy hasn't helped matters. "Brand-product marketing has been a hole here," says Nigel Stokes of Markham, Ont. database-software maker DataMirror Corp. "If Microsoft is just a branch plant [here], they don't have a world mandate." In other words, many Canadians work in offices where marketing just isn't a concern—it's handled in New York or Atlanta. And the picture is getting worse, says Marchand. Major U.S. firms that once did Canadian market planning here—such as Kimberly-Clark and Procter & Gamble—have pulled their strategic marketing operation back to the States, closing down what once was a major training ground for Canadian marketers. "You have brand managers [in Canada] who are not in charge of marketing anymore," says Marchand.

Then there's our national modesty. "Americans are born marketing machines—there's no disgrace in it to them," says Mary K.

Marsden, founder of the Mar.Com Group, a strategic marketing firm in Austin, Tex. " But Canadian humility gets in the way. Canadians just cannot say, 'We're the best!'"

Marsden, an Ottawa native, speaks from the heart. Her father worked in marketing for a U.S. firm, and she moved south "for the sole purpose of learning how to market," she says. "I couldn't do it in Canada." Most of the Canadian marketing campaigns she's seen were pretty lame. "We'd say, 'Okay, let's run two ads in San Jose,' and that would be it. It was hit-and-miss. It's not disciplined."

Discipline in marketing means a carefully crafted approach. "You need to sit down and say, 'Here is what we want to achieve,'" says Keith Warne, director of Warne Marketing & Communications in Toronto. "You need to consider it from every angle: the product, the audience, the image. Unless you reach your target audience, you're wasting your money."

But Canadians, according to Marsden, are largely reluctant to commit resources to brand-building. To be blunt, we're reluctant to spend. When U.S. companies mount a marketing campaign, they do so through various media: television, radio, print and much, much more. "They put display signs on grocery-store carts," says Marsden. "There is no stone unturned." But companies in Canada have no way of knowing that throwing money at an ad campaign will pay off; in the U.S., they do. "At Campbell's, we would use what's called 'marketing-mix modelling,'" says Marchand. "We would know exactly what spending $100,000 more on ads would get in results. Canadians don't have the same tools." Why? It takes a company many years of marketing research, and many dollars, to model its markets. Canadian companies haven't been willing to invest.

One of those tools should be research. While marketing research is a growth industry in the U.S., it suffers from Canada's national malaise. PROFIT canvassed marketing profs at universities across the country to try to locate statistics or research studies that might speak to how bad—or good, for that matter—Canadians are at marketing. None could even suggest where to look.

In fact, the experts agree that any Canadian company that wants to mount a serious marketing effort will have difficulty finding partners who are up to the challenge. "It's not really fair to say that these companies can't market, because a lot of what goes into marketing—advertising, PR—is done by third parties, and there's a lack of quality third-party agencies in Canada," says Peter Buchanan of Operon Partners, a strategic-marketing firm in Washington, D.C. Buchanan has worked with top Canadian firms such as Telus and BCE, and says that his clients had to go to the U.S. to get the marketing strategy and vision they needed. "No Canadian PR firm comes to mind... there's not one company that I thought was really good," he says.

Ouch—that hurts. You could dismiss Buchanan as just another American dissing the competition... if only many Canadian marketers weren't saying the same thing. "With a lot of the advertising, you see people trying to display their brilliance and coming off stupid," says Warne. "Everyone's going around in circles." David Fong, president of ad agency TBWA/Chiat/Day in Toronto, has recently called Canadian advertising "underwhelming."

Now that really hurts.

WHERE DO WE GO FROM HERE?

Marchand worries that the best and brightest marketers are going to the U.S., where the action and money are. But Chrapko—another Canadian who has worked in the U.S. and returned home—sees a more open border as the solution to our marketing morass. "We need to let Canadians go to work for U.S. companies, and we need to be more welcoming to Americans here," he says. "The tie between product development and marketing is better understood in the U.S. We need that understanding, [to] beat them at their own game." And ex-pats will return if given a chance to do sterling work.

Brett Marchand did. His "Rant" triggered a cultural phenomenon at home and was even copied abroad—and he credits his U.S. experience for much of his success. Marchand had worked in Toronto for American firms ("I like to say I earned my MBA in marketing at Procter & Gamble," he says) before heading to the U.S. But he was lured back to Canada by the world-class opportunities offered by the job at Molson. "If you work in marketing in Canada, it's best to work in beer," he says, alluding to the big budgets and the brewers' commitment to building brands. The "Rant" was just one part of a broad marketing strategy that included TV ads, a cross-country Joe Canadian tour and "I am Canadian" merchandise—T-shirts, hats, you name it. (It's worth noting that Glen Hunt, the ad exec who wrote "Rant" for agency Bensimon Byrne D'Arcy in Toronto, also did a U.S. tour of duty.) Marchand has since started up Onsidekick.com, a Toronto-based e-commerce portal for the sportswear industry. Once we lure great marketers back to Canada, it seems they may actually find a reason to stay.

Warne sees growing potential in the Nepean, Ont.–based Canadian Institute of Marketing, which is beginning to work with Canadian universities to create stronger homegrown marketers. "Marketing professionalism hasn't been recognized in Canada," he says. He points to the Institute's British counterpart as a role model and inspiration. "In Britain, marketing people go back to school every two years. There is ongoing education and training." But all that is still in the future here.

While Marchand agrees with the need for education, he also sees a role for the feds. "It would be great if the Canadian government would give tax credits to companies for brand development, the way they do for product development," he says. "That would really be putting them on a level playing field."

Marketing makes the difference between a simple product and an enduring brand that can sell at home and abroad. There is no question that Canadian companies can build the products. Now they need to rev up their marketing. The question is: can we do it?

The last word goes to Nickerson, who is now involved in telemedicine and investments in early-stage Net companies. While he says Canadians "reek" at marketing and business development, he believes there's hope: "I do think that Canadians tend to be better, well-rounded managers, and better motivators in general. So I think we have a definite role in general management, engineering excellence and ideas and research."

All we have to do is sell that notion to the world.

Steps to Global Success

by Susanne Baillie

Thinking of taking your brand global? If Canadians are to succeed on the world stage, we'd do well to learn from the best—the McDonald's, Coca-Colas and Volvos that have branched out from their home countries to thrive on the world stage.

So how do you win in international markets? Start out by winning at home. "I don't think there are any global or international brands that are not extremely strong in their domestic markets," says David

Arnold, head of the international marketing management program at Harvard Business School.

Real success abroad often stems from combining national and brand identities, he adds, especially with consumer products. Coca-Cola, Levi's and Marlboro cigarettes, for example, have made the spirit of America part of their image. Sony, Panasonic and Mitsubishi capitalize on the world's perception of the Japanese as electronics specialists. "Nearly all of the world's leading consumer brands are strongly associated with their country of origin," he says. "So if a Canadian brand is going to succeed globally, it should play off what the world thinks Canada is good at." For instance? "Maybe outdoor clothing, lumber, agricultural products... those types of things," ventures Arnold. You'll have to figure out how to balance brand consistency and adaptation to local markets. "People used to think that global uniformity was the fixture of marketing," says Arnold, but "that line is moving in favor of the local company." As long as you have the same visual identity of the brand and its logo, he says, adapting to local markets actually improves sales. "Management can get infinitely more complex if you allow local alteration," he says, but "that's what the market wants."

Take McDonald's. It maintains brand recognition by using its golden arches and red-and-yellow color scheme consistently and rigorously. However, the menu and store layout vary to make McDonald's relevant to the local market. "This is a very good model of how it should be done," says Arnold.

Finally, selecting the right distribution partner abroad is critical for building your brands, says Arnold. Don't choose a local partner who will only make a few quick sales to obvious customers before petering out, he warns: "Pick someone who has a marketing capability as well as a sales capability."

Teacher's Pets: Canucks Who Make the Grade

by Kali Pearson

Don't have a marketing MBA? No problem. We asked professors from Canada's top marketing programs to give you a crash course on which Canadian companies do the best job at marketing—and how they do it.

Get People Talking

Adrian Ryans, director of the executive marketing program at the University of Western Ontario, gives Research in Motion top honors for doing an exceptional job generating a very un-Canadian buzz for its BlackBerry wireless technology.

"Initially, they started with a pretty small budget, relative to their competitors worldwide," says Ryans of the Waterloo, Ont. company. "But they built the buzz by sampling to some very key people." RIM offered its BlackBerry pagers selectively to key analysts, journalists and executives. Michael Dell has one, Bill Gates has one, and people started to notice.

"Now they're spending the money advertising in targeted media," says Ryans. "They've created the buzz; now they're taking it to a mass-market level."

Serve Your Niche Relentlessly

Donald N. Thompson, a professor at the Schulich School of Business at York University, likes Loblaws and Holt Renfrew—companies that have nailed what he says is the key marketing fundamental: identifying a niche and serving it relentlessly.

"Holt's has found their niche in the high-end fashion market and they aren't moving," he says. Although stores such as The Bay and the new Eatons have tried to market high-end fashions, they aren't as focussed. "From the start, Holt's placed themselves above both Eatons and The Bay," says Thompson. "They stayed the right size, got the right buyers, and they price based on what their market will pay."

Loblaws avoided being displaced by larger, discount food retailers by reinforcing its brand with the President's Choice line of specialty products. It also renovated stores to create a higher-end look, emphasizing fresh foods to differentiate itself from the big-box stores. "It took a business that, a decade ago, you would have said was being squeezed out by Costco and Wal-Mart and Price Club," says Thompson, "and has evolved into one of North America's top two or three food retailers."

Hire the Right People

Charles B. Weinburg, professor at the University of British Columbia, says great marketing comes down to service. Above all, have the right people serving your market. His favorites: Canadian Tire and Mountain Equipment Co-op.

"Canadian Tire faced a big problem with the introduction of Wal-Mart and the big-box stores," he says. "But they were smart enough to know they had to revitalize or die." Canadian Tire retrained staff to ensure top-notch service. "It used to be if you went to Canadian Tire for a hammer, someone would grunt and point at an aisle," says Weinburg. "Now they'll take you there and find you exactly the model you need."

Vancouver-based outdoor-equipment chain Mountain Equipment Co-op demands that everyone, from president to floor staff, provide great service. "They have a real consistent sense of mission," says Weinburg. "They carry strong, well-made, well-respected product lines, and they hire people who really care about what they do."

Know Thy Customer

University of Toronto business professor David Dunne cites Toronto online grocery service Grocery Gateway.com as a marketing phenom. "It understands its market—the time-strapped urban shopper—stunningly well," he says. "It knows when they shop, their constraints and their habits, and it tailors its product to that. It spends next to nothing on promotions, thanks to tremendous word of mouth."

Clarifications

Celtic Tiger: A reference to the new "roaring" economy of Ireland, which, according to a story on CBS's *Sixty Minutes*, is the world's leading exporter of computer software and Europe's fastest-growing economy. The story notes: "There are 3.5 million people in the Republic of Ireland, and a staggering 70 million people of Irish descent worldwide. All that is beginning to change. The Celtic Tiger is calling its cubs to come home." Read more of the story at *www.cbsnews.com* by searching for "Celtic Tiger."

Wal-Mart eclipses Eatons: The article mentions that Wal-Mart has eclipsed "such established rivals as Eatons, The Bay and Zellers." Since the article was written, Eatons has gone out of business.

Branch plant economy: Many large international companies have branches here—so much so that our economy may seem to depend on the whims of outside corporations. In 1983, the year before he became prime minister, Brian Mulroney was quoted as saying: "We'd be swamped. We have in many ways a branch plant economy in certain important sectors. All that would happen with free trade would be the boys cranking up their plants throughout the United States in bad times and shutting their entire branch plants in Canada. It's bad enough as it is." What did Mulroney do about free trade once he became prime minister? Read the story on the CBC Web site at *www.tv.cbc.ca/national/pgminfo/freetrade.*

Talking Points

In a group, list what you remember about the television ad campaigns of some of the larger Canadian companies (Nortel, Canadian Tire, Bank of Montreal, London Life, or the Bay). What is it about a campaign that makes it memorable? Humour? Music? How many of you are aware of the term "Freedom 55"? Which of the companies mentioned here came up with that campaign? Compare notes with the rest of the class.

How does Brett Marchand differentiate between an ad and brand creation? Have any of the companies mentioned above been successful at creating a brand? How?

The title of the article is "Why Canadians Can't Market," and the first subheading is "Why We Stink." How do these very negative headings affect your reading of the article? Is the writer playing on the same "national reticence" she mentions in the article to encourage you read her article, which is ultimately about how to market?

An expert is quoted as saying: "Nearly all of the world's leading consumer brands are strongly associated with their country of origin....So if a Canadian brand is going to succeed globally, it should play off what the world thinks Canada is good at." What might the world think Canadians are good at? How can we use our image abroad to build better brand recognition for our companies?

Web Research

Dr. Ralph Wilson's Web Marketing Info Center is at *www.wilsonweb.com/webmarket/.*

Profit magazine's Profitguide Sales & Marketing Centre is at *www.profitguide.com/sales.*

Guerrilla Marketing is at *www.gmarketing.com/Learning*.

The Canadian Institute of Marketing is at *www.cinstmarketing.ca*.

The on-line home of *Advertising Age*, the U.S. ad industry bible, is at *www.adage.com*.

Marketing Online, the on-line version of Canada's weekly *Marketing* magazine, is at *www.marketingmag.ca*.

Strategy, the biweekly Canadian newspaper of marketing and strategy, has a Web site at *www.strategymag.com*.

Research the Hudson's Bay Company and Wal-Mart on the Canoe Money site at the Canoe financial portal, *www.webfin.com*. The stock symbol for the Bay is HBC, while Wal-Mart's symbol is WMT. Check the relative performances of these two companies since the article was written.

Writing That Works

Introduction—startling statement: "'We're probably the world's worst marketers,' says new economy entrepreneur Ken Nickerson…." The comment is made by the former Canadian general manager of Microsoft, the world's biggest and most successful company, which gives the introduction an extra punch.

Instruction and process: The two small articles following the major one by Hilary Davidson are both "how-tos," or instructions. Davidson has stated the problem and given some reasons for its existence; the other two writers then follow with suggestions for change.

A Land of Excellence

by Peter C. Newman

Maclean's, July 1, 2000

In any country that has more trees than people, like this one, excellence tends to strike by inadvertence.

Yet, we have more than our share.

So deferentially inclined that we would rather raise killer bees than sing songs of self-praise, we tend to downplay our home-grown excellence. That's what makes us feel inferior, not the absence of excellence itself. Indeed, the onset of the millennium finds this country overflowing with leaders in every field of endeavour, from pioneering diabetes research to the world of country music divas. Excellence may have collective consequences in raising national prospects, but its essence is exercised individually. One by one, we are finally creating an exciting and highly competitive new global identity.

One obvious mark of excellence is invention, the intuitive leap required to think up a new idea that turns into useful innovation. The lengthy list of Canadian firsts is impressive, and even when we don't invent the ultimate product—such as the Internet—we come close. In 1968, a group of National Research Council scientists patented a touch-sensitive screen and pioneered an extraordinary interactive computer system to test and educate students with learning disabilities. Based on a central computer in Ottawa, the computer linkup, one of the first of its kind, connected educators across the country and revolutionized the teaching of the children. Since those early days, Canadians have so overwhelmingly taken to their computers that we log on to the Internet for 15 hours a month and exceed the U.S. home penetration figure by 40 per cent to 32 per cent. According to a blue-ribbon, government–private sector roundtable report released earlier this year, 180,000 Canadian jobs will be created by the Internet in the five-year period ending in 2003, while another study says domestic e-commerce will reach nearly $148 billion in 2004.

The galaxy of firsts that few Canadians know about include the steam foghorn, washing machine, zipper, paint roller, electronic synthesizer, carpet sweeper, kerosene, electron microscope, tuck-away-handle beer cartons, advanced space-vision systems and, in 1860, a mechanical skirt lifter that helped Calgary ladies cross muddy streets. And, of course, there are the ones most of us do know about: insulin, Pablum, the snowmobile, Superman and Trivial Pursuit. That list leaves out the telephone, which every Canadian schoolchild knows was perfected by Alexander Graham Bell in Brantford, Ont. Bell modestly credited his 1876 invention to not knowing enough about electrical theory to realize the phone couldn't work. He was a true Renaissance Man, having also pioneered the gramophone, film sound tracks, the electric eye, iron lung, a saltwater converter, a pre-X-ray method for detecting bullets inside bodies, a functioning hydrofoil craft, a vacuum jacket to ease childbirth, Canada's first manned flight, and a new breed of sheep that gave birth to more than one lamb.

Excellence in Canada has always been measured according to one criterion: would it make the cut in the United States, that empire to the south of us that validates so much of what we do and dream. Until very recently, the meaningful accolades were: "She studied at Harvard," "I bought it on Fifth Avenue," "We got our tan in Palm Springs," "His book was respectably reviewed by The New York Times," "She had her hysterectomy at the Mayo."

Economies of scale still allow Americans to pick the winners in many categories, especially the entertainment industry, which depends less on quality than on numbers. But excellence is now sprouting independently on our side of the 49th parallel. Within the global economy that obeys no rules except those of the Darwinian jungle, Canada has been remarkably successful. In two of the past three years, the Canadian economy has grown faster than that of the United States. That's a remarkable show of excellence, because 40 per cent of our gross domestic product is exported. In other words, what we do and what we make is competing successfully in world markets that are open to all comers on increasingly equal terms. One example: Ontario is about to become the number 1 auto-producing region in North America, surpassing Michigan, which now accounts for 18 per cent of the continent's vehicle manufacturing.

We must be doing something right.

What we're doing right is educating our young. Except for our tragically dysfunctional health-care system, no public-sector activity is the subject of harsher criticism than education. Yet a higher proportion of Canadians is successfully completing postsecondary education than the citizens of any industrialized country on earth. Michael Dell, the computer wizard, recently rightly observed that "Canada is a hotbed for new technologies, with an advanced communications infrastructure and a Net-savvy population that makes it a leading competitor in the New Economy."

Despite the volatile political climate that has created a leadership vacuum in Ottawa, Canadians are taking their future into their own hands and declaring that this will be their century. Thirty million characters in search of an author, we have on this Canada Day, 2000, realized something highly significant: that Canadian excellence is not an oxymoron.

Being Canadian has become less of a journey than a destination. We have arrived at last.

Clarifications

Oxymoron: A figure of speech in which contradictory words or phrases are used together either inadvertently or for a particular effect; for example, "jumbo shrimp"; "you have to be cruel to be kind." An excellent place to research words is *www.word-detective.com*. The author of that Web site explains that an oxymoron comes from the Greek *oxymoros*, or "pointedly foolish." His examples include "increasing declines" and "eloquent silence." A favorite of mine is the RV manufacturer that advertises "mandatory options."

Gross Domestic Product (GDP): Gross Domestic Product is a measure of the total production and consumption of goods and services in a country. For information on Canada's GDP search the Statistics Canada Web site at *www.statcan.ca*.

Thirty million characters in search of an author: This phrase refers to a play called *Six Characters in Search of an Author*. Who wrote the play? Using the Internet, find out the last time it was performed in Canada at a major theatre.

Talking Points

Newman gives a list of firsts that Canadians don't know about. The items in the list seem to swing from one extreme to another—from the sublime to the seemingly ridiculous. What effect does this have on the reader?

Find out how much time per month each member of your group spends logged onto the Internet. Calculate the average time for your group, then compare your average with other groups and with the average mentioned by Newman in the fourth paragraph.

Newman has a wonderful way with a phrase. Note the following phrases: "excellence tends to strike by inadvertence"; "that Empire to the south of us that validates so much of what we do and dream"; "Being a Canadian has become less of a journey than a destination." Rewrite these phrases in your own words, and discuss whether your version or Newman's version sounds better.

What is a Renaissance Man, and why does Newman consider Alexander Graham Bell one? Can you think of any twentieth or twenty-first century Canadians who might be considered Renaissance Men (or Women)? Pierre Trudeau is too easy.

Web Research

Newman mentions a "mechanical skirt lifter." Find out if this item was ever patented. (Hint. You will need to check the Canadian Intellectual Property Office on the Strategis Web site (*www.strategis.ic.gc.ca*)).

Peter C. Newman has written several books. Find out more about Newman and his books on the SchoolNet Web site at *www.schoolnet.ca.*

Writing That Works

Metaphor: "Being Canadian has become less of a journey than a destination;" "The galaxy of firsts"; "excellence is now sprouting independently."

Lists: "The galaxy of firsts that few Canadians know about include the steam foghorn, washing machine, zipper, paint roller, electronic synthesizer, carpet sweeper, kerosene, electron microscope, tuck-away-handle beer cartons, advanced space-vision systems and, in 1860, a mechanical skirt lifter that helped Calgary ladies cross muddy streets." Notice how this list combines the everyday with the scientific, ending on a humorous note.

Expert opinion: "Michael Dell, the computer wizard, recently rightly observed that "Canada is a hotbed for new technologies, with an advanced communications infrastructure and a Net-savvy population that makes it a leading competitor in the New Economy." Many writers explain why the expert quoted qualifies as an expert. Newman contents himself with saying that Michael Dell is "the computer wizard," probably assuming that most people will know that Dell is the founder of Dell Computers.

TOPIC *3*

CANADA WORKS AT HOME

INTRODUCTION

Since French actress Brigitte Bardot was photographed on the ice floes protecting baby harp seals in 1977, much of the work Canada does on its own soil has been embroiled in controversy. Work related to our history as a country rich in natural resources is the very work that a modern world often dislikes: fur trapping, clear-cutting forests, fishing and mining have all been sources of ethical discussion.

In recent years, native land claims, and mineral and fishing rights, have also become controversial. In "Licence to Whale," the two issues come into conflict in a story about the Inuit asserting their right to hunt whales in the face of a moratorium on commercial whaling that has been in effect since 1986.

Recently the Canadian workforce has become more and more high tech, depending less on natural resources, fishing and farming. The move away from these primary industries has meant loss of work for some Canadians, especially in provinces where workers rely on such occupations as fishing and mining. A *Globe and Mail* article from February 23, 2002, based on a report from Statistics Canada, notes that "the number of Canadians who derive their main income from farming—313,000—represents a 26-per-cent drop from 1998, and is a mere shadow of the post-Second World War farming work force, when 1.2 million Canadians made their daily bread by working the land."

Pressure from the United States, where water, oil and gas are all needed desperately, may mean that Canada will have to make some difficult choices in the future. In the meantime, government subsidies have sometimes put us at odds with our neighbours to the south. For example, in May 2002, a U.S. trade panel upheld its government's decision to impose import tax of more than 27 per cent on Canadian lumber in retaliation for what it saw as unfair Canadian government subsidies to the lumber industry.

As Canada moves away from primary industry and into areas like high tech and medical research, it has not escaped newer controversies. Gene therapy, genetic modification of crops such as corn, and the involvement of companies like Nortel and JDS Uniphase in the stock market meltdown of 2000–01 have kept this country on the front page of foreign newspapers. On the brighter side, Canada has become "Hollywood North" with thriving film industries in both Toronto and Vancouver. Recently, Toronto mayor Mel Lastman announced plans to construct the world's biggest sound stage. The last article in this chapter chronicles the rise of one of Canada's most successful media companies. However, government subsidies and tax breaks also play a part in that discussion.

Food Fright
by Michael Smith

ROB Magazine, October 29, 1999

On a cloudless July day, biologist David Dennis points proudly through the glass wall of a rooftop greenhouse on the Queen's University campus. His plants, thriving in the summer heat, are nothing much to look at—no profusion of blooms or spectacular fruit. They're mostly pretty standard-looking canola—thin stalks topped by pale-yellow flowers—with a few other species thrown in. But for Dennis, they are the future: Thanks to genetic engineering, some resist drought, some thrive in poor soil, some need less fertilizer, others grow larger than usual. "We are developing new crops for the world's farmers," Dennis says in a soft north-of-England burr, repeating the mantra of his biotech start-up, Performance Plants Inc.

Performance Plants, with about 30 employees split between the Queen's campus in Kingston, Ont., and a lab in Saskatoon, is one of the few Canadian companies practising the type of agricultural biotechnology that creates new plants by manipulating genes. It's a high-stakes game, with enormous potential for profit. International giants like Monsanto, Novartis and DuPont have invested billions in genetically modified crops, and expect to spend billions more. A small company with some good ideas can expect to attract interest—and cash—for its science. Performance Plants, for example, has a $2.2-million deal with Dow AgroSciences Canada that gives Dow the right to sell seeds under licence. Dow will pay Performance Plants a royalty fee out of the profits—when there are any. Dow also has an option to buy a 7% stake in Performance Plants.

Although the future looks bright on this sun-drenched day, there are clouds on David Dennis's horizon: whipped-up public fear of a technology he sees as immensely beneficial. "In Britain, you can read the most horrendous articles," he says, "and there seems to be no one challenging them, saying 'This is nonsense.'"

Could public opposition in Canada and elsewhere consign Performance Plants to the compost heap of history? Dennis says he hopes not, but he adds it's up to the industry to make sure it doesn't come to that. "We have to calm things down and explain the science," he says. "It's not like England here." He pauses. "Yet."

July 26. Lyng, England. About 30 people, garbed in decontamination suits, descend on farmer William Brigham's fields, snip open pad-locked gates with bolt cutters and begin ripping up his corn, which is part of a government-sponsored test of genetically modified crops. The white-suited activists are, they say, "decontaminating" his field. Police arrest the leader, Peter Melchett, a Labour member of the House of Lords, a former government minister and now executive director of the British branch of Greenpeace, and hold him overnight.

It's a scene that has been repeated many times over the past year, as the British campaign against so-called GMOs—genetically modi-fied organisms—gains in fury and hysteria. After his stint in the hoosegow, Melchett is released on bail, with a condition that he not organize similar raids. But he is unrepentant, and no one thinks the raids will stop.

Although not as vehement as it is in Britain, the backlash has spread to North America. In October, American GMO opponents notched a major victory when St. Louis, Mo.–based Monsanto Co. announced that it will not commercialize the chillingly nicknamed Terminator technology. It consists of seeds that cannot reproduce themselves after one generation. Monsanto didn't develop the tech-nology. But the company will gain control of it as part of its proposed acquisition of Delta & Pine Land Co. The technology would safeguard the company's intellectual property by preventing farmers from saving its patented seeds from year to year, or buying them from the black market. Farmers would have to come back to Monsanto for more seed.

In Canada, opposition to GMOs has so far been muted, but it is growing. In September, Ottawa announced plans to create standards for the voluntary labelling of genetically modified foods. Shortly after that announcement, Greenpeace Canada and the Council of Canadians launched a protest campaign asking the Loblaws super-market chain to remove genetically modified ingredients from its pop-ular President's Choice and No Name brands. They also want international brands such as Kraft and Cadbury to offer Canadians GMO-free products.

Will opposition in Canada continue to grow? Unlike the British, we tend to trust our government regulators to make sure foods are safe (see below), and our farmers not to poison us. "It comes down to con-sumer confidence," says Doug Powell, an assistant professor of plant agriculture at the University of Guelph, Ont. In Britain, he says, the public has been rocked by food scandal after food scandal, including the infamous Mad Cow debacle. Britain has also seen regular out-breaks of bacterial infections, such as so-called hamburger disease—abdominal pain, diarrhoea, vomiting and fever. "They just have problems with food," Powell says.

In such a climate of distrust, it's not surprising that the public is worried. There has also been what Powell calls an "information vacuum" left when regulators lost their credibility and scientists kept their mouths shut. Into that vacuum leapt protest groups.

GMOS—dubbed "frankenfoods" by the always-colourful British press—are living things that have been genetically altered in some way. For example, more than half of the canola planted in Canada is classified as transgenic (genetically modified)—in most cases to make it resistant to herbicides such as Monsanto's popular weed-killer Roundup. To achieve that end, scientists took a gene from a soil microbe called agrobacterium and used it to insert a gene that trans-fers herbicide resistance to the canola. The result is a plant identical in almost all respects to its forebears, except that it can live through a rain of Roundup.

Herbicides are expensive, and some are toxic, but farmers use them because they need to get rid of weeds. Until recently, that meant dif-ferent herbicides for different kinds of weeds, increasing the cost of—and the exposure to—what are, after all, poisons. But Roundup is what's called a "non-selective" herbicide; it kills most plants, including normal canola. Cheap and widely used by farmers and homeowners for many years, Roundup was of little use to canola growers once their crop was planted, until the genetically engineered version of canola came along. Now, according to Monsanto, farmers can throw away all the other herbicides and spray once, or perhaps twice, with Roundup. The result: a weed-free crop that costs less to produce because it uses fewer chemicals, making it better both for the farmer and the environment.

Regardless of how much of that you believe—and activist groups such as Greenpeace don't believe much of it—farmers have leapt on the new technology. According to federal government estimates, Canadian farmers planted 1.7 million hectares of transgenic canola, corn and soybeans in 1997. The estimated total for 1999 is 3.9 million hectares.

Supporters of the technology, such as farmer Mary Lou Garr of Grimsby, Ont., say they need genetically modified crops to save money, produce higher yields and reduce the use of herbicides and pesticides. Garr is a vice-chair of AGCare, a coalition of 16 Ontario farm groups that has been working for years to reduce the use of chemicals on crops. In a series of news conferences this summer, AGCare stepped into the battle over GMOs, arguing that the genetically modified corn now in the fields is, in Garr's words, "the best thing we've seen in the past few years" to reduce pesticide use.

But there are clear risks as well. The corn Garr talks about has been designed to carry a bacterial gene that produces a toxin called Bt, which poisons an insect known as the European corn borer. Bt is harmless to humans; it's even used in spray form by organic farmers. But spraying Bt doesn't work on the corn borer. As the insect's name implies, it bores into the stalk and ears, where it chows down on parts of the corn untouched by the spray. The Bt corn, though, has the toxin in every cell; there's no more free lunch for the borer.

If such an innovation happened in the normal course of evolution's arms race, the corn borer would soon develop resistance to Bt. Plant and insect would be back to square one. That's a realistic fear in this case as well, Garr says. That's why she and other farmers are setting aside refugia—land where they plant non-Bt corn as a haven for the corn borer. The idea is that even if some superborers survive their Bt-laced lunch long enough to breed, they'll breed mostly with normal insects from the refugia, and widespread resistance won't develop.

There's also a risk to what Garr calls "non-target species." Earlier this year, Cornell University researchers found that if they put pollen from Bt corn on milkweed, it would harm Monarch butterfly larvae that feed on the plants. How likely that risk is outside the lab is another question—one that's under study at the University of Guelph. Will butterflies eat tainted milkweed if they have a choice? Even if they do, will a nearby cornfield produce enough pollen to cause harm? Garr doesn't know, and while admitting that no new technology comes without risk, she says, "The secret is to manage those risks in a responsible manner."

For the opposition, that's whistling past the graveyard. The risk, they say, is simply too great to be managed, so great that the technology has to be stopped completely and never used again. There are really two main arguments. In the first place, we don't really know what we're doing when we modify plants, and once they are out in the world, they can't be recalled. Their genetically modified pollen will have spread, they will have contaminated their non-engineered cousins, and the novel genes will have jumped to closely related species. Whether all this is immediately harmful, or not, isn't the issue. There may be unintended effects, perhaps decades down the road, and it will be too late to do anything about it. "Suppose something goes wrong," says Peter Tabuns, a former Toronto city councillor and now executive director of Greenpeace Canada. "How do they call it back?"

The second argument is more political: The modified plants are being made by giant multinational corporations whose goal is to dominate agriculture worldwide and turn farmers into peons dependent on the company. Monsanto is painted as the big villain here: Its main GMOs are crops that are resistant to the herbicide Roundup, which is made by—conspiracy theorists rush to point out—guess who? Monsanto's second-quarter results for 1999 showed earnings of $344 million (U.S.) on record worldwide sales of $2.6 billion, led by strong sales of Roundup.

To environmentalists, Monsanto's talk of increasing crop yields to help feed a hungry world and reducing herbicide and pesticide use is a smokescreen. "The primary concern of these corporations is in fact to make money and to bring farmers to the market every year to buy seed and to buy chemical inputs for farming," says Lucy Sharratt, who's heading up the antibiotech campaign for the environmental group Sierra Club of Canada.

It also doesn't help, in the eyes of critics, that Monsanto has been aggressively protecting its engineered crops, by requiring farmers to sign an agreement that they won't save seed from year to year and threatening them with legal action if they do. In the first case to make it to court anywhere, Saskatchewan farmer Percy Schmeiser is being sued for growing Monsanto's canola without a licence; his defence is that modified seed blew onto his land and took root.

But Monsanto Canada Inc. president Ray Mowling argues that the licences are an essential part of a strategy that will ensure the company can continue to develop new genetically engineered products. It's akin to software companies fighting to suppress pirated copies of their programs. "We're really protecting the interests of the other 20,000 growers who have signed these agreements in good faith," says Mowling.

A third argument—one that's not emphasized very much, but which underlies the whole debate—is what you might call the theocratic view: that God (or Nature) created species to be separate. If you put a bacterial gene into a corn plant, you enter some sort of natural no-fly zone. "We're creating very new organisms," says Sharratt. "We're crossing the species barrier, the kingdom barrier—something that's never been done before." In the June 13, 1998, edition of Britain's *Daily Telegraph*, no less a personage than the Prince of Wales gave the clearest expression of this view: "I happen to believe that this kind of genetic modification takes mankind into realms that belong to God, and to God alone...do we have the right to experiment with, and commercialize, the building blocks of life?"

The last argument isn't really susceptible to rebuttal—either you believe or you don't. So the major logical debate is about risk: One side says you can't make an omelette without breaking eggs; the other says we'll have to live without the omelette because cracking the eggs is just too dangerous. And risk is notoriously difficult to communicate, especially when—as in the case of most of the gene-altered crops to date—the benefit for consumers is indirect. Sure, if farmers get bigger yields at lower costs, food prices will stay low. And the environment may well benefit from less pesticide and herbicide use. But how will those arguments play against the mysterious, unknown dangers cited by Tabuns? Interestingly, Prince Charles made an exception for genetic engineering for medical purposes, perhaps because he understands that consumers will not be willing to give up the potential for new medicines.

David Dennis and his colleagues are hoping their technologies will be seen in the same light as medical genetics. The problem, as Doug Powell argues, is that "people don't buy technology." Instead, they buy food. The much-touted transgenic Flavr-Savr tomato of a few years back failed in the marketplace—not because it wasn't a good tomato, Powell argues, but because it couldn't compete. The Flavr-Savr's advantage was that it could be picked in California, be shipped to Ontario and still last, red and ripe, on the shelves for several days. Unfortunately, hothouse tomatoes from Leamington, Ont., also have a long shelf life, because they don't have to be shipped thousands of kilometres, and they're cheaper. End of story. End of transgenic crop.

For Performance Plants, the target market is still the farmer, not the consumer. "The next phase of agbiotech," Dennis says, "is modification of plant metabolism—actually changing the plant to produce...more oil or higher-quality oil or new products or better protein." So Performance Plants is working on ways to make plants that grow larger with the same nutrients, grow in drier conditions, produce low-fibre seeds that will make better-quality cattle feed, and flourish with less fertilizer. Such modifications are more difficult than today's single-gene insertions, but they are not pie in the sky either: Performance Plants has more than 250 lines of canola growing in test fields, as well as alfalfa, corn and soybean crops in various stages of testing. "You've got to get it out in the fields and show it works," Dennis says.

In the company's cramped boardroom, accompanied by company vice-president Dan Lefebvre and business manager David Gauthier, Dennis flashes a slide of two heads of experimental lettuce. One is normal and one is transgenic, using the company's so-called GET technology, which enhances growth by improving the efficiency of photosynthesis. The heads were grown in the labs upstairs, under low light—and "lettuce hates low light," Dennis says. The difference is striking: The light-starved transgenic lettuce looks fine—green, bushy and vibrantly healthy—while the normal head, equally light-starved, appears almost dead. The same technology, applied to canola plants, appears to produce up to 15% more seed and a plant that's 25% bigger than normal, Dennis says.

Canola, of course, is one of the company's target crops, along with corn, alfalfa and soybeans. Together, these four crops have a yearly farm-gate value in North America of about $50 billion (U.S.), so that a 15% increase in yield would mean big money. Farmers would get most of it, Dennis concedes. But the company that developed the technology—Performance Plants, if all goes well—could also expect to come out with a pretty good cash flow.

There are other reasons to do the work, as well. Improving the insect resistance of soybeans is all very well, but it doesn't do much to vindicate the real promise of agricultural biotech: feeding more people more easily. "The fact is," Dennis says, "that the world's population is growing; it's going to double in 35 years and one can't ignore that." More productive plants, using fewer resources to grow the same food at the same or lower cost, should be easy to sell to the general public—assuming a public outcry doesn't stop the research in its tracks. "What we need," says Gauthier, "is the time to develop things that [consumers] want and need." The company's technologies may ultimately prove more acceptable to the gene opponents as well, because they mostly involve modifying the plant's own genes, rather than introducing foreign DNA.

But at the moment, the scientists are on the defensive. Greenpeace Canada, according to Peter Tabuns, will step up its protest campaign. Will it involve the kinds of demonstrations that have landed his British counterpart in jail? "I'm not ruling it out and I'm not ruling it in," Tabuns says. A rumour running through the biotech industry is that Greenpeace has earmarked $50,000 for its campaign—a large amount for environmentalists—on the grounds that Canada may be an easier target than the United States. Tabuns laughs, and denies the figure. "We haven't set a budget yet," he says.

Monsanto Canada's Ray Mowling is grumpy about the beginnings of a backlash here in Canada. "It becomes a self-fulfilling prophecy—gosh, they've got problems in the U.K., therefore we're going to have problems here," he says. "I don't think that's necessarily true." Mowling would prefer to emphasize the future of biotech. "It's hugely exciting...when you talk about improving yields, improving how crops are grown, producing more food on less acreage," he says.

But those considerations may not win over consumers in a grocery store. The next wave of products will have some consumer benefits, such as reduced cholesterol. That, Mowling says, will make the job of defending them easier.

Greenpeace's Tabuns begs to differ. It's his view that Canadians and Americans are just becoming aware of the issue. "I would say the battle in North America is just going to be joined in the next year or so." The storm cloud, Tabuns thinks, is about to rain on David Dennis's parade.

The Road to the Dinner Table

What proportion of Canada's crops are genetically modified? Are foods made from those crops safe?

Good questions. The answers are: a) lots, and b) probably.

The proportion of genetically modified plants varies by crop. The main ones are soybeans, canola, corn and potatoes.

According to federal government estimates, 57% of this year's canola crop was genetically modified, 45% of the corn, and 25% of the soybeans.

Also, it's highly likely that any product in North America with soy in it has some gene-modified components. Ditto for canola oil.

In Canada, genetically modified foods must clear several regulatory hurdles. Stop 1 is the Canadian Food Inspection Agency. Margaret Kenny, acting director of the agency's biotech office, says the first task is an environmental assessment. Until this stage, the plant has been grown in isolation in a lab or in a greenhouse. Among the issues examined is the potential for the plant to become a weed or to have its pollen spread to other species.

The next step is outdoor field trials conducted by the manufacturer. Agency inspectors are supposed to make sure the company follows the rules it agreed to in its assessment.

Finally, the plant's makers can apply for a licence to sell it. At this point, Kenny says, there's another environmental assessment—one for a commercial crop. The whole process generally takes four to seven years.

If the crop is intended for animal feed, the agency also does a feed safety assessment. If the crop is intended for human consumption, Health Canada conducts a similar examination.

Critics argue that those studies are not enough. The raw data for the studies are supplied by plant developers, leading environmentalists to charge that Health Canada and the food inspection agency are little more than pawns.

Kenny replies that "we set the information requirements ... it's the company's responsibility to get that research carried out."

Gene Splicing

Evolution is really nothing but genetic engineering: nature tinkering over billions of years with the inheritance of all creatures great and small.

But it was only with the discovery in 1953 of the structure of deoxyribonucleic acid (DNA) that genetic engineering by scientists became theoretically possible. It took decades for the theory to become reality. In 1999, while gene splicing is not exactly routine, it is common.

DNA, a long, chainlike molecule found in all living cells, is basically simple: Four sub molecules, called bases, are arranged in various orders along a backbone of what is essentially sugar, arranged like a spiral staircase. If the bases are ordered just right, they are called genes. They are used by the cell as the blueprint for proteins, which do most of the work in the body.

A gene whose bases are disordered in some way usually produces a defective protein, or none at all, with sometimes fatal consequences. The disorder may also have no substantive effect (my brown eyes and your blue eyes), or it may actually enhance the organism's abilities in some way.

The first goal of genetic engineering was to correct the human body's mistakes: Researchers hunted for—and found—the gene defects responsible for such diseases as cystic fibrosis and muscular dystrophy. Repairing defects proved to be orders of magnitude harder: To date, no human gene therapy has become commonplace, at least partly because experimenting on humans is frowned on.

In the plant and animal kingdoms, genetic manipulation has worked. Pigs have produced human insulin, corn plants produce their own insecticide, and bacteria produce human growth hormones. A Quebec company is even trying to get goats to produce spider silk in their milk.

In Canada, about 40 so-called transgenic crops are approved by the federal government, although not all are grown here. The biggest crops are canola and soybeans, modified to be resistant to the herbicide Roundup. There are also corn varieties that resist the European corn borer, and potatoes that resist the Colorado potato beetle. As well, modified tomatoes, wheat, flax, squash and cotton have been approved.

Blowin' in the Wind

Percy Schmeiser, a 68-year-old farmer from Bruno, Sask., is the target of the first lawsuit aimed at protecting genetically engineered plants that will actually go to trial. The case is scheduled to go to court in Saskatoon next June.

Monsanto Canada filed the lawsuit in August, 1998, alleging that Schmeiser grew its genetically modified canola in 1997 without a licence from the company. Monsanto alleges as well that Schmeiser harvested seed from his first crop and planted a second crop in 1998.

According to his lawyer, Terry Zakreski, Schmeiser did no such thing. He says that seed from genetically altered canola drifted onto Schmeiser's land, 100 km east of Saskatoon, and took root. A truck carrying the seed probably spilled some of its load.

Critics of genetically modified crops around the world are alarmed. They say that Schmeiser's defence confirms their worst fears about such plants—that they can and do spread modified genes beyond farmers' fields and into the ecosystem.

But supporters of the new technology are worried as well, because of the legal implications for intellectual property. Monsanto sells its seed under a Technology Use Agreement, which is much like a user's agreement for computer software.

The buyer agrees to grow one crop and not keep seed from it for subsequent use.

Monsanto Canada president Ray Mowling said the lawsuit is aimed at creating a "level playing field for the farmers who have signed agreements." It's also aimed at protecting Monsanto's intellectual property, of course, in the same way that software companies prosecute alleged pirates.

The agreement is a new form of control on seeds, and one that farmers appear to be accepting: Mowling says about 20,000 Canadian farmers signed the agreements in order to grow the company's plants in 1999.

But if Schmeiser wins, it could make enforcing the agreements more difficult, since transgressors could argue they were the innocent recipients of drifting seed.

Clarifications

Hoosegow: Slang word for jail, from the Spanish word *juzgado,* meaning tribunal or courtroom.

Mad cow disease: Otherwise know as BSE or bovine spongiform encephalopathy, an infectious degenerative brain disease occurring in cattle which is believed to pass to humans who eat infected meat. You can read more about the disease on the CDC Web site at *www.cdc.gov/ncidod/eid/vol7no1/brown.htm.*

Hamburger disease: Haemorrhagic colitis, commonly known as hamburger disease, is an illness that comes from eating undercooked hamburger infected with E. coli. Read more about the disease at *www.hlth.gov.bc.ca/hlthfile/hfile02.html.*

Prince Charles: The son of Queen Elizabeth is a well-known conservationist; his home, Highgrove, is managed organically and he is patron of the Henry Doubleday Research Association in the UK. The lecture mentioned in this article, "Respect for the Earth—A Royal View," was part of the BBC's 2000 Reith lecture series.

Talking Points

Should we be taking chances by genetically modifying food?

In regard to terminator technology, should a company be allowed to protect its intellectual property in this way, or is there a greater good that must be considered?

Which side of the argument do you feel the writer is taking? What can you point to in the article that indicates a position?

Web Research

Read a special report on genetically modified foods, which was presented on the CBC-TV show *Marketplace,* at *www.cbc.ca/consumers/indepth/gmos.*

The Canadian Health Coalition (*www.healthcoalition.ca*) has an extensive Web site with articles on genetically modified foods and other issues concerning Canadians' health.

Regulations for food products derived through technology are posted on the Canadian Food Inspection Agency site (*www.inspection.gc.ca/english/ppc/biotech/bioteche.shtml*) and are managed by the Inspection Office of Biotechnology.

The Sierra Club of Canada, mentioned in this article, has an informative Web site at *http://fishtomato.com.* It includes links to several scientific sites, including The Royal Society of Canada, where there is a report by an "Expert Panel on the Future of Food Biotechnology."

No research on this subject is complete without a visit to the Greenpeace Web site at *www.greenpeace.ca.*

Writing That Works

Definition: "Terminator technology. It consists of seeds that cannot reproduce themselves after one generation." Notice how brief the definition is. A definition that is too long is distracting.

Definition: "GMOs—dubbed 'frankenfoods'…—are living things that have been genetically altered in some way. For example, more than half of the canola planted in Canada is classified as transgenic (genetically modified)—in most cases to make it resistant to herbicides such as Monsanto's popular weed-killer Roundup."

Definition: "DNA, a long, chainlike molecule found in all living cells, is basically simple: Four sub molecules, called bases, are arranged in various orders along a backbone of what is essentially sugar, arranged like a spiral staircase. If the bases are ordered just right, they are called genes. They are used by the cell as the blueprint for proteins, which do most of the work in the body."

Classification: The opposing arguments are categorized, beginning with the paragraph that starts, "For the opposition, that's whistling past the graveyard." The three arguments are apocryphal, political and religious. The writer attempts to debunk each one.

Comparison: The article compares the situation in Britain with the situation in Canada. Both classification and comparison are used as methods for arguing the case in a subtle and reasoned way.

Expert opinion: The discussion moves from one side to the other, using expert opinion from each side. However, the author appears to have weighted the argument towards the "pro" side.

When Water Kills

by Andrew Nikiforuk

Maclean's, June 12, 2000

Long after the dead have been buried in Walkerton, Ont., rural Canadians who rely on groundwater will continue to feel and smell the impact of a largely unreported revolution: the growth of factory farms. This new industry, or what governments call "intensive live-stock operations, "has unsettled farm communities from New Brunswick to Alberta. Unlike the family enterprises of old, which proudly cared for 20 pigs or 60 cattle, these new facilities operate on an entirely different and largely unregulated scale.

Let's begin with the industrialization of Alberta's fabled beef herds. Thirty years ago, thousands of farmers throughout the province regarded the care of 100 cattle as a big deal. Today, 50 beef barons, largely concentrated north of Lethbridge in an area known as Feedlot Alley, fatten and manage 80 per cent of the province's slaughtered beef. As a result, just one feedlot will have as many as 25,000 cattle in a maze of outdoor corrals on a piece of land the size of a city block. As Cor Van Ray, Alberta's undisputed feedlot king, puts it, "Everyone likes to think they can get their chicken or beef on a cozy farm somewhere. But unless you get big and run it like a business you are squeezed out. This whole corporate thing is just snowballing."

Factory farming has also radicalized the country's multibillion-dollar hog industry in Ontario, Quebec and the West. One of the fastest growing in the world, Canada's hog sector employs 100,000 people and exports more than a third of its production to 35 countries. In 1976, 18,622 Ontario farmers raised an average of 103 pigs each. By 1996, 6,777 (many of them white-suited swine technicians) managed an average of 418 animals each in crowded high-tech barns, while just two per cent of Ontario's hog factories accounted for nearly a quarter of the 5.6 million hogs produced in the province. And big just keeps getting bigger. An Asian firm, the Taiwan Sugar Co., for example, proposes to build an 80,000-hog operation outside Lethbridge. Local citizens are concerned about the amount of untreated waste it will create—equivalent to that produced by 240,000 people. They are also concerned that, like most of Alberta's intensive livestock operations, it will be regulated and taxed like a family farm.

The monstrous size of these profitable operations has raised troubling questions about water quality and threats to public health from coast to coast. Manure from factory farms often contains a variety of heavy metals, lake-choking nutrients and deadly pathogens such as E. coli 0157. In fact, wherever factory farms have concentrated industrial piles of manure in small spaces, big trouble has followed. No one knows this better than Dr. Paul Hasselback, the medical officer of health for Alberta's Chinook Health Region, home to Feedlot Alley and the nation's largest concentration of livestock—and a region plagued by chronic health and water problems. "Walkerton has demonstrated to the public that there is a substantial risk out there," he notes. "There just isn't a framework to develop these industries in a sustainable fashion."

The market forces now erecting animal factories across Canada are simple. They include a federal commitment to support low food prices and new economic realities. For starters, it is far cheaper to export steak and pork than to ship grain or corn. Thanks to abundant feed grains, Western Canada can now produce bacon more profitably than any other region in the world. In addition, the world's key pork producers, Taiwan and Holland, recently pushed production into the danger zone, causing severe water pollution and animal disease outbreaks. But their environmental disasters have had an effect here: hog barns managed by Europeans or funded by Asian investors are popping up all over the country.

Such factories, however, have generated intense opposition in rural Canada. Living next to one can be unpleasant: in addition to the stench of manure, neighbours routinely complain about increased traffic, flies, dust and noise. Most Canadian provinces now boast some kind of coalition battling beef feedlots or hog barns—and the resistance generally focuses on fears about water pollution. And for good reason. The growth of animal factories—aided by provincial incentives such as subsidies in Quebec and the Prairie provinces—has created industrial-scale waste problems. A single 500-sow farm producing 20 piglets per sow a year creates as much effluent as a town of 25,000 people without a waste treatment system.

Hog waste, which contains a host of heavy metals because of mineral-rich feeds, simply goes to open-air lagoons before it is sprayed on the land. Beef factories aren't much better. A 25,000-head feedlot produces in excess of 50,000 tonnes of dung—or more fecal matter than 250,000 Calgarians excrete over a year. It, too, is just spread on land bases often too small to absorb all the nutrients. Alberta's livestock industry may hold a national manure record: dung heaps equivalent to the waste of 48 million Canadians. Very little of this dung is properly treated, regulated or monitored. In Alberta, to the dismay of public health officers like Hasselback, last month the provincial government unceremoniously shelved proposed legislation to crack down on and monitor intensive livestock operations. In many provinces, government downsizing has also foisted the responsibility for regulating these facilities on those least equipped to do the job: municipal governments.

In Quebec, where, according to government statistics, probably a third of all hog operations don't comply with provincial environmental standards, a coalition of 18 farm and environmental organizations even took their case to NAFTA's Commission for Environmental Co-operation. The governments of Mexico and Canada, however, voted against investigating allegations that Ottawa and Quebec weren't protecting waterways from manure runoff. Ontario is also in bad shape. Dr. Murray McQuigge, the outspoken public health officer who blew the whistle on the Walkerton outbreak, warned last September that "poor nutrient management on farms is leading to the degradation of the quality of groundwater, streams and lakes." Ontario has no specific legislation governing factory farms.

Les Klapatiuk, who runs a Calgary firm specializing in water treatment, says there isn't a single government in Canada with adequate legislation to deal with these volumes of animal waste. "The leakage from lagoons is incredible, and when you spread millions of gallons of waste on a field it just runs into the surface water," he says. "If a city or an oil company operated this way, they would be shut down."

All this manure has already taken a costly toll on waterways in Quebec, Ontario, Manitoba and Alberta. A 1998 federal study found half of 27 Alberta streams in key agricultural production areas exceeded water guidelines for nitrogen, phosphorus and disease-carrying bacteria. According to a 1991 study, about 30 per cent of rural wells in Ontario were contaminated with pathogens. In the United States, the Environmental Protection Agency estimates that agricultural runoff from animal factories and traditional farms is the leading source of water pollution in that country.

David Schindler, one of the world's leading experts on water and an ecologist at the University of Alberta in Edmonton, believes Canada is no different. He thinks the nation's notoriously cavalier attitude towards water quality will prove calamitous. In a scientific paper to be published this fall, he predicts that pollution from agriculture and other sources, as well as habitat destruction, will end all freshwater fishing within 50 years, while the nation's drinking water supply will be in dire straits within a century. "Whenever you don't pay attention to factory farms and their waste, you end up paying for it in spades in health services and waste-water treatment," Schindler says. "Country after country has gone down this path. Why aren't we learning from other people's mistakes?"

Is health being compromised? In a study published last year, Health Canada mapped cattle densities and the incidence of Escherichia coli 0157 infections in rural Ontario, only to discover that six rural Ontario counties with the highest number of cattle—and Walkerton is located smack dab in the middle of them—routinely registered the highest rates of E. coli 0157 infection between 1990 and 1995. Pascal Michel, the Health Canada veterinarian and epidemiologist who did the E. coli 0157 study, says he was surprised by the scale of the Walkerton tragedy—but not by its location. "We knew we could expect more cases of infection in these counties than anywhere else in the province," he said.

Alberta's Feedlot Alley, which produces untreated waste from 1.3 million animals that is the sewage equivalent for a population of eight million people, has also been plagued by Walkerton-like troubles. Conclusive proof that health problems there are the result of animal waste does not exist. But area residents routinely run to the bathroom with the highest rates of intestinal disease in the province. In one three-year period between 1989 and 1991, E. coli 0157 killed a dozen children and afflicted scores more in southern Alberta's cattle country. In recent years, the Chinook Health Region has repeatedly raised pointed questions about the bacterial contamination of drinking water, the fouling of irrigation canals, clogged water treatment plants and nitrates in the groundwater.

The public health costs of hog factories are equally daunting. A U.S. survey published this spring found that people living downwind from hog farms in North Carolina—where such factories first originated—experienced more headaches, runny noses, sore throats, excessive coughing, diarrhoea and burning eyes than residents of a community without hog factories. None of this is surprising: according to other U.S. studies, 25 per cent of all workers employed by hog barns suffer from bronchitis due to the corrosive nature of hog waste. A 1997 Iowa study found that the methane, ammonia and hydrogen sulfide spewing from a 4,000-hog operation caused respiratory illnesses in people living up two kilometres away.

In the United States, where factory farms have polluted parts of the eastern seaboard and poisoned scores of communities, state and federal governments have gotten tough. Kansas and Nebraska, for example, have banned large animal factories and Iowa has declared a moratorium on future developments. The EPA has also targeted factory farms for top priority inspections. Canada, however, hasn't followed suit. With the exception of a pending national program for uniform standards for hog operations, and funding on manure research, Ottawa is largely absent from the debate over factory farms. Nor are provinces picking up the slack.

Critics agree there are some obvious reforms. Provincial governments should cap livestock density in many regions, while many rural Canadians want to see animal factories regulated and taxed for what they are: industries. Canada also needs laws that recognize that E. coli 0157 and other pathogens have forever changed the nature of manure. Many experts also recommend that animal waste should be properly treated before the dung ever leaves the barn. Most producers support higher standards for the simple reason that disasters like Walkerton aren't good for business. Last but not least, Schindler, Canada's top water scientist, would also like to see federal funding for freshwater research restored (it is now, he says, at an all-time low) and comprehensive management plans for the nation's watersheds. "Walkerton," Schindler concludes, "should be a wake-up call—for the entire nation."

Clarifications

Escherichia coli 0157: A strain of the E. coli bacterium that produces a powerful toxin and can cause severe illness or even death. E. coli 0157 is the strain involved in the Walkerton tragedy.

NAFTA: The North American Free Trade Agreement was launched in 1994 under the Mulroney government. Read about the treaty at the Department of Foreign Affairs and International Trade Web site (*www.dfait-maeci.gc.ca/nafta-alena*).

Talking Points

Given that it was not a factory farm that caused the problem in Walkerton, is it fair for the author to frame his argument with the example of the Walkerton tragedy?

Family farms are in trouble in many parts of Canada. Is the move to factory farming inevitable, or should the government be increasing subsidies for farmers to allow them to continue to operate in the more traditional style?

Would higher standards for factory farms make them a more acceptable alternative than family farms? Research the problem on Canadian Government Web sites. Has any change taken place since this article was written? Are standards now being considered?

Web Research

There is an extensive Web site on the Walkerton inquiry at *www.walkertoninquiry.com*.

The Concerned Citizens of Walkerton Web site is at *www. walkertoncwc.org*.

The Grace Factory Farm Project (*http://factoryfarm.org/international-canada.html*) has some interesting links on the Taiwan Sugar Corporation's proposed hog farm in Alberta.

The Canadian equivalent of the EPA, the Canadian Food Inspection Agency, is on-line at *www.inspection.gc.ca*.

Better Farming magazine, dedicated to better farming practices in Ontario, can be found on the Web at *www.betterfarming.com*.

Read various articles about the horrors of factory farming and other animal rights issues at *www.factoryfarming.com*.

Health Canada's Drinking Water Guidelines are at *www.hc-sc. gc.ca/ehp/ehd/catalogue/general/iyh/dwguide.htm*.

Writing That Works

Lists: "Manure from factory farms often contains a variety of heavy metals, lake-choking nutrients and deadly pathogens such as E. coli 0157"; "Chinook Health Region has repeatedly raised pointed questions about the bacterial contamination of drinking water, the fouling of irrigation canals, clogged water treatment plants and nitrates in the groundwater"; "…people living downwind from hog farms in North Carolina—where such factories first originated—experienced more headaches, runny noses, sore throats, excessive coughing, diarrhoea and burning eyes than residents of a community without hog factories."

Question and answer: "Is health being compromised? In a study published last year, Health Canada mapped cattle densities and the incidence of Escherichia coli 0157 infections…"

Appeal to emotions: The threat of "invasion" by pork producers from Holland and Taiwan appeals to our sense of patriotic outrage, with a touch of racism as well.

Analogy: An analogy that can't help but speak to us is Nikiforuk's comparison of the amount of animal waste to the number of humans needed to produce the same amount of waste.

Expert opinion: The writer quotes many experts and gives their qualifications. One is University of Alberta professor David Schindler. Read more about him on the university Web site at *www.biology.ualberta.ca.*

Studies: The writer makes extensive reference to studies. Frequently, however, only basic details of the study are given. When they are cited in journalistic pieces published in national newspapers, we can assume these studies do exist. In your own writing, though, you should make specific reference to the studies—where they were done, by whom, etc.

Licence to Whale

by Michael Vlessides

Canadian Geographic, January 11, 1998

At a few minutes past five on a brilliant August afternoon in 1996, a bowhead whale was breathing its last on the waters of Repulse Bay, a remote, ice-freckled firth straddling the Arctic Circle. Surrounded by boats filled with Inuit hunters from across the eastern Arctic, the whale bore the wounds of 14 harpoons and countless bullets that had been fired into its 15-metre-long frame. As life ebbed from its body, the bowhead spouted a V-shaped plume of bloody water some five metres into the air, leaving a scarlet curtain lingering long after it had submerged.

It would be two days before enough gas built up inside the decaying 45-tonne body to raise it to the surface. As the leviathan was towed to shore by the triumphant hunting crew, celebrations were already beginning in the hamlet, population 557. After more than a generation in which bowhead hunting had been virtually reduced to a memory, the Inuit had forged a link between their rapidly disappearing hunting past and their uncertain future.

Although the Inuit have hunted whales for millennia, few residents of the emerging territory of Nunavut have actually killed a bowhead, which was officially listed as an endangered species in the 1930s. Only a few of the whales have been taken in the eastern Arctic since 1979, when legislation was passed prohibiting bowhead hunting without a licence. The most recent was in 1994, by three Igloolik hunters who were said to have acceded to the wishes of an elder who longed for one last taste of bowhead maktak. Charges were laid by the Department of Fisheries and Oceans (DFO) but then stayed.

During the negotiations leading up to the 1993 Nunavut Land Claims Agreement, however, the Inuit fought for and obtained the right to hunt bowheads, subject to approval by DFO. In late 1995, the Nunavut Wildlife Management Board (NWMB) set a total allowable harvest of one bowhead for the following year. On February 2, 1996, then–fisheries minister Fred Mifflin approved the decision allowing the hunt. For Nunavut's Inuit leaders, getting the licence was viewed as a significant victory, demonstrating their increasing political authority. (Nunavut will officially become a territory in 1999.) Preparations for the first hunt in more than a generation were soon underway.

At the time of the hunt, I was the editor of a northern magazine and the only print journalist invited to observe the event, which was planned for late summer. I was convinced that this was a cultural rebirth, the long-awaited return of that piece of Inuit identity virtually obliterated by short-sighted and profiteering whalers in the 18th and 19th centuries. My article was to be decidedly rosy. Any lingering concerns about hunting an endangered species were allayed by DFO officials, who said that although bowhead populations in the region had fallen from more than 10,000 at the turn of the century to some 700 in 1996, taking a single whale would do little harm to eastern Arctic populations. Furthermore, anecdotal reports from the Inuit indicated they were seeing more bowheads than usual in local waters.

So in the early morning of August 13—an idyllic arctic day of crisp air, infinite skies and endless seas—13 men from across Nunavut boarded four motorboats and ushered in a new era. Historically, Inuit bowhead hunts were conducted by men from the same community, each intimately versed in the abilities and inabilities of his companions. In 1996, however, hunters were selected by local political organizations to represent each of Nunavut's three regions and were either flown or boated in to Repulse Bay for the event. Most were meeting for the first time.

The youngest was 18-year-old Moses Ikkidluaq, a shy Kimmirut resident who represented Nunavut's future whale hunters. The oldest, 72-year-old Repulse Bay resident Abraham Tagornak, had been assigned the honour of serving as hunt captain. When Tagornak hunted bowheads as a young man, he did so in a sealskin-covered boat called an umiaq, and used only his intimate knowledge of the sea to guide him. "If I had one wish," he said through an interpreter, "it would be that we hunt for bowheads in an umiaq using the same harpoons that we used many years ago, without guns."

Spraying icy mist over the wakes of their high-powered outboard motor boats, the hunters sped toward a small, rocky group of islets called the Harbour Islands, less than an hour from town. Here, where 19th-century British and American bowhead whalers once sought protection from the boat-crushing ice, the hunters, clad in orange survival suits, reassembled to finalize their strategy. After a brief meeting, they dispersed again, using satellite-fed global positioning system receivers to pinpoint their location and high-frequency radios to communicate with each other.

The day passed rhythmically. The boats motored and drifted, motored and drifted, as watchful eyes scanned the horizon for sign of a bowhead. They talked. They laughed. They hunted for seals. As the sun dipped toward the horizon, we camped on the shores of an ice-clogged inlet. Several hunters disappeared across the spongy tundra, rifles in hand. They returned a few hours later, each carrying a portion of a caribou. As the first day wound to a close, it was apparent that spirits were not dampened by a failure to spot even a single bowhead.

Despite the easy-going atmosphere aboard the boats, not all Nunavut Inuit were convinced of the hunt's validity. Some had argued that it was motivated more by Nunavut leaders, intent on making a political statement about the independence and uniqueness of their new territory, than by the wishes of the people. Repulse Bay residents played a minor role in the planning of an event that would turn their community upside down for more than a week; some suggested that only the politically connected had any hopes of being named to the hunt crew.

Others believed the hunt was a necessary step in recapturing the spirit of purpose, community and dignity that existed when Inuit survival depended largely on hunting. Still, the hunt raised insistent questions. Is it possible to revive a cultural heritage by resuming a practice all but dead? And is it wrongheaded for contemporary Inuit society to try to turn back the clock while simultaneously embracing industrial and technological innovation?

"In the old days," an elder once told Norman Hallendy, a long-time traveller and student of the North, "we always followed in the footsteps of our ancestors. Travelling, we killed every living thing that we or our dogs could eat. Such was The Great Necessity."

Taimaililaurtugut kisianaiungmat (tie-ma-lee-LAU-too-goot kisi-anai-ung-mat). The Great Necessity. Of all the words in Inuktitut, perhaps none so completely describes the traditional Inuit mindset as this melodic term. The Inuit have survived for more than 4,000 years in one of the world's harshest environments with little more than ingenuity, hard work and brutal determination. Inuit reality was founded on a simple, immutable rule: to live, you killed.

British and American commercial whaling altered that reality. With the breakneck expansion of the industry in the 18th century came the advent of shore-based whaling stations and the over-wintering of whaling ships, vastly increasing contact between the two cultures. Animals, seen by the Inuit for millennia as food, clothing and shelter, soon became commodities to be bartered for firearms, cloth, tobacco and alcohol. Small, nomadic bands of Inuit, once scattered across the landscape according to the availability of subsistence resources, became concentrated in ever-increasing densities near whaling stations to capitalize on employment and trade opportunities. More and more, the Inuit relied on food from the whalers' larders. Diseases to which Inuit had little or no immunity ravaged entire communities.

Between 1791 and 1911, some 28,000 bowheads were killed by whalers in the eastern Arctic. As the bowhead population was depleted, the commercial hunt ground to a halt. At the same time subsistence bowhead whaling by the Inuit ceased throughout most of the region. What had been a vital activity for eastern Arctic peoples for thousands of years became a secondary undertaking at no more than a few locations.

A mere 21 of the whales were taken between 1919 and 1979, when hunting bowhead without a licence became illegal. Some say the Inuit voluntarily curtailed hunting to help save the bowhead population. Others suggest subsistence bowhead hunting slowed because the Inuit tradition had become inextricably linked with commercial whaling and, once that enterprise died, the Inuit saw no further economic reason to hunt bowheads.

The hunters broke camp slowly, almost leisurely on the second morning and headed for deeper waters. The four boats, along with a larger supply vessel, scattered throughout Repulse Bay and Roes Welcome Sound. We encountered a wealth of marine life: seals, a pod of narwhals, a polar bear mother and cub. Nobody spotted a bowhead.

Nightfall came with a flourish of pastels in the western sky. We again set up camp, fishing for arctic char in the chilly evening, drinking coffee, and scanning the rocky hillsides for caribou. Radio communications with the other hunters were regular; there was as much talk of seals and caribou as there was of bowheads. The hunt was being billed as a turning point in the history of the Inuit, but all the hype seemed far from the hunters' minds.

John Amagoalik, an Inuit leader who has often been called the "The Father of Nunavut," says the hunt is critical to cultural survival. "If you don't practise something, it dies. We are a hunting society, a society tied to the land and the animals. It's important that our people experience bowhead hunting not just by having someone describe it to us, but by actually taking part in it."

Taking part in what some people consider the needless killing of an endangered species has won Amagoalik and his political peers few friends in the wildlife conservation community. For these activists, cultural practices such as bowhead hunting have no place in modern society.

Paul Watson, leader of the Sea Shepherd Conservation Society, an environmental group that has long targeted the Japanese and Norwegian whaling industries, sides with those who believe that some cultural traditions should be allowed to die.

"If hunting a bowhead whale is coupled with the return to the traditional values and beliefs of yesterday, then it would make more sense," says Watson. "But you can't live in a modern society and say

'O.K., we're going to resurrect our culture by killing something.' That's the only thing they'll be doing, killing something. So I don't see any contribution to anybody's culture."

But University of Alberta anthropologist Milton Freeman says only the Inuit have the right to determine if they should hunt bowheads. Freeman, who has worked with the Inuit since the 1950s and witnessed the 1991 hunt by Inuvialuit residents of the western Arctic community of Aklavik, says that since DFO has indicated there are no conservation concerns with the hunt, then the outsider's view is irrelevant unless you support cultural imperialism—where one group dictates what another group's culture should be. "Obviously, we can all think of cultural examples we'd rather see die, but the fact is, this is a fairly innocuous expression of a people's culture," says Freeman.

"I don't think there's a single answer why we should hunt bowheads, " says Jose Kusugak, president of one of the most influential political organizations in the region, Nunavut Tunngavik Incorporated, who witnessed the hunt from a supply vessel. "The arviq is a big animal and it's worthy of the challenges of hunting. It has an incredible amount of meat. It is a real delicacy. It wasn't every day that you had arviq, as you do caribou or seals. It was like a very good cut of beef that you have once in a while."

Kusugak likens the excitement of the hunt to a deal brokered on Wall Street. "The idea of hunting a bowhead is exactly that same way. It's a huge animal and there's great pride and a thrill of being one of the people to catch it. I would have loved to have put my harpoon in it."

And that thrill is not altered by the use of modern technology, something some critics call cultural bastardization and others call evolution. "Just because we may not do things exactly the way we used to doesn't mean we're losing our identity," says Amagoalik. "Just because every Scotsman doesn't wear a kilt doesn't mean they're not Scottish anymore."

George Wenzel, a McGill University anthropologist who has been visiting Baffin Island for almost three decades, agrees that the tools used in the pursuit of an activity are less important than the social components surrounding the act. When Wenzel hears that sonar devices were used in the search for the bowhead after it sank and that hunters carried satellite phones and wore the latest in survival suits, he shrugs.

"As southerners, we often think that adaptation means becoming like qallu-naat (non-Inuit)," he says. "Inuit culture is quite dynamic and adapting to the times. But Inuit can still call themselves Inuit because of what they retain."

Shortly after 11 a.m. on day three, while the hunters were searching waters about 100 kilometres away, a bowhead was spotted by Repulse Bay residents in shallow waters within sight of town. Residents, who had been previously ordered by the event's organizers to stay several kilometres away if and when a bowhead was struck, corralled the mammal with their boats, preventing it from moving to deeper water until the hunt crew arrived. Children in the school heard the news and temporarily abandoned classes to gather on a narrow spit of land, pointing and cheering each time the whale surfaced.

Far from town, radios aboard the boats crackled to life with the news that a whale had been sighted. The atmosphere was instantly transformed. Leisurely cups of coffee were abandoned. We were off.

It took several hours for all the boats to arrive, the roaring engines drowning out the exuberant cheers of children. As the hunters waited for the whale to surface, Paul Malliki, a sombre Repulse Bay artist in his 40s who had been given the honour of throwing the first harpoon, readied the harpoon heads he had made earlier in the week. Twice the whale appeared. Each time, Malliki's boat came up alongside the bowhead too late and his harpoon hit only water.

When the bowhead rose a third time, though, Malliki's harpoon found its mark, burying itself a few feet from the whale's blowhole. At that moment, a chorus of cheers arose from the shore and the 20-odd boats scattered throughout the bay.

Abraham Tagornak stood beside Malliki. But instead of issuing directions to the hunters, he paused, taken aback as the cheers rang out. "I felt it was wrong for them to feel that way before the bowhead died, " he said later. "In the traditional way of hunting bowheads, the cheering and celebrations would happen after the bowhead had died and been brought to shore."

Once the first strike hit, any semblance of a buffer zone evaporated. The whale dove, pulling the harpoon and its bright orange float down with it; each time the whale surfaced, boats raced furiously toward it, jockeying dangerously for position. Harpoons were thrown, bullets flew in every direction. Just after 5 p.m., the whale dove for the last time.

For the next 20 minutes, boats crisscrossed the waters, hoping the whale would rise in their vicinity. Soon it became obvious what had happened: the bowhead's lungs had been punctured; with blood and water replacing the air in its lungs, the behemoth sank to the bottom of the sea. The once-joyous mood of the hunters turned confused, despondent.

For the next 48 hours, the hunters concentrated on raising the bowhead to the surface. We stared hopefully at the fuzzy screen of an underwater sonar device, desperately searching for some sign of the bowhead and 14 floats attached to 14 harpoons. A remote-operated underwater camera was even flown in from Rankin Inlet to aid in the search, to no avail. Then, on Saturday afternoon, just as the last boat was giving up the search and talks began to focus on whether the hunters would seek a second whale, the bowhead floated to the surface.

The hunters' mood changed immediately upon hearing the news. Morose for the past two days, they were now elated. Several of them even rode on the whale as it was towed to a rocky beach not far from town. Nearly 100 people were waiting there to help drag the bowhead ashore. After slicing a blanket-sized ceremonial piece of maktak from the whale in the day's fading light, hunters, residents and politicians retired to the Repulse Bay community complex to feast and celebrate. On Sunday, the flensing of the whale—the process by which the blubber is cut away from the body—began. It would never be finished.

The planners of the 1996 hunt say their goal was to make it something in which all Inuit could share. To that end, hundreds of cardboard boxes had been shipped to Repulse Bay and were sitting on the beach waiting to be filled. Fresh maktak was to be sent to all 27 Nunavut communities. But little was distributed. Most spoiled on the beach or rotted in boxes not refrigerated quickly enough.

Shortly after the celebrations ended on that chill August evening, hunters and organizers—whose flights had been previously booked—hastily departed Repulse Bay, leaving the community to conclude an event over which it previously had little control. For about four days, residents sporadically continued the flensing, although there was no organization to their efforts and little enthusiasm for the undertaking.

Joani Kringayark, a 37-year-old Repulse Bay resident, is one of the hunt's more outspoken critics. In a letter to the editor of *Nunatsiaq News,* the most widely read paper in Nunavut, Kringayark called for the resignation of the event's organizers. Like many Inuit, he does not question the right to hunt. Instead, he challenges the motives of the event's organizers.

"The hunt was more like a symbolic image representing the creation of the Nunavut territory," he says. "But the cultural aspect of it, the tradition of it, should come from the people, not the politicians, not the government. If we feel we need to get a bowhead whale, then we'll ask for it."

George Wenzel agrees. "It's the social component that seemed to me to be not very traditional, and that's a very key element in the argument. None of those things that give traditional coherence to Inuit communities—how the hunt was organized, how food was distributed and so forth—was part of this hunt."

Mistakes were made, admits Paul Kaludjak, president of the Kivalliq Inuit Association, a major player in the organization of the hunt. But future hunts should not be stopped because they are a unique way for the Inuit to retrieve a historic right, insists the well-respected hunter and politician.

And the heart of those values, even today, is The Great Necessity. Only now, what was once a quest for survival seems to be a search for a sense of purpose, of community, and of dignity that traditionally defined Inuit society.

A week after the flensing began, the bowhead whale—tonnes of flesh still clinging to its once-majestic frame—lay rotting in the waning days of arctic summer. Repulse Bay residents, paid to dispose of it, cached huge quantities of meat in boxes and under rocks on a nearby point. Late the following spring the meat was dumped onto rapidly melting ice floes far out at sea. The remainder of the bowhead was eventually burned.

Clarifications

Leviathan: A huge creature described in the Bible, possibly a crocodile or a dragon although more like a combination of the two. The creature was described as having sharp teeth, scales, eyes "like the eyelids of the morning" and smoke and flames coming out of its mouth. The Book of Job says the creature "maketh the deep to boil like a pot" and "the sea like a pot of ointment." Now *leviathan* is used to describe something that is very large.

Narwhal: A grey-coloured Arctic whale that has a twisted ivory tusk protruding from the left side of its head. At one time it was hunted for its tusk, which was believed to have magical qualities.

Tundra: A treeless plain lying along the Arctic Circle.

Nunavut: Canada's newest territory, Nunavut came into existence on April 1, 1999. Read about the new territory on the Government of Nunavut Web site at *www.gov.nu.ca*.

Talking Points

This article deals with a complicated issue, and both sides clearly have strong arguments. Research the issue further, divide the class and debate.

Emotions about animal rights may complicate the discussion. Can this argument be carried on without an emotional element entering in? Do we have a tendency to think of whales as being more like us than say, sharks? How would your feelings on the discussion change if the story was about an endangered species of lobster?

Web Research

The Web site of the Canadian Museum of Civilization (*www. civilization.ca*) has excellent articles and links on whaling, fishing and First Peoples. To get a good sense of the history of the area, go to the History section and read Inuit and Englishmen: The Nunavut Voyages of Martin Frobisher. The site also has a page entitled The Whaling Station.

Greenpeace (*www.greenpeace.ca*) has ongoing news stories on topics such as this.

The World Council of Whalers has a Web site at *www. worldcouncilofwhalers.com*. The site includes news stories and discussions on the issue of whaling from the viewpoint of traditional, rather than commercial, whalers.

Writing That Works

Introduction—anecdote: The opening of this article, like the article as a whole, is quite literary. In fact, the author seems to be using a technique known as *in media res*—in other words, he starts the story in the middle. In some ways, of course, it is the end of the story, as the whale dies, but the real story is only half over.

Point of view: Unusually, this writer slips into the first person in the fifth paragraph. He does so because, at this point, he is declaring a pre-existing bias and indicating that he may have changed his mind since covering the story.

Definition: "Taimaililaurtugut kisianaiungmat (tie-ma-lee-LAU-too-goot kisi-anai-ung-mat). The Great Necessity. Of all the words in Inuktitut, perhaps none so completely describes the traditional Inuit mindset as this melodic term. The Inuit have survived for more than 4,000 years in one of the world's harshest environments with little more than ingenuity, hard work and brutal determination. Inuit reality was founded on a simple, immutable rule: to live, you killed." Notice that this definition also includes a—very necessary—guide to pronunciation.

Expert opinion: "John Amagoalik, an Inuit leader who has often been called the 'The Father of Nunavut,' says the hunt is critical to cultural survival. 'If you don't practise something, it dies. We are a hunting society, a society tied to the land and the animals. It's important that our people experience bowhead hunting not just by having someone describe it to us, but by actually taking part in it.'"

The Accidental Moguls
by Sarah Scott

ROB Magazine, November 24, 2000

White stretch limos deliver bulging older men and their twentysomething girlfriends onto a red carpet, where they stroll past flashing cameras and shouting reporters into the opening of a new Canadian movie, *Stardom*. It's the opening-night gala of the 2000 Toronto International Film Festival, an affair designed to stroke the egos of all concerned—above all, the egos of those who helped the movie's distributor, Alliance Atlantis Communications Inc., become Canada's premier entertainment company.

The firm's 44-year-old chairman and CEO, Michael MacMillan, has made sure that all the players are here tonight at Roy Thomson Hall. Sheila Copps, the federal culture minister, mugs for the camera in her shiny suit. Her government, along with Ontario's, gave Alliance Atlantis and its production partners nearly $100 million last year. And there's *Stardom's* charming producer, Robert Lantos, with his arm wrapped around his date. Just two years ago, he pocketed close to $60 million when he sold his movie and TV company, Alliance, to MacMillan's Atlantis. Most people on Bay Street think he laughed all the way to the bank.

Way off in the corner is a middle-aged woman in a plain black dress, Phyllis Yaffe. The fans and the cameras ignore her. Yet this one-time librarian from Winnipeg runs the division of Alliance Atlantis—broadcast, operating low-budget, high-profit specialty channels—that matters much more to the company's future than the handful of movies it makes each year. As she pushes her husband's wheelchair into the theatre, one of the stretch white limos nearly runs her over.

Stretch limos are not MacMillan's style. Alliance Atlantis arranged that each of the movie's principals—star, director, producer, distributor—arrived at the premiere in one of a series of primary-colour Volkswagen Beetles. It is a studied moment, to be sure, but not a false one. After all, MacMillan himself drives a VW Cabriolet, not a Porsche or Mercedes as other moguls do. He's not afraid to go against type. This fall, as Canada's media and communications companies paired up in the name of convergence, many analysts, investors and media observers expected Alliance Atlantis to join the dance, lest it wilt like a wallflower. But it abstained. "It's not essential to be owned by a telephone or cable company," MacMillan says.

Common sense, perhaps. That MacMillan said he'd sit out didn't surprise anyone who subscribes to the standard take on his talents: He's a Scot bean counter, he only cares about the numbers. Not like his foil Lantos, the continental who only cares about the art. The caricature is at best only partly true. Michael MacMillan may have abandoned his dream of becoming a movie director, but there's more to his makeup than bean counter. The strategist in him won't rule convergence out: "I never say never to anything."

Atlantis Films, the firm MacMillan founded in 1978 with four Queen's University buddies—of whom only Seaton McLean and Janice Platt stayed on—made small documentaries and dramas that were pure CanCon in a time before there was money in it. When, in 1982, Platt produced "Boys and Girls," a half-hour drama for the CBC based on an Alice Munro story, it was a step up from *Manitoulin Island: Gateway to the North*—but still, the production cost only $156,000. And even that budget almost broke the company. Before shooting began on the show, last in a series of six, MacMillan realized,

"We were going to run out of money, and the Royal Bank was going to call our loan. I was dejected; we were all dejected." MacMillan's wife, Cathy, came home late one night to find her sleepless husband reading the want ads in bed.

Royal didn't call the loan. But it was such a close thing that, come the spring of 1984, the MacMillan-McLean-Platt trio had to pinch themselves to believe they were sitting in L.A.'s Dorothy Chandler Pavilion waiting for Michael Caine to reveal the winner of the Oscar for best short drama. When Caine announced the winner—"Boys and Girls"— "We all jumped out of our seats for about half a second," says MacMillan. "But the time I was up in the air seemed like an eternity. And while I was up there, I can remember thinking, this will keep the Royal Bank quiet for at least a few months."

Not that the movie made much money. At that point, the three-some were paying themselves around $100 a week each. But the Oscar—emblem of world-conquering American dream factory that it may be—would pay off big time shortly, when Ottawa decided that it was time to boost Canada's own film and TV industry. Independent TV producers were to be encouraged to make more Canadian content. In 1983, Ottawa put in place the supports that still buttress the business today. Telefilm Canada, the central support agency, funds up to half of production costs; on top of that, lucrative tax breaks often are available. Ottawa had already obliged Canadian broadcasters to devote part of their prime-time schedule to visibly Canadian fare. In other words, government now provided both market and means.

The Oscar acclaim made Atlantis eligible to become a vehicle of cultural nationalism. But MacMillan recognized opportunity too in another development. Seeing that cable networks were a growing force in the U.S., MacMillan and company started feeding them sci-fi adventures, beginning with Ray Bradbury Theater in 1985. These shows, and their descendants—*The Outer Limits, Psi Factor, Earth: Final Conflict*—still got tax breaks worth around 8% of the budget. And not only could they be sold in the U.S., where fees are higher than in Canada, but they could also readily be sold around the world.

The company's ambitions didn't sit well with Platt, who leaned more to Canadian stories than American cable fare. "It just wasn't me," she says. "I couldn't see my signature on anything any more." Besides, she yearned for a life in the country. She broke up with her partners during a dinner in 1989 at MacMillan's house. "There were lots of tears," Platt says. "It was a very big deal for all three of us." Platt, who now raises cattle at her farm in Northern Ontario, still likes and admires her former partners. "Michael has the hunger that never ends," she says. "He's like an explorer. There's always something else to be learned."

By the time Atlantis went public in 1993, MacMillan and McLean had new partners: Ted Riley, another pal from Queen's days who had joined the firm in 1984; and Peter Sussman, who became a partner in 1989 after doing legal work for the firm. Together, the four friends, who control almost two-thirds of Alliance Atlantis's voting shares, worked collegially under MacMillan's leadership. "He's the smartest guy I ever met who still continues to listen," says Riley. MacMillan looks at a deal "as if it's in three dimensions, because there's always something you can pull in from out in the ether that gives a new context to a deal, that helps push it forward." MacMillan focuses so intensely on the big picture that he sometimes neglects the little details of life. He once left a car running at the Toronto airport while he ran to catch the plane—and remembered it only when he got back to town.

By 1998, Atlantis was one of Canada's biggest TV producers and distributors. Its main rival, Lantos's Alliance Communications, was close to twice as big, and had cracked the lucrative U.S. prime-time TV market with *Due South*. Unlike Atlantis, Alliance was also in the film business: It had just garnered a couple of Oscar nominations for *The Sweet Hereafter*. Between them, the two companies dominated the Canadian TV and film production and distribution market. And they were both in a jam. The expansion of the TV universe that had initially created so much opportunity was now cutting into margins. With far more channels on the air, fewer people were watching each show, which translated into lower revenues per airing. Alliance and Atlantis had both developed distribution arms that could sell and resell their shows to more than 400 buyers around the world, eventually making a profit. But in this ever-more fractured TV world, "eventually" was receding farther into the future. You needed deep pockets to afford to wait that long, especially with drama that could easily cost $1 million an episode, and with customers who kept turning into competitors (big ones), thanks to a wave of TV-industry mergers. Neither company's pockets were deep enough.

Lantos made the first move. In 1997, he recalls, "I called Mike, and I proposed that we buy him. I said, I feel small, so you must feel smaller.

"He said he agreed with me, but he was not selling. I said, well, I don't see how you can buy us. He said, would you consider selling? I said, I'm not married to my job."

Translation: Lantos might sell, at the right price. So began a long dialogue between two unlikely collaborators.

Lantos is a Hungarian-born movie producer, a worldly Lothario who is the closest Canada has come to producing a central-casting film mogul. His purported reason for growing Alliance Communications was to win himself the freedom to pursue his interests—just one of which is making the sort of movies that matter, the stories that are "food for the soul." He parks his topless Mercedes outside a swish fortress of an office that he made a point of building beside his tennis club, which he rarely uses.

MacMillan, on the other hand, runs every morning at 6:30 to blow stray thoughts out of his mind. Born in the anonymous Toronto suburb of Scarborough to parents who worked in insurance and real estate, MacMillan has been together with lawyer Cathy Spoel since university (they married in 1981). Despite his wealth (he now makes $853,000 a year and is worth, as of early November, around $20 million), MacMillan is a very grounded guy—he sends the two youngest of his three daughters to public school, goes home every night to cook dinner for the family. (In his social time, mind you, he's a famously hearty partier.)

MacMillan proved to be a determined suitor. Between January and June of 1998, MacMillan and Lantos talked every other day. Lantos finally told his board what he was up to. They were astonished. "Robert," one director pleaded, "give me a month to talk you out of it." Lantos agreed, and slipped out of touch with his opposite number at Atlantis.

MacMillan, chafing, finally called Lantos and put it on the line: "Either right today right now, let's do this or not. 'Cause we're not going to wait around." So they did it.

Technically, Alliance bought Atlantis; every share of Alliance was worth two shares of Atlantis. But as part of the deal, MacMillan and his management team took over, while Lantos sold all his shares and options at $28 and $29. He netted nearly $60 million, factoring in his severance pay and $5 million toward film development costs—as part of the package, the merged company agreed to finance and distribute up to $100-million worth of Lantos movies. "Robert made off like a bandit," one analyst observes under the cover of anonymity. That was the gossip on the Street: Michael got snookered by a wily old pro.

High hopes and rosy promises for the merged company did not materialize. The stock got hammered. Alliance Atlantis non-voting shares slid from $32.30 in midsummer 1998, right after the deal was announced, to $11.35 at the end of 1999.

"They failed to meet the Street's expectations on TV program delivery and earnings, and management credibility suffered as a result," says analyst Susan Reid at Research Capital Corp. The merged company was making far too much TV drama. Margins in the TV division had sunk to 8%. Yet TV drama had always been Atlantis's core business, the engine of its growth. This despite the fact that MacMillan has never produced a bona fide hit. "The great weakness of this company is that we've never had a hit show," says Peter Sussman, who heads TV production. "I mean like *ER*, shows that made hundreds of millions. The great strength of this company is that we've never had a hit show. We've had to learn how to make it work, brick by brick."

The company, in fact, has been working on two construction projects—one for Canada, the other for the rest of the world. The Canadiana shows are heavily subsidized and not very profitable. Take *Traders*, the closest thing to a hit that the Atlantis side of the company has produced for the Canadian market. It's a visibly Canadian show about Bay Street shenanigans. Last year, in its fifth and final season, it picked up 1.3% of the viewing audience in Toronto, compared with 9.3% in the same time slot for *ER*.

The typical cost of an episode of an American prime-time show is $1.7 million (U.S.). *Traders* cost about $900,000 (Canadian) per show. Nearly half of that amount, $400,000, was funded by the Canadian government. Broadcaster CanWest Global paid about $200,000 in fees per show, leaving a deficit of $300,000. Atlantis managed to break even by selling *Traders* to two dozen countries. The U.S. was not one of them, save for one season on one station. Mentions of "Bay Street" and glimpses of multicoloured cash are a big turnoff stateside. Says Sussman: "The lion's share of the U.S. broadcast market has a very narrow view of the world, and they're reluctant to air things that don't feel local for America." *Boys and Girls* or *Traders*, CanCon is never going to be the company's ticket to payday.

Indeed, as much as government support is important to Alliance Atlantis, Canadiana is now only a small part of its TV business. By MacMillan's count, 15 of the last 20 series have been predicated on export.

In the 1990s, MacMillan's team redirected its attention in the U.S. from the cable market to the first-run syndicated market—essentially a collection of independent stations that like cheap, sexy no-brainers like *Baywatch*. "First-run syndication is a business where shows run at times of day where people watch with one eye, not two," says Sussman. "You're busy getting dressed to go out while you're watching." Sussman hoped that Peter Benchley's *Amazon*—a $1-million (U.S.) per-hour thriller about a bunch of good-looking young people who survive a plane crash in the Amazon—would be low-brow enough to satisfy the one-eye criterion. But it got too plot-heavy, and was cancelled this year after one season. Sussman's conclusion: "A really, really good idea that nobody wants to watch is a shitty idea."

The company is counting so heavily on the U.S. market that it has based Sussman in Los Angeles. About 80 people work in the L.A. office generating ideas, writing scripts, selling product to U.S. buyers and marketing TV and movies. That doesn't sit well with Ian Morrison, president of Friends of Canadian Broadcasting, which lobbies for Canadian programming: "I see a de-emphasis on programs that have a Canadian cultural-flagship objective," he says. "They're milking resources from the federal government for purposes that are distant from the original."

That sort of criticism infuriates Peter Sussman: "The fact that we actually produce more things triggered by U.S. interest than Canadian interest doesn't make us any less Canadian. In fact, it makes us more Canadian. It allows us to take the success of that activity and take it back to Canada, whether it's literally bringing a [made-for-TV] movie like *Nuremberg* to shoot in Montreal, or whether it's making us a stronger company, giving us the wherewithal to launch *Traders*."

The truth is, Sussman's side of the company is becoming less important. The centre of gravity is moving toward another front, one also protected by a federal government trying to secure Canadian space in the era of globalized entertainment.

Several years before the merger with Alliance, MacMillan had figured that the splintering of TV audiences offered not only danger (the declining margins in TV drama) but also opportunity (owning a splinter of one's own).

Although they may only capture a small share of the market, specialty channels are lucrative in Canada. Cable companies are obliged by the Canadian Radio-television and Telecommunications Commission to carry them. The resulting steady stream of subscriber fees usually covers most or all of the channel's program costs—a surer and quicker way of making money than TV production. With the cable revenue in your pocket, any ads you can sell may be gravy. Finally, when you do generate your own shows for these sorts of channels, production is cheap. There's no need for egotistical directors or high-priced actors. You can count instead on regular folk who know how to prune a bush or make a soup. "It's hard to spend more than $20,000 on a daily food show," says MacMillan.

He insists that the pursuit of the specialty opportunity is not just about the money. MacMillan has a strategic reason to move into broadcasting. In a world with hundreds of channels, it would be foolhardy to be only a producer of content, he says: "If you're only a producer-creator, and you have no method of packaging it up and presenting it to viewers—you don't own the channel brand—you've got a problem," he says. (MacMillan doesn't mention it, but focusing on specialty channels is also a good hedge against the day the political winds in Ottawa shift away from pouring money into film and TV production.)

MacMillan made his first move into broadcasting in the mid-'90s by bidding for a CRTC licence for Life Network, a mix of travel, cooking, gardening and people stories. There were plenty of contenders for the few choice licences up for grabs. But Atlantis had the edge. It turned out that those Canadiana dramas served their purpose after all: Once again, Atlantis could leverage its cultural brownie points.

After the Life start-up, Atlantis launched another specialty channel, HGTV Canada. Platt returned to lend a hand on both. Actually, HGTV (Home and Garden Television) originates with The E.W. Scripps Company of Cincinnati. But American companies aren't allowed to broadcast in Canada without the CRTC's blessing. A Canadianizing partner makes it culturally acceptable. Hence, HGTV Canada.

The broadcasting division has been growing like crazy. MacMillan acquired two more channels—History and Showcase—in the reverse takeover of Alliance. The CRTC approved his purchase of a 48% stake in Headline Sports in the fall of 1999. Another two channels launched in January, 2000: The French-language Séries+ and Historia are 50% partnerships with Montreal's Astral Communications Inc.

In October, Alliance Atlantis launched a Canadian version of the Food Network, the popular U.S. cable channel covering a topic close to Macmillan's heart. Again, this is a Canadianization of a Scripps channel. For the past three years, Alliance Atlantis has been the Canadian agent for the Food Network, which occupied one of the last analogue—which is to say, widely carried—channels available in Canada. Food Network Canada retains the same spot on cable, but it's 51% owned by Alliance Atlantis and runs Canadian shows half the time.

All told, Alliance Atlantis's band of channels captured 3.6% of the English-language Canadian viewing audience this fall. "And we ain't finished yet," MacMillan says. What's next? The company has its eye on Family Channel and Sportsnet, both of which will come on the market soon to satisfy CRTC rulings. Alliance Atlantis is hoping for green lights from the CRTC in December for The Independent Film and Documentary Channel, The Book Channel, Signature Television (a biography channel), plus Canadian versions of the Scripps channels D.I.Y. and Fine Living, not to mention offerings from new partners: BBC Canada, BBC Kids, National Geographic Channel Canada and The Health Network Canada (a joint venture with Healtheon Web MD and News Corporation).

It was the broadcasting division, not movies or TV, that was the hit of the Alliance Atlantis annual meeting in September. MacMillan rattled off the stats: Specialty channels and pay-TV account for about 42% of Canadian TV viewing, up from 15% five years ago. Broadcasting is still a small fry that generates only 12.1% of the company's revenues. But its expenses are so low that it produces gross margins of 57% and accounts for 30% of gross profits.

Not surprisingly, MacMillan wants to spend more money and time on broadcasting and less on TV production. He's cutting the number of hours of TV drama and boosting lower-cost genres that travel well in time and space: non-fiction (to which end Edmonton producer Great North Communications was acquired earlier this year) and children's programming, especially animated shows.

These moves are supposed to improve the results in TV. In fiscal 2000, TV production and distribution was still the biggest chunk of Alliance Atlantis's business, generating 53.4% of revenues. The division also had the highest direct operating expenses—84.2% of revenues, leaving 15.8% gross profits.

The movie division MacMillan inherited from Lantos generated nearly 30% of the company's revenues, with 20% gross profits, mostly from distributing movies from the U.S. and abroad. It's been a slow year, says McLean, now the head of movie production. Lantos's departure "was like losing the captain of the ship." Since McLean took over the division in early 2000, he has spent a lot of time wondering why Canada has failed to produce a *Full Monty*–style low-budget hit. "A whole generation of Canadian filmmakers grew up in a subsidized environment," he says. They were encouraged by the system to make smaller, personal movies. McLean doesn't want to stop making that kind of movie—indeed, it's a company objective, dovetailing with its art-house cinema chain—but he hopes to aim for a wider audience with some pictures. His first big effort is a movie shot in England with a major-league star, Samuel L. Jackson. At $40 million, it's the most expensive Canadian movie ever made. Its title is bound to drive the Canadiana supporters crazy: *The 51st State.*

Since the merger, MacMillan's moves to slash 164 jobs, cut TV production and reposition the company as a broadcaster have improved the balance sheet. The firm reported $39.1 million in net earnings on $772 million in revenues in 2000, compared with net losses in 1999 of $27.3 million. Susan Reid, the Research Capital analyst who revised her recommendation downward in 1999, says "the company has subsequently delivered on its strategic plan." Other observers are less complimentary: "One-third of the company [the specialty channels] is a good asset, and the rest is crap," says a Bay Street observer. "What is it? Film and TV. Do you know anyone who plans their day around watching an Alliance Atlantis show?"

Investors, still spooked by film accounting, aren't that thrilled about the improved balance sheet. This year they bid up the price of the stock to almost the merger price for an entirely different reason— the frenzy to converge, to own both content and the pipes that shoot it into homes.

"We're not for sale," MacMillan insists. He's received plenty of offers, and is not ruling anything out. Neither MacMillan nor his three partners sound like sellers. And they're not likely to fight over it. They make corporate decisions by consensus, they say; not once has there been a 3-to-1 vote that could isolate or anger one of them.

While everyone else is converging—or wondering how getting together will make them more money than staying apart—MacMillan is testing his own version of the concept on the internet. Although no one has tried anything like it before, MacMillan jumped at the idea the very day the three creators pitched it. That's one advantage of independence, he says. "We can respond and not be afraid of these things. We're willing to take creative chances."

He's investing $10 million in a net TV station, U8TV. It's reality programming: Eight young hipsters live in a loft in downtown Toronto, their every move monitored by cameras. They'll host segments such as Shower Hour and Casting Couch; a half-hour digest will be broadcast on Life Network each day. The rest of the time, you can tune into every second of their unscripted lives on the internet.

It will be intimate, if the September auditions in Toronto are any indication. As the cameras roll, the station's creators pop questions to each of the prospects: What's the wildest thing you ever did? The most embarrassing moment? Thirty seconds on sex? What's the one thing you don't want the camera to see?

The kids are eager to answer. "I love being the centre of attention," says one 20ish woman. "I have a thousand thoughts on my mind and I have to get them out. I believe that watermelon is the only fruit that you can taste its colour."

It's a long way from Alice Munro. But if letting loose a thousand thoughts is where TV is headed, Michael MacMillan will make sure that Alliance Atlantis is there.

Clarifications

Continental: Someone from what the English call "the Continent," that is, Europe. A European, sophisticated.

Bean counter: A somewhat derogatory slang term for an accountant.

Lothario: A lady's man, a man who seduces women. Named after a character in the play *The Fair Penitent* by Nicholas Rowe, a late–seventeenth century dramatist.

Meet the Street's expectations: The Street refers to either Wall Street (in New York) or Bay Street (in Toronto), the financial districts of each city. To "meet the Street's expectations," a company must announce earnings that match the expectations of financial analysts.

CanCon: Canadian Content.

Talking Points

The article reports that the federal government is "trying to secure Canadian space in an era of globalized entertainment." Should this kind of company be subsidized with taxpayers' money? How necessary is the type of Canadian content they provide?

The Lofters, the show mentioned at the end of the article, is now a popular reality show. Reality shows became popular in 2000, especially after the success of *Survivor.* What is it in reality shows that appeals to people?

Web Research

Telefilm Canada has been funding independent filmmakers since 1967, when it was called Canadian Film Development Corporation. The Web site is at *www.telefilm.gc.ca.*

See what Alliance Atlantis is up to now on U8TV at *www.u8tv.com.* The Web site shows live feeds of the TV "lofters" 24 hours a day.

Check *www.stockhouse.com* to see how Alliance Atlantis (symbol AAC.b) is faring on the stock market. Since the article was written, the company has been involved in the making of the *Lord of the Rings* trilogy, from which it has made and can expect to keep making lots of money.

Writing That Works

Definition: "The frenzy to converge, to own both content and the pipes that shoot it into homes." The term defined here is "convergence," a business/technology expression that describes the integration of those who provide access to the Internet and those who provide content. A good example is the takeover of TimeWarner by AOL.

Structure—process: The article is structured in chronological order, and tells how the company became successful. Note the time cues that appear in the first sentence of several paragraphs: "In October"; "After the Life start-up"; "In the 1990s."

Conclusion—summary: The conclusion frames the company history. The writer returns to the first success of the company, the drama "Boys and Girls," then points to the future. This conclusion is a good summary for an article that has been organized chronologically.

TOPIC *4*

CANADA WORKS WITH THE WORLD

INTRODUCTION

Many Canadian companies compete globally with large American and European companies and are successful at what they do. Canadian companies are building major highways in Israel (the Derech Eretz Consortium), installing telecommunications networks in China (Nortel), building regional jets for Germany and rail cars for Australia (Bombardier), and providing data security for the U.S. National Security Agency (Kasten Chase), among other activities. At the same time, however, our exports face problems, the worst case being companies involved in the softwood lumber dispute between Canada and the U.S.

Some companies have run into trouble with the work they do in other countries. Talisman Energy has been accused of helping to fund the war in the Sudan, and Derech Eretz faces opposition from Palestinians and environmentalists as it builds the Cross-Israel Highway. Others are on the more positive side of the argument. Winspear (now DeBeers Canada) and Ekati Diamonds compete proudly and ethically against companies mining "blood diamonds" in war-torn countries.

Canadian workers abroad often work in difficult surroundings. Oil company workers have been kidnapped in Ecuador and casino executives in Venezuela worry about becoming targets of hit men. Often the countries these people work in are areas where poverty is extreme.

Canadian consumers, meanwhile, are often asked to boycott certain products because of their source. The treatment of local workers, specifically those who work in sweatshops or for poverty wages, is an issue for many. The issues of free trade, fair trade and corporate social responsibility all have to be dealt with by Canadian companies and by consumers.

Feeling the Pain
by Ken MacQueen

Maclean's, December 3, 2001

It was a Thursday afternoon, less than a week before American lumber giant Weyerhaeuser Co. pronounced a death sentence, when manager Dave Sebellin walked through the eerie, sprawling silence of the Canadian White Pine mill in Vancouver. He strolled to the edge of the Fraser River, where, as they have for eight decades, booms of western red cedar logs rode in water as still this day as grey glass. He followed the raceway to the jackladder, which, in better times, hauled logs out of the river and into battered wooden buildings the size of aircraft hangers.

The air was thick with the perfume of cedar. After 21 years in the business, "wonderful" is the only word he could find to describe the scent. He climbed the stairs and catwalks, past the giant barker, past the headrigs where the logs are sawn into slabs, past the edgers where the slabs become lumber. Nothing moved.

The saws at Canadian White Pine are stilled by the softwood lumber dispute with the United States, the mill's biggest customer. Countervailing and anti-dumping duties imposed by the U.S. commerce department have added an average 32 per cent to the cost of Canadian softwood—pricing Canadian timber, and especially premium B.C. cedar, out of the U.S. market. The dispute has caused 18,000 layoffs of mill and forestry workers in British Columbia alone, and closed mills in Quebec, the next largest softwood exporter.

Negotiations between Canadian and U.S. officials have been as productive this fall as the moribund White Pine mill. Trade officials seem unable to reconcile two profoundly differing visions rooted in the fact that Canadian timber comes primarily from provincial Crown-owned land, while U.S. timber is largely in private hands.

The Coalition for Fair Lumber Imports, a politically powerful lobby dominated by southern U.S. mill and forest owners, has led the 20-year fight to limit Canadian imports, claiming they are subsidized by artificially low stumpage or harvesting prices set by provincial governments. "Until Canada's lumber production is market-based," says coalition chairman Rusty Wood, president of a family-owned lumber company in Perry, Ga. (and well aware of the amusement about his name), "the United States cannot let unfair trade practices destroy our mills, our jobs and the forest landowners who rely on our industry."

The claims of protectionism cut both ways. NAFTA, the free-trade agreement, is, in the jaded view of Canadian timber producers, an acronym for Nearly Always Favouring the Americans. They see the U.S. lumber lobby as violating trade law in order to shelter their inefficient operations from competition. The U.S. also wants an end to British Columbia's restrictions on raw log exports. Provincial forest workers consider that tantamount to exporting their jobs to U.S. mills.

The duties hit hardest in B.C., which sells 70 per cent of its softwood to Americans—half of the $10 billion in annual Canadian softwood exports to the U.S. About 125,000 B.C. workers depend on the forest industry for employment, and it generates nine per cent of the provincial economy. It's the only game in town in many coastal and northern communities.

White Pine, which sells 60 per cent of its production to such American customers as Home Depot Inc., has operated sporadically since the summer, needing to meet its contractual obligations, but often losing money by doing so because of the trade sanctions. The duties, says Sebellin, "have a major impact on our ability to operate."

Just eight of 400 hourly employees were working the day Sebellin, 44, took his walk. A maintenance worker approached him by the bin sorter, which separates boards by size. He couldn't let the manager pass without asking the question on every worker's mind: "Got any good news for me, Dave?" Sebellin had little to give but a few sympathetic words and a shrug.

Strategies in B.C. for resolving the dispute vary wildly. Washington state–based Weyerhaeuser—which in 1999 bought B.C.'s giant forest company MacMillan Bloedel Ltd.—has been circumspect. While denying its Canadian subsidiary is dumping cheap lumber in the American market, its corporate statements have straddled the fence, mindful that the core of its $24-billion annual operation is based in the U.S.

Far more impatient is David Emerson, the outspoken president and CEO of Canfor Corp., Canada's largest softwood lumber producer. Just back from a fruitless trip to Washington, Emerson hiked a foot onto a coffee table in his 30th-floor Vancouver office, and complained that U.S. trade law is an embarrassment. "It's really nothing more than a punitive instrument of narrow protectionist interests in the industry in the U.S., and compliant actions and decisions made by people in government." He's spending half his time on the dispute, time he'd rather spend growing Canfor so it isn't left as easy prey for a foreign takeover, as MacMillan Bloedel before it.

Emerson met in Washington with Marc Racicot, the special envoy picked by President George W. Bush to settle the dispute, and offered to fly him to a B.C. timber community like Fort St. James to see the damage firsthand. Racicot made a return visit to B.C. last week for talks with industry and government leaders, but he limited his visit to Vancouver, which is, of course, the province's largest clear-cut. Both Racicot, a former governor of Montana, and B.C. Premier Gordon Campbell left a meeting with only faint hope of major progress by Christmas. Yet people "with faces and homes and families" are being hurt on both sides of the border, said Racicot, whose home state is also reliant on timber revenue. He said a lasting resolution—"open fair trade based upon free-market principles"—requires negotiation rather than litigation. But litigation may be unavoidable.

Canfor's Emerson has attained near-hero status in the province by opening, in frustration, another front in the sanctions battle. Canfor has launched a $250-million (U.S.) lawsuit against the American government for what Emerson calls "capricious, arbitrary and punitive" violations of the free-trade agreement. He worried that the suit—which will take years to resolve—might be seen as fracturing the united Canadian negotiating front. Instead, he was "blown away" by the huge measure of public support he's received. He interprets it as a sense of relief that "somebody, somewhere, was actually standing up and trying to gain back some control."

The logs for White Pine mill come from the coast, from Vancouver Island and from the rain-swept Queen Charlotte Islands. They come from Deborah Mantic, 45, and her husband, Andreas Uttendorfer, 58, who live in splendid isolation in the bush outside tiny Queen Charlotte City. He is a faller. She measures and grades timber.

They met more than 20 years ago at a Remembrance Day dance. "She was a young and beautiful log scaler," he says. "I asked her to dance." Their love affair with logging stretches back further still. They speak of it in spiritual terms. Mantic grew up in logging camps where her father was a high rigger. Uttendorfer says, simply: "It's just my life." Sometimes he stands before a tree he will cut and imagines its future. He sees it living in another form: perhaps supporting a Japanese temple, or as a fine piece of furniture, or in an American home.

They work for Weyerhaeuser. Their current layoff will stretch deep into January. Or longer. They, like many on the Charlottes, are living off their savings, and the salmon and venison in their freezer. They are not so much angry at their American neighbours as they are puzzled.

It didn't go unnoticed that the U.S. imposed its latest duty in the same October week that HMCS Vancouver and 235 Canadian personnel left Vancouver Island to join the American-led war on terrorism. What, after all, was the lesson of the Sept. 11 tragedy but the value of building new alliances and strengthening old ones? asks Uttendorfer. "What I'm hoping for is that people come to their senses and see that it is important for us to stick together, to make our relationship work."

Not everyone is as diplomatic. "Turn back the frigates," demanded a letter writer to Vancouver's *Province* newspaper. During a conference call, provincial Forests Minister Mike de Jong appealed to American journalists. Tell the U.S. commerce department, he urged, "that we're actually on your side. You know, we're one of the good guys."

Making that point is an expensive proposition. B.C. timber companies alone are spending $35 million annually on lawyers and consultants, and to lobby the issue onto the personal agendas of the leaders of both countries, the only hope for a lasting resolution. Simply getting the issue on the radar in a preoccupied Washington is a challenge. Companies like Home Depot, home builders associations and other groups have formed their own lobby, American Consumers for Affordable Homes, to make the case for cheap lumber imports. The tariff on Canadian lumber, which accounts for a third of the U.S. market, adds an estimated $1,500 to the cost of a home, says spokeswoman Susan Petniunas. "The U.S. is pushing Canada around," she says. "The important thing, we really believe, is for Canada to stand firm. We really think there is a huge chance to win on this."

So far, though, the battle is political rather than consumer-driven. The well-financed U.S. timber lobby has a list of its own mill closures and failed businesses. It also has a powerhouse advocate in Montana's

Max Baucus, chairman of the Senate finance committee and an outspoken critic of Canadian timber imports.

The thousands of Canadian layoffs that resulted from the anti-dumping duty levied on Oct. 30 was front-page news for days in B.C. In the influential *Washington Post,* it merited a single business brief deep in the newspaper.

When the news did come, it was bad. On Nov. 14, Weyerhaeuser's Vancouver office announcing the permanent closure of Canadian White Pine by March. It had operated since 1923—the first mill owned by H. R. MacMillan, and a foundation of the former MacMillan Bloedel empire. A nearby particleboard plant, employing 100, shuts in January. White Pine's work will go to five other company mills in B.C. A Weyerhaeuser news release blamed an "unprecedented number of serious challenges" facing the B.C. coastal forest industry. Among them, the softwood lumber tariff, which left too many mills for too few markets.

Company staff had time to phone most workers with the news, but some heard it on the radio. Letters outlining settlement packages were hand-delivered later that day to workers' homes. Dave Rodway, a lift-truck driver with 32 years seniority, said he'll clear $20,000 severance after taxes. "I don't know what I'm going to do," he said, the shock still setting in. "Who's going to hire me at 56?"

He gave a bitter laugh at the Weyerhaeuser letterhead on his severance notice. "The future is growing," reads its motto. But not in B.C.

Clarifications

Moribund: Approaching death or about to become obsolete.

Politically powerful lobby: A lobby is the entranceway or hallway of a house, or a waiting room. It has also come to mean a group of people trying to influence a vote in, for example, a parliament—because originally this was achieved by meeting with the legislators in the lobby of the parliamentary building. An example of a powerful lobby group is the tobacco lobby.

Softwood lumber: Types of softwood lumber include pine, spruce and fir.

Punitive: Something that aims to punish. Punitive damages are damages that are awarded in court in order to punish the person or company against whom they have been levied.

Talking Points

This article appeals to the reader's emotions and sense of patriotism and justice. As a biased reader, what effect does the style have on you? What effect would the article have on a reader whose family was involved in the industry on the other side of the border? To develop a sense of being on the other side of the argument, read what Rusty Wood's Coalition for Fair Lumber Imports has to say on its Web site at *www.fairlumbercoalition.org*. Can you see more merit in one side of the argument or the other? Then form two groups of "workers," one from each side of the border, and debate this issue.

A recent news story on the CBC outlined the possibility of India becoming a major trading partner for our softwood lumber. Should we be trying to sell our lumber to new markets, or should we continue to focus on the U.S.?

Web Research

Natural Resources Canada at *www.nrcan-rncan.gc.ca* has an excellent section of forestry information and links.

Forest Information at *www.forestinformation.com* has an extensive Web site. It is claimed that a seedling is planted for every visitor to this site, which is funded by the forestry industry.

The largest industry news site is Forest Web at *www.forestweb.com*.

The Weyerhaeuser Web site at *www.weyerhaeuser.com* has information and links on the softwood lumber dispute.

Writing That Works

This article does not feature the impersonal "expert opinion" or "statistical studies" seen in many of the articles in this reader. Instead it includes description and personal examples designed to appeal to the emotions of the reader.

Description: "The air was thick with the perfume of cedar. After 21 years in the business, 'wonderful' is the only word he could find to describe the scent. He climbed the stairs and catwalks, past the giant barker, past the headrigs where the logs are sawn into slabs, past the edgers where the slabs become lumber. Nothing moved."

Personal example: "Just eight of 400 hourly employees were working the day Sebellin, 44, took his walk. A maintenance worker approached him by the bin sorter, which separates boards by size. He couldn't let the manager pass without asking the question on every worker's mind: 'Got any good news for me, Dave?' Sebellin had little to give but a few sympathetic words and a shrug."

Personal example: "They met more than 20 years ago at a Remembrance Day dance. 'She was a young and beautiful log scaler,' he says. 'I asked her to dance.' Their love affair with logging stretches back further still. They speak of it in spiritual terms. Mantic grew up in logging camps where her father was a high rigger. Uttendorfer says, simply: 'It's just my life.' Sometimes he stands before a tree he will cut and imagines its future. He sees it living in another form: perhaps supporting a Japanese temple, or as a fine piece of furniture, or in an American home."

Diamonds and Blood
by Barry Came

Maclean's, July 31, 2000

In the jargon of the diamond trade, they are known as "conflict" or sometimes "blood" gems. No one knows exactly how many of the 860 million diamonds cut and polished every year may fall into the category: perhaps four per cent of total world production, perhaps as much as 10 per cent. But there are plenty of people, like Canada's Ian Smillie, who are acutely aware that the diamonds that are being mined and sold illegally are fuelling ferocious civil wars in African trouble spots from Sierra Leone to Angola. For the past year, Smillie has been in the forefront of a global effort to stamp out the illicit traffic. And last week in Antwerp, the old Flemish city in northern Belgium that has been the world's diamond capital for the past 500 years, Smillie had reason to celebrate. "We've turned the corner," he said, with satisfaction. "What we have witnessed here may be the beginning of the end of something that has brought misery to so many for so long."

Smillie's optimistic remarks were prompted by the outcome of the latest World Diamond Congress, twice-yearly gathering of the notoriously secretive industry's major traders, cutters and polishers. For four days last week, some 350 delegates from around the planet assembled in Antwerp to engage in often acrimonious debate over how to confront mounting international pressure to tackle the volatile issue of conflict diamonds. "It was a real bun fight," remarked Smillie, who monitored the discussions on behalf of Partnership Africa Canada, a coalition of a hundred non-governmental organizations (NGOs), which earlier this year published a hard-hitting investigation of the illegal trade. "But at the end of the day," he added, "agreement was reached on a program that will mean major changes in an old industry that has not really experienced much change at all for the last 100 years."

The nine-point plan envisages a global certification system for parcels of uncut and unpolished diamonds that, once in place by the end of the year, will track the precious stones from the moment they leave the mines to the time they arrive at international trading centres. Every package of rough gems will have to be shipped in sealed bags, with the contents of each entered into an international database. To give the procedure teeth, a new body, provisionally entitled the International Diamond Council, will be established to ensure that no diamonds from illegitimate sources are traded. Composed of representatives of producers, manufacturers, traders, governments and international organizations, the proposed policing authority will have the power to automatically expel traders who knowingly violate the system from industry organizations.

Over the longer term, traders in illicit gems may also face criminal charges if governments in producing and importing countries act on the proposals recommended by the Diamond Congress last week. The industry wants host governments to enact legislation encompassing the measures set out in the nine-point program, including criminal penalties for any violations. Government co-operation, in fact, is critical to the success of the industry's plans. To that end, industry and government representatives met last Thursday in London to evaluate the results of the Antwerp gathering, in itself the continuation of a consultative process that began last April in South Africa and will culminate at the end of the year with a ministerial-level conference, also scheduled for South Africa.

For a business that is still largely conducted behind closed doors, often on the basis of nothing more than a nod and handshake between long-time confederates, the pace of change has been nothing short of remarkable. "I've never seen an industry change gears so fast," noted Smillie, formerly executive director of the Canadian University Service Overseas and now a private international aid consultant based in Ottawa. Until quite recently, many in the diamond trade refused to even acknowledge that blood gems were a problem.

But pressure has been brought to bear on the industry, much of it coming from Canada, which did not even have a rough diamond trade until 1998, when the three million-carat-per-year Ekati mine opened 300 km northeast of Yellowknife. Two more promising mines, also in the Northwest Territories, are under development, raising the prospect that Canada will be producing 10 per cent of the world's diamonds by 2010.

It is one reason why there was a significant Canadian presence in Antwerp last week. Robert Fowler, the Canadian ambassador to the United Nations, addressed the gathering, as did the Northwest Territories' resources minister, Joseph Handley. Both warned the assembled delegates that failure to grapple publicly with the issue of conflict diamonds risked invoking a consumer backlash, one that could threaten not only the $9-billion-a-year trade in rough diamonds but, even more chilling, the $90-billion business in the sparkling finished product. "In Canada in the 1970s," warned Fowler, "we watched our fur industry, the business upon which our country was founded, destroyed by a small number of very shrill and very effective animal-rights activists. A vibrant, 400-year-old industry was all but annihilated by an extremely deft manipulation of consumer consciousness. Many do not like this parallel but it is, I will continue to argue, germane to your discussions here."

Canada, of course, was not alone in applying pressure. Fowler was speaking for the United Nations in his capacity as chairman of the Security Council committee on Angola sanctions, which is currently engaged in a program to cut the diamond funding of Jonas Savimbi's Unita rebels in that country. Smillie represented the Canadian contingent of a worldwide NGO coalition marshalled to clamp down on the illicit diamond trade that is fuelling ongoing armed rebellion in six African states.

No matter what the source, the collective pressure clearly had an impact on De Beers, the South African–headquartered mining conglomerate, which controls 70 per of global trade in uncut diamonds. De Beers also purchases 35 per cent of the rough stones mined at Canada's Ekati operation. It is also engaged in a hostile takeover of Winspear Diamond Inc. of Vancouver, which hopes to open a diamond mine south of Ekati. And to assure consumers that their diamonds were mined legally, De Beers will offer written guarantees to that fact.

Some diamond manufacturers are already engaged in even more effective practices. Jamie Ben-Oliel, whose family has been in the trade in Toronto and Vancouver for 25 years, purchased a $200,000 laser last year when he opened a business in Yellowknife to cut and polish gems, many from the new Ekati mine. Every diamond that Ben-Oliel ships from the facility is now burned with the tiny symbol of a polar bear, so small that it can only be seen with a magnifying glass. "We wanted to put it on Canadian diamonds," he said, "so people will know that they are pure." According to Ben-Oliel, the system has "gone down well" with both jewellers and consumers—neither of whom want any connection with conflict diamonds, whose gleam is stained with the blood of thousands.

Clarifications

A real bun fight: *Bun fight* is a British term for a party, often a church tea party. However, the expression is also used (as in this article) to mean a fight.

De Beers: This South African company is the premier diamond-mining company in the world. In fact, the company was instrumental in tying the engagement ring to diamonds in the public's mind, with the "A Diamond Is Forever" campaign, thereby ensuring the continuing value of diamonds. Last year the company spent $68 million on the campaign in the U.S. alone. The ads do not actually mention the company name.

Talking Points

The Canadian ambassador to the United Nations compared the diamond industry to the fur industry, which was "destroyed by a small number of very shrill and very effective animal-rights activists. A vibrant, 400-year-old industry was all but annihilated by an extremely deft manipulation of consumer consciousness. Many do not like this parallel but it is, I will continue to argue, germane to your discussions here." Discuss.

The polar bear could be seen as a form of branding. Discuss this in the context of the articles in Section 1. How is a polar bear an appropriate symbol in this case? Would a maple leaf have been a better one?

Web Research

Ekati Diamonds has a very cool Web site at *www.ekati.com*. Read the entire Ekati story there. Try running your cursor over the diamonds as well. They're enough to make you want to get engaged.

As noted in the article, Winspear Diamond Inc. was bought out by De Beers in 1999 and renamed De Beers Canada. With its purchase of Winspear, DeBeers bought a two-thirds interest in a mine in Snap Lake, Northwest Territories. The Web sites are *www.debeersgroup.com* and *www.debeerscanada.com*.

Find diamond news and information on the Diamond Registry at *www.diamondregistry.com*.

The Big Bet
by Raizel Robin

Canadian Business, 25 June, 2001

Deep in the heart of Venezuela, halfway up the Orinoco River, lies a place called Ciudad Guayana. From the air at least, the city's steel mill and oil refinery, as well as its massive hydroelectric dam, appear to be carved out of the dense surrounding jungle. Ciudad Guayana is an orderly place that was created through amalgamation in 1961 in the Venezuelan government's top-down approach to creating an industrial heartland. Early on a Monday evening in May, at a time when Caracas, the nation's capital, would be buzzing with traffic and street vendors, Ciudad Guayana appears dead. Its wide streets lie empty in the stifling heat, and only a handful of its 700,000 residents are out.

Most of the activity centres around the newest of the town's many malls, a two-storey, open-air arcade. Old men, sipping demitasses of viscous black coffee, slump at tables in a pastry shop. In the drugstore next door, two teenage girls in skintight jeans sigh into a makeup mirror as they sample wilted lipsticks. Everyone seems burdened by the excessive humidity—not to mention the rigors of trying to get ahead in a developing economy. But the executives at a bizarre Canadian gaming company called International Thunderbird Gaming Corp. (TSE: INB) have a different take on Ciudad Guayana. As they see it, the locals are simply bored. They want some fun; they want an air-conditioned fiesta with lights and music. Thunderbird says the people want to gamble.

The company thinks it can solve Ciudad Guayana's entertainment problem—and make some cash in the process. So Thunderbird's three principals have come to Venezuela to facilitate the opening of Fiesta Casino Guayana, the latest in its chain of nine casinos. Unlike the locals, their look is strikingly '80s prep school: polo shirts, jeans and chinos. The men are here to meet with Antonio Escalona, who runs the local Inter-Continental Hotel, where Thunderbird's casino is supposed to be opening any day.

In the Inter-Continental's sleek dining room—dominated by a huge window that overlooks a palm-fringed azure pool and a cage full of riotously colored parrots—they are poring over last-minute logistics. Deferential waiters glide through the room, their jet-black hair slicked back, delivering platters of seafood and fruit. The casino opening, trumpeted in an April press release, is weeks behind schedule. But that's the least of Thunderbird's worries. The company has been awaiting a final permit from Venezuela's newly formed casino commission, which has been mired in internal politicking. And Thunderbird must open this casino—and fast—because it's in serious need of revenue. The company's operations in Panama and Guatemala are generating some cash—US$16 million in 2000 and almost US$4 million in the first quarter of this year. But it's not enough to cover costs.

As if the cash flow headaches weren't enough, company executives are also worried about employee security in Ciudad Guayana, an area notorious for kidnappings. Thunderbird's ruddy-faced vice-president of international operations, Clay Hardin, even refuses to allow his photo to appear in the local press for fear of becoming a target. As the discussion turns to that topic, Escalona, the hotelier, becomes impassioned. "I've dealt with worse people," he explodes, pulling open his shirt to reveal a chest peppered with bullet-hole scars. It's hardly your typical business luncheon, but Hardin, a casino vet from Nevada, takes it all in stride. "Yeah, he likes to show those when he gets upset," Hardin later says. "But there were just three bullet holes, a flesh wound."

Chances are you haven't heard of the guys at Thunderbird before. And why would you? From an office in San Diego, this group of Americans, while trading on the TSE, operates under the laws of the Yukon to circumvent regulations in other provinces that stipulate that a majority of board members must be Canadian. Thunderbird builds and operates gaming houses in Latin America—five in Panama, two in Mexico, one in Guatemala and one in Nicaragua—and expects to open its Ciudad Guayana location soon. The company's strategy is first to meet with local businessmen, usually the economic elite of the countries in which it operates—but only after they have been "checked out" by private investigators, a routine procedure in the casino industry. It then approaches local banks and financiers for money, and finally builds and opens its casinos.

Thunderbird's target market, however, has a twist. Because the areas it operates in are usually saturated with tourist-oriented casinos, the gaming company targets locals—in countries where the vast majority of people live below the poverty line and the monthly minimum wage is usually just a few hundred dollars. And like its small-time customers, Thunderbird's $19-million market cap is relatively puny. Its stock trades at less than a dollar; no analysts cover it; it has no institutional investors; and every major bank in Canada and some in the US have slammed their doors in the company's face when it has gone knocking for money. As a result, Thunderbird's posse of executives has turned its attention as far south as Venezuela, cobbling together funds through banks and business partners who want a cut.

But with loan interest being sucked out of company coffers as fast as coins into a slot machine, its operations based in risky and often corrupt Third World oligarchies and with competition that includes, as one Thunderbird executive puts it, "thieves and crooks," investing in the company is a pretty big gamble. Besides, would you buy into an operation that takes from the dirt-poor and gives to the filthy rich?

"Bring your money!" Thunderbird CEO Jack Mitchell shouts in his nasal, Midwestern drawl. "And leave without it!"

The lanky former real estate lawyer from Missouri has squeezed his long limbs into the back seat of a company car—an SUV with tinted windows—and is being chauffeured from the airport in Ciudad Guayana to the site of Thunderbird's newest casino at the Inter-Continental. With him is Donald Snyder, a small, lean man with a pensive air and a thick head of wiry chestnut hair.

Snyder is also a lawyer, from Washington, DC, and he advised the Panamanian government on the privatization of its casinos in the late 1990s. In early 2000, he joined Thunderbird as the company's director of international development. Also along for the ride is Gustavo Márquez, a wealthy Venezuelan investor in the company.

Mitchell's face is beaming, and it's not just from the sweat that has accumulated on his brow since he crossed the airport tarmac to his waiting car in the furious midday sun. What's making him fidget with glee on this rare trip to Ciudad Guayana is the unexpected news that the town is a mere hour away from the state's capital, Ciudad Bolivar, which has a population of roughly 300,000. Mitchell is buoyed by the thought of thousands of bored and underpaid government workers pouring into his casino, their monthly paycheques of about 200,000 bolivars, or US$280, in hand.

As the carload of Thunderbird execs speeds toward the hotel, the men share a joke about erecting a sign on the highway to Ciudad Guayana. It would read "Follow the Yellow Brick Road," Snyder suggests—and the car erupts in laughter. Márquez is swept up in the jubilant mood. "Why do people say spending money in casinos is bad?" he muses. "You go to the supermarket to spend money." A hush falls over the group.

"I don't know how long you could use that analogy," Snyder says, gazing out the window. "At the supermarket you get to take food home."

"Yeah, and at the supermarket you'll spend $10," says Mitchell. "We want you to bring $1,000. We want all your money!"

The Thunderbird team has planned a birthday party for operations manager Clay Hardin, who is helping get the new casino under way. There have been a few glitches, aside from the licensing issue, though. The company is still scrambling just to equip the place. And days before Mitchell and Snyder arrived, two transport trucks went missing on the way to the casino. They turned up in the next town, the lost drivers parked on the side of the road, taking a siesta. But tonight is a night for fun. Hardin is turning 43 and has allowed his presidential suite at the Inter-Continental to be overtaken by Thunderbird employees, who munch mozzarella sticks and belly up to an open bar for five-fingered Cuba Libras.

A handful of Thunderbird's hostesses—tall, gorgeous young women who the company says will eventually work in the casino when it opens—mill about the room. One of them, a stunning blonde with hazel eyes and luscious red lips snuggles against "Papa Clay," as she calls Hardin. She presses a unique birthday present into his hand: a dagger with serrated edges.

"You can see the kinds of gifts we get here," Hardin remarks.

"You could cut some serious string with that," a nearby guest jokes.

"Yeah," a straight-faced Hardin retorts. "Or throats."

Everyone has a story at the party, especially Hardin. His voice is hoarse and gravely—the result of getting a puck in the throat in a hockey game when he was a teen—perfect for a tale he likes to tell. Back in 1979, when he was a 22-year-old greenhorn casino bar manager in Vegas, Hardin says he found himself at a party brimming with mafiosi. At one point, they asked him to leave. "I thought, 'Oh no, I'm in trouble with the boys,'" he recalls. But it turned out someone had tipped the Mob off: the FBI was going to raid the soirée. "They told me, 'You're a good boy,'" Hardin continues in a mock Italian accent. "They said they didn't want me to get mixed up in anything."

Thunderbird's operations manager says he learned a lot from working around the Mafia. "They really had two sides to them," he recalls the next morning over breakfast, as he sips his fourth cup of coffee. "But they understood respect—more than a lot of young people in North America do now. You knew who your boss was. Maybe you respected him out of fear, but you respected him."

The story of Thunderbird Gaming doesn't begin in Las Vegas, or in Venezuela, or Panama, or Guatemala. Nor in the Yukon, where it is incorporated, nor in Toronto where its stock trades, nor even in San Diego. The company got its humble start in 1994 in Vancouver, where Hari Varshney and Raj Chowdhry—two accountants with a reputation for packaging companies and taking them public—joined forces. Their goal in forming Thunderbird? To make a mint manufacturing and selling slot machines to Indian reserves in California.

These were reserves most gaming companies wouldn't touch. The chances of losing money were high because the tribes had refused to sign a compact with the US federal government, as required by the Indian Gaming Regulatory Act. Without one, their casinos were illegal—although Washington turned a blind eye to the operations. It was risky business; but as long as nobody complained, Thunderbird made money. The revenues weren't bad for a start-up either: about $35 million in 1996.

But the good times didn't roll for long. In 1997, then-California-governor Pete Wilson unleashed a legal battle against the Indian casinos, arguing that they had to share their revenues with the state. The tribes counterattacked, maintaining they should be subject to federal, not state, law. As the legal battle raged, the statehouse in Sacramento applied pressure to gaming suppliers to stop outfitting the casinos so California could force the natives into signing a revenue-sharing contract that would formalize its Indian gaming industry. "We respected the state's wishes," says Alex Winch, a Thunderbird shareholder at the time, who today sits on the company's board and is its Toronto-based investor relations director.

Thunderbird closed its slot-machine business in 1998. By then, Jack Mitchell had been in the company two years. Shortly thereafter, Varshney and Chowdhry resigned and the head office relocated from Vancouver to San Diego, where Mitchell resides. Varshney and Chowdhry weren't the only ones to leave the company. Thunderbird underwent a complete overhaul; Mitchell says not one of the company's original 300 employees remains, except for him.

Thunderbird used to trade on the Vancouver Stock Exchange. Under Mitchell's management, however, the company has moved to the TSE, although it still operates in areas where few big-name casinos would dare to tread. But then again, at a billion dollars a pop, Thunderbird could never afford to open a casino on the Las Vegas strip. Best to start small, but the company still has a long way to go before it hits the jackpot. In the past six months, Mitchell estimates that Thunderbird has raised US$25 million through loans and project financing, which will help cover the company's US$2.6 million in payments that come due at the end of this year.

If Thunderbird can't borrow enough money to make loan payments, CFO David Michelson, a former salesman of military communications equipment, says it should be able to make the payments in due course from the cash flow of its operations. In essence, that means making money from its customers, most of whom are Panama's working poor, to pay back banks and independent financiers in the US and Latin America. Michelson acknowledges that if the Venezuela casino is delayed much longer, making the payments "could be a challenge." Still, he says he is confident the company will be able to raise the necessary funds through private lenders.

Compounding its debt problem, Thunderbird operates in countries where revenues are drained by complex layers of taxes and which, incidentally, also receive low scores on the annual Corruption Perceptions Index published by the Berlin-based anticorruption think tank Transparency International. The organization, which surveys business people, country analysts and the public on how likely they think they are to encounter corruption among public officials and politicians, has awarded Venezuela a dismal score of 2.7 out of 10. "It's difficult to get things done when you play by the rules," Snyder says. "Which we do."

But the rules aren't always clear, as even Thunderbird principals will admit. "There's some interpretation that goes on," Mitchell acknowledges. "So in many cases it becomes a negotiation with the official. At the end of the day, you come up with a number you can agree on and you can make a profit on." So does Thunderbird haggle with bureaucrats over tax rates? "Definitely," says Mitchell, shaking his head in exasperation. "Definitely."

It's no surprise then that financing in Latin America is about as tricky as rolling a natural seven. According to the US State Department's International Narcotics Control Strategy, Venezuela is a prime area of concern for money laundering, and as cash businesses, casinos are a prime target. "All the countries we operate in have a history of illegal gaming," says Mitchell. "It's incredibly hard to finance gaming projects here."

Thunderbird has had to look for unconventional lenders. It is now stuck paying interest rates ranging from 9.9% to 18%—up to three times the prime rate—to such financial institutions as Panama's Pribanco and Banco Bilbao de Viscaya, Banco Del Sur of Venezuela, San Diego-based Borrego Springs Bank and four independent financiers whose names it revealed only as the story was going to press. "We would secure cheaper loans if we could," says investor relations director Winch, a Torontonian who gained notoriety in the city's financial circles for shorting Livent Inc. before the entertainment company's meltdown. "When I first learned what we are paying, I was surprised," he says in a reference to Thunderbird. "I spoke to all the big Canadian banks, several large American banks and private corporations that are engaged in corporate funding. The answers were consistent rejection."

Thunderbird has also encountered opposition in some communities, where opponents of gambling have criticized it for targeting impoverished locals instead of well-heeled tourists. But the company makes no apologies for its strategy, which has earned it a return on investment of more than 140% in Panama and 70% in Guatemala. "There are people who will bet $50,000 or $100,000 in a night," says Snyder. "But most people lose $50 to $200 a night. Revenues from tourists make up maybe 2% of our business in Panama." (According to Mitchell, tourists account for 25% to 30% of Thunderbird's total business.) Thunderbird goes after locals, Mitchell explains, because studies have shown that the tourist casino market in Latin America is becoming saturated.

To counter its critics, Thunderbird has launched extensive media education campaigns in areas where it operates, as it has in Mexico, Guatemala and Panama. It has also made philanthropy a vital part of its marketing strategy. "We support a lot of charities because it's good business," says Hardin. "It's good for our image. Put it this way: on Mother's Day in Panama, Jack [Mitchell] and I were with the Monsignor of Panama and he accepted a cheque from us for his charity. In the beginning the Church was like, 'Oh my God, casinos are horrible.' But we put $100,000 toward the homeless of Panama, and it's funny how things change."

Over coffee at the Inter-Continental the morning after the birthday bash, Hardin and Mitchell appear bright-eyed as they expound on the virtues of their 1,200 employees in Latin America, who hail from all over Central and South America—and even Europe. Some of them are "warriors," says Mitchell. "We tend to take people from the really dangerous places like El Salvador and Nicaragua," he explains, noting that a "guy from Belfast" is currently scouting properties for Thunderbird in Medellín, Colombia, home base of the infamous cocaine cartel. "No problem—he can handle it."

Hardin weighs in. "We get a few Colombians," he says. "They're the best workers. A lot of problems in their country, though."

He looks up to flag a passing waiter, impatiently waving his finger at his empty cup. "Señor! Mas café!"

On a warm evening in Caracas earlier that week, Snyder has decided to dine on a rooftop patio with Thunderbird's local partner, Gustavo

Márquez and his wife, Marielisa. A whisper of a breeze flutters through the restaurant's white curtains. Márquez, with his dark pomaded hair and sharp black suit, looks straight off the set of Miami Vice. He runs Tamanaco Entertainment, a subsidiary of a shell company, Hotel Tamanaco CA, that trades on the Caracas Stock Exchange and which owns a grand old hotel in the Venezuelan capital, now managed by Inter-Continental. The company's closely held stock hasn't traded since 1998.

Marielisa has huge blue eyes, a plunging neckline that reveals ample cleavage, and blond ringlets that perfectly frame her smooth, tanned face. As she samples her passion fruit mousse, her husband explains why he is eager to work with Thunderbird. Not only does he hope the company will one day open a casino in his hotel; he also says North Americans know how to get things done, while most Venezuelans lack initiative. "Europeans—the Italians, the Germans—they work hard," he says. "But here, you live by the beach; you can eat mangos and bananas."

Márquez expresses some sympathy for his compadres, however. His voice grows hushed and his handsome features break into a momentary frown as he relates how 80% of Venezuelans live below the poverty line. The elites of the oil-rich country have billions, he says, and the poor have nothing. "But don't write that in the article," interrupts his wife with a smooth smile.

The comment snaps the more media-savvy Snyder back to attention. "So, what is going in your article?"

"Everything."

"Yeah?" Snyder asks, pausing for a moment. "Fortify your house."

The table falls silent for a few seconds until he finally cracks a smile. "I'm kidding," he says. "I'm kidding!" Before setting off for Ciudad Guayana, Mitchell and Snyder take a brief detour to the beachside resort of Higuerote, a two-hour drive from Caracas. Casinos and bingo halls are now illegal in the Venezuelan capital, so Thunderbird plans to serve the capital by opening another gaming establishment in Higuerote's fanciest hotel, which is now being renovated.

After another lavish business lunch, Thunderbird's Higuerote associate, Antonio Benito, invites the Thunderbird crew for a boat ride. Benito is part-owner of the hotel and several of the town's buildings, which his construction firm built, and boasts that he is its main employer. Among his company's many holdings is the local marina, where he kicks two unsuspecting couples out of a 30-foot pleasure boat, but not before asking for and getting some of their beer, and invites the Thunderbird executives to sit down on the vessel's white pleather seats. As the boat crashes through the waves, Mitchell and Snyder savor the scenery—ocean, sun, and a flock of pelicans overhead. "We don't usually live like this," Snyder insists.

But it's a charmed existence while it lasts. "We've had a lot happen," Mitchell will tell you. "We've had people try to bribe us, we've run into organized crime. At this point, it's just another day in the Third World. A lot of people would be terrified of some of the stuff we've dealt with, but it's an adventure to us." Both partners balk at the thought of ever returning to a desk. Says Mitchell: "I'd rather be shot at."

Clarifications

Deferential: Polite, respectful, somewhat submissive.

Politicking: Talking about or being involved in politics, usually partisan or one-sided.

TSE: The Toronto Stock Exchange. The Web site is *www.tse.com* and you can check the price of the Thunderbird stock at any time. The fact that the company is listed on the TSE rather than on the CDNX means it has achieved a certain amount of credibility.

Mafiosi: Members of the Mafia.

Talking Points

Although Thunderbird, the gaming company, is technically Canadian and was founded by Canadians, it is now fully owned by Americans. Does Canada have some sort of responsibility for what seems like a distasteful business—building casinos for people who live in poverty?

Web Research

Transparency International, the "global coalition against corruption," is found on-line at *www.transparency.org*. Check where Canada ranks on the Corruption Perceptions Index in a list of 91 countries.

Writing That Works

Literary allusion: The introductory paragraphs, describing the river going deep into the heart of Venezuela, the stifling heat, the "old men sipping demitasses of viscous black coffee," has echoes of Joseph Conrad's *Heart of Darkness* and the movie *Apocalypse Now,* with an additional hint of Graham Greene's *Our Man in Havana.*

Literary allusion: "A company that takes from the dirt poor and gives to the filthy rich" is a reference to Robin Hood, who stole from the rich to give to the poor. Notice the additional touch of the "dirt" metaphor: *dirt poor, filthy rich.*

Simile: "But with loan interest being sucked out of company coffers as fast as coins into a slot machine...."

Simile: "It's no surprise then that financing in Latin America is about as tricky as rolling a natural seven."

Conclusion—narrowing focus: The opening paragraph starts at the country level, then moves down the river to a local level. By the conclusion, the focus is on the two men involved in the business. The technique is a literary version of inductive reasoning: moving from the general to the specific, from country to single man. A similar shape is found in Conrad's *Heart of Darkness.*

The Coffee Crunch
by Chris Cobb

Ottawa Citizen, November 25, 2001

Note: This article is broken into two parts; students may be assigned to read either part.

PART ONE

In the dim shadows, you can make out four or five photographs pinned to the ill-fitting wood-plank walls of the house: two pictures of a benevolent-looking Jesus Christ and a photograph of a young man and woman in traditional dress, perhaps on their wedding day. Her striped outfit is bright, bold and a colourful mix of reds, blues and greens; his tunic plain and white. In another photograph, the couple is older, with several of their children standing beside them. The photographs are wrapped in loose-fitting, stained plastic and fixed haphazardly with small nails.

Jose Hernandez, his wife Maria and their eight children live here. Jose, 39, is a coffee farmer in Majoval, a community of coffee farmers high in the mountains of Chiapas. Majoval is part of Mut Vitz (Bird Mountain), a co-operative of indigenous coffee farmers. It is here, on the lush, warm, rain-blessed Mexican mountainsides where some of the finest coffee in the world is grown, and where, for the price of a cappuccino at any North American designer coffee house, a man could feed his family for a week.

The shaft of light that captured the cockroach streams from a room next door where a baby with a hacking cough occasionally recovers enough energy to cry. Comforting words from the baby's parents, spoken in the local language, Tzotzil, drift from the room. Seven children sleep on the other side of the wall where the family pictures are pinned. They have been silent and unseen in their pre-bedtime rituals, doubtless warned to behave in the company of strangers.

Five of us visitors are crammed into one of the three tiny, dirt-floor rooms of the Hernandez home: my interpreter, Monika, and her 16-month-old daughter Kamila. Caroline, travelling with her husband, Rafael, is four months pregnant. She represents the Fair Trade organization in Paris and is in Mexico to determine whether Mut Vitz, and three other coffee-growing co-operatives in Chiapas state, can join Fair Trade. Membership has its privileges: a few pesos more for the coffee beans, courtesy of supportive western consumers, and a small measure of stability and marketable prestige.

Caroline, on her first trip to Mexico's coffee country, is dressed more for a stroll down the Champs Elysees than a tromp through mountain mud. Earlier, on our way down a muddy slope to the Hernandez house, she slipped and rode on her backside, passing through a stream of effluent oozing from a pig pen. Her ankle-high pumps were probably ruined and the dark stain on the rear of her pants severely compromised her Parisienne style.

Jose watched Caroline's slide with a puzzled look on his face and commented proudly to the rest of us that the four pigs are shared by 50 families.

Community leaders chose the Hernandez house for us because of the washroom—a cobbled-together wooden structure across the yard from the house. Inside there is an old, cracked, seatless toilet bowl, and a water tap and bucket for flushing. The toilet waste spills down the mountainside, powered by gravity alone.

Like the clothing and running-shoe factories in the Far East, this is a Third World sweatshop dependent on First World consumption. It's a place of struggle, poverty and illiteracy and, like many coffee-producing communities around the world, is slipping into economic disaster.

Coffee is the second most traded commodity in the world after petroleum products. Most coffee drinkers don't know that, partly because prices at local coffee shops have either stayed constant or increased. If coffee were gasoline, there might be a consumer revolt, but getting hot under the collar about the price of a cup of coffee hardly seems worth the energy.

Coffee drinkers around the world consume $90 billion-worth of crushed or processed beans annually but, according to estimates of international coffee-growing federations, producing countries see barely 15 per cent of that revenue. Farmers, in turn, receive only a fraction of that. If a North American consumer buys a bag of good quality coffee for $15, the U.S.-based Consumer's Choice Council figures, the farmer will get between 50 and 70 cents.

Economies of coffee are volatile and complex but not just about trans-national corporate business and coffee-dependent economies of Third World countries. Coffee also is about human rights, the environment, politics, exploitation, affluent western lifestyles, misguided foreign aid, community dislocation and human tragedy.

The tragedy, for example, of 14 male Mexican "coffee refugees" in their 20s and 30s who perished from dehydration in the 46 C heat of the Arizona desert last June. Relatives said they were attempting to enter the United States to find work because they could no longer afford to feed their families. Depressed coffee prices, at an historic low of 60 cents a pound, meant they could no longer make a living on their farms.

In the grim words of an official from the human rights organization Global Exchange: "The coffee we enjoy every morning is tainted with suffering."

The bad news for coffee farmers today is that the commodity market price of coffee has dropped more than 60 per cent in the past three years. This is due mostly to increased production from relatively new coffee producing countries that are flooding the market with cheaper beans. Since few of the advantages of depressed prices are passed on to consumers, roasters and retailers (often one and the same) have been able to increase profits. The crisis for the farmers is the result of the rock-bottom market prices. The situation is so bad that many farmers are already shifting some of their land and energy to vegetables. A family can survive on vegetables, but what use is coffee, they say, if it's costing more to produce than the market is willing to pay?

In nature, coffee grows best under shade. But it can be grown quicker and more economically in open sun and with the assistance of copious amounts of insecticides and pesticides. This is how most coffee consumed in the western world is grown—on plantations throughout the Third World producing for a handful of major transnational corporations which control the coffee business: Nestle, Philip Morris and Procter and Gamble prominent among them.

According to analysis, the poisons do not make it into our cups, partly because the beans are so well protected by their natural outer coat and partly because harmful residue evaporates in the intense heat of roasting. But the environment, and workers using the poisons, don't escape so easily. Hundreds of workers have been poisoned, some have died, but according to aid agencies, the casualties are much higher because most cases go unreported. Contaminated drinking water in many coffee producing countries has been linked to birth defects and developmental problems in children.

A study by the Smithsonian Institution in Washington, found that the destruction of forests to make way for coffee plantations in Central and South America has reduced the population of some migrating birds—Baltimore orioles included—by almost half.

For a humble bean, coffee has a remarkable, far-reaching universal impact.

The car ride through the mountains, to the town of San Cristobal de Las Casas, takes several hours from the nearest airport at Tuxtla. The drive demands a significant measure of skill on the part of the driver and blind faith on the part of the passenger. After passing the first sheer drop-offs and unfenced snaking curves you appreciate why local drivers construct elaborate, miniature altars on their dashboards. They need all the help they can get. Accidents are commonplace.

The mountain roads weave and rise through dense clouds and past angled fields of corn so tall they tower over the diminutive Mexican farmers. The corn, often contained within steel fences bearing the names of multinational chemical companies, obviously is genetically modified.

Corn and other vegetable farming is still a minor part of the local economy. This is coffee country where they grow mostly arabica, the superior of two coffee species. Robusta, a hardier plant but a more bitter coffee, is grown mostly in Africa and Asia whose coffee industries are aided by the World Bank and International Monetary Fund. Traditional coffee-growing nations blame Vietnam and its sponsors specifically for much of the current misery and economic havoc low prices are wreaking.

There are 110,000 farming families in Chiapas whose livelihoods depend on coffee. The average family has six members which means that more than 600,000 people here alone rely on coffee pickings. Others do too: during the harvest, when beans must be plucked quickly to preserve their quality, farmers are often forced to supplement family labour with outside help, further diminishing their incomes.

Farmers, most with a hectare or less of land, comprise 95 per cent of coffee growers in Chiapas and represent about half the coffee-growing land in the state. Five per cent of growers—owners of industrialized plantations who produce most of the coffee—hold the other half of the land.

This is a big day at Mut Vitz, a co-operative of 72 local coffee farmers based at La Estacion, another two-hour car climb from San Cristobal de Las Casas.

The co-op is already a provisional member of the Fair Trade organization and today, elected officials are gathering to make their case for full membership to Caroline, from Fair Trade's Paris office. She is especially concerned about their business plans. Full membership offers no extra money but carries some guarantee of long-term security and a local prestige that will attract much-needed new members to the co-operative. The money, roughly an extra 25 cents per pound for the co-op, is the same for both provisional and full members.

The meeting is held in a simple, white concrete building. Naked lightbulbs dangle from ceiling wires but there is no electricity to turn them on. A dozen rows of wood benches face a long wooden table where five officers of Mut Vitz are about to make their case for Fair Trade permanency. The half-light in the room comes from one small window and from a back door that opens onto a yard. The rain clouds rolling in over the mountains gradually take away more light as the meeting begins.

The interior walls are mostly bare and painted white. There is a map of the region on one wall and a poster on another explaining in simple, child-like pictures what needs to be done to the land to make it "organico." The accountant, who knows most about the business plans, is sick and hasn't arrived. It's a bad sign.

Mut Vitz president Juan Perez Hernandez, a 39-year-old farmer with eight children and three years of formal education, offers coffee to everyone. Like most brewed coffee in these parts, it is best laced with sugar to disguise the insipid taste. The best beans are exported. Mut Vitz second-tier beans are roasted locally, packaged beautifully and sold to tourists in San Cristobal de Las Casas and Tuxtla.

I ask Juan whether the coffee is from their fields.

"I don't know," he laughs. "I think we import it." The joke amuses his colleagues and is obviously layered with an irony that only they understand.

A pack of scrawny dogs hovers at the door waiting for scraps from the chicken soup the women have prepared for us. The dogs are tentative and cowering but their begging is clever and unrelenting. Dogs here work hard for their scraps.

Once the meeting begins, I take a walk with Monika, my interpreter. Across the street are two shacks, both brandishing Coca-Cola signs and both, apparently, in competition even though their shelves are almost bare and most potential customers have no money.

Coca-Cola can be found in every nook and cranny of the region.

"They may not have clean drinking water," says Monika, "but they do have Coca-Cola."

A gaunt young man in ragged clothing and stubble beard approaches me at the threshold of a medical clinic with his hand outstretched.

"Buenos tardes," he says, coughing uncontrollably. I assume he is a patient but no, he is the community doctor. He points to two female patients on beds behind him. They are his patients but he looks sicker than either of them. The clinic has little in the way of medical supplies, or medicine, except for a shipment it received from an Italian aid agency. Most of the medicine is useless. They need headache and stomach medicine but the agency has sent prescription drugs for specific ailments they have no training to diagnose. And the labels are all in Italian, which nobody can read.

At the meeting house, a group of children has gathered outside, apparently drawn by the foreigners. They are handsome, good-natured and seem chronically happy and giggly. Their demeanour is in stark contrast to the sad, tattered clothing that hangs from their bodies and the grim futures that await them: the boys will eke out an existence in coffee and the girls will marry as early as 15 and pop out babies in rapid succession.

One of the farmers appears and I remark about how happy the children are.

"It's how we all are," he says, "we could laugh ourselves to Afghanistan."

The coffee growers use the word "coyote" a lot. It is the pejorative description for the coffee middle man, the person who buys the beans from the farmer, sells them to the exporters or roasters and generally lives off the labour of others. In a few cases, coyotes will roast the beans themselves and sell them abroad directly. Roasting is where much of the value is added to coffee and where the various blends get their names.

To the farmers, coyotes are the scum of the Earth—parasites who not only cheat on prices but humiliate farmers into submission. The resentment is exacerbated because farmers, even those who are part of co-ops, must deal with coyotes to survive.

"Selling to the coyotes is always a bad experience," says Juan Hernandez. "They tell us our coffee is bad and poor quality so if the price is five or six pesos a kilo, they can drop the price even more. They will tell us our coffee is too wet and heavier because of the wet. Then they can pretend there is less coffee than there is. And when they put the coffee on the scale, the scale is not properly balanced."

Every farmer has a coyote story but the reality is that every farmer also needs fast cash. Many get loans from the coyotes because until harvest time, they often have no money to feed their families. The loans, at interest rates of 20 per cent or more, are against a portion of the crop.

After the meeting, Caroline emerges skeptical about their business plan. She confides that she probably won't recommend full membership to the Fair Trade office. But perhaps the ailing and absent accountant will change her mind when they meet later. (The accountant did not turn up for the other meeting either.)

Fair Trade is a bright hope for coffee farmers but the organization has its problems, including ineffective marketing, and seven different labels, which conspire to confuse consumers. They are currently developing a universal symbol.

"In the future," says Caroline, "I think we will only be allowing organic farmers to join Fair Trade."

She means certified organic farming which for the small producer means money they often cannot afford. Most of them already farm organically and under shade, because they can't afford chemical fertilizer and insecticide. To be certified organic takes three years and a minimum $6,000 to $7,000 U.S. depending who is doing the certifying. Foreign importers have favourite organic certifiers who perform periodic, random spot checks looking for such things as natural composting and testing the plant and land for chemical use.

Chemicals take a heavy toll on the soil and plants—coffee plants that aren't modified to tolerate and thrive on it. Some farmers are repulsed by the use of chemicals. The day before, in the nearby community of Acteal, I met Juan Perez Santiz, of Las Abejas (The Bees), a group dedicated to preserving their native traditions.

"Chemicals are easier but it is not good for the plants," he said. "The plants get too used to receiving it and it damages them and the land. A well-tended coffee bush can last 30 or 40 years but not with chemicals. The government was promoting the use of insecticides, pesticides and artificial fertilizer but we noticed it was making the children sick. It is also a violation of Mother Earth and part of our tradition is to keep our land pure."

As night falls rapidly, we drive in the back of a flatbed truck to El Brillante, a community that is part of the Mut Vitz co-operative. We go to a classroom where Caroline is scheduled to give a short talk about Fair Trade and where we will be fed dinner.

Someone mentions sleeping arrangements.

"You could sleep in one of the houses but they are full of fleas," says one of the community leaders with disarming honesty. "We will find somewhere better."

The farmers pack the classroom and ask Caroline why Fair Trade can' t pay co-ops money upfront so they don't have to borrow from the coyotes. She tells them the co-op has to better establish itself and develop a track record.

After a night spent on the concrete floor in a partially finished community centre, Andres Ruiz Gomez takes us to his fields. The soil is dark and rich, sustained by natural compost. The coffee plants, shaded by banana trees, look healthy.

Andres is 39 and a little more prosperous than most. He grows a little corn as well as coffee and owns two hectares. He recently gave his eldest son one hectare. He has two daughters aged 14 and six, neither of whom can speak and, consequently, do not go to school for even the minimal level of education offered to other children. The youngest Gomez child, a daughter, is three.

The family has a turkey, a few chickens, a pig and a horse. He sees a brighter future if farmers unite in a co-op but even so, the most fervent co-op supporters must sell to the coyotes to survive.

"The coyotes cheat everyone," he says, "but some people don't see it—they don't see how they weigh the scales. Still, most people here sell only to the coyotes because there is a lot of hard work if you're a member of the co-operative. They want everything to be certified organic. Not many people here use chemicals anyway because if one uses them, everybody is affected."

Harvest begins in December. On the farms, the work is dawn-to-dusk picking—painstaking, labour-intensive work that involves gathering the ripened beans from the bushes and throwing them into baskets strapped around the waist. The beans are then fed through a hand mill that removes the skin and the pulp underneath it. The pulp becomes compost and the seeds—or actual beans—go on to be fermented, washed and dried. Coffee farmers have a flat, concrete surface outside their homes where the beans dry. A parchment-like cover remains to protect the bean.

The harvest will end in February and another cycle will begin. Farmers work their fields with machetes and hoes. The machetes to clear away undergrowth and the hoes to work in the compost.

Like his father before him, Andres has always been a coffee farmer and says his children have no other choice than to rely on it for their futures.

"It's my work," he says. "Coffee is all I know. If you don't have coffee around here, you don't have much."

I ask Andres if he ever thinks of the people who drink what he grows—people in Canada and the United States.

"No," he says. "That all seems very far away. I don't know what happens to my coffee after I sell it."

Another Mut Vitz farmer, Mario Perez Diaz, figures he makes about $1,200 a year after expenses. He has seven children and has farmed his single acre of land for 15 years.

"We get very little for our labour," he says. "It's very difficult to get ahead. I try to hold as much of my coffee as possible for the co-ops because we get a better price but we all have to sell some to the coyotes because we need cash to feed our families."

Mario says he doesn't want his kids to be farmers. The family's eldest, a 19-year-old daughter, is studying theology at a church school in Guadalajara.

"My children are studying, thank God," he says. "It is expensive for us because there are supplies and notebooks we have to buy and living in the city is expensive. We find the money by working hard. We grow fruits and vegetables and sell them in the town. We don't have any land to give to our children. I want them to study and learn to defend themselves and have a better life away from here."

Mario reads and writes a little but is frustrated by his own inability to function in the wider world.

"Spending your life in the fields and not being able to learn Spanish," he says, "is no way to be and no way to defend yourself in the world."

I casually suggest that being surrounded by the beauty of the mountains is better than being one of the 20 million in the ugly, polluted sprawl of Mexico City.

"I don't know," he responds. "I have never been to Mexico City. We have no money to travel so we have to stay here. But I like it here. It is fine for me."

Many farmers are skeptical about joining co-ops, says Mut Vitz president Juan Perez Hernandez, because they've fallen victim to some unscrupulous leaders—their own people—who sold a few of the co-op's bags on the side.

Politics is another reason.

"Our communities are divided politically," he said, "and people tend to group according to political and philosophical affiliation." By political affiliation he means those who support the ruling government and those who don't. Or, more specifically, those who have supported the indigenous rebel Zapatistas and those who moved to the government side.

When co-ops have stuck together and worked well, the coyotes have raised their buying price in an effort to break the competition.

"This is another problem," says Juan Hernandez, "but we tell our members to be careful; if we become weak, the coyote price will go down even lower than it was before. That's the way they operate."

But loathe them as he does, even Juan has to sell to the coyotes.

"To say that I earn enough to look after my family is an exaggeration," he says.

PART TWO

Guillermo Gutierrez Viladroza is a coyote but doesn't look like a person who would fix a weigh scale to rip off a poor farmer. I had walked into his Spartan roadside office in San Cristobal de Las Casas unannounced and asked for an interview.

"I hope you have something to wipe your eyes," he smiles. "It is a very sad story I will be telling you."

Viladroza, dressed casually in shirt, sweater and slacks, is in sharp sartorial contrast to the tattered farmers who grow what he buys. He is a pleasant man and a salesman to the core. On his simple wooden desk is a calculator and a telephone. Two colleagues sit with him. He obviously isn't busy.

He buys and roasts coffee beans and deals mainly with Nestle. These are bad times for farmers who grow the best beans, he confirms, because the market is being flooded by low-rate robusta from Africa and Vietnam.

"All the coffee gets lumped together," he says. "Organic coffee has become fashionable but it is an insignificant part of the market and really, farmers around here have been organic for many years. It doesn't help if you don't have the market to sell to."

Predictably, Viladroza rejects charges that coyotes cheat and maintains it's the market that dictates prices. The world price is exacerbated, he says, because unlike Colombia and the mythical Juan Valdez, Mexico doesn't promote its coffee very well. Consequently, when Mexico's coffee coyotes sell they are forced to do so at a discount.

Roasters and retailers make the big money, he says, because they rarely have to drop their prices: "Consumers in North America don't keep a watch on coffee prices."

At a major processing plant an hour's drive away in Tuxtla Gutierrez, they select beans for Starbucks and other big North American clients. In massive warehouse-style buildings they have machines to strip away that final parchment from the beans and mechanical tubes spotted with holes that gradually get larger—first releasing broken and tiny beans and gradually retaining larger ones. (U.S. consumers like to buy big beans, though big isn't always best.) In the most modern processing plants, beans pass through a series of electronic eyes that can detect discolouration, which usually means a fermenting bean that can destroy a whole sack.

The modern, airy building stands behind a tight security fence in an industrial park on the outskirts of the city. Several men work in one glass-walled anteroom, roasting and grinding small quantities of green beans, then brewing and sipping like wine tasters—cupping it's called in the coffee trade.

Octavio Hernandez Torres was trained in the craft of cupping in the United States and tells me without bravado that he can taste a sample of coffee and tell immediately from where in Mexico the beans originated. His job is to ensure the right beans go to the right clients, who will then roast and blend them into the various types of coffee for drinkers in Canada and the U.S.

His boss, Roberto Estrada, says low coffee prices affect all levels of the business and predicts gloomily that unless things improve, only the largest industrial growers and roasters will be left. The small farmer is in danger of losing everything, he says.

The best hope for coffee farmers seems to lie in educating consumers and persuading them to become more selective in their coffee buying.

But Estrada's view is bleak.

"Our whole industry in Mexico could disappear," he says. "The big companies are the only people making money from this situation and it's because of the millions of bags of coffee that are being dumped on the market. We might have the best coffee in the world but it doesn't matter."

The night before I left for Mexico, I bought a pound bag of Mexico Shade Grown in an Ottawa Starbucks store. It was done up in a brightly coloured package with a warm and fuzzy environmental message. The coffee is from the El Triunfo Biosphere Reserve in Chiapas—one of the world's finest coffee-growing regions—and produced by what the packet described as "a dedicated farmer who plucks a ripe coffee cherry from its tender bough ..." The one pound (454 g) of coffee is certified organic and marketed by Starbucks in partnership with Conservation International, a high-profile, well-funded Washington D.C.–based environmental group. The packet costs $16.95.

Luis Herrera Solis, director general of Comcafe, the Chiapas state-sponsored coffee marketing board, says he knows the Starbucks–Conservation International venture well. I show him the bag, tell him how much it cost and he immediately begins jotting down a calculation on a piece of scrap paper.

"I know the producers," he says, "and we support this kind of initiative and wish there were more of them."

Solis says the initiative, which has obvious advantages for the Starbucks image, involves the purchase of 5,000 sacks (110 pounds each) for $238 from a small group of about 200 producers. The retailer, he estimates, gets the package of coffee to its customers for about $7, of which the farmer group shares about $2 from each package sold.

"There is a profit in there for someone," he adds, "but not for the farmers. When you look at the numbers, you understand that there could be a fairer distribution of the wealth and more help given to the farmers."

(Two weeks ago, Starbucks announced a pilot project with Conservation International they say is designed to help farmers worldwide who grow coffee according to strict environmental standards.)

Solis and his organization are fighting battles on several fronts in a desperate effort to stop the total collapse of the region's coffee industry.

"The situation in Chiapas is particularly dire," he says, "because most of the people who grow coffee here depend solely on it for their income. But in all coffee-growing regions of the world the situation is more or less the same."

Among the battles are efforts to get some kind of compensation fund to see farmers through especially hard times. He is also lobbying to ban the importation of foreign coffee into Mexico. Nestle, he says, imports Vietnamese coffee into its Mexican plants to make instant brew.

"But why would Nestle bring coffee all the way from Vietnam, if Mexican coffee is so cheap?" I ask.

"Because it is even cheaper," he replies.

Mexican farmers have started to grow the cheaper, easier-to-cultivate robusta beans to compete with foreign growers and in recognition of the fact that commercial coffee blends that were once 70-percent arabica are now the reverse.

"Organic coffee is important for many producers," says Solis, "because they own their land and growing organically is the best way to preserve it. But only six per cent of coffee we export is certified organic. If you consider all the small initiatives ... shade grown, bird friendly, organic etc., you have a total six per cent. The market is not strong enough to sell coffee under those labels."

Solis shows me a coffee package with the word CHIAPAS stamped boldly across the front. He's made a deal with a Chicago company that has agreed to distribute the branded coffee throughout the U.S. and Canada.

"This is the first step in a dream," he says.

Solis hopes that branding the state name will be less confusing to consumers and give them a clear choice if they want to buy coffee that comes directly from the producers.

"There is nothing to suggest the situation is going to get better," he says. "We just have to hope it doesn't get worse. There is little sensitivity among consumers about what happens to producers when prices go so low because most consumers don't even know it's so low. But I don't want to blame consumers too much. What is worse are people in the industry who take advantage of the situation."

Shortly before leaving the mountain farmland, I asked Juan Hernandez what message he would like to send to Canadian coffee drinkers.

He thought hard before replying.

"I would ask them to think about where the coffee is coming from and how some of us are treating our plants very well to produce the best quality coffee. We are doing our best but it isn't just Juan who is doing it, it's Juan and his whole family working together in the fields."

He paused again: "I don't know what else I can say."

Clarifications

Indigenous: Belonging to or produced by a particular region.

Fair Trade: Read about fair trade on the Café Campesino Web site at *www.cafecampesino.com/fair.html*. The site notes that "according to the Fair Trade Federation there are seven principles to fair trade: Fair Wages, Cooperative Workplaces, Consumer Education, Environmental Sustainability, Financial and Technical Support, Respect for Cultural Identity, and Public Accountability."

Third World: The "Third World" is made up of developing nations; the term was first used after the Second World War to refer to countries that had gained independence from colonialism. Now it is often used to mean poor or underdeveloped countries.

Sweatshop: A factory or workplace that employs people at low wages and in poor conditions. Sweatshops are usually associated with Third World or poorer countries or immigrants from those countries.

Talking Points

Read the Fair Trade standards at one of the Web sites below, find the symbols that represent fair trade, then check out the coffee brands on the shelves at your local supermarket. How many are "shade grown"; how many are "100% arabica"; how many are "blended"? How much difference do these notations make to the price of the coffee? You may find that a shade-grown arabica, technically and ethically the best coffee to buy, is actually one of the cheaper coffees. President's Choice Organics line, sold in Loblaws, Maxi and Provigo stores, has a coffee that fits this category. In addition, a U.S.-based natural food supermarket chain, Whole Foods Market, has recently opened stores in Canada in which it sells an organic brand named Allegro Coffee (*www.allegrocoffee.com*).

It would be easy for coffee consumers to demand shade-grown, fair trade coffee. Why has this movement not done better than it has? How many students in your class were aware of the fair trade movement?

Web Research

The Fair Trade Federation is on-line at *www.fairtradefederation.com*.

Global Exchange has an interesting Web site at *www.globalexchange. org*.

The organization that grants Fair Trade certification in Canada is Transfair. The Web site is at *www.transfair.ca*.

Oxfam Canada's Web site at *www.oxfam.ca* has a Fair Trade Coffee Workshop Kit which names the coffee shops in Toronto and elsewhere selling Fair Trade coffee.

Find out at *www.songbird.org* how you can make a difference to songbirds when you buy fair trade coffee.

Writing That Works

Introduction—anecdote: The first paragraph grabs the reader's attention with a snapshot (both real and figurative) of a family life. Anecdotes run through the entire article as well, personalizing the situation for the reader.

Comparison: "It is here, on the lush, warm, rain-blessed Mexican mountainsides where some of the finest coffee in the world is grown, and where, for the price of a cappuccino at any North American designer coffee house, a man could feed his family for a week."

Analogy: "Like the clothing and running-shoe factories in the Far East, this is a Third World sweatshop dependent on First World consumption." The writer paints a quick picture by comparing the situation in Mexico to a situation that readers may be more familiar with.

Comparison: "If coffee were gasoline, there might be a consumer revolt...."

Faceoff: Point/Counterpoint
by Sherry Cooper and Linda McQuaig

Canadian Business, April 30, 2001

POINT: SHERRY COOPER

Since the end of the Second World War, impediments to free trade have been markedly reduced, triggering an era of unprecedented economic growth and prosperity.

International trade has expanded far faster than the world economy. Imports of goods and services as a percentage of global gross domestic product have doubled, from 12% 40 years ago to 24% today. For Canada, the uptrend has been even more impressive. In the past decade alone, Canadian exports of goods and services have risen from 26% of GDP to 46%. This has been an enormous source of jobs, income and tax dollars. It has boosted our stock markets, helped to eliminate our government budgetary deficits and taken our jobless rate down to its lowest levels in many years.

Of all the major industrialized countries, Canada is the most dependent on exports as a source of growth. And more than 80% of our exports go to the US. Expanding NAFTA to include the rest of the Western Hemisphere would broaden our markets, helping to diversify our customer base. It would also help bring the clear benefits of NAFTA to South America, improving and stabilizing the many troubled economies of the region.

As centrally planned economies floundered in the past 20 years, we have seen the spread of market capitalism throughout the world. The evidence is clear that this has led to a rise in living standards in virtually all countries that have participated. That is not to say that free trade—and the enhanced global competitive pressure that it brings—is without costs. Dislocations and creative destruction in declining industries and sectors can be painful. But the use of protectionist measures is even more disruptive, preventing the appropriate allocation of capital to its most productive use.

Free trade promotes the underlying competitive forces of the division of labor and comparative advantage. This fosters stronger growth and rising living standards. One of the real dangers, however, is overselling the benefits. While free trade increases income levels, it does not appear to narrow the gap between rich and poor. This is where the disappointments and protests come in: inequality in the world economy has not diminished.

The key to economic advantage in the Information Age is knowledge—a well-educated, hardworking labor force. With rare exception, richer countries have a better-educated population than the poorer ones. The key to success in raising income levels has largely been the provision of good public education for all. But that is not so simple. It requires a significant degree of political stability and it also requires sound government financing, presupposing a solid macroeconomic foundation.

Economists once preached that as global trade increases, average output per person should become less disparate around the world. Unfortunately, it just has not happened—at least on a broad scale. Not because trade has failed, but because of the continuing gap in the ability of many emerging economies to provide a well-educated and technically savvy workforce. The most notable success stories have been the so-called Asian tigers. We have seen the enormous progress in East Asia—Singapore, Taiwan, South Korea and Hong Kong—leaping from Third World to First World status with the freeing of trade and the provision of good public education for all.

Nevertheless, the bulk of the emerging world remains relatively poor; income inequality has been roughly stable for more than a century. This explains why globalization has generated such negative sentiment in some circles. We have witnessed the protests of the past few years in such places as Seattle, Washington, DC, and Prague—the turbulent and sometimes violent street theatre of incensed young middle-class Westerners who defame multinational corporations for exploitation and environmental rape. Ironically, the emerging countries that are supposed to be the victims of global capitalism do not support such protests. The poor countries fear that labor or environmental restrictions will reduce their competitiveness and slow the inflow of foreign business.

Yet globalization undeniably has created millions of jobs and enhanced training opportunities from Bangalore to Brazil. It has developed whole regions, bringing electricity, phone service and sewage treatment to some 300 million families in developing nations. It has transferred nearly US$2 trillion from rich to poor countries through financial markets. It has had tremendous political effect as well, toppling dictators and making information freely available in once sheltered societies. Today, the Internet has obliterated much of the power of censorship of information. It has the power to narrow the commercial and cultural gulfs separating rich and poor nations.

Trade and inflows of private capital are essential for achieving strong, sustainable growth and reducing poverty. Key also is the spread globally of mandatory education for everyone. In too many developing countries, quality education is available only for the wealthy or elite. In addition, too much of the foreign investment in many developing countries is subject to little if any environmental or human rights restrictions.

Still, the benefits of globalization are so potent, so obvious, that the threat of the protesters becomes all the more serious. It is essential that the progress continue. It is also crucial, therefore, that the costs of globalization be addressed, mitigated and, where possible, eliminated. We need better corporate and government policy. Multinationals—which account for the bulk of direct cross-border investment and one-third of all trade—have a social and moral responsibility. This is especially true in countries where basic human and worker rights are not guaranteed. Multi-governmental efforts should continue to assure and enforce this responsibility, rather than quell the forces of progress and growth.

COUNTERPOINT: LINDA MCQUAIG

Let's get one thing out of the way, quickly. Being opposed to NAFTA and the FTAA does not mean one is opposed to international trade. In fact, opposition to the trade deals is about something completely different, and can be stated simply: the deals greatly expand the power of corporations and shrink the power of governments. In many ways, these deals are only peripherally about trade. What they are really about is redesigning the international economy in a way that enhances corporate power.

Corporate power has, of course, always been extensive. But before the new trade regime began about a decade ago, there were limits imposed. And for good reason. It was recognized that, in a democracy, the real power should rest with the people and their elected representatives. This, let's not forget, is what democracy is all about. The shortcomings of government are legendary, but the truth is that government is still the only vehicle ordinary people have to shape their world. The idea that democratic governments should have precedence over private corporate interests has not only been discarded by those designing the new trade deals; it has been turned upside down. In an enormous transfer of power, corporations have been given wide-ranging new rights that essentially give them the power to challenge the authority of governments—even in areas that affect the ability of governments to defend important rights of their citizens.

Consider what happened, for instance, when Metalclad, a California-based company, decided it wanted to build a toxic waste facility in a town in Mexico. The town feared the plant might pollute its water supply—a reasonable fear, one might add—and so denied Metalclad a building permit. In the days before NAFTA, that would have been the end of the matter. But under NAFTA, Metalclad was able to sue Mexico and take its case to a NAFTA tribunal, which ruled that the Mexican government must pay Metalclad US$16.7 million in damages. Similarly, a Canadian company, Methanex, is suing the US government for a staggering US$970 million because California banned a gasoline additive that the company produces—after some of the additive leeched into municipal wells in the city of Santa Monica, contaminating the local water supply.

The sheer audacity of these lawsuits is enough to take one's breath away. Imagine what must have been in the minds of the executives at

Methanex when they hit on the idea of filing a lawsuit to protest the ban on their product—after that product had contaminated a city's drinking water!

And in a case with far-reaching implications for this country, UPS, the American courier company, is suing Canada for $230 million. Its grievance is that Canada Post's courier business uses some of the publicly funded facilities of its letter business. In fact, there's good reason for this blending of operations; it creates greater efficiency, allowing the Crown corporation to provide comprehensive, uniform mail and courier service at reasonable rates across a vast country. If the UPS lawsuit succeeds, will we then face lawsuits from private health care companies complaining that they are at a disadvantage because they have to compete with a medicare system that uses publicly funded facilities? Would these companies sue if, for instance, they had to perform cataract surgery in private clinics while medicare provided cataract surgery in publicly funded hospitals?

What makes this new set of corporate rights particularly startling is that corporations get to make their claims to NAFTA tribunals operating in secret. Even though issues like the safety of drinking water and the future of our medicare systems are clearly of broad public interest, no member of the public is allowed to attend these tribunal hearings, no transcripts are released, and no reasons are given for the decisions.

This transfer of power to corporations under the new trade deals is part of a whole new attitude towards corporate power. In the past, corporations were recognized as powerful special interests, and it was understood that governments, working in the public interest, had to be vigilant with them. This was the thinking behind the Canada–US auto pact. Signed in 1965, the pact allowed Canada to demand that US automakers produce cars in Canada if they wanted to sell cars here tariff-free. The deal was a huge boon to Canada; it ensured that we got a lucrative piece of North American car production. But the business sector didn't like having to live up to these sorts of requirements. So this approach—in which governments demanded real-world guarantees from corporations for jobs and investment—has been banned in the new trade deals. The auto pact itself was terminated earlier this year, after the World Trade Organization ruled against it.

It's often suggested that we should endorse these trade deals because, well, what's the alternative? The question implies that the trade deals are really about trade, and that without them international trade would decline, if not grind to a halt. But that's absurd.

International trade flourished throughout the decades following the Second World War, when a NAFTA-style regime was nothing more than a gleam in the eye of a few ambitious corporate managers. The difference was that, back then, the rules of the international trading system also permitted democracy.

The realm of corporate power is expanding, and the territory occupied by democratically elected governments is shrinking. It's fashionable these days to think this has something to do with mysterious forces operating in the global economy beyond our control. But it has more to do with the fact that we keep signing treaties that facilitate this transfer of power. It's also fashionable to dismiss anything that happened more than 10 years ago. But some things that happened long ago are still worthwhile. Like democracy.

Clarifications

NAFTA: The North American Free Trade Agreement was signed in 1992 by Canada, the United States and Mexico. The agreement took effect on January 1, 1994. The agreement removed tariffs for certain exports and encouraged cross-border trading, especially in such industries as agriculture, automobile manufacturing, energy and trucking. It replaced the so-called "Auto Pact" that had been in effect since 1965 and was responsible for the growth of car manufacturing, especially in Ontario.

Macroeconomics: The study of economics at the national level.

Talking Points

Read the comments below on the writing style of the two authors, and discuss which argument you find most convincing. How did the way each author wrote influence your opinion? Did you already have a strong opinion on this issue? If so, did either of the arguments sway you?

Web Research

The Department of Foreign Affairs and International Trade has information on NAFTA at *www.dfait-maeci.gc.ca/nafta-alena.*

Learn what the opposition to NAFTA has to say on the Stop the FTAA site at *www.stopftaa.org*.

Writing That Works

Both authors write well, but their styles are quite different. In fact, much can be learned about their arguments from the way they argue. Here are some brief comments about each writer's style.

Sherry Cooper: As her Web site (*http://sherrycooper.com/index.php*) says, Dr. Sherry Cooper is "a global economic strategist and executive vice-president of Harris Bank (Chicago) and Bank of Montreal (Toronto)." She is therefore the only expert she consults in her article. Her assertions are believable and sound true—"In the past decade alone, Canadian exports of goods and services has risen from 26% of GDP to 46%." Facts like these can be checked, but she does not give any source. Her writing is clear, balanced and to-the-point.

Linda McQuaig is a journalist who writes for the *National Post*. She has also published several books, the most recent of which is *All You Can Eat: Lust and the New Capitalism*. Her writing style is more literary than Cooper's and she uses examples, such as Metalclad, Methanex and UPS. McQuaig appeals to the reader with her obvious outrage: "The sheer audacity of these lawsuits is enough to take one's breath away." She also uses rhetorical questions: "Would these companies sue if, for instance, they had to perform cataract surgery in private clinics while medicare provided cataract surgery in public funded hospitals?"

TOPIC 5

THE BUSINESS OF MANAGEMENT

INTRODUCTION

Although some forms of management theory or "science" have been around since the beginning of the Industrial Revolution, it was the twentieth century that saw the emergence of the first real business theorists. The grandfather of management as a science was Frederick Winslow Taylor, who put his ideas in writing in his 1911 book *The Principles of Scientific Management*. Interestingly, the book is still available and has sold in the region of 30,000 copies on Amazon.com. (For comparison, this is about 5,000 more than Margaret Atwood's modern classic novel *Lady Oracle*). Taylor's book focuses on time management, particularly in steel mills.

The father—sometimes called the godfather—of management theory is Peter Drucker, an Austrian-born American economist still writing in his late eighties as we go to press. Drucker has written more than thirty books, including *The Practice of Management* (1954), and the recently published *Management Challenges for the Twenty-first Century*.

Another candidate for paternity of management theory is W. Edwards Deming, who went to Japan in the 1950s as it rebuilt after the Second World War. Although Deming was often credited with saving Japan's economy, he was not well known in North America until NBC aired a documentary about him in 1980 entitled "If Japan Can, Why Can't We?" Deming became a popular lecturer and consultant, and his book *Out of the Crisis*, published in 1986, introduced his fourteen points of quality management. (Read about these at *http://caes. mit.edu/deming/14-points.html14.*)

Various management theories are discussed in the first article in this chapter, "Distilled Wisdom: Buddy, Can You Paradigm?" Today, with the issue of globalization on everyone's mind, business theory often concentrates on the way a business looks to the outside world. For example, "Samaritan Inc." discusses corporate social responsibility, an idea that is in some ways a response to globalization. Economic downturns, the subsequent layoffs and the importance of resiliency and loyalty in "human capital" are discussed in "Creating a Resilient Organization." The final article, "Ms. Versus Mr.," looks at the differing management styles of women and men.

Distilled Wisdom: Buddy, Can You Paradigm?

by Brian Dumayne

Fortune, May 15, 1995

Management must be one of the most unnatural activities in the world. Why else would managers sustain a vast publishing and consulting industry with a huge component of blather whose main function is reassurance rather than the transmission of knowledge? Like diet and golfing books, the hundreds of management guides that come out every year really function as corporate security blankets. Managers, like obese people and duffers, feel so perpetually anxious about themselves that they will tolerate an almost incredible torrent of balderdash in the hope of self-improvement.

Managers can spend an eternity searching for panaceas in the pages of such books, but they won't find them. They may for a few months or even years think that they've found a piece of the true Cross, but eventually the advice, trend, or tool will devolve into just another fad or folly. Yet if you look hard at the history of the Fortune 500 over the past 40 years, there emerges through all the static a set of golden management rules that have surviving power. They don't have labels—once you stick a name on something, it's fast on its way to becoming a flavor-of-the-month disappointment—but are broad management principles. They are (1) Management is a practice. (2)

People are a resource. (3) Marketing and innovation are the key functions of a business. (4) Discover what you do well. (5) Quality pays for itself.

Still, the question nags: Is any of this real? Has it actually generated wealth? As with golf and dieting advice, some fundamentals have proved themselves over time. While no one can measure the precise financial impact of these ideas, the argument that they paid off can be made with confidence. Stanley Gault, who has been to the Fortune 500 over the past decade what Joe Montana is to football, says that basic management principles like empowerment, strategy, and quality contributed greatly to his successes at GE in the 1960s and 1970s, and to his turnarounds at Rubbermaid and Goodyear in the 1980s and 1990s.

The very idea of management as a practice, like medicine or navigation, didn't even exist when Fortune published its first 500 list in 1955. Until Peter Drucker published his classic *The Practice of Management* the previous year, management had been seen largely as the expression of rank and power. People managed subordinates; they didn't manage businesses. Says Drucker: "When my book came out, nobody had even thought of managing a business. It led to the whole idea of objective, of what is the mission of a business."

Drucker's insight has had nearly endless ramifications. Once companies like General Electric, Du Pont, and Sears started thinking about management in this way, everything needed to be redefined. What, for instance, was the appropriate role of top management? Rather than trying to control everything, Drucker taught, senior executives should focus on strategy and let the rank and file carry out their objectives. With Drucker's help, General Electric in 1956 opened its now famous Crotonville, New York, training center and has since taught generations of managers this philosophy.

Odd as it may seem in an age when downsizing has depopulated entire office towers, one of the most important and enduring ideas about management is that managers should treat workers as a resource rather than a cost. Says PepsiCo CEO Wayne Calloway: "It seems to me that over the last 40 years the biggest idea is the notion that management doesn't have the monopoly on brains or judgment. It's this idea of utilizing all the strengths of a corporation."

The shift away from command and control didn't happen fast. It has taken decades to get people—at least some people—to take initiative, to learn, to change constantly. True, in the 1970s, self-realization movements like est got out of hand. PacBell had to abandon its costly leadership program after employees complained that it was a "dress code for the mind." But more recently companies have put "empowerment" to better use. Hewlett-Packard in the 1980s used it to reduce cycle times, requiring employees to team up and design, develop, and market products and services at record speeds. For instance, in 1988 H-P developed the DeskJet printer in just 22 months—a job like that used to take twice as long.

In the early 1990s books like Peter Senge's *The Fifth Discipline* took empowerment a step further, arguing that people are more than cogs; they are individuals with feelings, thoughts, and insights that need to be aired and understood. What Senge and others articulated was that motivated people are good for business. Says Goodyear's Gault: "The empowerment revolution has allowed our nation to record unprecedented progress in the areas of productivity, creativity, technology, product development, and overall competitiveness in a global market."

This notion has exerted a powerful effect on corporate structure. If people were to have more autonomy, they didn't need as many middle managers looking over their shoulders. Thus, a company could shed organizational layers. Lincoln Electric started experimenting with the flat, or horizontal, organization in the 1950s, but it wasn't until the restructuring movement of the late 1980s that corporate America really began to see the light.

In the management of products, as opposed to people, a similar change has turned out to be a winner. In the Fifties and Sixties, with Japanese and German industry still in ruins, U.S. industry could make virtually whatever its engineers or marketers pleased, the customer be damned. But in the 1970s, especially in the auto industry, global competition began to intensify. American corporations slowly realized they would have to start organizing around the idea of serving the customer. Says Theodore Levitt, Harvard business school professor emeritus and marketing expert: "We call it the marketing concept. It made us run businesses around the principle 'Put the customer first, and then profits will follow.'"

A strong customer focus led companies to adopt disciplines like test marketing, surveys, and focus groups that helped them keep in touch with customers and create new products. Says Andrall Pearson, a partner at the New York LBO firm Clayton Dubilier & Rice: "The idea of a marketing discipline was revolutionary. Before, we had no scientific focus. We were just pissing money away on the market." That attention to marketing detail spread in the 1970s and 1980s and helped build such service giants as L.L. Bean, Nordstrom, and Federal Express. Drucker sums it up best: "You get paid for creating a customer, and you get paid for creating a new dimension of performance, which is innovation. Everything else is a cost center."

Our fourth nominee for a great management idea, strategic planning, took a wrong turn for a decade or so. Although the Pentagon had been doing strategic planning through the 1950s and 1960s, not until the 1970s did the idea gain broad currency in corporate America. Before strategic planning, executives essentially sat around and played what-if: What if our competitors did this or that? Then, starting in 1969, GE began to teach strategy as a discipline. The new idea was to conduct a comprehensive analysis of competitors—their past, present, and anticipated future. GE's strategy course also taught managers to allocate resources based upon how you would categorize your business: Is it a growth business or a harvest business?

The beauty of this kind of planning was that it helped managers focus on what they did best, on competencies (although they didn't use the word at the time) that gave them a competitive advantage. Obvious, perhaps, but the point got lost in the conglomeration-mad Sixties and Seventies. Seeing the inefficiencies that resulted and realizing—with the help of Wall Street raiders—that their best strategy was to focus on what they did well, companies in the Eighties began deconglomerating.

Implicit in the idea of jettisoning the unnecessary was focusing on the essence. Thus it was that corporate strategy came back full circle to one of today's most popular ideas: core competencies. Consultants Gary Hamel and C. K. Prahalad argued that every company has a core strength—be it marketing, manufacturing, or R&D—and that it should focus resources on what it does best. Nike, for instance, concentrates on marketing and design, farming out the manufacture of its athletic shoes.

Sometimes a truly good idea needs an apostle. Before the "quality revolution" of the 1980s and 1990s, managers basically thought that investing in high quality was a cost that couldn't be recouped. More than anyone else, consultant W. Edwards Deming disabused them of that notion. In the 1960s and 1970s, Deming worked in Japan and taught the Japanese that by continually improving the quality of a product or process—kaizen, as it's called—a company could save time and money, reduce waste, and give the customer better products faster.

For years Deming couldn't sell his message in the U.S. Then, on June 24, 1980, at 9:30 p.m., he appeared on an NBC show about Japanese quality called "If Japan Can, Why Can't We?" A manager at Ford happened to be watching and brought Deming and his ideas to Ford. The result was Team Taurus, a quality-driven project that helped Ford turn itself around and eventually led to the development of the company's best-selling car.

After that, quality spread wildly throughout the rest of corporate America. Yes, there were abuses, as some companies like Florida Power & Light got carried away in the 1980s and turned their quality programs into self-sustaining bureaucracies. But overall it works. Stressing high quality makes lots of money for companies. Some 15 years after Deming appeared on NBC, Motorola, one of the great disciples of the quality movement, makes such good pagers that it is now a formidable player in the Japanese market.

1955 Corporations start adopting ideas in Peter Drucker's new book, *The Practice of Management.*

1956 GE opens Crotonville training center, identifying management as something to be taught.

1958 Lincoln Electric experiments with flat management, pledging not to lay off workers and obtaining flexible work rules.

1960 Douglas McGregor publishes *The Human Side of Enterprise,* which outlines Theory X (employees are machines) and Theory Y (employees are extended families).

1963 Harold Geneen embarks on course of acquisitions that will make ITT one of America's largest conglomerates.

1969 GE, struggling to cope with a raft of acquisitions, becomes one of the first big companies to adopt a strategic plan.

1971 Werner Erhard launches Erhard Seminars Training, the taproot of touchy-feely management.

1980 Rand Araskog becomes ITT chairman; to reduce debt, he begins selling some of the 250 businesses acquired by Geneen.

1980 W. Edwards Deming appears on NBC TV documentary; Deming is hired as a consultant by Ford.

1980 Japan overtakes the U.S. as the world's leading producer of automobiles.

1982 T. Boone Pickens, chairman of Mesa Petroleum, makes his first hostile takeover attempt, for Cities Service Corp. It fails.

1985 Ford introduces Taurus, one of the first American automobiles to be designed and built using cross-functional teams.

1987 Manpower becomes largest private employer in the U.S., with over 465,000 temporary workers.

1988 Hewlett-Packard develops DeskJet printer in just 22 months.

1990 C.K. Prahalad and Gary Hamel publish "Core Competence of the Corporation" in *Harvard Business Review.*

1993 Michael Hammer and James Champy publish *Reengineering the Corporation: A Manifesto for Business Revolution.*

Clarifications

Panacea: A remedy that cures everything; a simple remedy for a complex problem; or a band-aid solution.

Rank and file: This term initially referred to enlisted troops, as opposed to officers. Now it usually refers to the workers in an organization, excluding management.

est: The Erhard Seminars Training courses of the seventies seem now to be a parody of seventies culture. The training sessions consisted of weekend-long stays at "space stations," where the object was to tear people down emotionally and then put them back together. You can read an interesting collection of articles on est and its founder Werner Erhard at *www.rickross.com/groups/est.html.*

Command and control: A form of management consisting of a boss who tells people what to do, and the rank and file (see above) beneath him who do what they are told. Find Margaret Wheatley's article "Goodbye, Command and Control" on Peter Drucker's Web site at *www.pfdf.org.*

Talking Points

What is the difference between workers being treated as a resource and being treated as a cost? In what kinds of work situation are workers treated in each of these ways?

Nike concentrates on marketing and design, farming out the actual manufacture of its athletic gear. Read what Naomi Klein has to say on this practice in her article "The Tyranny of the Brands" (page 53).

Web Research

For on-line business news read the *Financial Post* at *www.canada.com;* *ROB Magazine* at *www.robmagazine.com;* the *Wall Street Journal* at *www.wsj.com,* and Canoe's financial Web site at *www.webfin.com.*

Writing That Works

Classification: The article postulates a set of "golden management rules that have power" and then proceeds to classify those rules: "They are (1) Management is a practice. (2) People are a resource. (3) Marketing and innovation are the key functions of a business. (4) Discover what you do well. (5) Quality pays for itself." Each rule is then explained using examples and citing expert opinion or best-selling books: (1) Peter Drucker's *The Practice of Management,* and General Electric; (2) Peter Senge's *The Fifth Discipline,* and Hewlett Packard; (3) experts Theodore Levitt and Andrall Pearson; (4) General Electric and experts Gary Hamel and C.K. Prahalad; (5) W. Edwards Deming and Ford Motors.

Notice how the structure is not numbered until the discussion of the "fourth nominee," giving the article a subtle quality.

Conclusion—summary: The conclusion consists of a brief summary ("after that, quality spread wildly...")

Samaritan Inc.
by Hilary Davidson

Profit: The Magazine for Canadian Entrepreneurs, May 1, 2000

Bruce Poon Tip built his business on a foundation of environmental, ethical and social responsibility. Since 1990 his Toronto company, G.A.P Adventures Inc., has been specializing in ecologically minded tours, providing travellers with unique, authentic cultural experiences. G.A.P's guiding principle of sustainability dictates that tours are kept to small groups of 12 and visitors stay in guest houses or private homes instead of hotels, thereby interfering with the environment as little as possible. Respect for the local people and the environment, says Poon Tip, is the sine qua non of the company's philosophy. "Being responsible is at the top of our agenda," he says. "We are constantly evaluating ourselves so that we can be as responsible as we can be. The mentality is, we can always do better."

Not your typical corporate mantra, yet those principles have attracted like-minded travellers and helped boost G.A.P's 1999 sales to $12.9 million, up from just $500,000 five years ago. But they've also been the source of some gut wrenching decisions that came at a steep price. Last year Poon Tip reluctantly shut down a popular tour to Burma, when conditions there violated his company's philosophies. He's also scaled back trips to other destinations where sustainability proved questionable. "I can't even begin to add up the losses," Poon Tip admits. "We're bottom-line driven, we're profit-driven. But we don' t only consider the bottom line. It's a question of what's right."

Poon Tip is not alone. Doing the right thing is top of mind for many businesspeople today. The buzzword is "corporate social responsibility," a grassroots movement that believes values, ethics and community well-being should be part of everyday business.

It means abandoning the notion that a business's only responsibility is making money, and encouraging companies to adopt a mindset and culture that considers their relationships with all "stakeholders," including shareholders, employees and communities. Admittedly, CSR encompasses some wide-ranging terrain: ethical behavior can include donating to charity, adopting fair labor policies, protecting the environment, truthful advertising, fair pricing and supporting community projects.

At its core, CSR is about sustainability, both economic and environmental, says Tobi Davidge, executive director of Canadian Business for Social Responsibility (CBSR), a Vancouver-based not-for-profit group. It's about fostering mutually beneficial relationships among business, governments and consumers to preserve and enhance the quality of life in the long term. "This is part of a culture shift," says Davidge. "Businesses are made up of people, and people care about these issues. There's momentum building here [in Canada], in the U.S. and the U.K."

Still, CSR is stirring immense emotional debate as businesses grapple with donning the mantle of "corporate citizen" and becoming more active players in Canada's social fabric. Many businesspeople fear CSR represents a slippery slope that leads head-on into increased government regulation.

One thing remains clear: CSR is a hot button that's not going away anytime soon. As momentum grows, how your company deals with the challenges of becoming a good corporate citizen may ultimately determine its success. And ignoring CSR may help move the issue from voluntary to compulsory.

The momentum of corporate social performance is seen in the explosion of CSR-oriented groups, media coverage, books and conferences (including a series this month hosted by the Conference Board of Canada). Founded in 1992, the CBSR has grown to more than 100 members—up from 45 in 1998—and now includes heavyweights such as MacMillan Bloedel, BC Hydro and Alcan. The CBSR's mandate is simple: foster awareness and provide resources to help firms adopt CSR policies.

What's driving the whole social-responsibility trend? For starters, says Davidge, "consumers are demanding it." According to a Conference Board of Canada study to be released this month, 60% of Canadians say they have chosen to do business with a company because it was more socially responsible than its competitors. Indeed, the survey found that 81% of Canadians prefer to buy from, 79% would rather work for, and 77% want to invest in companies that demonstrate a strong commitment to the environment.

Add to that mix a heightened awareness of environmental and labor abuses, and lingering misgivings about business actions in the past. "A large part is a reaction to the hideous way many companies treated their employees in downsizing in the early '90s," says Barbara Moses, author of *The Good News About Careers: How You'll Be Working in the Next Decade*. When they get back to work, says Moses, "people want their company's values to match their values."

In fact, there are increasing signs that businesses that do good do well. A 1997 study by DuPaul University's Institute for Business and Professional Ethics in Chicago found firms with a commitment to ethical behavior do better financially, based on sales and profits. The Jantzi Social Index, introduced last December to track 60 socially responsible Canadian companies, has gained 7.2% since its inception, compared with 4.9% for the S&P/TSE 60. In the U.S. the Domini

Social Index, which tracks 400 ethical stocks, has recorded three-year annualized returns of 32.3%, versus 27.6% for the S&P 500.

Many entrepreneurs, such as G.A.P's Poon Tip, have practised social responsibility for years. Poon Tip traces his social conscience back to two trips he made to Thailand 10 years ago. The first was a tour in an air-conditioned coach, the second a $10-a-day solo adventure. On his second trip, he says, he found the country "so different from what I thought it was. I felt ripped off. I think it was irresponsible [of the tour company] to show the country from a Western view." Poon Tip's response was to form G.A.P. Today the company operates tours in 21 countries, visiting such exotic locales as Borneo and Tibet. Last year, his company signed a partnership agreement with Washington-based Conservation International, a non-government organization committed to environmental sustainability. The partnership articulates G.A.P's commitment to sustainable tourism, with minimum impact on the local environment.

Poon Tip carries CSR policies into his own office as well. G.A.P's 68 employees have a voice in how the company is run. There's ongoing training and team-building exercises, plus four weeks' holidays and a free G.A.P trip each year. Poon Tip doesn't view this as generosity, just clear-headed business. "We want the best out of everyone," he says.

That's the sunny side of the picture; there's a downside to CSR, too. G.A.P's mandate is to work exclusively with local communities, a policy that proved all too difficult in Burma, where G.A.P was forced to deal with federal government officials. Ultimately, Poon Tip decided to end his Burma trips despite the loss of revenue. And his commitment to environmental sustainability has prevented Poon Tip from adding trips to some already popular areas even while he's watched less ecologically minded competitors move in to fill the demand.

Still, Poon Tip believes that an increasingly savvy public can tell the difference between a company that operates responsibly and one that tarts itself up to appear enviro-friendly. "We certainly have a lot of customers who are devoted to our company, and we get a lot of respect," he says. "As long as they don't have to pay more, they'd prefer to travel with a company that's environmentally sound."

"You cannot trade on CSR alone," agrees George Khoury, director of the Conference Board's Canadian Centre for Business in the Community. "You have to be competitive on other issues. Everything being equal, people will buy from a socially responsible company."

Khoury wants the Conference Board to take a leadership role in business's move toward CSR. "This," he says, "is the business issue of the 21st century." Globalization, technological advances and government cutbacks are changing consumer expectations of business, he says. He believes the Board's members generally approve of CSR principles. "The only objection I have heard is, "We can't afford to do it," says Khoury. His response: "You can't afford not to."

Indeed, it's hard even for critics to oppose the principles of CSR. "How can you argue against social responsibility?" says Peter Foster, an editorial writer at the *National Post.* "What are you in favor of—social irresponsibility?" But the fact that CSR remains ill-defined is a sticking point. "A lot of these things that are called corporate social responsibility are really just in a corporation's self-interest ... you look after your employees, you look after your shareholders, your customers, the people in your environment," says Foster. To take on these responsibilities is just good business sense; however, to cast the net wider and take on formal social responsibilities, Foster says, is a recipe for business disaster.

Foster cites Nobel-winning economist Milton Friedman, who believes social responsibility is up to government, not business—and that if business takes up the task, it will face no end of obligations. Eventually Foster believes business would end up subject to a barrage of regulation.

Such fears are well founded. In the U.K., the recent Turnbull Report is ringing alarm bells for companies listed on the London Stock Exchange. Produced by the Internal Control Working Group with the blessing of the government and the Institute of Chartered Accountants, the report requires LSE listed companies to itemize and account for all their "risks"—financial, environmental, social, ethical—and report on them at their year-end, starting this December. There are already fears that such reports will make it hard for many firms to insure themselves, and that they could open company directors to personal lawsuits.

Could it happen here? Asked about the chance of federal regulation, Khoury cites the Turnbull Report. "If there's a government intervention, it would be in this area [reporting risk]," he says. "By and large, there is a readiness on the part of the government to create an environment to foster corporate responsibility."

The thought of government stepping in sends shudders through many of those who support CSR. "Our constituency doesn't believe government is all that effective in solving these problems," says Catherine Swift, president of the Canadian Federation of Independent Business, an advocate of CSR principles. "I don't think the government has much moral authority anymore." In recent years, governments have drastically cut social spending, notes Swift. "They don't have the authority to tell business, 'You should do this [adopt CSR].'"

Jason Mogus believes in CSR, but he too rejects the idea that government should compel companies to adopt such principles. "It needs to come from the marketplace," says the president of Vancouver-based Communicopia Inc. "We need to vote with every dollar we spend. What makes a company tick is money."

Mogus has made his six-year-old website design firm a model of social responsibility. Its policies include providing services at a discount or free of charge to non-profit groups, and adopting "ethical and environmental" purchasing policies. Mogus even declines clients whose goals are not in line with Communicopia's.

He says adopting CSR has worked to Communicopia's advantage. "There are no bones about the benefit," he says. It even helps attract good staff: "People are here for the mission as much as the job."

Linda Lundstrom agrees business has a mission. "I believe a company is a lot like a person," says Lundstrom, president of the Toronto-based clothing-design firm Linda Lundstrom Ltd. "It has a conscience, a spirit, a sense of stewardship. The evolution of [my] company coincided with the evolution of myself and of key people here. We share common values."

Lundstrom advises business owners to focus on values that are important to them. She supports causes such as First Nations artists, the environment and breast-cancer research. "We look at doing what we can to have the greatest impact," she says. Initiatives include allowing staff to do volunteer work on company time, donating stock to charities and using environmentally safe fabrics.

While many advocates suggest companies start on CSR by donating 1% of pre-tax profit to the community, cash is just one way to give. "I don't think it costs a great deal of money to go down this road," says Davidge. "You can start by creating a recycling program for your company."

David Horowitz began his company's initiative by writing letters. Horowitz's company, Anjou, Que.–based Priva Corp., makes adult diapers. It receives countless letters from product users—or the people who care for them—describing their health difficulties. In 1996, those

TOPIC 5: The Business of Management

letters sparked an idea. "We wanted to create a program to support and reward caregivers," he says. "And we wanted to do it in a direct relationship [with consumers]." So Priva created a Caregiver of the Year award to give the people who look after Priva's customers some recognition—and to give a grand-prize winner a week-long cruise to get away from it all.

For Horowitz, community involvement is key. "It puts a human touch to the company," he says. And while he admits the cost of running the awards is "absolutely high" he has no regrets. "It's a way of giving back," he says. "And because we all feel so good ... there's a passion, an enthusiasm that shows in all we do, and people flock toward you."

Barbara Moses agrees. She sees more friends shying away from what they perceive as "soulless" companies. "The environment isn't their issue," she says. "They just don't want to work for a company whose sole goal is profit. Who does?"

CSR Checklist

Wondering how your company can incorporate some CSR-inspired principles? Canadian Business for Social Responsibility suggests some easy steps to help you get started:

- Donate 1% of pre-tax profits to your community
- Give priority to local suppliers and employees
- Develop an employee volunteer program
- Ensure that employees and suppliers are fairly and promptly paid
- Promote from within and institute fair performance packages
- Create professional-development programs for employees
- Develop an ethical purchasing policy
- Offer employees flexible working hours
- Create opportunities for employee ownership and profit sharing
- Comply with environmental regulations—Practise the three Rs: reduce, reuse, recycle
- Refrain from using goods or services produced with child or prison labor
- Ensure advertising is truthful
- Audit your social and environmental performance regularly
- Work in partnership with community groups to achieve mutual goals

Ethics by Demand

What do consumers think of corporate social responsibility? A survey to be released this month by the Conference Board of Canada suggests that Canadians' expectations of business are changing. The bottom line? Consumers want businesses to think beyond making money and incorporate socially and ethically responsible behavior into the business process.

Here are highlights from the CBOC's study:

Percent of Canadians who would more likely invest in, buy from or work for a company that commits resources to social and community concerns:

- Invest money: 68%
- Buy goods and services: 72%
- Type of company you would like to work for: 71%

Percent of Canadians who would more likely invest in, buy from or work for a company that demonstrates a strong commitment to being environmentally responsible:

- Invest money: 77%
- Buy goods and services: 81%
- Type of company you would like to work for: 79%

Percent of Canadians who believe companies should engage in socially responsible behavior even if it means:

- Higher prices for products and services: 57%
- Less money for employees: 9.3%

Have you ever chosen to do more business with or buy more products from one firm over another just because the company is more socially responsible than its competitors?

- Yes: 60%
- No: 38%

56% of Canadians believe social and environmental issues are the responsibility of private businesses, as well as government.

41% of Canadians believe successful businesses should focus on social and community issues, rather than profits.

Clarifications

Sustainability: The ability of land to sustain stresses from activities such as agriculture or tourism, and to keep supporting its people.

Sine qua non: A Latin term meaning, literally, "without which not." Translated, it means the essential element. In this article, Mr. Poon Tip believes responsibility to the people and the environment are the essential elements of his business.

Mantra: A word or phrase repeated as a prayer or magic spell.

Stakeholders: Originally a stakeholder was the person who held the money until a bet was settled. However, it has come to mean people who have a stake in the outcome. In other words, the current meaning is the exact opposite of the original meaning.

Talking Points

In his book *Capitalism and Freedom,* economist Milton Friedman said that the "one and only one social responsibility of business [is] to increase profits so long as it stays within the rules of the game, which is to say, engages in open and free competition without deception or fraud." Discuss.

No Canadian company has been in the CSR spotlight as much as Talisman Energy, a company that has been drilling for oil in the Sudan. Read what that company has to say about CSR at *www.talisman-energy.com* (click on "Responsibility"), and test what it says against the Janzi Social Code. Does Talisman seem to be a socially responsible corporation? Why is the company so reviled in the press? Test other company Web sites against the guidelines as well.

Web Research

Read more about the travel company profiled in the article at *www.gap.ca.* Also check out *www.profitguide.com/profit100/2001, Profit* magazine's guide to Canada's fastest growing companies. G.A.P was number 63 on the list in 2001.

Check Michael Janzi's Web site and read his Social Code for Ethical Investments at *www.mjra-jsi.com.* Download sample company profiles including the London, Ontario–based water purification company, Trojan Technologies.

The Conference Board of Canada (*www.conferenceboard.ca*) has an area dedicated to corporate social responsibility.

Writing That Works

Introduction—example: The writer uses an example that most people will be able to relate to—a travel company. The phrase used by Bruce Poon Tip—"respect the local people and the environment"—is a good summary of corporate social responsibility.

Structure—process: Once the author gives the example and explains CSR, she goes on to explain how a company can adopt CSR as a policy.

Definition: "The buzz word is 'corporate social responsibility,' a grass-roots movement that believes values, ethics and community well-being should be part of everyday business." In fact, the entire article is really a definition of CSR, using one good example. Notice how much more interesting this method is to read than would be an essay, report or article without examples.

Expert opinion: "At its core, CSR is about sustainability, both economic and environmental, says Toby Davidge, executive director of Canadian Business for Social Responsibility (CBSR), a Vancouver-based not-for-profit group."

Parallel structure: Notice the CSR checklist, which is in parallel structure. Each point starts with an action: Donate, Give, Develop, etc.

Creating a Resilient Organization
by Peggy Doe

Canadian Business Review, June 6, 1994. Peggy Doe is a Principal with Mercer Delta Consulting Ltd. and works with CEOs and executives in leading organizational change.

The realities of today's economy and the globalization of markets are driving organizations to change the way they do business, not only to retain or improve their competitive position, but to survive. Process improvement, re-engineering, information technology installations and restructuring initiatives abound in the business world as companies look for ways to reduce costs without affecting service or product quality. Virtually every organization in Canada has undergone some form of change related to these management initiatives in the past few years, and downsizing continues to play a role in achieving results.

CONSIDERING THE INDIVIDUAL

Research indicates that 90 per cent of change initiatives that fail do so because the human factors were not adequately taken into account. In the event of downsizing, organizations may fail to consider the emotional impacts on the remaining employees. Though the organizations may look leaner and more efficient at first glance, the downsizing can backfire through the demoralization of the workforce, and the benefits may be lost.

Many senior executives do not understand the need to consider survivors. A "you should just be happy you still have a job" philosophy often prevails, but motivation cannot be mandated, and people driven by fear will not perform well. Organizations and individual managers at all levels must understand the natural emotional response to downsizing and learn to manage this response in order to realize the operational and technical goals of the downsizing effort.

Downsizing affects remaining employees in many ways. An increased workload for fewer employees puts pressure on them to work faster. This can result in increased stress, which leads to decreased quality, and this compounds itself throughout the production or service delivery cycle. New duties or tasks are assigned and the use of new technologies is required, but the training and support given to the employee may be limited or non-existent. In many cases, the prime source of information for the people with these new responsibilities—the outplaced employees—has gone.

Remaining employees have just lost valued colleagues. They very often have feelings of insecurity, powerlessness and lack of confidence in leadership. They experience guilt and apprehension about remaining. No longer sure of the stability of their employment, the employees feel a significantly reduced sense of loyalty to the organization. It is normal for them to experience a series of emotions—denial, anger, depression, testing and acceptance—and these feelings can be fuelled by the lack of a good communication strategy.

Helping employees to understand these emotions and their impact on performance is essential. This process begins with educating senior managers on the concepts of human response to change and effective strategies for managing that response. Awareness of and sensitivity to these issues in the top-level group of an organization goes a long way towards ensuring that employees' concerns are handled effectively.

A simple exercise is often used to assist senior executives in understanding their employees' response to change. During awareness training sessions, four or five executives are selected to stand at the front of the room facing their peers. Each individual is given a set of three beanbags. The instructor tells them to start juggling on the signal "Go" and continue until told to stop.

Without further explanation, the instructor gives the signal. Except for the occasional "ringer," most people fumble, throw and drop the beanbags repeatedly. Some refuse to try. Some laugh nervously and keep trying. Once the signal is given to stop, the instructor asks them, "How did you feel?" Usual responses are "embarrassed," "stupid," "angry," "humiliated," "ridiculous." This is effective in teaching senior people to understand through experience the emotions that employees feel when they are given new job responsibilities, new tools or technology with which to work. The results provide a powerful message to those executives who ask employees to perform in front of their peers and superiors with no training, no support and no opportunity to ask questions or ask for help.

RESILIENCE—THE KEY TO SURVIVAL

The ability to adapt to changes in the work environment varies among individuals, and it is influenced by other changes in their lives that are happening simultaneously. People have the capacity to assimilate change, but when too much occurs at once, the aggregate impact can create problems. As employees reach and pass the threshold beyond which they can no longer assimilate change, they start to exhibit such behaviours as irritation, frustration, low productivity, poor quality work, negative attitudes and chronic absenteeism. In extreme cases, sabotage, physical or psychological breakdowns and even violence or suicide can occur.

Individuals must not only have the capacity to adapt to change, but they must learn to be more resilient to change. Resilience means that the employee will expend less effort in assimilating the change and will thus be more productive. Resilient individuals are people who are "opportunity" driven rather than "danger" driven. They view change as an opportunity to grow, learn and achieve new results rather than as a threat to themselves and their environment. A resilient organization requires a resilient workforce. Organizations, through selection and assessment techniques, can ensure that they are hiring and keeping resilient individuals. Chances are that the surviving members of an organizational downsizing are those who demonstrate resilience in their ability to be flexible and adapt to new situations. Even these individuals, however, can benefit from support. By working with them to increase their resilience, the organization will improve its ability to adapt to changes and seize opportunities more quickly than its competitors.

Research has in fact suggested that people often change behaviour purely as a result of the attention paid to it. Thus, training employees on management of change, typical responses to change and personal resilience often results in individuals who exhibit more flexibility, adaptability and willingness to take risk. These behaviours must be continually reinforced, rewarded and supported by the organization and its senior management.

CONSIDERING THE HUMAN FACTORS

Aside from promoting individual resilience, organizations can successfully manage downsizing initiatives to reduce problems associated with the individual's response to change. Senior managers must recognize that, just as it is critical to have a structured, well-thought-out approach to implementing technical and operational solutions, managing the human aspects requires careful planning and ongoing monitoring throughout and after the downsizing effort. This planning should consider the following factors.

Communication: How will decisions and information regarding the downsizing be communicated to employees at all levels? When and how frequently? Keep in mind that it is almost impossible to over-communicate. Even when the message is that some people will lose their jobs, employees respond better to openness and explanations of the need for such actions. One senior human resources executive puts it clearly: "We've closed down whole plants—and we've done it both ways. The open approach is by far the better. We'd never go back to the traditional approach of waiting to the last minute possible by law or collective bargaining to announce the closure."

Executive fears of sabotage and lost productivity if employees are informed of decisions in advance are rarely realized. Most companies have an active grapevine, and employees get wind of what's happening anyway. Without proper information, often the fear and anger associated with downsizing are amplified. Early, honest and ongoing communications go a long way in assisting people to deal with the situation. And remember, management does not have to have all the answers or have all decisions made. Employees can accept that these decisions take time—just keep them informed.

Employee involvement: Involve employees at all levels in decisions that will affect them. One successful organization used a team of employees to make decisions on severance packages, outplacement consultants and other issues related to terminating employees. This initiative involved efforts in both the Canadian and U.S. operations. Interestingly, this approach seemed to work better in Canada. Whether this is reflective of differences in organizational or national culture is not clear, but Canadian organizations seem to operate with a more participative management style than their U.S. counterparts. This type of involvement allows an organization to give some control back to employees.

Organizations that have used this approach have indicated that it often results in a permanent shift in culture. Employees and managers learn to work in teams, provide input and resolve issues effectively. The skills and techniques often carry forward and remain after the downsizing. In some cases, cross-functional teams continue to operate, managing day-to-day activities; in others, problems are automatically solved by mobilizing the appropriate resources to form a problem-solving team.

A transition plan: Careful planning of who and when to terminate requires a clear understanding of the restructured organization. Do you consider only the position in making termination decisions or the ability, skills and experience of the individuals? Some organizations choose the first option to avoid making judgements on employee performance and maintain objectivity in the eyes of employees. However, this may result in the loss of valuable contributors. A well-thought-out transition plan will allow an organization to keep the employees who have the required skills, abilities and opportunity for advancement and who fit with the structure and environment of the new organization. This plan should consider the long-term goals of the organization. If the company wants to learn from the experience and become a more flexible and resilient organization, individual resilience should be a consideration in the transition decisions.

A transition plan can involve a variety of options for both terminated and remaining employees. In general, the trend is to take a more holistic approach and to consider career planning. Often, the decision is not to "axe" as a first step, but to attempt to redeploy people. In a redeployment plan, employees have a chance to be evaluated and, if considered suitable, retrained to work elsewhere in the organization. Aside from some of Canada's Schedule A banks, other forward-thinking employer organizations that have provided internal job relocation centres are Ontario Hydro and Imperial Oil. This growing attention to in-placement is in part due to the realization among downsized organizations, once the dust has settled, that they may have cut too deeply. This type of careful planning assists in avoiding termination of valuable individuals.

If, in the final analysis, the best solution is for the employee to leave, then that person should be considered for career transition guidance and ultimately given career change counselling.

As well as providing redeployed and terminated employees with valuable support during downsizing, this process is helpful to those left behind, who will see their colleagues and friends treated fairly and with respect by the organization. This will alleviate some of the anger and fear that the surviving employees may be feeling.

Support and training: Remaining employees must be given the skills and support that will enable them to make it in the new organization. This means technical training to handle their new responsibilities, continual feedback and encouragement on their performance, and reward and recognition for incremental results as they occur. It is essential that senior management play an active role in this. They must be visible, openly supportive and understanding of what their employees are going through. Since this may not come naturally to all managers, awareness training on change management and emotional response to change can go a long way towards giving them the skills to handle employee concerns.

Human resource policies: Individual goals and objectives must be tied to organizational objectives. This requires a review of the human resource policies and practices that shape behaviour: compensation and reward systems, ongoing communication strategies, performance management, training and education, and management style. If you require your employees to be resilient and opportunity driven, ensure that they are rewarded and supported when they exhibit these behaviours.

BENEFITS TO THE ORGANIZATION

Effective and sensitive management of downsizing can have benefits to the organization in addition to improved morale, productivity and performance. When employees feel that they and their departed colleagues have been treated fairly, the organization gains in terms of its public image. One organization felt that the best measure of how well they were managing a plant closure was what their employees were saying to the media. Reports were generally positive, indicating that—given the situation—the company was treating people as fairly as possible. This went a long way in building the firm a solid reputation as a fair and sensitive employer.

In times of economic downturn, image may not seem a critical factor. However, as the economy picks up and employers must once again compete for highly skilled resources, it will have a direct impact on their ability to attract and retain the best people. Good people are selective about whom they work for, and fairness and recognition of the value of employees is now an important consideration in the job search.

The ability of an organization to continually adapt to change has a direct correlation with the ability of each employee in the organization to adapt effectively to change. A growing number of business leaders recognize that their organization's success in these turbulent times depends on the people they employ at all levels. Understanding the individual emotional responses of remaining employees and managing this response in a structured and sensitive way are critical to realizing and sustaining the benefits of downsizing. Otherwise, the costs—reduced service and product quality, reduced employee loyalty, insecure and stressed-out workers—are just too high.

Clarifications

Resilience: The ability to recover quickly from an illness, change or loss; the ability to "bounce back."

Sabotage: Usually, to destroy property or disrupt operations in time of war. The root of the word is *sabot,* a kind of wooden clog. Originally *sabotage* meant to walk noisily or deliberately bungle something.

Talking Points

Discuss the "bottom-line" or profit-first approach to downsizing that is described in this article.

How many ways can you say "fired," in addition to those used in this article ("outplaced," "downsized"). Why is the word *fired* so little used in these situations?

The article mentions a series of emotions that take place when people are laid off, including denial, anger, depression, testing and acceptance. These are the same emotions that psychologist and author Dr. Elisabeth Kübler-Ross has identified as the stages of bereavement. Why the similarity?

In small groups, try the beanbag exercise described in the article. If one group has a student who is able to juggle, have that group work co-operatively to learn how to juggle. Then as a class discuss the way each group felt druing the exercise. What are the implications to a business facing change?

Web Research

Read about stress at work on the Canadian Institute of Stress Web site at *www.stresscanada.org.* This institution was founded by Dr. Hans Selye, Alvin Toffler, and other luminaries including Marshall McLuhan.

The Human Resources Development Canada Web site is at *www.hrdc-drhc.gc.ca.* Here you can read the rules that apply to people who have been laid off or "downsized."

CanadaOne has an extensive HR Guide for Canadian Employers at *www.canadaone.com/tools/hr_guide.html.* Articles posted there include tips on how to find employees and how to keep them happy.

Writing That Works

Introduction—anecdote: The opening anecdote gives a quick picture of the type of company the article is about. The anecdote leads in to a definition of corporate social responsibility.

Structure—process: This article is a very clear, to-the-point essay on how to keep a company resilient in the face of layoffs and downsizing. The article is structured very much in the way a student should structure a business report.

Headings: The headings lead the reader through the article. Notice that the second heading, "Resilience—The Key to Survival," points to the definition of resilience given in this section.

Ms. Versus Mr.

by Rhea Seymour

Profit: The Magazine for Canadian Entrepreneurs, December 1, 2000

When the breakfast rush dies down at Hockley Valley Resort near Orangeville, Ont., guests might catch a glimpse of something you don't often see at a posh resort: the company's president clearing dishes in the dining room. "If the servers are late cleaning up, I'll vacuum and wash dishes—whatever it takes to get ready for the lunch sitting," says Nancy Adamo, owner of the 104-room resort and conference centre. "My staff knows I'm one of them. I'm not into hierarchy," she says.

Adamo has no problem sharing power at the company she began building 15 years ago. "In the last 10 years, I've never made a decision totally on my own," says Adamo. "I meet once a week with my managers. I'm adamant about listening to people. We may disagree but I can listen to their perspectives—they may offer something I haven't thought of."

Adamo's approach has certainly worked for Hockley Valley. After purchasing the bankrupt 28-room hotel in 1985, Adamo remodelled and revamped the hotel, adding 76 rooms, a conference centre, and a golf course and other facilities to target the business market. Hockley Valley's 1999 sales reached $12.4 million.

Still, more women than men will relate to Adamo's management style. That's because women and men have distinct styles when it comes to managing their staff and their businesses. According to research by the Ottawa-based Centre of Excellence for Women's Advancement and The National Foundation for Women Business Owners in the U.S., men are more likely to think in hierarchical terms and focus on establishing rules and procedures, while women business owners tend to emphasize creative thinking. Like Adamo, women are typically more nurturing, better communicators and are more willing to share. And in today's changing workworld, where the emphasis is on teamwork and open and easy communication, these characteristics may give women a competitive edge.

"The male style of management—called command and control—involves top-down decision-making. The people at the top know best and tell everyone else what to do," says Judy Rosener, a professor in the Graduate School of Management at the University of California and author of *America's Competitive Secret: Women Managers.* "Women, on the other hand, tend to be interactive leaders, basing decisions on who has the most information and sharing power. There is lots of anecdotal data that women are more flexible, are multi-taskers and tend to be comfortable sharing power and information—all attributes that are effective in today's fast-changing, service-oriented, entrepreneurial, global work environment."

Barbara Orser, program manager for Centre of Excellence for Women's Advancement, agrees that women bring special strengths to the workplace. In a recent study, "Creating High Performance Organizations: Leveraging Women's Leadership," the centre found that 76% of men and 90% of women interviewed cited differences in the management and leadership style of men and women. "Women are particularly strong in managing interpersonal relationships and their approach is more consensual," says Orser. "In an economy where businesses are entering into strategic partnerships, mergers and alliances, for example, these are particularly useful."

In a study conducted by the Washington, D.C.–based National Foundation for Women Business Owners, 66% of women entrepreneurs surveyed said they gather information from business associates and advisors before making business decisions, versus 56% of men. That finding doesn't surprise Ron Burke, professor of organizational behavior at York University's Schulich School of Business in Toronto. "Obviously, all men aren't the same, nor are all women, but men are more task-oriented and women are more people-oriented. Men are more likely to say 'I did this,'" he says, "rather than 'we.'"

Perhaps surprising, both men and women believe consensus decision-making offers real benefits. By gathering and considering others' points of view, management teams are better able to address issues in an informed way. And when decisions are executed, says Orser, "employees are more likely to feel like they have been part of the decision-making process and are key players in implementing solutions."

In fact, that's why Cindy Eeson consulted her staff before deciding to open a new unit of her Calgary-based manufacturing and retail business, Kids Only Clothing Club Inc. Wanting to launch a new division producing women's clothing, Eeson first ran the idea by her staff. "I'm very consensus-oriented," says Eeson. Before redirecting 20% of Kids Only Clothing's sales into a new division, Eeson first spoke with her designers, asking for feedback. Next she discussed her idea with her executive team. "Even had they thought it was a bad idea," says Eeson, "as the company's visionary I wouldn't have necessarily buried it. But I wanted their input."

Orser says women are also more nurturing: "They're far more likely to praise, less likely to be critical of employees, and more compassionate." And women are often more willing than men to deal with people issues. "I styled my entire concept for this company on the care system—the importance of listening to people, getting to know them and finding out what motivates them," says Denise Meehan, president of Lick's Concepts Inc., a fast-food franchise with 23 outlets in Ontario. The payoff: "If you have good people, the place practically runs itself."

In Meehan's restaurants, all of her 1,000 employees are evaluated during every shift by their managers and are encouraged to discuss their assessments. It's a model that women accept more easily than men. "I have an easier time instructing women managers to nurture the staff," says Meehan. "They tend to have more empathy and tune into the concept more." The focus on regular communication and nurturing extends to Lick's Toronto head office, where Meehan employs 18 people. "We're like a family here. I have an open-door policy. I'm always available to them, and people can express their views," she says. That makes it a fulfilling place to work. "You bond with people, so the work environment is not hostile. And we have very low turnover in the stores and the office."

The rewards of creating a flexible, collegial workplace can definitely boost the bottom line. Bethesda, Md.–based Watson Wyatt Worldwide's Human Capital Index analysed and measured human resource practices at 400 public companies in Canada and the U.S. Those companies that scored high (75 out of 100) on the index by encouraging trust, teamwork and co-operation, flexible work arrangements, high employee satisfaction and less formal authority structures saw average shareholder returns of 103% over five years. That was twice the 53% gain recorded by companies with a low index rating (less than 25).

Still, the concept that men and women manage differently solely on the basis of gender has met some opposition. "The within-group differences among women are greater than the between-group differences of men and women," says Eileen Fischer, professor of marketing at York University. "I'm skeptical that there's a pure management style and that you're going to find it in firms run by women." She agrees that "leaders have an impact on a firm's success, but so does the rest of the management team and other external service providers like accountants—it's unlikely they're all going to be the same sex."

"This issue is very controversial," admits Judith MacBride-King, associate director of research for the Conference Board of Canada's Centre for Management Effectiveness in Ottawa. "Some people, including women, say we're raising a new stereotype. They worry that highlighting that women are stronger in certain areas—as nurturers, for example—may result in women being pigeonholed into particular positions in the workplace." But organizations that understand gender differences can capitalize on them, she says. "Knowing women have a particular strength in relationship-building, for example, may help you decide who to appoint to a management team during a merger."

Fifteen years ago, pointing out gender differences may have indeed pigeonholed women into "soft" areas such as human resources, says Peter Gregg, president of Calgary-based consulting company The President's Team. But there is nothing second-string about soft skills today. "There's a whole new set of rules coming in for managers and leaders based on traits—being intuitive, creative, emotional—that have always been associated with women," says Gregg. The typical male CEO is still locked in command-and-control while women want more feedback and involvement, he says. Gregg believes women will have an advantage in the new economy, "where people will need to be flexible, to move in and out of relationships easily and to inspire people to do things without using power. Men are going to need to learn skills that they'd never get in an MBA program. They'll need to be more feminine in the way they manage."

They might look no further than Cindy Eeson, who believes in a "feminine" style of managing. "We cry, we laugh, we praise, we bring in family issues," she says. "We can't leave a meeting where there's been any dissension without doing some emotional patching-up." And, yes, it's starting to spread to her male employees. "I really see younger men working to fit into our environment which includes traditional female values."

In the end, finding a balance between the two management styles may be the key to success. "Women have the emotional sensitivity, but sometimes we apologize too much," says Denise Meehan. "You have to have a balance—empathy plus the ability to put your foot down. Men are going to have to be more like women, and women can learn a few things from men."

Clarifications

The Centre of Excellence for Women's Advancement is part of the Conference Board of Canada, which is an independent applied research facility. The Centre's Web site can be found at *www.conferenceboard.ca/cewa.*

Talking Points

What makes a good manager? Do you agree that women tend to have certain skills that would make them good managers?

Read what Cindy Eeson has to say about women's management styles ("We cry, we laugh…," etc.) Is this true of most women, or is it simply stereotyping? Also discuss what Judith MacBride-King has to say in this article.

Web Research

Research Watson Wyatt's Human Capital Index on their Web site at *www.watsonwyatt.com*. Read their magazine, *Strategy@Work*, also to be found on this Web site.

The Conference Board of Canada (*www.conferenceboard.ca*) has a wealth of information and discussion (found under "Knowledge Areas"), including such topics as Corporate Social Responsibility, Innovation, Human Resource Management, and Organizational Excellence. As noted above, information on the Centre of Excellence for Women's Advancement is also found at the Conference Board site.

The Women's Executive Network at *www.wxnetwork.com* has an interesting paper entitled "Moving Forward: Canadians' Perceptions of Workplace Advancement Among Men and Women."

Writing That Works

Introduction—example: The example of the company president clearing dishes in the dining room quickly establishes the topic: women prefer equal relationships at work.

Expert opinion: "'The male style of management called command and control involves top-down decision-making. The people at the top know best and tell everyone else what to do,' says Judy Rosener, a professor in the Graduate School of Management at the University of California and author of *America's Competitive Secret: Women Managers*."

Expert opinion: "Barbara Orser, program manager for Centre of Excellence for Women's Advancement, agrees that women bring special strengths to the workplace."

Studies and statistics: "In a recent study, 'Creating High Performance Organizations: Leveraging Women's Leadership,' the centre found that 76% of men and 90% of women interviewed cited differences in the management and leadership style of men and women."

TOPIC 6

CANADIANS ON THE JOB

INTRODUCTION

What's a good job? When I ask students this question they frequently answer that money is the most important factor. Perhaps it is because they are just starting their work lives and see post-secondary education as a way out of the minimum wage "McJobs" ghetto. I once asked a group of students if they would shovel meat off the floor in a dog food factory for $100,000 a year, and every member of the class was quite sure he or she would do the job "until I saved enough money." Setting aside the fact that such jobs with such salaries don't exist, no one ever saves enough money in an unpleasant job.

A report on the excellent Canadian Policy Research Networks Web site, entitled "What's a Good Job? The Importance of Employment Relationships," discusses the social and psychological elements of employment relationships. The report points out that perceptions of what is a good salary can vary, and notes that "the perception of whether a job pays well" has a bearing on all the elements of an employment relationship. The article identifies the elements as trust, commitment, influence and communication. Read more on this issue in the first article in this section, which is a summary of the original report.

A recent survey by U.S. research company Walker Information found that of thirteen countries surveyed, Canadians are the most committed employees with the highest level of job satisfaction. Finnish workers were second on the list, followed by those from Spain and the United States. On the bottom of the list were British and German workers.

Other articles in this section cover some of the more negative aspects of employment relationships, including what to do about a bad boss, the difficulty of managing family and work, and harassment on the job. Clive Thompson's article discusses the trend towards instant messaging in the workplace and how it changes interpersonal relationships.

Labour Researchers Define Job Satisfaction

by Darryl Grigg and Jennifer Newman

Vancouver Sun, February 16, 2002

Getting a good job isn't what it used to be. Once, a good job was permanent and full time. It offered secure work with decent pay and benefits.

But today, almost half of the Canadian labour force works at more than one job or finds jobs that are part-time, temporary, on contract and include flex time and fewer benefits. And one big change: more and more people are working at home.

So do these trends mean there are fewer good jobs out there?

Not so, say Graham Lowe, professor of sociology at the University of Alberta and researcher Grant Schellenberg. The researchers conducted a national survey for Canadian Policy Research Networks (CPRN), an Ottawa-based independent, non-profit research organization.

CPRN projects are funded by federal, provincial, association and corporate sponsors like Human Resources Development Canada, British Columbia Public Service Employee Relations Commission, Canadian Union of Public Employees, Home Depot, Canfor and Scotiabank.

The researchers wanted to know what workers defined as a good job and how the ingredients of a good job were relevant to policy makers, business and unions.

They surveyed 2,500 people by phone and conducted eight follow-up focus groups after the survey.

Respondents were currently employed men and women aged 18 to over 55 years. They included both permanent and temporary employees, the self-employed and multiple jobholders. Participants included aboriginal people and visible minorities.

Lowe and Schellenberg discovered that people didn't define a good job by a detailed contract or job description, or whether it included union, staff or association membership.

Interestingly, participants in the study had a somewhat negative view of contracts and indicated that they would rather not formalize their working conditions into a contract.

Instead, the quality of the working relationships was identified as the most important aspect of people's definition of a good job.

Relationships, particularly with immediate supervisors and co-workers, were considered more important to overall *job* satisfaction than pay and benefits and contracts.

As one respondent said, "Of course money is important, but that's not what's going to make you jump out of bed in the morning."

So, what makes people jump out of bed ready for work?

It seems that having influence at work, including having a say in decisions affecting one's work, some input into work schedules and power over how work gets done, make for a good job.

Clear communication at work was important, especially when workers had a good idea of their role and the information and skills needed to perform it.

Recognition and regular feedback were also essential to a good job.

Getting respect from the boss was the crux of good employee-employer relations.

One person noted, "Everyone here would take more money and more time off—that's a given. But some of the things that really make the job a good one or a bad job are your relations with your boss.

If your boss gives you a project and supports you and lets you do it your way and gives you lots of feedback, you take on a sense of ownership. And that's the key."

Above all, survey participants highlighted the importance of commitment and trust between co-workers and employers to the making of a good job.

Commitment was seen as a two-way street.

Respondents noted that the needs of the employer and employee were similar since their jobs were tied to employer profitability. At the same time, workers believed that employers had an obligation to recognize that people had family responsibilities and other needs that went beyond the workplace.

Workers pointed to respect and dependability between co-workers as important. And they didn't like to pick up the slack for under-performers.

When workers can identify with an organization and its goals, they are more motivated at work. Workers reported good jobs were ones where their values meshed with those of the organization.

Another prerequisite for a good job was feeling proud working for the employer and being willing to go the extra mile to help the employer succeed.

Trust between employers and employees takes time to develop, according to respondents. Being able to depend on supervisors and managers entailed leader honesty and openness.

Fair treatment by supervisors was important to workers who emphasized being treated equitably. Playing favourites in particular was considered antithetical to garnering trust at work.

In our practice, we have observed that efforts to improve human relationships at work yield positive results. Besides being considered the hallmarks of a good job, having influence, clear communication, trust and commitment at work results in more satisfied, skilled and effective employees.

This is important for employers. Productivity is increased through better skill use, higher staff retention, better morale and less absenteeism. And that makes everybody happy.

Lowe and Schellenberg's research carries important implications for employers and unions alike.

Employers can:

- Provide employees with the resources and training to do their jobs, give workers more say over their work and schedules, and keep the work interesting.

- Commit to ensuring that trust between supervisors, managers and co-workers is a cornerstone of the business.

- Build in ways to respect work-life balance for staff.

- Be fair and deal quickly with people who don't pull their weight.

- Be clear, honest, and up front in your communications.

Unions can:

- Review the emphasis on formalized employment contracts as the main union offering to employees. Workers do not appear to consider the legal aspect of employment to be a major concern. Their relationships with the employer and one another seem more pressing. This is important when serving existing members and recruitment are a concern.

- Address worker needs for healthy relations between themselves and their employer. Improving psychological working conditions such as building more trust between management and workers, increasing mutual commitment between co-workers and the employer and facilitating clear communication benefits workers.

It seems that Canada's economic viability, as well as union and business success rest on enhanced workplace relationships. Workers identify the most important working condition to be the quality of their human interactions at work—how people relate to one another and how they are treated on the job.

Talking Points

This article summarizes a larger report written by expert researchers—but the writers also appear to be experts, since they talk about "our practice." In many ways, this is a descriptive summary. However, it also departs from the "rules" of descriptive summary writing in many ways. Evaluate the article using the rules for descriptive summary writing found in the Types of Written Work section. Does the fact that the article appears to have deviated from these rules make this a less effective summary? Rewrite the article in a more standard format.

Although most of the articles in this reader are written by journalists, most do not use the one-sentence-per-paragraph style seen in this article. Generally, I avoided selecting articles written in that way. How does the short-paragraph style affect your reading? Do you find it easier to read this kind of style?

Web Research

Workplace surveys are available at *www.workplace.ca/survey.*

The report on which this article is based can be found on the Canadian Policy Research Networks Web site at *www.Cprn.org.*

Bad Bosses and How to Handle Them

by Barbara Moses

This article is excerpted, in slightly different form, from What Next? by Barbara Moses. Barbara Moses is an organizational career management consultant, speaker, Globe and Mail workplace issues columnist, and author. Her latest book is The Good News About Careers: How You'll Be Working in the Next Decade. She can be reached at www.bbmcareerdev.com.

He goes from strength to strength, even though everyone knows he has the spine of a jellyfish. He won't lobby for the resources you need, or stand up for you on critical issues. The result is that you are doing work below your own standards, but he doesn't seem to care—so long as it gets done within the budget.

At the first sign of a conflict, he runs. He tolerates toxic behaviour from your co-workers and perhaps even encourages petty rivalries. He is a classic example of the weak manager, and a very bad boss.

Bad bosses—whether jerks, bullies, or micro-managers—have always been with us. Today, however, we're seeing more bad bosses than ever before. As a result of institutionalized leanness, overextended managers are both short-tempered and too busy or ill-trained to provide staff with the support they need.

No one has as much power as a bad boss to unnerve you and wreak havoc on your sense of self-esteem. This is why it is commonly said that people don't quit jobs, they quit bosses. And by the time you are in your thirties, the chances are that you will have at least one.

What makes for a bad boss? Some are just plain nasty, but often, a bad boss is all in the eye of the beholder. One person's boss from hell may be another person's pinup. If you need regular direction, for example, you will be miserable with a hands-off, absentee manager, but if you have strong needs for autonomy you will flourish under the same regime.

Then again, the problem could be simply bad chemistry. She's an introvert and you're an extrovert. You like direction, she thinks you're "needy." You like to go home at six, she's a workaholic. So before you assume your boss is a complete jerk, ask yourself: Does she get along with others? Does she pick on everyone, or just you?

The key to getting on with a boss is to manage him by understanding his underlying motivations, which may be different than you think. Here are some common types of bad bosses, their motivations, and strategies for dealing with them. If you're a manager, look for yourself in these descriptions:

THE WEAK MANAGER

She won't stand up for you. She aggressively avoids taking risks. She's vague and her commitments have the sticking power of water.

But the underlying causes of her behaviour can vary. Often, she simply wants to be liked by everyone, and can't stand conflict. It's also possible she's too busy to understand when there is a problem, or too burned out to care. Frequently, such managers are reluctant to be managers at all, and would much rather be getting on with their own work as individuals.

They may also be ill-trained, and lacking management skills.

If you are dealing with a weak manager, identify the problem. For example, if your manager needs to be liked by everyone, avoid communications that suggest contentious or highly charged emotional issues. Where you can, solve conflicts yourself. If her problem is that she is spineless and refuses to take on any leadership role, talk to your boss's boss.

If your boss is too burned out to care or is a reluctant manager, work around her. Take the initiative to set out the parameters of the work. Give yourself the feedback you need. Pin your boss down by e-mail to a suggested meeting time.

Make her life easy by only talking to her about critical issues. If your boss is lacking management skills, tell her what you need from her to do your job and the impact of not receiving the support you need. Then cover yourself by sending an e-mail.

THE OBSESSIVE MICRO-MANAGER

She trusts you the way you'd trust a five-year-old behind the wheel of the car. No matter how much detail you give her, or how many times you do redo a piece of work, it's still not right. You're completely demotivated and have lost your sense of competence.

Why is she so untrusting? Is she anxious about failing to please her boss, or is she simply a control freak? If the problem is her own insecurity, anticipate issues that will make her anxious by reassuring her that you have covered all the bases. Say, for example, "in completing this I spoke to Jane Doe and took the following issues into account …" Write it down as well, as she may be too anxious to fully process what you are saying.

THE POLITICAL MANAGER

He has an unerring ability to know what will make him look good. He will go to bat for you only on issues that serve his political agenda. He's sneaky and plays favourites. He won't think twice about using you as a sacrificial lamb to support his own career goals.

Support his high need for recognition by making him look good on strategic projects. Focus your own efforts on "high-value" work. Be prepared to share the limelight, even if it kills you. Don't trust him to have your own interests at heart. Pitch him on work you want to do by emphasizing its profile and importance to senior management.

THE BLACK-AND-WHITE MANAGER

He just doesn't get it—either because he has the IQ of an eraser or he is as concrete as they come. He doesn't understand context, nuance, or high-level ideas.

If his problem is intellectual deficiency, indulge him like a mis-guided child. Better yet, ignore him if you can. But if the problem is one of cognitive style, shape your communications to his needs. If he is fact-oriented, don't waste your time painting compelling arguments based on ideas. Simply state the facts and provide information unembellished.

THE INVISIBLE MANAGER

You have no one to go to for direction. She doesn't have a clue about the volume or pace of your work. You're killing yourself, but no one notices or gives you feedback.

This manager shares many of the underlying motivations of the weak manager. She may be invisible because she's too busy, or is a reluctant or unskilled manager.

If she is pressed for time, do your homework before you meet with her to make the meeting as efficient as possible. Be strategic on issues where you need support. Give yourself direction and feedback by setting milestones and regularly evaluating your effectiveness against them. Thank yourself for a job well done. Establish a mechanism for getting direction, whether it be weekly or monthly meetings at an agreed time. Hold her to her commitment.

THE TASK MASTER

He doesn't have a life, and doesn't expect you to either. You're drowning in work but he keeps heaping on more. His time-lines are ridiculous. Sometimes an extremely task-focused manager is simply shy or preoccupied, or so focused on getting the work done that he's not aware of the impact of his behaviour on the people around him. Is he aware of your work load?

If you've talked to him and he still doesn't get it, create your own standards for evaluating what is realistic and doable. Don't be apologetic about wanting time for a personal life. Work-life balance is your right, not a privilege. If your organization wants to "be an employer of choice" remind your boss of the incongruity between policy and behaviour.

THE NASTY MANAGER

She's ruthless. She seems to take pleasure in watching you squirm. She has pets and you are not one of them.

Sometimes an apparently nasty boss is simply so task-focused that she is oblivious to how her behaviour makes you feel. Underneath a gruff exterior, as the saying goes, may be the heart of a pussycat. When you confront her, does she apologize, or become aggressive?

Regardless of what type of boss you have, your first line of defense is to speak to him, as he may not be aware of his behaviour. Don't make sweeping generalizations about his personality. Rather, talk to the specific behaviour in question and tell him how it makes you feel. You can soften your comments and avoid defensiveness by allowing your boss to save face. Introduce your statements with "You may not be aware ..." or "You may not realize ..." or "You may not intend ..."

If none of these strategies work, you have two choices. If you have good personal reasons for staying in your job—you love your work, you're learning a lot, you like the people you're working with—you can hold your nose and ignore your boss as best you can. Or, you can quit: life is too short to deal with this kind of abuse.

Clarifications

Sacrificial lamb: A sacrificial lamb is a lamb that has been killed as a gift to a god or supreme being. It is used figuratively in this article to describe how an unscrupulous boss might use his workers to help his own career along, not caring what happens to them. A search on Google will show you that this expression is used frequently in the media: Arthur Andersen (the accounting firm) was a "sacrificial lamb" in the Enron scandal; a student caught using Napster was a "sacrificial lamb" in the "MP3 Wars" between Metallica and Napster.

Share the limelight: Limelight was an early way of lighting a theatre stage. When we "share the limelight" we get equal attention or light shone on us.

Talking Points

In your work experience, have you encountered one of these types of bad managers? What did you do about it? Can you create a similar list of types of good bosses?

Although they are not bosses, do teachers fit into these categories?

Barbara Moses' Web site (*www.bbmcareerdev.com*) has other articles that make for good discussion. One article notes: "Employees at all levels and life stages want the opportunity to look after themselves economically, be challenged at work and honour commitments to children, parents and significant others. Finding an employer who recognizes their overcommitted and complicated lives is a crucial determinant for job satisfaction." Discuss this article as it relates to the article above.

Web Research

Barbara Moses, Ph.D., is an organizational career management consultant, speaker, and workplace issues columnist for the *Globe and Mail*. Her latest book is *The Good News about Careers: How You'll Be Working in the Next Decade*. Many other excellent articles are included on her Web site (see URL above).

The Canadian Policy Research Networks Web site at *www.cprn.com* has many articles on work, health and family, and is an excellent place to do research.

Another excellent database of work-related information can be found at *www.workplace.ca*.

Writing That Works

Definition: "He goes from strength to strength, even though everyone knows he has the spine of a jellyfish. He won't lobby for the resources you need, or stand up for you on critical issues. As a result, you are doing work below your own standards, but he doesn't seem to care— so long as it gets done within the budget." The topic, what to do about a bad boss, is introduced by the definition of a bad boss. Notice also how this opening uses the second person "you." Anyone who has ever had a bad boss will be drawn instantly into this article.

Classification: Every type of bad boss you can imagine is classified in this article. Note particularly the thesis statement and map, which shows that the article is going to classify bad managers and then tell you how to deal with them: "The key to getting on with a boss is to manage him by understanding his underlying motivations, which may be different than you think. Here are some common types of bad bosses, their motivations, and strategies for dealing with them."

Definition: "The weak manager: She won't stand up for you. She aggressively avoids taking risks. She's vague and her commitments have the sticking power of water."

"Hey. Wassup?" "Nothin'"

by Clive Thompson

ROB Magazine, December 29, 2000

For Leon Stiel, it usually begins like this:

The first message pops up. you there?

He bashes out an instant reply: yeah. what's up?

you call the client?

no. i'll do it later

cool

And thus concludes one of several dozen typical "instant messaging" exchanges that Stiel will have with co-workers, all day long, as chief strategy officer of Oven Digital Inc., an internet firm with offices in Toronto, New York and worldwide. Few of the conversations are particularly gripping or deep; few are even grammatical. But they form a sort of social glue holding his network of co-workers together as they work across the globe—in offices as far-flung as San Francisco and London.

"Once you get a couple of people all sending messages, it can pretty easily take the place of a lot of phone calls," Stiel notes. "And then everybody wants in. You get a project manager using it, she gets another manager using it, and pretty soon everyone's messaging." Indeed, when I visited Stiel's office earlier this year, easily half the staff were zapping away on instant-message applications—from ICQ to Yahoo!'s Messenger to America Online's popular Instant Messenger. All work the same way: Other users can send you short text messages which pop up on your screen, on top of whatever else you're doing. Brief and urgent, they cater to a type of rapid-fire chattiness that outdoes even e-mail.

Yet the messaging trend is quickly overtaking the business world. The Gartner Group estimates that almost half of all North American corporations already use messaging—a number projected to grow to 90% in barely two years. Companies as big as Chase Manhattan Bank are hooking up their employees, and AOL has more than 61 million people using its messaging system, many of them "free agents" working out of home offices. Messaging is thus poised to subtly alter the way workers keep in contact with one another and do everyday business. What exactly is the lure?

In one sense, messaging is the internet's answer to a problem the internet itself created—far-flung workers. Sure, you can outsource all sorts of work to Goose Bay, Nfld., but you lose out on the breezy, water-cooler repartee that knits a team together. Enter messaging. "I see it as the replacement for standing up and hollering over the cubicle," says Gartner vice-president Joyce Graff. "We're all so mobile now, we're in different buildings, so you can't just lean over any more and yell, 'Bob, did you get that disk?' It's short, so you can send these one-word messages—like 'yo,' stuff you wouldn't bother sending in an e-mail." Messaging's real-time vibe gives it a verbal quality—which is what endeared it to gossip-swapping teenagers, the tool's first and most fervent users.

Messaging is a sort of elegant midpoint between the phone call and e-mail; fast, yes, but still with the quasi-literary quality of all text. Aficionados say that at its best, this mix can actually produce a richer, smarter form of dialogue. "When you're talking on the phone, your brain is working a bazillion miles a second about what to say," notes Rich Wall, director of internet technologies for IBM Corp. "But with instant messaging, you have a few seconds to think about what it is you're saying before you type it. You wind up seeming smarter, wittier."

There are other, less obvious social aspects. For example, most messaging tools display a list of who in your coterie of workers is currently on-line. In the messaging biz, this is called "presence"—a spatial sense of who's "around" you, virtually. "I log on and can immediately see who on my team is available to talk. You can't do that with a phone or e-mail," says Joseph Carusone, managing director of StockHouse Media Corp., a financial news site.

Still, the social vibe cuts both ways. Now your friends and colleagues have yet another way to send you URLs or interrupt your workday with pointless banter. Terrific. Yet another digital tool to help pound your attention span into tiny little splinters.

A study by one psychologist found that messaging significantly degraded users' abilities to focus on the type of data-searching tasks— such as scanning through a spreadsheet or a list of files—that typically comprise most computer work. "It's particularly a problem with older workers" less attuned to computers and the internet, argues Mary Czerwinski, the researcher at Microsoft's Adaptive Systems and Interaction Group who conducted the study.

Not all users agree. "On the contrary, I'd say you don't get interrupted as much. A phone call is much more disruptive than a message," argues Edward Gray, manager of central services for Tucows Inc., a Toronto-based digital distributor and domain reseller. And as he points out, you can just toggle yourself into "off-line" mode whenever you want. As with all things technological, a generation gap emerges: Czerwinksi suspects that the problem may ease as younger workers—weaned on messaging—move into the workplace. They're more "interrupt-driven," to use her gorgeous and (unintentionally, I think) backhanded phrase. "They're just fine with it, though maybe it's at the cost of an ability to focus—we don't know," she adds.

Other technological hurdles abound, including the fact that rival messaging systems, ICQ and Messenger, for example, don't work with one another—they aren't "interoperable." No one service wants to give away its user base, its most bankable asset. You can, of course, download all the different platforms and try to cross-manage them, at the risk of becoming rather more interrupt-driven than you'd prefer. Or you can use emerging third-party companies with software that crosses all systems, such as the Foster City, Calif.-based Facetime Communications Inc.

But either way, it seems likely that messaging will grow explosively—not only in use, but in forms of media. Wireless devices are already introducing short text-messaging; in Britain alone, for example, wireless messaging shot from 500,000 messages a month in August, 1999, to a mind-boggling eight billion in August, 2000. And as broadband grows more widespread, some predict video messaging is poised to take off—since almost every current messaging tool either allows for it, or will soon.

"Originally, the phone was just a person-to-person tool. Only later did it become a corporate tool, and only later still did we get richer services like conferencing. Messaging's going to go the same way," argues David Hsieh, Facetime's vice-president of marketing. In this sense, messaging's social aspects could help it finally usher in the long-ballyhooed rise of virtual collaboration—with remote team members working together in real time, swapping ideas, talking via video, and sharing documents simultaneously.

And trading really bad jokes.

Clarifications

Breezy, water-cooler repartee: Traditionally, the office water cooler has been the place where people gather to chat and gossip.

Fervent: Strong, passionate or ardent.

Aficionado: Comes from a Spanish verb meaning to induce a liking for. Used in English, it means a fan or enthusiast.

Coterie: A group, usually a select group, who hang out together. The word originally meant an association of tenants, or cottagers.

Banter: Light, teasing talk. Give and take.

Talking Points

The article notes that "a study by one psychologist found that messaging significantly degraded users' abilities to focus on the type of data-searching tasks—such as scanning through a spreadsheet or a list of files—that typically comprise most computer work." In your experience, is this the case?

Towards the end of the article, the author discusses the concept of virtual collaboration. How many of you have collaborated virtually? How does it work? Do the students in class who have used ICQ feel that they would be able to move from chatting to collaboration in this medium?

Web Research

The Gartner Group's Web site is at *www3.gartner.com.* The site is an excellent resource for researching new and developing business technologies.

StockHouse Media Corp. is a financial news company with a Web site at *www.stockhouse.ca.*

Microsoft's Adaptive Systems and Interaction Group does research on the interaction between humans and computers. The Web site is at *http://research.microsoft.com/adapt.* The body of research here is quite impressive.

The company mentioned in this article, Facetime, has an excellent Web site for research on this issue at *www.facetime.com.*

Writing That Works

Introduction—example: The introduction gives an example of a conversation using instant messaging.

Parallel structure: "Few of the conversations are particularly gripping or deep; few are even grammatical." The second part of the sentence, paralleling the first, operates almost as a punch line.

Pop culture allusions: The title of the article alludes to a popular television commercial for Budweiser, where a group of young black men phone each other about nothing. The introduction then ties into this allusion, showing a conversation about nothing.

Statistics: "Yet the messaging trend is quickly overtaking the business world. The Gartner Group estimates that almost half of all North American corporations already use messaging—a number projected to grow to 90% in barely two years. Companies as big as Chase Manhattan Bank are hooking up their employees, and AOL has more than 61 million people using its messaging system, many of them 'free agents' working out of home offices."

Battle Wary

by Harvey Schachter

Chatelaine, July 1, 1997

As a young girl, Leona Alleslev-Krofchak dreamed of growing up to serve her country in the military. Her grandfather was part of the Danish underground, her father was a major-general in the Canadian air force, and she spent her childhood living on bases. She entered Royal Military College of Canada, the country's premier military university, in 1987, just seven years after women were first admitted. Members of RMC's last all-male class had expressed their view of the new coed era by sporting graduation rings engraved with the acronym LCWB. Meaning: Last Class With Balls.

The hostile machismo expressed in that slogan would plague Alleslev-Krofchak's future military career. After graduation from the Kingston, Ont., college, she was posted to CFB Comox in British Columbia as the officer in charge of getting all supplies to the base.

Her second-in-command greeted her by ranting about how he'd never taken orders from a woman and wasn't about to start. Over her nine years of military service, Alleslev-Krofchak enjoyed some of her work and made good friends, but her fond memories are outweighed by the bad. Aside from enduring overt antiwoman sentiments, she was also troubled that the military was slow to redesign uniforms and develop child-care policies to accommodate women. Last year, she took a buyout. In fact, she says, more than half of the 20 women in her RMC class have left the military.

"I had a love of the military before I joined," says Alleslev-Krofchak, a cheerful effervescent woman. "All the reasons I joined—to serve my country—are still there. And I'm happy I did. But the day-to-day life was awful at times." Her conclusion on the Forces: "It's an organization whose philosophy hasn't changed to include women."

Can Canada's military make women feel welcome? The question gained urgency last year after publicity about Capt. Sandra Perron. She was the first woman to become an officer in the Canadian infantry, the part of the army geared for frontline combat. During a bizarre training exercise in 1992 in Gagetown, N.B., she was tied to a tree, subjected to a mock execution and left barefoot out in the snow. After a haunting photo of the scene was leaked to the media last year, Perron declined to comment, though one media account said that she felt the incident was being blown out of proportion. But the photo captures a grim truth: Perron eventually left the army because male colleagues treated her so miserably.

An inquiry into Perron's whole military experience determined that she was an excellent soldier, respected by her subordinates and supported by her bosses. But, as inquiry leader Lt.-Col. Denis Mercier was shocked to discover, she was resented and harassed by some other young officers who were competing with her for promotions. "They do not want to see a female officer in the infantry, let alone in combat," Mercier reported. "To them, the infantry is 'the last tavern.'"

Officially, the tavern is under attack. In 1989, following much stormy debate, a human rights tribunal decreed that in gender terms, the Canadian military must be "fully integrated" by 1999. Before this, most combat-focused jobs had remained closed to women. While the tribunal wasn't clear on the exact final goal, it did direct the Forces to open up all employment areas to women (save for submarines, judged not to offer sufficient privacy). Early this year, the military itself added momentum to the cause when the army set a goal of making women

25 percent of its future recruits. Currently, women comprise only 10.7 percent of the Canadian Forces, and are poorly represented in senior military ranks and frontline combat roles. That makes the new recruitment goals and ongoing integration plans very ambitious—and controversial.

"You don't tell Team Canada to add women," says Scott Taylor, the feisty ex-infantryman who edits *Esprit de Corps,* an Ottawa-based magazine that champions the lowly infantry grunt. "War is the ultimate competition. Your life is on the line and so is the fate of the nation." To Taylor, women simply aren't suited for combat, a view still dominant in the nation's legions and mess halls.

Back in 1980, Sandy Cotton, then a lieutenant-colonel, wrote a PhD thesis that identified a critical group of men within combat ranks as what he called "beleaguered warriors." They were tough guys who were resistant to change and imbued with a "masculine warrior mindset." Among other things, they would tend to believe their job was to protect women, not march into battle with them. Sandra Perron met those warriors head-on. And her ultimate downfall highlights the obstacles women face not just in being comfortable in the service, but in taking command.

Top jobs in the army, which sets the tone for overall military culture and policy, are usually filled by experienced combat-arms officers who typically take 25 years to reach a top rank such as general. With Perron gone, and no one else closing in on her level of achievement, women will take decades to assume true power. "There hasn't been enough time to grow a combat general," says retired Maj.-Gen. Lewis MacKenzie. "And maybe we messed up our best chance with that gal tied to a tree."

In wartime, Canadian women actually have a strong tradition of military service, starting with the nurses who served in the 1885 North West Rebellion and the Boer War. But for many decades in peacetime, our forces imposed strict caps on women members. Gradually, however, through the gender upheavals of the 1970s and 1980s, more women started joining, with many taking up more nontraditional roles.

Cmdr. Deborah Wilson, who coordinates gender integration for the Forces, likes to emphasize that Canada's current 10.7 percent representation of women is second only to the United States. "We are world leaders," she says. But skeptics say Canadian women really haven't made strides where it counts, and haven't achieved true acceptance. "There are a lot of people in the Armed Forces who think that integration is just a trial and that it will be over someday," says Shirley Robinson, a retired lieutenant-colonel who heads the Association for Women's Equity in the Canadian Forces. "I don't think they have done an effective job at integration. They've been dragging their heels as much as possible."

Division of labor in the military is sometimes described by the phrase "tooth and tail." People such as infantry soldiers and fighter pilots form the tooth—the part that goes quickly into frontline battle. Others form the tail: some follow up in combat, others never see battle. Encouragingly, women now hold 11.3 percent of the military's officer posts, more than their total representation in the Forces. But they work mostly in the "tail"—in supply, administration, personnel and medicine. To measure gender integration, the Canadian Human Rights Commission focuses on women's progress in several so-called "monitored occupations"—all in the "tooth." In these occupations, women comprise just 2 percent of the lower ranks and 4.6 percent of officers.

If acceptance in combat roles is the truest measure of functioning integration, the whole issue is plagued by thorny debates over what you might call the two s's: sex and strength. Women aren't physically strong enough for combat, say critics such as Scott Taylor, and they may distract men from getting the job done. A former infantry private, Taylor tells the story of a visit he made as a journalist to Canada's peacekeepers in Bosnia, where 400 women served. At one point he was in a small contingent that came under fire. As the soldiers were preparing to flee their tent, one of the men noticed that one of the women was in her underwear. "None of the soldiers bolted for safety right away," Taylor recalls. "They stayed around for a few seconds to catch a glimpse. The sexual element is still there under fire."

Lewis MacKenzie, commander of UN forces in Bosnia, came away with the opposite conclusion. "After my experience in Sarajevo, I have no doubt that gender integration can work," he says. "You think about your equipment and people—sex is the furthest thing from your mind." MacKenzie recalls being in a gender-mixed group that performed superbly when it had nearly been hit by an antitank round. "People acted more bravely than I would have anticipated," he says. "The guys didn't want to be showed up before the gals and the gals didn't want to be showed up before the guys." He even remembers the case of a female surgeon calmly reassuring two men who were terrified they were about to die when coming under fire on the road to Gorazde.

Women may be brave, but are they strong enough for battle? The issue has ignited many controversies. In fitness tests at RMC, for example, chin-ups have been replaced by push-ups, in part because women's lower centre of gravity makes chin-ups more difficult for them. To graduate, RMC women must meet minimum fitness standards that are lower than those for men. For instance, women must run a mile and a half in 12 minutes—compared with 10 minutes, 16 seconds for men. People such as Taylor are outraged by the double standards. But those managing integration say the new standards pose more equitable challenges to men and women, based on their differing physiques and physiology.

Some experts argue that, in fact, fitness alone is no fair measure of women's combat potential. Ron Dickenson, a retired lieutenant-colonel who was involved in early trials of women in combat areas, observed women applying brains over brawn to move heavy material. To do a job a man might do solo, women would have two people share the load or use ropes and pulleys. "The military had tunnel vision," he says. "The women showed us there were alternatives to brute force."

The latest surprising perspective on this issue comes from a 1996 U.S. study showing that the military could take tips from pro athletics to make even civilian women strong enough for "very heavy" military tasks. The experiment involved 41 civilian volunteers. By training with sports-oriented weight-lifting techniques, almost 80 percent of them met the U.S. army's heavy-training standards—compared with 20 percent who typically do so after traditional military training. Principal investigator Everett Harman concludes, "Far more women than we previously thought could be trained to do a very heavy, physically demanding job."

Contrary to popular belief, women have been successful combat warriors throughout human history. In this century alone, more than 800,000 Soviet women were in combat for the Soviet Union in World War II; in the 28-year guerrilla war fought against Ethiopia by the Eritrean People's Front, about a third of the fighters were female, many commanders. "There is an ignorance about what women have done in war," says Linda Grant De Pauw, an American professor who directs the world's only PhD program in women's military studies. "The archetype is man as warrior, woman as mother. The reality is that while no man can give birth, women can kill. Women can do both, but that disappears from history."

Canadian Dee Brasseur of Nepean, Ont., a dynamo who went from a typewriter to the controls of a CF-18, is a living example of the struggle to shatter the archetype. In 1979 she was one of the first four Canadian women to begin military flight training. "Most of the fellows were 21 or 22," she recalls. "Whether it was testosterone, age or maturity, we seemed to threaten their young male egos. They had trouble with us doing the same things as they did. They couldn't imagine their mother, sister or girlfriend doing that."

She wasn't accepted—even by some students she taught as a flight instructor—until one night in 1983, when she was flying with a student and a bird zoomed into her craft's engine, destroying it. Though her steering mechanism was dead, leaving her in a state comparable to a car driver who's lost automatic steering, Brasseur expertly manoeuvred the plane back to the base rather than ditching it. Even the young bucks now had to admit she belonged. But Brasseur is annoyed that she needed the incident to gain respect. "It's assumed guys could handle that situation. Women weren't granted the assumption of capability."

Brasseur left the military in 1994, after 22 years of service, feeling that downsizing had diminished her chances to remain an active pilot. Women today still face some of the barriers she did, she says, but less intensely. "We have proven ourselves," she says. "A lot of the apprehension and fear and ingrained prejudices of men have fallen away." She would recommend military life to other women. "If you want challenges and change and the opportunity for personal growth, the military is wonderful."

Not all women who have toughed it out in the Canadian military can be so forgiving, especially those who claim to have suffered overt abuse. Administration clerk Kimberley Franke, for instance, claims she faced lewd comments and sexual advances from a superior at CFB Comox. When she grieved to his boss, a woman, not only was the complaint treated lightly, she says, but she was accused of being licentious; she received poor job appraisals, suffered harassing phone calls and was accused of being psychologically unstable. Eventually she took her grievance to the Canadian Human Rights Commission, and she did develop emotional problems that left her unable to work. "It's like Somalia," she says. "The whole system is based on camaraderie.

Everyone protects everyone else. If you break with that, you are an outsider and have to be punished."

Franke is currently in group counseling in Courtenay, B.C., where she met Nancy Knight, a former military radio technician who is suing the Armed Forces for what she says was about six years of sexual harassment and physical assault during her time at a base in Trenton, Ont. When she complained, she says, superiors either condoned or participated in the abuse. And, she claims, the military addressed her problems by transferring her—rather than the alleged aggressors.

Last year, there were 126 formal complaints of harassment in the Canadian military, sexual and otherwise, and 60 percent came from women—almost six times what would be expected from their numbers alone. A 1992 survey found that 26.2 percent of women in the Canadian military felt they had experienced sexual harassment. The military addresses complaints with a procedure that follows the norm in other major institutions. But Matthew Fahey, who is Nancy Knight's lawyer, says the system doesn't work. "She's suing because she wants to change the system. She wants to open the way for women to serve their country."

In the struggle to make women totally comfortable in the Armed Forces, there are two key target institutions: RMC, which grooms future officers, and the army, home of the fiercest warrior culture. On both fronts there are heartening signs.

At RMC, women comprise just over a quarter of the student population, strong numbers compared with the days of Leona Alleslev-Krofchak. In the 1996–97 academic years, most of the cadet officers—the leaders chosen to oversee student activities and some training procedures—were women, because they were the top performers. When Cybele Wilson, a 21-year-old cadet from Hull, Que., researched an essay on military women for a course she takes at neighboring Queen's University, she was surprised to find that former female RMC cadets felt much bitterness toward their school. "They were telling me things I have never encountered—like women finding excrement in their sinks and being teased about eating dessert, as it would make them fat," she says. "I have no doubt my classmates see me as equal."

For its part, the Canadian army now holds focus groups to explore why women have quit. When Sandra Perron spoke at one, many senior officials were stunned by her mistreatment. Shirley Robinson, who is highly skeptical of the military's work in gender integration, says this is at least a first step. "For too long," she says, "they didn't ask why women left."

The army's new goal of recruiting 25 percent women upsets many critics because it smacks of a quota. The target was chosen because studies of minorities in large institutions—such as blacks in the U.S. military—show they must achieve such a critical mass before they're accepted by the majority culture. Though a critical mass may be necessary, it may be unattainable, particularly in the army. The simple fact is, not many Canadian women want to spend their working hours wallowing in slit trenches. The 25 percent is a "stretch goal," says Cmdr. Deborah Wilson, but it is at least forcing the army to increase its appeal to women. That will involve redesigning marketing programs, probably stressing the camaraderie of army life rather than the chance to play with electronic gizmos.

For the last several years the military has been preoccupied with downsizing, at the cost of other priorities. These days, it seems to be turning a serious eye to women's issues. Gender-sensitivity programs are being planned; and uniforms are being steadily changed to accommodate women: shirts will no longer be see-through; flak jackets will be better contoured to the female body. "The easy part is over in terms of opening areas up to women," says Cmdr. Wilson. "We now have to do the hard part to make changes to the organization so we will reflect gender equity."

All of the latest initiatives have come too late, however, to salvage the military career of Leona Alleslev-Krofchak. Instead of carrying on the family tradition, she now works alongside her father, as a management consultant based in Ottawa. And she remains disappointed that her dreams were destroyed. "I was treated in ways that I would not expect people to treat me," she says.

While many women do enjoy fulfilling military careers, eight years after the call for full integration, many others do not. Sandra Perron is gone. Kimberley Franke is gone. Nancy Knight is gone. As the military fights to gain back the public respect that's required of an institution of such vital national importance, Canadian women are watching to see if it can march into a more sensitive and sensible new age.

Clarifications

Danish underground: During the Second World War, many resistance movements developed in Europe. One was the Danish underground. Read about the movement on the PBS Web site at *www.pbs.org/ weta/forcemorepowerful/denmark.*

Machismo: A Spanish word meaning aggressive, overassertive male pride.

The last tavern: This expression is used as if it is a common one. However, I could find no reference to it anywhere else. Presumably, the last tavern is the last place that allows only men to go there.

Like Somalia: In 1992, Canadian soldiers were part of a massive relief effort in Somalia. However, a scandal erupted when pictures of Canadian soldiers torturing a Somali teenager were shown on television. Eventually, a commission of inquiry was struck. Read the details on the CBC Newsworld Web site at *www.newsworld.cbc.ca/ flashback/1996.*

Critical mass: Critical mass is the smallest amount of fissionable material that will sustain a nuclear chain reaction at a constant level. Used in non-nuclear terms, it refers to the amount of anything needed to achieve a desired result or effect.

Talking Points

During the war in Afghanistan in 2001–02, female pilots flew fighter planes and took part in bombing raids. However these officers, stationed on air bases in Saudi Arabia, were asked to wear the dress of the local women when off-base, although their male counterparts were not expected to do more than "dress conservatively." Discuss.

Search for articles from the period of the Gulf War and compare them to articles from 2002. How have attitudes to women in the military changed over that period?

Web Research

A messy but interesting Web site on women in the military can be found at *www.geocities.com/Athens/Troy/3825/country/militarywoman/ milwoman.htm.* This is not the kind of site that students should refer to in a report, as it is obviously a personal Web site; however, it may have links to other more appropriate sites.

The Department of National Defence site is at *www.dnd.ca*. It does not seem to provide much information about women in the military.

A Web site that deals with various issues related to women in the American military can be found at *www.militarywoman.org/homepage.htm*.

Many pages exist for military spouses. Because they are often personal pages, I have not named them here. A Google search using the terms *military* and *spouse* will turn up plenty of interesting pages.

Writing That Works

Framing story: The opening anecdotes are picked up in the closing paragraphs, giving the article a frame.

The Work–Family Crunch: How Are We Coping?
by Deborah Jones

Chatelaine, April 1, 1996

Sometimes, you forget to breathe. It might happen on the day you skip lunch to make a meeting so you can finish work in time to collect the children from swimming, buy groceries, cook and eat, and wave to your partner or baby-sitter coming in the door as you rush out to a parent-teacher meeting. It could even be in bed, late that night, as your drift into blessed sleep is interrupted by thoughts about the messy house, and how you avoided your boss for fear she'd ask for overtime, and how long it's been since you visited your parents, and how you skipped the kids' bedtime story because the laundry needed doing.

If this describes me, a full-time writer striving to match up the puzzle pieces of work and family, it seems to apply equally to the 1,237 readers who responded to *Chatelaine's* survey on the work-family crunch last August. Your responses—and several hundred appended stories scrawled on hospital notepads, computer paper from home businesses and scrap paper at the family cottage—painted a vivid picture of how Canadians with double (and sometimes triple) duties struggle to care for their children and parents, pay their bills, nurture their careers, and do it all, somehow, even if it means sacrificing necessities like sleep.

In compelling detail, you described your workplaces and homes, your day-care solutions and lifestyle downshifts, your nightmares and hopes, your lifesaving tips. ("Scrub the bathtub while having your own shower each evening," suggested one working morn. "Win a lottery!" advised another.) You reported that the need to balance work against family caused either "a lot" of stress (41 percent) or at least "some" (55 percent). And no wonder, given the changing face of today's Canadian family. It's not merely that the number of families with both parents employed soared from almost 33 percent in 1967 to more than 61 percent in 1991, with a full-time homemaker in a scant 13 percent of today's families. It's also because traditional support networks of neighborhoods and extended families have vanished. Jobs have become more scarce and less secure, making it riskier than ever for someone to opt out of the "rat race." Meanwhile, those who are employed work longer hours and bring home tax-shrunk paycheques.

The result: families that made do on one income 20 years ago now require two. For many survey respondents, this harsh reality raised concerns for children nurtured on the fly, and an enduring legacy of guilt that overshadowed daily triumphs over laundry, commuting, scheduling. "I feel guilty for not spending enough time with my kids, guilty because I can't give 150 percent at work and put in the 12-hour days that many of my coworkers do, and I feel guilty because I can't always be there for my husband," wrote Joy Ward of Waterdown, Ont. She echoed many others in asking, "I wonder if I'm the only one who feels like they do so much, but they do nothing really well?"

What follows is not merely a report on the survey results, but an attempt to find new strategies for coping with the crunch. Our chief sources are your survey responses and interviews with women across the land. We only hope you find time to read on ... and to breathe.

MAKING WORK WORK

The shape of the Canadian workplace is changing rapidly—and none too soon for families. Many Canadian parents enjoy previously undreamed-of options about where and when to work, and job support systems that help take away some double-duty stress.

A Few Good Bosses

Canadian employers are paying more attention than ever to family issues, partly because a younger generation has reached management, and mostly because stressed employees are less productive and take more days off work. "Let's face it, our first priority is always our families, and if they're taken care of, you can spend the rest of your time giving the very best to your work," says Maddy Tiller, a supervisor with Human Resources Development Canada in Vancouver.

Tiller, herself a single mother of two teens and a caregiver for her elderly mother, helps to run an unemployment-insurance telecentre that is something of a model of the modern family-friendly office—its policies include flexible hours, part-time shifts and willingness to help workers when possible. Last fall, for example, employee Mireille Massincaud was allowed to start work nearly two hours late for five mornings so she could take her children to school while her parents, who normally care for them, were away. "I did not feel I had to beg for that," says Massincaud, "which made me feel very good."

The City of Vancouver is one of a number of employers who offer four-day workweeks in which workers stay longer hours in return for each Friday off. School boards commonly allow two teachers to share one job. Several banks, where women far outnumber men on the payroll, offer flexible working hours and part-time shifts designed to coincide with the hours of school. In Ottawa, a nonprofit program offers emergency child care, partly subsidized by employers like the Ottawa Civic Hospital, Ernst & Young, Bell-Northern Research and the Carleton Board of Education, so workers are not left in a pinch when their regular child-care arrangements break down. And cafeterias at some large workplaces, such as British Columbia's Children's Hospital in Vancouver, will sell employees baked goods for the family or even entrees to take home on busy days. One of the more innovative companies is PepsiCo, which replaced a company concierge who ran laundry errands for employees with an on-site dry cleaner—unfortunately, only at its head office in New York state.

Sociologist Kerry Daly, associate professor of family studies at the University of Guelph, says there's a big difference between how men and women use family-friendly policies. "Even when companies offer family leave, men don't take advantage of it to anywhere near the extent women do." Daly believes men encounter subtle barriers to playing a greater role in household and child care—coworkers may make jokes at the watercooler about "Mr. Mom."

But according to your survey responses, the real key to a family-friendly workplace is a supportive boss. "I work for an employer who offers no benefits other than those required by law," wrote Barbara Moser, a professional mechanical and aircraft engineer in Markham, Ont., whose three kids range from 11 months to 10 years. "However, my boss is extremely accommodating and flexible.... I have discovered that all the official policies, benefits and even financial considerations (within reason) are not as important as the attitude and practices of your direct superiors."

Unfortunately, understanding bosses are not as plentiful as we'd like: many survey respondents wrote notes about how they feel they must lie and tell their employer they are personally sick on days when family takes them away from work. Stuck with a boss who just doesn't get it? Tiller suggests trying to raise family issues through negotiation ahead of time. If you must take your daughter to the dentist, talk to your boss beforehand and offer to work late or through lunch in return for time off. Ask a coworker to offer to help cover your work. Assert your needs clearly, but be diplomatic and consider how you can avoid making other workers, or your boss, feel they are unfairly carrying your load.

Go Ahead, Employ Yourself

For more than 650,000 Canadian women, the best way to handle the boss is to be your own. Self-employment contributes flexibility to the work-family crunch, says flower-and-gourmet-foods shop owner Laura Dean of Coquitlam, B.C., mom of Kali, 6, and Cameron, 12. But, she warns, "It also requires more hours—sometimes when the children are sleeping."

Being your own boss brings a degree of freedom and a few tax advantages—for example, you may be able to write off part of your household and your car as business expenses if you run a home office. But, says self-employed Vancouver accountant Randall Dang, self-employment is not for people who prefer a secure paycheque, and the pluses must be weighed against the lack of benefits like drug and pension plans, and a patchy safety net: self-employed people are ineligible for unemployment insurance, even during maternity leave.

Home Work: The Job You Never Leave

When her family moved to a cottage in Ontario's Muskoka area near Rosseau, chartered accountant Michele Fraser negotiated a deal that lets her work three or four days a week for most of the year and spend summers off with her two sons, David, 5, and Cameron, nearly 2. Year-round, Fraser receives 60 percent of her regular salary from an area firm, Harris, Cull, Gordon, Gingrich. On workdays, her children go to a friend's house; Fraser either drives to clients' offices or brings her work home. "I've found a job that is perfect for me and my family," says Fraser. Today's home workers—an estimated 743,000 Canadians—include many who work for big companies such as banks and insurance companies, thanks to fax machines and modems. The benefits are obvious: you're there for family emergencies, there are no transportation costs, and money can be saved on business clothes.

But it's no panacea. Unions worry that telecommuting employees might work longer hours, and self-motivation is critical. Home offices work smoothly for those caring for older children or dependent adults, but young children's needs are all-consuming. Trudy Engel, a Saskatoon accountant and mother of two, gave up her home office after just five months. "I always felt that neither work nor home-life duties were getting done," Engel says. Hairstylist Lutine Bjornson of North Vancouver sold her Vancouver salon when her daughter, now 4, was born, to work out of her home. The arrangement can be frustrating, such as when her daughter escapes her sitter and runs into the home salon demanding attention while Bjornson wields sharp scissors on a client—but Bjornson says she'd do it all over again.

Is a home office for you? Assess whether you can perform your best surrounded by endless diversions and no supervisors. As a writer who has worked from home for 17 years, I've found it crucial to separate work and household tasks—telephone calls over the roar of a dishwasher sound unprofessional. Your work area should have a door to prevent work from invading family life. Compensate for the lack of an office culture by scheduling coffee or lunch with friends or associates.

SHARING THE LOAD

For Kim Porter of Pictou, N.S., a respiratory therapist and mother of four, work is more than a necessary evil. "I stayed home for three years, then went stir-crazy," she says. "My children and my husband suffered more when I stayed home and had the house spick-and-span and the meals ready on schedule." Porter started her own respiratory home-care business, enlisted her parents and in-laws to help care for her children, and reports that she and her family are much happier now that she is out in the workforce. But no one says that child-care solutions are simple.

Grannies and Other Strangers

"Today's generation of grandparents are failures," a friend of mine declared recently. Her family had just bought a house, and she was livid that her parents, who never help out with her work-family crunch despite living nearby, refused to care for her two children during her hectic move. But is this harsh judgment fair? Readers (of whom 26 percent helped to care for an elderly friend or relative) offered mixed reflections on help from grandparents and other relatives. Sometimes having a grandmother care for a child caused friction between in-laws. One working mom asked her own mother to live in and care for her daughter four days a week, but found that the care needed by the aging granny—down to cutting toenails—worsened the crunch.

Others reported ideal family situations. After her grandmother died, Ottawa's Colleen McAuley, a single mom who often works overnight as a retail supervisor, moved in with her 79-year-old grandfather. "My son stays at home with my grandfather while I am working," wrote McAuley. "Our extended family is quite convenient for me, and it also allows my son to learn our family history and enjoy the company of his great-grandfather."

Friends, Neighbors and Nannies

For many readers, informal arrangements with friends and neighbors are vital child-care strategies. When Mireille Massincaud of Vancouver's unemployment-insurance telecentre needs backup help, she leaves her three school-age children in the care of a friendly neighbor at 6:45 a.m. Neighborhood baby-sitting cooperatives exist in most Canadian cities, set up informally by groups of parents. It's a concept that can be expanded to include elder care as our relatives age, or even food preparation. (Confession: I tried this for a few weeks, but I don't think my friend's husband liked my cooking.)

Still, with extended families scattered around the world and close-knit neighborhoods increasingly rare, more than 51 percent of kids under age 13 are in the care of someone other than a parent at least once a week. Some working women have found ways to make this situation work to their advantage. For 10 years, Patti Tetreau of Kelowna, B.C., has employed the same baby-sitter for her four kids, now ages 7 to 13, to everyone's benefit. "She has been like a third parent," wrote Tetreau, a cashier. "She is wonderful to all of our children. She has taught them manners, great respect for others, etc."

But many readers mentioned they had problems finding a caregiver they were satisfied with, and ongoing concerns about their child's care. Worried one mom with a 15-month-old daughter, "What kind of a man is my baby-sitter's husband? He looks okay, but what if he turns out to be a child molester?" And for many, the cost of hiring a nanny is prohibitive.

Oh, Yes, Them

And husbands? Well, somehow the subject didn't come up in most of your stories. It was telling that for all but a few readers, it was working moms who took responsibility for running the household and caring for others. "No matter how much my husband offers his help and support," wrote Jayne Graham of London, Ont., "I know (despite what he might say) that I (like so many other women) do the lion's share of the work in our home." Among the exceptions was Sue McCaw, a nurse in Newmarket, Ont., who described a hectic work-family schedule but added: "Fortunately, I have a wonderfully supportive and capable husband, Rob, who is able to take over all the day-to-day needs of the children as soon as he sheds his suit and dons his sweat gear."

Statistics Canada reported this year that despite a small reduction in the disparity between male and female household contributions, men still spend around two hours less, each day, on unpaid chores than women. Sociologist Kerry Daly says men tend to view some of their time at home as leisure time, while women do not feel they can give themselves "permission" to relax because there are always chores to be done. He suggests that both sexes change their attitudes to meet in the middle. Meanwhile, it's no secret that we women can be our own worst enemies be cause of our insistence on controlling the domestic scene. (Confession Number 2: my husband's macaroni-dinner technique drives me nuts.) Advises reader Susan Vassel of Don Mills, Ont., who is grateful for a supportive family in the face of recent personal health problems: "I used to hate the way my husband would fold the towels and I'd criticize him every time. Now, I realize it does not matter how the towels are folded, as long as someone does it."

STRIKING A BALANCE

"My grandmother said that she would be up until 11 o'clock cleaning, doing laundry and ironing," says Christina Walton, a funeral director in Hamilton, Ont., who's expecting her third child in May. "She was shocked when I told her that I am too. She said: 'But you went to university!'" The truth is, it's harder than ever for working mothers to balance their priorities. But it's not impossible.

Get Real, Mom

Eight years ago, Calgary chartered accountant Diane Fleming decided that her biggest double-duty problem was her own unrealistic expectations. Today, Fleming works part-time, earns less money and considers herself lucky. "Although I haven't advanced in my field, I enjoy my work and find it challenging and interesting," she says, noting that her reduced schedule allows her to spend time with her three children, ages 3 to 8. "I am not willing to sacrifice my family time for more prestige, money or responsibility," Fleming says bluntly.

Likewise nurse Katherine Brisbin. Last fall, fed up with working full-time in Comox on Vancouver Island and trying to make ends meet, Brisbin, her husband, Rodney, a shop foreman for a car dealership, and their toddler moved back to their hometown of Moose Jaw, Sask., to be closer to family members and in a town with a lower cost of living that allows her to work part-time. "We are making some sacrifices but we both believe that it will be so much better for our family. I don't have to work full-time—it is such a relief to write those words!"

It's a truism that those who cut back on work or quit for a while place themselves on the "mommy (or daddy) track" and damage their career prospects. But not everyone wants to reach the top of her career. And employers are increasingly willing to discuss downscaling options: Apple Canada, for instance, offers "sabbatical" leave programs that allow some stressed parents to enjoy the whole summer with their families.

Get Real, Canada

For so many of us, the ideal family is still something pretty close to that reflected in the old (and never realistic) American sitcoms we grew up with. The truth is, postwar families of the Cleaver type were an aberration of history. The western world rose to unprecedented levels of wealth after World War II, and a brief period ensued when upper-middle-class Victorian ideals were embraced by an ambitious and war-weary middle class. These ideals included tightly defined sexual roles: men work, women parent. But before and since that time, few people have had the luxury of devoting the entire resources of one adult to raising children and keeping house. Both my rather middle-class grandmothers worked—one ran a post office and helped her husband farm, the other owned a candy store—while raising families much larger than today's average of 1.2 children. Ever since the industrial revolution, moms have taken in boarders, cleaned other people's houses, and been paid to take care of the children of other women who worked in factories. The biggest difference is that today, those of us who hold paying jobs must often do so without the support systems of close communities, extended families and churches.

Meanwhile, we cling to an equally idealized and outdated vision of the economy. First-year economics students are taught that the economy is the system set up to provide goods and services to people. But many family advocates argue that in reality, it is people who are fed to the economy. "The system is greedy," says Robert Glossop, director of programs for the Vanier Institute of the Family in Ottawa. "If we don't continue to increase our appetites as consumers, then the Conference Board of Canada will remind us about the level of consumer confidence. Then, we'll worry about building new homes because if we don't, the B.C. lumber industry goes down the tubes, and if we don't buy a new car every few years, auto jobs in Mississauga will be lost."

If your survey responses are any indication, many Canadians have had enough of the growth-at-all-costs idea and certainly are not willing to sacrifice their families to the economy. You are willing to make dramatic lifestyle changes to improve your maxed-out lives, and you are looking for less-costly ways to enjoy daily life—ways much more practical and effective than the daily bubble baths, 90-minute workouts and weekly date nights prescribed by advice columnists. For some of you, life will be easier if you simply make friends with the dust balls under the furniture. As Lynn Potter, a bank employee and mom in Calgary, wrote: "My fondest memories as a child are not of how clean my house was." For others, happiness is a family board game in front of the fireplace, a jaunt in a local park, or reading aloud the Sunday funnies.

But first, take a deep breath.

Clarifications

Panacea: A cure-all, something that cures all diseases.

Telecommuter: Someone who works at home and stays connected to the company network by computer.

Talking Points

Four-day work weeks, job sharing, flexible working hours—these are a few options that, according to the article, make women happier about their jobs. PepsiCo's head office apparently has an on-site dry cleaner. What other options would women in the class like to see in their future workplace? Should options like these be limited to women?

Are men pulling their weight at home? This article was written several years ago. Is it considered acceptable today for a man to stay home and take care of the children while his wife works?

Recent research has indicated that men who are stay-at-home dads die younger, on average, than men who work outside the home. What might be the reason for this finding?

Is telecommuting (working at home via computer) an option for parents, or is an integral part of the workday—companionship—too important to give up?

The current generation of working women has been called the "sandwich generation," because often they must take care of aging parents as well as children. How is this problem likely to develop in the future?

The writer frequently puts her own experiences into the article. What is the effect of her doing this?

Web Research

Chatelaine has an excellent database of articles about women, family and work at *www.chatelaine.com/work*. Fill in the Wheel of Life to see how satisfied you are with the balance of work and family in your life: *http://spotlight.chatelaine.com/wheel/wheel.html*.

The Canadian Policy Research Networks Web site includes an excellent paper entitled "Work-Life Balance in the New Millennium: Where Are We? Where Do We Need to Go?" Select "Work" from the drop-down menu and then search for the 92-page article.

Writing That Works

Point of view: The second person used in the opening paragraph—"Sometimes you forget to breathe"—pulls the reader personally into the situation. The writer continues by identifying herself with the situation, and then details "your" stories that "you" sent to *Chatelaine*. In effect, the writer uses herself as an expert.

Statistics and surveys: The article is based on a mail-in survey that *Chatelaine* carried out in 1995.

TOPIC 7

IMMIGRATION AT WORK

INTRODUCTION

When I arrived in Canada as a landed immigrant in 1973, I was part of a trend. As a New Zealander who met a Canadian in Istanbul and later married him, I was part of the baby boom generation that spent years backpacking in Europe and forming intercultural relationships and marriages. I joined a privileged group of immigrants who could come to Canada because we had married Canadian citizens. This group included the 50,000 war brides who came to Canada after the Second World War. However, most new Canadians do not find it so easy to enter the country.

Canada was first settled by non-aboriginal peoples in the sixteenth century, with the foundation of the colony of New France. New France was initially made up of the shores of the St. Lawrence River, Newfoundland, and Nova Scotia (also known as Arcadia), but spread to include much of the Great Lakes region. The British, meanwhile, were laying claim to the Hudson Bay area and much of what later became known as Atlantic Canada. In the eighteenth and nineteenth centuries, immigrants from England, Scotland and Ireland flooded in, often because of problems in their home countries. In Scotland, landlords cleared the highlands of tenant farmers to make room for sheep, sending many poor farmers to Canada, and in Ireland the potato famine of the mid-nineteenth century did the same. After the American Revolution of 1776, United Empire Loyalists—Americans who wanted to stay loyal to the British throne—came to Canada as well, including the ancestors of my husband.

In the mid-nineteenth century, many Chinese men were brought in as a source of cheap labour to build the railways. Like other groups, these Chinese immigrants left a poor economic situation at home. The Chinese also came as part of the California gold rush of 1849, to what they called Gold Mountain. When California's gold dried up, they moved to B.C.'s Fraser River valley in 1858. Between 1923 and 1947, the Chinese were the only people excluded from immigration because of their race. Read more about this group of immigrants on the CBC Web site at *www.cbc.ca/news/indepth/chinese*.

In the 1970s, after the end of the Vietnam War, came the Vietnamese "boat people," a group with perhaps the saddest stories of all immigrants to Canada (read some at *www.boatpeople.com*). For the rest of the twentieth century, the aftermath of war continued to be a supplier of new Canadians. In the late 1990s it was refugees fleeing Kosovo who came here. But while war has always brought us refugees, it is often economic need that brings people to our shores. Canadians tend to be less welcoming of people who come here for economic reasons, especially people who pay to be smuggled in—who are sent home if discovered. However, as the first article in this section indicates, we are no longer in a position to turn people away so easily. It is now Canada who needs immigrants for economic reasons.

Opening Our Eyes to Immigration

by Steven Frank with reporting from Ruth Abramson, Deborah Jones, Susan Bradley, Melanie Collison, Laura Eggertson, Kim Guttormson, Lisa Hrabluk and Leigh Anne Williams

Time Canada, May 7, 2001

Baher Abdulhai is on the fast track—in fact, he's creating it. The Cairo-born civil engineer is one of the world's top experts in a field known as intelligent transportation systems, which aims to improve urban and highway traffic flows by networking cameras, computers and electronic message boards placed along the way. Abdulhai was on a team at the University of California at Irvine that developed an ITS network that's now being set up on California's jammed highways. In the ever more congested world of the future, ITS will be an invaluable tool for urban planners, traffic cops and busy commuters. "It's a multi-billion-dollar business that's very popular in the States, Europe and

Japan," says Abdulhai, "and now it's catching up in Canada, Australia and Asia."

Abdulhai, 35, is on the cutting edge of Canada's future. As the country bids to fortify its position as a leader in the knowledge economy, brains and talent like his are the nation's most important resources—and they are an imported good. Abdulhai got his undergraduate degree at the University of Cairo and immigrated to Canada in 1991. He and his wife Nayera adjusted to Canadian life (and –40 degree Celsius temperatures) while he studied highway and pavement engineering at the University of Alberta in Edmonton, before Abdulhai was lured to get his Ph.D. in California. He was fervently recruited by the University of Toronto, which decided Canada needed his expertise to become a world leader in the field. "U. of T. must compete internationally," says Barry Adams, who heads the university's civil engineering department. "Our objective is to bring the best worldwide to U. of T."

Canada has long attracted the best and the brightest from around the world to staff its universities, build its industries and enhance its quality of life. But the need for that talent is acute and growing fast. The country is about to reach the climax of the most important demographic event since World War II. The mammoth baby-boom generation, roughly one-third of the population, is starting to approach retirement age. Many boomers are reducing their hours or giving up high-powered positions. Others are planning to drop out altogether once their financial future is secured by pensions or investments. Statistics Canada confirms that the average retirement age has already declined, from 62.3 in 1996 to 60.7 in 1999. "Boomers will be exiting their jobs in big numbers in the next five years," says Deborah Sunter, StatsCan's director of labor statistics. The full effect will crest in 15 to 20 years, when the peak of the boomer wave hits its 60s.

What does that mean? Among other things, that people like Baher Abdulhai will be more important than ever. In a normal cycle of population aging, the next generation of native-born Canadians would take up the slack as the boomers fade away. But the native-born generation is nowhere near big enough. The natural rate of population growth in Canada, without immigration, is less than half a percentage point a year, and falls to almost zero in some provinces, says Ernie Stokes, a former federal Finance Ministry economist who heads an Oakville, Ont., consultancy. At current rates, population growth would actually start declining in 2008 to 2010 without immigrants.

As a result, a worker shortage is developing that can only get worse without new recruits from abroad. And in highly mobile professional areas where the new, knowledge-based economy is centered, the so-called brain drain of Canadian talent to the U.S. is making matters worse. Mahmood Iqbal, chief research economist of the Conference Board of Canada, says that in the welter of conflicting statistics on the brain drain, there's one important number: for every seven Canadian professionals going to the U.S., only one American comes to Canada. "That's a huge drain that could affect our living standard," says Iqbal, an immigrant from Bangladesh.

That's why attracting highly skilled immigrants to Canada—and keeping them—is perhaps the country's greatest challenge. New Canadians are crucial to the country's future, and they are shaping it in increasing numbers. Newcomers make up 20% of the general work force, a proportion that will probably increase when StatsCan completes its five-year census this year. From 1991 to 1996 the immigrant population increased 15.5%, a rate three times that of the Canadian-born. Federal Human Resources Minister Jane Stewart puts the situation into stark perspective: "Seventy percent of the additions to our labor force in the past few years have come from immigration."

The future is people like Nirmala Naidoo-Hill, an anchor for Global News in Calgary. The ethnic Indian, born in Durban, South Africa, came to Canada at age two when her parents were recruited to teach in High Prairie, Alta. She earned a journalism degree at Carleton University, then freelanced for NSC in London during the Gulf War. She met her husband in Britain before moving back to Canada and settling in Calgary. "I'm so proud to be Canadian," she says, "but I know there's a whole other world out there. It comes of being from an immigrant family. You don't put any limits on where you can go or how high you can go."

Tens of thousands, even hundreds of thousands, of people like Naidoo-Hill are going to be badly needed in the years ahead. Canada's recent spurt of economic growth has created a dearth of skilled workers in high technology, medical sciences, nursing, teaching and computer programming. A survey by the Canadian Federation of Independent Business put the national shortage of such people between 250,000 and 300,000 in small and medium-size businesses alone. The Association of Universities and Colleges in Canada predicts that Canadian universities will need to hire about 30,000 faculty members over the next 10 years, but the country is producing about 4,000

Ph.D.s a year, of whom only a fraction will seek university positions. ("We figure that between 2000 and 2006, about 30% of our faculty will be retiring," says University of British Columbia commerce professor Michael Goldberg.) The Canadian Federation of Nurses Unions expects that by 2011, Canada will be lacking well over 100,000 nurses. The Canadian Medical Association says that the country has a short-fall of 500 doctors each year. If the situation doesn't change, the Conference Board of Canada foresees a national shortage of 1 million skilled workers by 2020.

Only in the past few years have governments responded. The federal government, for example, has offered up to $2 billion to the Canada Foundation for Innovation to allocate over the next decade, and $600 million to the Canada Research Chairs Program to be spent be between 2000 and 2005. In broader terms, the Liberal government has been promising since 1993 to push annual immigration rates to 1% of the Canadian population, or about 300,000 people annually. Yet the number still remains stuck at around 225,000. That's not enough, says Stokes, who argues that immigration should be quickly ratcheted to 300,000 a year, and then to 500,000 by 2015.

Some provinces need help already. Manitoba, which has a low unemployment rate and birthrate, is desperate to attract immigrants. The province is short of workers ranging from welders, machinists and machine-tool operators to registered nurses, computer program-mers and accountants. If it can't attract more newcomers soon, University of Manitoba economist Norm Cameron sees the province heading into crisis. "Businesses are choosing to go to Vancouver, to Calgary, and it's not because there's cheap labor, but simply because labor is available," he says. Nervous at the prospect, the provincial gov-ernment has launched recruitment programs via advertising and web-sites. Winnipeg Mayor Glen Murray sees the situation as a microcosm for the whole country. "Without immigration, Canada is in trouble," Murray says. "I think the economy would stall very quickly if we don't get the immigration levels of 40, 50 years ago."

Back in those days, relatively unskilled manual and agricultural labor was enough to fill the job gap. The situation is much more com-plicated now. Without specialists like Thomas Ducillier, 31, a French born photonics engineer, companies like Ottawa's JDS Uniphase, the world's largest maker of fiber-optic components, would never have been able to expand to world-beating status in the 1990s. Ducillier was working for the French IT giant Alcatel when he decided to move to

Canada and joined JDS. He couldn't be happier. Says he: "Here, things are yet to be done."

Ducillier had no trouble qualifying to enter Canada. But for many, getting into the country and finding a job in their field of expertise has not been so easy. In 1996, the last year for which detailed statistics are available, recent immigrants were significantly less likely to be employed in their chosen professions than people born in Canada. Colombia-born Alejandro Jadad, 37, endured a marathon of struggle before emerging as one of his adopted country's foremost experts in the field of pain relief. Jadad won a fellowship to Oxford University, where he did research on his specialty, practiced as a physician and completed a Ph.D. in informatics. He came to Canada in 1995 to do postdoctoral work at McMaster University and then at U. of T. Even then it took him three years to get a Canadian medical license—and only by becoming a full professor at McMaster first.

Halifax-based land developer George Armoyan faced the same uphill struggle when he first started out in business two decades ago. A Syrian-born Armenian, Armoyan moved to Canada in 1977 as a teenager and started what he admits was a "very aggressive" push into real estate when he was in his early 20s. Says Armoyan, 40: "I am still not accepted by a lot of people in Halifax." Nowadays his companies own residential and commercial properties throughout the Maritimes, Quebec, Ontario, Alberta and British Columbia, as well as Maine, and employ 550 people.

It takes up to 10 years for the average immigrant to become fully integrated into the labor force. The more highly educated the newcomer, the longer it may take to find appropriate employment. But once established, highly educated immigrants tend to stay employed and often have more energy and entrepreneurial spirit than their native-born counterparts. Immigration Minister Elinor Caplan calls it "that old bootstrapping, hard-work, give-me-a-chance ethic that built this country." And these days, the expertise, knowledge of languages and networking abilities that immigrants bring add even more to their value in an export-driven economy. "That is a huge competitive advantage for a trading nation like Canada," Caplan says.

Suromitra Sanatani, 36, is part of that advantage. The Vancouver-based vice president of the Canadian Federation of Independent Business is one of the most thoughtful and articulate voices for business in the West, advocating tax relief and propounding ways for businesses to cut through red tape. Born to well-educated Bengali parents in Bonn, Sanatani lived in Germany, India and the U.S. before moving to Canada—all before she was 16. She can speak better English, French and German than Bengali. But, she says, "I'm very aware of where I come from. I have a responsibility to continue that tradition. The emphasis is on making a contribution or succeeding in a profession."

Once adventuresome immigrants have arrived, Canada must persuade them to stay put. Areas like Atlantic Canada have long seen their native-born population move to richer parts of the country; now immigrant populations are on the same trail. The region accounts for about 8% of the total Canadian population, yet attracted less than 2% of the country's immigrants in 1998. "And that only indicates where they arrived, not where they intended to settle permanently," says Nabiha Atallah, program manager of the Metropolitan Immigrant Settlement Association in Halifax. "Secondary migration is a serious problem."

The problem is likely to get worse. These days, a boomtown like Calgary is not only competing against Edmonton and Vancouver for skills and talent, but it increasingly has to fight against the lure of such places as Dallas, Geneva or Tokyo in the straggle to retain a competitive edge. James Frideres, an associate vice president at the University of Calgary, says Alberta's universities are reasonably competitive in medicine, thanks to long-standing programs that provide grants and awards for medical research and equipment. A $330 million program for engineering and science will kick in this year. The province has created other funding agencies to support resources and teaching in the area of information, communication and technology. But Alberta universities have been less competitive in other areas, Frideres says, where they are having trouble matching the salaries and research funds that Ph.D.s are demanding and getting elsewhere. The University of Calgary ranks 3rd among Canadian universities for salaries. Poaching from the U.S., other institutions in Canada and the private sector, says U.B.C.'s Goldberg, is rampant. ("The low Canadian dollar and Canadian taxes don't help," he adds.)

But while much of the debate about brain drains and knowledge deficits focuses on areas of advanced education, other kinds of drive and talent are also required to keep Canada prosperous. Consider Zhu Hui, 32, who came to Canada with his young family from Beijing in October 1997. After 10 years of baking croissants and pastries in five-star hotels in the booming but still repressive Chinese capital, Zhu feels honored to be frying burgers and egg rolls at the Diplomat

Restaurant in Fredericton, N.B. The flip side of having so many young people getting sucked into the knowledge-based economy is that service-sector employers are finding it difficult to keep skilled staff. That's why Zhu was able to fit into one of Immigration Canada's 1,800 job categories—which range from accordion repairman to high-tech worker. Still, it took Zhu two years to wend his way through the Canadian immigration process. For a long time, he thought he would never make it. When he finally did arrive in Fredericton after a 30-hr. journey, Zhu was so excited he went straight to the Diplomat and insisted that he start his new job that very afternoon. His great hope is to send his two young daughters, Judy and Juliet, to a Canadian university.

Will there be anyone to teach them when they hit campus in 15 years or so, just as the boomer bulge finally goes bust? Immigration Minister Caplan is confident there will be. "Immigration built this country," she says, "and there are still a lot of smart, talented people who want to come here to keep building it." They will be needed more than ever.

Clarifications

Brain drain: The *American Heritage Dictionary*, found on-line at the Bartleby.com Web site, describes brain drain as "The loss of skilled intellectual and technical labor through the movement of such labor to more favorable geographic, economic, or professional environments."

Talking Points

Take a poll of the students in the class. How many are first-generation Canadians? How many were born in other countries?

What were your parents' or grandparents' job experiences, if they were immigrants? Did they come to Canada to seek a better life for their children, knowing that they themselves would have to work harder and be less successful than they might have been at home, possibly because of language difficulties? Would you be willing to make the same sacrifice for your children?

Web Research

The Conference Board of Canada Web site has an area devoted to Knowledge and Innovation at *www.conferenceboard.ca/inn.*

The Department of Finance has a Social Issues area that includes actuarial reports and information on unemployment trends.

Writing That Works

Question and answer: "What does that mean? Among other things, that people like Baher Abdulhai will be more important than ever."

Expert opinion: "Mahmood Iqbal, chief research economist of the Conference Board of Canada, says that in the welter of conflicting statistics on the brain drain, there's one important number: for every seven Canadian professionals going to the U.S., only one American comes to Canada. 'That's a huge drain that could affect our living standard,' says Iqbal, an immigrant from Bangladesh."

Statistics and studies: "Statistics Canada confirms that the average retirement age has already declined, from 62.3 in 1996 to 60.7 in 1999."

Skills That Go to Waste

by Ruth Abramson, Melanie Collison, Laura Eggertson, Kim Guttormson and Leigh Anne Williams

Time Canada, May 7, 2001

Daljit Singh spent five years working as a doctor in his native Punjab state in northern India before he emigrated to Winnipeg in 1990. Now he is one of about 100 foreign-trained doctors in Manitoba who can't get into the profession—even though there's a crying shortage of rural physicians. Instead, Singh juggles two part-time jobs as a home-care attendant and a telemarketer hawking credit-card applications. "I'm just wasting my skills," Singh says. "My life has been shattered."

Singh's skills are impressive even by the high standards Canada uses to judge them. He passed the Medical Council of Canada

Evaluating Exam, which tests basic knowledge of medicine and Canada's health system, as well as English proficiency tests and a medical qualifying exam that all graduates of Canadian medical schools must take. He also passed the U.S. equivalent of the test. Even so, Manitoba regulators don't view the training he got in India as equal to the training provided doctors in Canada—or in the U.S., Britain and South Africa. (Manitoba Health Minister Dave Chomiak says part of the problem is that some rules were made by the federal government and the province has to abide by them.) Singh calls that discrimination, and has taken his ease to the Manitoba Human Rights Commission, which has referred it to mediation.

Singh's plight represents one of the striking paradoxes of Canada's love affair with immigrants: it can be fickle. Even as the nation's actuarial tables point to an urgent demand for skilled people from abroad, regulations governing professional bodies and other barriers can force talented newcomers into lower-paid, lower-skilled occupations, leaving the nation still in need of skilled help.

Consider the case of Hsi Hsiao Tung, a nurse with expertise in anesthesiology. She and her family of four emigrated from Taiehung, Taiwan, to Victoria, B.C., in 1999, partly for the lifestyle and partly because British Columbia has a nursing shortage (100 in the capital region; 1,000 province-wide). The shortage is going to get much worse. The Registered Nurses Association of B.C. expects that half of the 9,800 nurses in the province will start to retire in the next few years, leaving a minimum shortfall of 4,000 nurses within a half decade.

Even though Tung has 20 years of nursing experience and good proficiency in English, she has yet to land a job in her field. She can't take her B.C. nursing-certification exam until she receives a top grade in the university-entrance English exam, which she says the Canadian embassy in Taiwan neglected to tell her about. "I had many friends who went to America to be nurses," Tung says, "and they got jobs within a couple of months of their arrival." Her husband, an experienced high school teacher, is also having trouble getting work. Meanwhile their life savings are dwindling.

Carlos Gaete, head of Victoria's Immigrant and Refugee Centre Society, sees a dramatic mismatch. Only about 15% of the professionals who have passed through his office recently have landed jobs in their field of expertise. "Professionals with years and years of experience are not able to use their skills here," Gaete says. "Immigrants lose, and Canada as a country loses too." Indeed, 1 in 5 new Canadians is unemployed, reports the federal Human Resources Department, even though 3 in 5 have a university-level education. And more than 1 in 5 is underemployed or working in a job below his or her qualifications. University of Toronto professor Jeffrey Reitz, currently a visiting professor at Harvard, says Canada is underachieving when it comes to integrating new immigrants. He estimates $36 billion as the annual cost of underutilizing and underpaying immigrants.

Why the waste? Part of it is the "normal" immigrant experience. Newcomers lack a network of contacts and are slowed in their job search because of unfamiliarity with local customs and procedures. Others are tripped up by more or less subtle forms of discrimination. Many often make short-term sacrifices by taking jobs that fall below their qualifications, according to Jane Badets, chief of immigration research at Statistics Canada.

But there are other reasons too. The world may be getting smaller, but Canadian employers and professional regulators still find it difficult to evaluate foreign credentials, especially those from developing countries. Another career killer for immigrants is red tape and bureaucratic misinformation. Yet another difficulty is that shortages can develop in a field that was once overcrowded, but the government may be slow to acknowledge that fact.

At least some of the irrationality is about to change. Under new federal regulations being mooted in Bill C-11, the Immigration and Refugee Protection Act, Canada will no longer focus on an immigration applicant's experience in a particular trade, because such classifications quickly become out of date. Instead, immigrants will be given points for "human capital," focusing on flexible skills and talents, including education, work experience and adaptability.

Canada has to compete more vigorously for highly skilled, educated immigrants, says Immigration Minister Elinor Caplan, "because the rest of the world is competing with us." Martin Spigelman, a social-policy consultant and immigration specialist, puts it more bluntly. "Immigrants have more skills, resources—and choices—than ever before," he says. "So it's not just a matter of Canada saying 'O.K., come.' If we want them to fill the voids, we have to begin welcoming them more openly."

Ottawa is working with provincial governments and professional organizations like the College of Physicians and Surgeons and various engineering associations to try to remove barriers to labor mobility by

July of this year. Ontario has set up its own initiative to help immigrants get credentials evaluated against Canadian equivalents. The College of Nurses of Ontario and other groups are forming CARE, (Creating Access to Regulated Employment), to be launched in September, which will help foreign-trained nurses prepare for licensing exams and find work in the province. And Manitoba last week announced a new program to assist foreign-trained doctors get their licenses to practice in the province within five years. It will send 10 candidates annually to work in rural areas with a conditional license.

Clarifications

Actuarial tables: Statistical tables used in the insurance industry that predict, for example, death rates demographically. In other words, they show when someone of a certain age is likely to die.

Mooted: Brought up a subject for discussion. *Moot* is a legal term meaning *hypothetical.* Law students argue cases at a "moot court," or practice court.

Talking Points

Read John Ibbitson's article "The Lonely Planet" (page 363) to see what he has to say about the future of population growth (or lack of it), and discuss the future of Canada and our need for immigrants. What changes do you think need to be made? Should we be encouraging more immigration? What other options do we have, apart from importing skilled immigrants? How about allowing students who come here to study to stay? Currently, these students must return to their home countries once they graduate.

Web Research

View the Immigration and Refugee Protection Act on the Citizenship and Immigration Canada Web site at *www.cic.gc.ca.*

Statistics Canada's Web site has population information at *www.statcan.ca/english/edu/theme.htm.*

Writing That Works

Introduction—examples: The example of the trained doctor who is unable to work in spite of a shortage of doctors makes for a strong introduction. His comment, "I'm just wasting my skills," is adapted to an effective title for the article.

Examples: "Consider the case of Hsi Hsiao Tung, a nurse with expertise in anaesthesiology. She and her family of four emigrated from Taiehung, Taiwan, to Victoria, B.C., in 1999, partly for the lifestyle and partly because British Columbia has a nursing shortage…"

Expert opinion: "University of Toronto professor Jeffrey Reitz, currently a visiting professor at Harvard, says Canada is underachieving when it comes to integrating new immigrants. He estimates $36 billion as the annual cost of underutilizing and underpaying immigrants."

Expert opinion: "Carlos Gaete, head of Victoria's Immigrant and Refugee Centre Society, sees a dramatic mismatch. Only about 15% of the professionals who have passed through his office recently have landed jobs in their field of expertise. 'Professionals with years and years of experience are not able to use their skills here,' Gaete says."

Question and answer: "Why the waste? Part of it is the 'normal' immigrant experience."

Welcome to Canada, Please Buy Something
by Showwei Chu

Canadian Business, May 29, 1998

It was Chinese New Year, and the Pacific National Exhibition fairgrounds in Vancouver were alive with celebration. In one building, throngs of visitors—mainly from the city's Asian community—stopped to sample specialties such as deep-fried dumplings and sweet lotus; in another, local businesses were promoting their wares. But probably one of the most popular venues in the entire site was a small stand in the Forum building, where a team of Chinese-speaking servers were busy handing out complimentary cups of Tropicana orange juice. The booth was such a magnet, in fact, that the servers quickly became overextended. "They were pouring like mad and their arms were so tired," recalls Diana Tang, account director at Hamazaki-Wong Marketing Group, the Vancouver firm that was hired by Tropicana Canada to run its Chinese marketing campaign.

That endless pouring was well worth it. By the end of the fair, Tropicana Canada had dispensed some 50,000 cups of orange juice and 30,000 redeemable coupons. The redemption rate was 40%—more than twice the average. " It's been a tremendous success for the company," says Andrea Graham, Tropicana Canada's senior product manager.

Two years later, Tropicana Canada is still reaping the benefits of its Asian campaign. Sales in Chinese supermarkets, such as those operated by China Can Enterprises Ltd, in Vancouver, have vastly improved; and Tropicana Canada has increased its revenue from all sources to $200 million from $88 million in 1995.

None of this came by chance. Long before Tropicana Canada set up its stand at the fair, it had researched its target market very carefully. It knew that its product would probably go over well with the Chinese—for one thing, oranges are considered harbingers of good luck in that culture. It knew, too, that by introducing its product during an event such as Chinese New Year, it would have immediate access to thousands of potential customers. Following the advice of Hamazaki-Wong, it also gave in-store demonstrations in Vancouver and Toronto, and ran print, radio and TV ads in Chinese media.

Tropicana Canada is not the only company that is catering to the Chinese market. Over the past few years, banks, car manufacturers, realtors and airlines have finally stood up and noticed what demographics have been telling them for much longer—namely, that the highly affluent immigrant Chinese population represents a huge market opportunity, just waiting to be tapped.

According to the 1996 census, there were approximately 900,000 Chinese living in this country. "This may not seem very large relative to the overall population," says Sonny Wong, president of Hamazaki-Wong. "But what's significant is how quickly this ethnic group has grown over the past five to seven years because of immigration."

Even more significant, perhaps, is the rate at which the population is still growing. The most recently available figures show that more than 50,000 Chinese immigrate to Canada every year. This makes the Chinese population the country's largest and fastest-growing ethnic group.

Naturally, immigrants from Taiwan, China and Hong Kong all have their own unique historical backgrounds, cultures, traditions, and languages or dialects, which they try to maintain in Canada. Depending on where they are from, their command of English also varies. But one trait they do share—and one that makes them highly attractive for marketers—is their relative affluence. According to a survey commissioned last year by CFMT International, a Toronto-based multi-cultural broadcaster, Chinese households in Toronto alone have $5.2 billion to spend annually. Another survey shows that three in four recent Chinese immigrants buy cars with cash, almost half own homes, and more than half own a personal computer. "They're into signs and symbols of wealth," says Wong. "Asians are conspicuous consumers."

Apart from their purchasing power, Chinese immigrants also share the distinction of being concentrated mainly in Toronto and Vancouver—which simplifies the task of running an ad campaign. Moreover, these immigrants tend to be highly mobile: some return to their country of origin for several months each year. Maintaining a cohesive family unit is very important to them, as is education and providing for the future. Many people from Hong Kong may even leave well-paid jobs to give their children better educational opportunities. "It's a way to move up," says Bobby Siu, a consultant with Toronto-based Infoworth Consulting Inc.

Because of their interest in education and future prosperity, Chinese Canadians tend to be great savers. Indeed, it has been estimated that the average Asian has a savings account that is twice the size of the average Canadian's. (It's worth noting, too, that anyone who wants to come to Canada as an entrepreneur immigrant must have a net worth of at least $350,000.)

The Chinese propensity for setting money aside has certainly not been lost on Trimark Investment Management Inc. In 1995, it launched a national program designed to educate the Asian community about mutual funds. "At the time, Chinese Canadians were pretty conservative investors," says John Yuen, vice-president of sales, who set up the program. "Most put money in bank deposits and Canada Savings Bonds." To help convince them to try other options, Trimark offered seminars in Mandarin and Cantonese in major cities, and advertised its investment philosophy in Chinese media, including TV. It also offered a free hotline and hired Chinese-speaking representatives for its offices in Vancouver and Toronto.

Today, there is no doubt in Yuen's mind that the program achieved its goal—and more. "In the past three years, the fastest-growing segment within the mutual-fund industry has been the Asian service segment," he says. Moreover, almost all the major Canadian mutual-fund companies have followed Trimark's example by instituting similar campaigns. As a result, the growth rate in assets among the Chinese community is almost double that of the market in general, Yuen says.

The influx of Chinese Canadians to Vancouver in the early '90s helped boost BC's economy and is even credited for Vancouver's property boom. One developer, Concord Pacific Group Inc., is building a $3-billion waterfront condo project on the former Expo 86 site that will hold between 8,000 and 9,000 suites. In designing the suites, it took certain Asian requirements into consideration. According to Jimmy Hung, vice-president of marketing and sales at Concord Pacific, even the 1,200-square-foot models have two bedrooms, plus a den, because Chinese families tend to stay together longer. The development will also feature 24-hour security so that they can "lock up and go." So far, Concord Pacific has sold more than 2,000 suites; 60% were bought by Asians.

One carmaker that has shown a great deal of ingenuity in its efforts to appeal to the Chinese market is Volkswagen Canada Inc. Three years ago, when it started researching that market, it came to a very simple realization: people from Hong Kong don't know what it's like to drive in snowy conditions. So it decided to offer driving clinics in Vancouver and Toronto, where it had Chinese-speaking drivers teach potential customers how to maneuver in bad conditions. It also employed an ethnic hook in its advertisements. In one print ad, it used three red eggs to represent VW and the other two members of the Volkswagen family—Audi and Porsche. Traditionally, red eggs symbolize birth. When a baby is born, a red egg is rubbed on its forehead to bring it good luck. According to Ron Lee, VW's district manager for sales in BC, the use of cultural elements in ads helped increase Volkswagen sales to Chinese consumers by 25% in Vancouver and 20% in Toronto.

In the final analysis, there is no great mystery behind the success experienced by Volkswagen, Tropicana Canada and others. Rather than pitch their product blindly to a group they didn't know, they set out to understand the values that shape the culture, as well as the habits that sustain it. Now that the initial groundwork has been laid, they can continue to build on that base. They might even find that, with the experience and knowledge they have gained, catering to other national or ethnic communities is a cinch.

Clarifications

Ingenuity: Creativity, inventiveness.

Cinch: Something that's easy to accomplish. The word comes from *cincha,* a Spanish word meaning *belt,* and has reached its current meaning from the act of cinching something tight. The bridge between the two meanings is the sense of having a tight grip or control on something.

Talking Points

Think of a typically Canadian product and create a marketing campaign aimed at different cultural groups. For example, try selling snow tires to recent British immigrants, or snow blowers to people from the Caribbean.

About.com has an article on the symbolism of Chinese food at *http://chinesefood.about.com/library/weekly/aa122199.htm.* Read the article and use it to create an advertisement for baked ham or brown beans.

Tear out ads from a magazine and try selling the product in group presentations to specific cultural groups. You may need to talk to class members from other cultures to discover what characteristics of the product you need to address.

Web Research

For an especially interesting part of Chinese Canadian history, read about the tunnels of Moose Jaw at *www.tunnelsofmoosejaw.com.*

The CBC Web site has extensive information on Chinese immigration to Canada at *www.cbc.ca/news/indepth/chinese/migrants1.html.*

Writing That Works

Introduction—anecdote: The Tropicana story is an example of marketing focused on a specific group. The anecdote at the beginning is a specific example of how focused marketing worked with that group.

Surveys and statistics: "According to a survey commissioned last year by CFMT International, a Toronto-based multi-cultural broadcaster, Chinese households in Toronto alone have $5.2 billion to spend annually."

Examples: "One carmaker that has shown a great deal of ingenuity in its efforts to appeal to the Chinese market is Volkswagen Canada Inc."

Conclusion—prediction: "They might even find that, with the experience and knowledge they have gained, catering to other national or ethnic communities is a cinch."

Building a Business Case for Diversity

by Christine Taylor

Canadian Business Review, March 22, 1995

Forward-thinking Canadian organizations have recognized that competing successfully in the new global marketplace requires more than the latest technology, most efficient production processes, or most innovative products. Canadian organizations' competitive strength is increasingly contingent on human resources. Competing to win in the global economy will require an ability to attract, retain, motivate and develop high-potential employees of both genders from a variety of cultural and ethnic backgrounds. The challenge facing today's corporate leaders is to foster an organizational culture that values differences and maximizes the potential of all employees. In other words, leaders must learn to manage diversity.

Canadian companies leading the way in the area of diversity management have discovered that by embracing the elements of ethnic and cultural diversity in their workforce they have enhanced their ability to understand and tap new markets, both within Canada and abroad. One in four senior executives responding to the Conference Board's benchmarking survey of the diversity management practices of over 150 Canadian companies views the increasing diversity of the workforce as "a competitive opportunity." These senior executives feel that workforce diversity is something their organizations can capitalize on to enhance their competitiveness.

These leaders have recognized that the cultural competencies needed to operate more effectively in today's global market exist within Canada's communities and labour force. They understand that, by working to create an organizational culture where valuing diversity is part of the way their company conducts its day-to-day business, they can develop a sustainable source of competitive advantage.

CANADA'S CHANGING MOSAIC

As a result of changing immigration patterns, major changes in the ethno-cultural composition of Canada have taken place over the past 20 years. Several key census statistics indicate this trend:

- Between 1986 and 1991, the proportion of the population reporting ethnic origins other than British/French/Canadian increased by 20 per cent.
- Over this same five-year period, the number of people reporting a mother tongue other than English or French grew by 17 per cent.

Nowhere in Canada has the impact of this change been more obvious than in the major urban centres, where many ethnic communities have grown to the size of towns or small cities.

- The population of Toronto's Chinese community is estimated to be over 350,000.
- Over 30 per cent of Chinese Canadians now live in greater Vancouver.
- Between 1986 and 1991, Montreal's Haitian community grew by 155 per cent.

Current statistics along with projections for the next decade indicate that ethnic segments of the population will continue to experience rapid growth rates. By 2006, when Canada is expected to have a total population of 30.6 million, the total population of visible minorities will be 5.6 million.

Canadian organizations undertaking diversity management recognize that, as they restructure to improve their ability to respond to the rapidly changing domestic and global marketplaces, their ability to tap the skills and insights of an increasingly multicultural and diverse workforce will play an integral role in their ability to compete successfully.

Until recently, increasing ethnocultural diversity in Canada has largely been viewed by mainstream Canadian organizations from the perspective of its impact on workforce demographics and its implications for human resource management. It has not been seen as a tool for tapping new markets or improving the effectiveness of international business. Increasingly, however, Canadian organizations are recognizing that valuing and managing diversity is a bottom-line issue. By linking diversity directly to other key business strategies and initiatives, particularly in the areas of marketing and international business, these organizations are improving their profitability and competitiveness.

THE BUSINESS CASE FOR DIVERSITY

Essentially, two key drivers underpin the business case for diversity in Canadian organizations—the globalization of world trade and the increasing ethnocultural diversity of Canadian markets.

Today, many customer-focused Canadian organizations recognize the need to incorporate the element of ethnocultural diversity into their marketing, sales and customer service strategies, and they are tapping the ethnocultural expertise in their workforce to gain access to lucrative "new" markets, both in Canada and abroad. Almost two thirds of respondents to the Conference Board's survey felt that their organization's senior management team had identified ethnocultural changes in its Canadian markets, and 71 per cent were considering ethnocultural diversity as an element in the development of their overall sales and marketing strategies. Over half of the respondents indicated they had taken advantage of Canada's ethnocultural diversity in developing new markets.

CREATING AN ENVIRONMENT FOR SUCCESS

The process of transforming an organizational culture into one with diversity as one of its core values is complex and lengthy. The most successful diversity initiatives will address attitude and behaviour change at the personal, interpersonal and organizational levels. Study participants repeatedly emphasized the need to proceed slowly—to understand that this is an evolutionary process. Moreover, there are limits to the scope of the changes that can, or should, be undertaken. These limits are imposed by the organization's mandate, its existing values and the availability of resources.

PUTTING PLANS INTO ACTION

Communicating the importance of managing diversity—both within the organization's workforce and, perhaps more importantly, within the community generally—has been a key to success for organizations engaged in the process. Of responding organizations with both internally and externally focused communication initiatives, 70 per cent indicated a "generally positive" employee attitude towards the diversity initiative. This compares with 54 per cent for those with only an internal communication component.

Training activities play an important role in incorporating diversity as a core organizational value. When diversity is integrated into core programs such as customer service, leadership training and development, employees become aware of the implications of dealing with diversity in the workplace, in the marketplace and in the community.

Using cross-functional teams to "drive" the diversity initiative brings together individuals from different parts of the organization who may be facing very different issues and challenges relating to diversity. Working together as members of a cross-functional team reinforces the employees' perception that diversity dynamics are an integral part of everyday life.

Several organizations interviewed for this project have also developed co-operative training initiatives with community-based organizations such as hospitals and ethnocultural community groups. This has proven to be both an economical and a highly effective practice.

THE LEADERSHIP IMPERATIVE

Leadership emerged in this study as the most critical variable in an organization's ability to successfully incorporate the value of diversity into its business strategy. Participants in the study stressed the need for a champion, in the form of a visionary leader, at the highest levels of the organization. This individual must be prepared to take a strong personal stand and willing to devote the time, energy and resources necessary to move the change initiative forward.

Diversity study participants also stressed that it is important to the overall success of the initiative that it not be perceived as a human resource program or policy. Rather, it should be seen as a business imperative. They indicated that, to ensure the buy-in of employees at all levels of the organization, the diversity initiative must be linked directly to the business objectives and goals of the most senior level of management. It is often necessary to show a causal link between managing diversity and the organization's profitability.

Findings from the survey further suggest that the majority of organizations currently undertaking diversity management initiatives have not clearly identified these as being linked directly to key business objectives, such as improved profitability. Diversity is still a human resource initiative in most surveyed organizations. In fact, 86 per cent of respondents stated that the individual with corporate responsibility for diversity reports directly to human resources management.

MONITORING PROGRESS, MEASURING RESULTS

Obviously, when undertaking any major change process, it is essential to monitor progress and provide quantitative and qualitative evidence of change. However, as many of the study participants acknowledged, quantifying the bottom-line benefits of a diversity initiative is very difficult, because the relationship between cause and effect is often unclear. Executives in pioneering organizations stressed that, while providing quantitative indicators of change is important, managers must achieve diversity objectives in the right way, by setting an example and creating an atmosphere that respects and values differences. Moreover, holding senior management and managers at other levels of the organization accountable for performance in relation to diversity is fundamental in establishing it as a core organizational value. Diversity pioneers insist that a failure to assess management's performance in relation to diversity goals will quickly become evident to all employees, because there will be no tangible evidence of change, and valuing diversity will not become an inherent part of conducting day-to-day business. Results of the survey show that among organizations with diversity management initiatives, just over half monitor or evaluate effectiveness.

LOOKING AHEAD

Today, many Canadian organizations are focused on simply ensuring their survival in the new global economy. Managing overall change is diverting both management's attention and the necessary resources away from the need to address the diversity issue, in effect, putting the issue on the back burner. However, a few Canadian organizations have recognized that there is a competitive advantage to be gained from embracing diversity within their business strategy. These pioneers have taken bold steps towards fostering an organizational culture that values differences. They are charting a new course for the future by responding to diversity as a business issue and developing individualized approaches that integrate it into their broader management objectives. Given the long-term nature of the cultural change required to transform an organization into one that truly values diversity, these firms may well develop a significant competitive edge in the future.

Web Research

This article is based on research done by the Conference Board of Canada on Effective Working Environments. The CBOC Web site is at *www2.conferenceboard.ca.*

Writing That Works

Introduction—thesis: This article begins with a clearer statement of the thesis than do most of the articles in this book: "The challenge facing today's corporate leaders is to foster an organizational culture that values differences and maximizes the potential of all employees. In other words, leaders must learn to manage diversity."

Structure—cause and effect: If companies manage diversity, then they will enhance "their ability to understand and tap new markets, both within Canada and abroad."

Studies and statistics: "One in four senior executives responding to the Conference Board's benchmarking survey of the diversity management practices of over 150 Canadian companies views the increasing diversity of the workforce as 'a competitive opportunity.' These senior executives feel that workforce diversity is something their organizations can capitalize on to enhance their competitiveness."

Conclusion: The final heading—"Looking Ahead"—shows that the type of conclusion used in this article is "pointing to the future."

TOPIC *8*

YOUNG CONSUMERS AND WORKERS

INTRODUCTION

The culture of youth probably started back in the nineteen-fifties, with the first generation of teenagers to be considered a generation, defined mostly by their music. By the sixties, the generation of post-war babies moved into their teen years and began to make their impact felt, not just as a generation but also as the defining demographic group of the times. The baby boom hippies of the sixties eventually turned into yuppies. No other generation has made itself felt as much as this one.

In 1991, in his book *Generation X,* Canadian writer Douglas Coupland defined the generation that came next: the one that had already been named the baby busters—the smaller group of children who followed the baby boomers. Coupland called them Generation X or slackers—people who had no real hope of getting jobs other than "McJobs," because of the size of the generation right before them. Without the ability to get long-term, permanent jobs, this generation saw the development of the temporary job, the consulting job, the sessional appointment at university.

Like all generations, however, Gen X has moved forward, and other generations have followed them, including Gen Y—the baby boom echo generation born in the late seventies and early eighties. Already, children born in the late eighties are starting to hit their teens and exert their influence on youth culture.

It's not year clear what the next generation of teenagers will be called. Patrick Brethour, in the first article in this chapter, calls them

Web Spawn. The slogan of the networking company Cisco is "Empowering the Internet Generation," but this is probably not referring to the same group. What is clear, however, is this generation's enormous purchasing power and its influence on popular entertainment. Like the generations before them, young people of today have a major say about what types of music are played, what types of movies are made, and what types of clothing are sold. What is different about them, however, is not the way that they spend their money, but the way they *don't* spend it. Communicating in chat rooms and on ICQ, downloading music, getting most of their information from the Internet, this group is destined to change the way we do business.

Web Spawn: The Keystroke Kids

by Patrick Brethour

The Globe and Mail, December 17, 2001

They have never known a world without personal computers at their fingertips. They were surfing the Internet before they'd lost all of their baby teeth. They are the first Web generation, young teenagers who use the global network as unconsciously as you or I would flip a light switch.

Teenagers have always lived in a different world: The existence of bobby socks, Mohawk haircuts and navel rings attests to that. But the gap between the Web generation and the rest of us runs much deeper than the usual teenage alternate reality. Unlike bobby socks, the Web's influence will endure, permanently changing the way that today's teens communicate with each other and how they act as full-fledged consumers.

Who makes up this virtual vanguard? Statistics Canada, in a study released last week, unearthed major differences in the on-line behaviour of 15- to 17-year-olds, even when compared to young adults just a few years older. (Canadians over 30 are beyond redemption, evidently.)

Those young teens see the Internet as part of the fabric of their everyday lives. It might be more accurate to say that they don't "see" the Internet at all—it's simply the way that they talk to their friends, research an essay or download a movie two weeks before it hits theatres.

They may not notice the Internet, but it is transforming their lives in a dramatic manner. The decades-old stereotype of teens tying up the telephone is going the way of the rotary dial, as the Web generation uses chat software to gossip after school, using a keyboard in their rapid-fire conversations.

According to Statscan, 71 per cent of 15- to 17-year-olds use on-line chat rooms, double the proportion of the only slightly older 20- to 24-year-olds.

I interviewed 17-year-old Kelly Andrews a few days ago, and asked her whether her chat-room conversations outnumbered those on the telephone. "I don't really talk to my friends on the phone," she said, in a kind tone reserved for those who ask innocuous but dumb questions.

Michael Antecol, a 33-year-old Forrester Research analyst who studies youth and technology, says most adults—himself included—view chat rooms as little more than a plaything. "I expect to get a phone call if it's important." That perceptual gap separates the Web generation and older Canadians, no matter how technologically adept the latter might become. It's akin to studying a second language as an adult: You may pick up the vocabulary, but you'll never be as fluent as the eight-year-old who learned it in daycare.

Cultural critics, not to mention parents, have fretted that the Internet isolates kids—an echo of the old maternal battle cry against television, "Why don't you go outside and play?"

In fact, the relationship of baby boomers to television has some parallels with the Web generation. Boomers grew up with TV, with their generation sharing experiences that their parents never would. Take the power of *Howdy Doody*, add on to that the instant communication of the telephone, and the ubiquitousness of the electrical system and you have an idea of the Internet's impact on today's teens.

Like any technology, the Internet is just a tool that can be used to good or ill effect. While virtual hermits are a theoretical possibility, the reality is that the Web generation uses chat rooms and e-mail to create an entirely new kind of communication, a fluid conversation that ebbs and flows as participants drop in and out.

The world of the chat room is anything but isolated. Much to the contrary: It is usually a flood of opinion, jokes, jabs that has more in common with coffee-house gabfests than anything else. According to Statscan, teens are cautious on-line, but nearly half of the Web generation has made a friend over the Internet.

"They're building a culture of access," says pollster Duncan McKie, head of Pollara Inc., who says the way teens use the Internet is dictated by their own lives, not the technology.

The same Statscan survey reports that on-line shopping is relatively rare among teens right now. That situation is as predictable as it is fleeting. Once they are able to tap their own credit cards, the members of the Web generation will turn e-commerce from a sideshow into a central part of the economy.

Already, the Web generation is making a name for itself in the e-tailing world. Forrester Research estimates that Canadians aged 13 to 22 will spend 13 per cent of their disposable income on the Internet this year, far higher than the overall share of e-commerce in retail sales.

Manufacturers are already launching products designed to capture the dollars of the Web generation—witness Apple Computer's launch of the iPod, a portable music player that can hold 1,000 songs downloaded from the Internet.

Telecommunications firms are also eyeing the opportunities that will emerge as Web teens mature. BCE head Jean Monty recently mused about how to boost revenue from "bandwidth hogs" of the Web generation, those who use the Internet for video, music and other capacity-hungry applications.

But the biggest change in the consumer behaviour of the Web generation from its predecessors won't be in the particular products that they buy on the Web. Instead, it will be in how they see e-commerce—or rather, don't see it at all. As with the Internet as a whole, the Web generation is going to view an e-tailing Web site as just another outlet for a retailer. If retailers mess up on-line, these consumers won't just shun their Web sites—they will walk away from them altogether.

For the Web generation, any distinction between a bricks-and-mortar store and its Web site will seem as bizarre as praising the peanut butter, but hating the jelly, in a sandwich. If you find that mindset puzzling, you are most certainly on the wrong side of the on-line generation gap, no matter whether you are 42 or 24.

Here's a quick quiz that will tell you which side of the divide you belong to: If you want to chat with a friend in another city, what do you do? If you think of picking up the telephone rather than a keyboard, welcome to fogeydom.

Clarifications

Web spawn: Spawn are the eggs of fish or frogs, but the word is also used to mean "give birth to." It is used in a derogatory way. The writer could also be making an oblique reference to the comic book character Spawn, created by Canadian artist Todd McFarlane (see *www. spawn.com*). If this is true, it is probably an attempt by the author not to sound like an old fogey. Is he successful?

Fogeydom: A made-up word meaning the state of being an old fogey—that is, a person with old-fashioned or outdated ideas.

Generation gap: The distance between what one generation and the next believe. Usually the expression refers to a lack of understanding between parents and children.

Chat room: These are places on the Internet where people can chat in real time by typing in messages. There are two types of chat room— Web pages and IRC channels. The writer appears to be referring to the Web page type of chat, although many of the "Web spawn" generation he writes about actually use IRC channels such as ICQ, which in some ways is like a telephone, in that a user can page another user. ICQ chats are more likely to be one-on-one.

Bricks-and-mortar store: A store that actually exists in the "real world," as opposed to a store that exists only on the Web—or one that exists both in bricks and in cyberspace, which is called a "clicks-and-mortar" store.

Bandwidth hogs: Could refer either to a large file that takes a lot of time to download, such as a graphic or music file, or a person who downloads such files. Some Internet providers have recently decided to charge a higher fee to "bandwidth hogs."

Talking Points

The writer makes the point that some people believe the Internet isolates kids. For those of you who spend at least two hours a day on the Internet, would you agree or disagree with this observation?

Ask your parents about the influence of TV on their youth. How much time did they spend watching television? Do they still spend more time watching television than they do on the Internet? How do they use the Internet? For what purpose?

How many students in your class have used chat rooms? How does the class statistic compare with the country as a whole? How many in the class download music from the Internet, and how has it affected the number of CDs that you buy?

What e-commerce sites do you know about and use? EBay? Stock sites? Booksellers? Compare e-commerce sites. What strategies do they use to aim at a particular age group?

Web Research

Forrester Research ("Helping Business Thrive on Technology Change") is found at *www.forrester.com*.

Pollara Inc. (*www.pollara.ca*) is the largest Canadian-owned public opinion and marketing research firm. It aims to help its clients "improve their performance through strategic research designed and analyzed by consultants who are experts in their fields."

To research Internet technology, go to Net Lingo at *www.netlingo.com*.

Writing That Works

Lists: "The existence of bobby socks, Mohawk haircuts and navel rings attests to that"; "A flood of opinions, jokes, jabs, that has more in common with coffee-house gabfests than anything else"; "Take the power of *Howdy Doody*, add on to that the instant communication of the telephone, and the ubiquitousness of the electrical system and you have an idea of the Internet's impact on today's teens."

Statistics: "According to Statscan, 71 per cent of 15- to 17-year-olds use on-line chat rooms, double the percentage of the only slightly older 20- to 24-year-olds."

Comparison: The writer compares the Web generation with the boomers who, unlike their parents, grew up with TV.

Analogy: "It's akin to studying a second language as an adult: You may pick up the vocabulary, but you'll never be as fluent as the eight-year-old who learned it in daycare."

Introduction—definition: "They have never known a world without personal computers at their fingertips…."

How Teens Got the Power

by Andrew Clark with Shanda Deziel, Susan McClelland and Susan Oh

Maclean's, March 22, 1999

A dozen teens sit in a fashionable Toronto office loft taking part in a focus group organized by Youth Culture Inc., a company that tracks trends. YCI's creative director Gary Butler and Sean Saraq, a demographer with Environics Research Group, want to know what exactly prompts kids to spend their money on CDs, movies, video games and fashion. Their responses? Annie Grainger, 16, says she is wary of commercials and marketing, yet spends $50 a pop for body-piercing. Eighteen-year-old Mike Landon proudly wears hip-hop clothes with the Phat Farm label and says: "Show me a commercial that says 50-per-cent off—that's a good commercial to me." Chi Nguyen, 18, says she would "like a world that didn't respond to advertising." So much for gaining insight into the mind-set of the "average" teen. The message: there is no such thing as an average teen. "The deeper people dig," says the 34-year-old Saraq, "the more they realize that teens are all over the map."

Why do companies want to pin kids down? Call it a Youthquake. Call it Teen Power. Whatever, for the first time since the baby boom, kid culture is king. Teens have more money in their pockets than ever before, and their influence is everywhere—in music stores with CDs by bands ranging from The Moffatts and Britney Spears to Korn and The Offspring; in clothing stores with labels such as JNCO and Snug; on TV with programs such as *Dawson's Creek* and *Felicity*; and in movies such as *Cruel Intentions* and *Varsity Blues*. MuchMusic's teen audience has grown 80 per cent since 1996. "It's all about pop culture," says Grainger, an eleventh-grader from Toronto. "And pop culture is all about buying."

Fact: never before has so much been pitched to so many who are so young. Advertisers are pursuing kids on TV, in print and even in schools. Their quarry comprise the so-called Echo or Y Generation (born between 1980 and 1995), the largest demographic in Canada next to their baby boomer parents (those born between 1947 and

1966). University of Toronto economics professor David Foot, author of the best-selling *Boom, Bust & Echo 2000,* says the Echo Generation is a nationwide phenomenon with its highest concentrations in Ontario and the West. Statistics Canada predicts that by July, there will be 4.1 million Canadians between 10 and 19 years of age. By the year 2004, that number will swell to 4.4 million. And don't doubt their clout: last year, nine- to 19-year-olds spent an astonishing $13.5 billion in Canada. "That number is going to do nothing but go up," says Lindsay Meredith, a professor of marketing at Simon Fraser University in Burnaby, B.C. "This is the gold rush."

Not that kids are doing nothing but shopping: more teens than ever are volunteering in hospitals and community centres; they are upbeat, socially aware and confident in their ability to make a difference. Nor are all teens part of the buying boom; many, obviously, don't have the means. But there is no doubting kids' overall economic power, and they are wielding it across the country, through TV and the Internet—a generation eminently connected to its shared (if diverse) culture. Rebecca Bruser lives in Yellowknife, thousands of kilometres from the fashion centres, but still keeps current: the 17-year-old Grade 12 student buys much of her wardrobe from Delia's (at about $200 per order), a New York-based online clothing catalogue. "It's better to have something no one else has," she says. "It shows you're an individual rather than just having the Gap." Her baby boomer mother, Deborah Bruser, is puzzled by Rebecca's spending. "In the '60s, I had little odd lusts, like wanting a mohair sweater, but it wasn't this ongoing 'I've-got-to-have-it' like I see today."

In North Vancouver, Maseioud Khandashti, 16, earns $300 a month working as a mechanic in the family automotive shop, and he rushes out to buy the latest hip-hop CD. "I just have to be there when it is released." When 16-year-old Vatice Wright shops in her home town of Halifax, her purchases "have to be a brand name, a label. It's just my taste." Her cousin, Shawn Wright, 16, spends his money on food, music and clothes, but "not brand names—I don't care what people think."

Advertisers and marketers divide the demographic into two distinct groups—nine- to 14-year-old "tweens" and 15- to 19-year-old teens. In Canada, there are 2.4 million tweens with $1.5 billion to spend, according to a Creative Research International Inc. survey commissioned by the cable channel YTV. Seventeen per cent of tweens have ATM bank cards, and each tween spends roughly $137 per year on back-to-school gear. Seventy-six per cent have Internet access either at home or at school. Susan Mandryk, vice-president of marketing with YTV, says the key to reaching tweens lies in understanding their "age aspirations—we never tell a tween that they are a tween." Tweens want to be teens; they buy products that make them feel sophisticated. Environics Research findings show that on average 12- to-14-year-olds want to be 18, while 15-to-19-year-olds want to be 20.

So while tweens spend to feel like teens, teens buy to cultivate their stature as "young adults." There are 2.5 million teens between 12 and 17 years old, according to Statistics Canada. And unlike Generation X, the 1980s teens who were maligned as "slackers" after running into the reality of inflation and unemployment, the current crop has high expectations. "They are totally optimistic," says Victor Thiessen, a sociology professor at Dalhousie University in Halifax. "Teens have not had an experience where the world kept them back. They take for granted that they are going to work." Meanwhile, they are going to spend: Youth Culture Inc.'s Butler estimates the average teen has a disposable income of $500 a month.

They also consider themselves immune to the tricks of the advertising trade. Bombarded from birth, they know they are being pitched and are suspicious. They recognize their own power. At the Youth Culture focus group, there are nods of agreement when 18-year-old Liane Balaban remarks: "I like the idea of a bunch of advertising executives sitting in a room sweating and pulling their hair out trying to figure out how to sell to us."

The resounding power of the Echo Generation seems to be a North American phenomenon. Europe did not have the same baby boom that North America experienced, so there is not the accompanying "boomlet." In the United States, however, the Echo market is staggering; Teenage Research Unlimited, a Northbrook, Ill.–based demographics firm, says there are 26 million teens who last year spent $141 billion (U.S.)—almost twice as much as a decade ago. That has U.S. companies battling for a slice of that pie, and their products spill over into Canada. *Teen People* boasts 10 million readers each issue. Launched in 1998, its circulation has grown from 500,000 to 1.2 million, making it one of the fastest-growing magazines in American publishing history. "It wasn't cool to be a teen in the '70s or '80s," says managing editor Christina Ferrari. "The teenage population hasn't taken centre stage like this since the '50s and '60s."

Where does their money come from? Studies show that while the popularity of after-school jobs is important, it is not the source of the vast majority of kids' cash. A recent report by the Canadian Council on Social Development showed the youth labour market is actually at its lowest point in 25 years—fewer than half of 15-to-19-year-old students worked in 1997, down from two-thirds in 1989. The big money instead comes from family sources. Foot calls teens "six-pocket kids" who get money from mom, dad, grandparents and often step-parents. Family money gets divided up into bigger chunks by fewer siblings, since Canadians are having smaller families (on average 1.7 children each).

To get at that potential windfall, advertisers are aiming their commercials straight at teens. Whatever the reasons—clued-in kids who grow up quicker and more assertive, indulgent parents who sometimes trade cash for calm—teens now exert what experts call "pester power" or "kidfluence." "I ask for money from my parents and sometimes bug them," says 15-year-old Chanta Carvery of Halifax. "If they give me a lot of money the day before, then I ask them the next day again." Now, more teens than ever make their own purchases—and even apply pressure on family acquisitions, such as advising their less-savvy parents on buying computers.

Marketers tap teen power with such tactics as "cross-referencing," in which companies unite to promote products. This month, Hostess Frito-Lay and the cable channel Teletoon launched the Cinetoon Trivia Challenge, a promotion with prizes such as Sony PlayStations and Cheetos snack foods. "There is an interlocking of movies with sports, TV and toys that previous generations never experienced," observes Meredith. "The movie sells the toy and the toy sells the movie. That means it's not as easy for a parent to say no. So you have the kid who screams his head off to a single mom who's barely getting by and she has to join the race." This concentrated selling technique fosters an acute awareness of brands and quality among teens. No other group cares more about what their purchases say about who they are. An Environics survey found that 66 per cent of 15- to 19-year-olds care "a lot" about whether their "clothes are in style." Seventy-four per cent say they always choose clothes "with great care."

There are striking divisions in the youth market. Tween buying habits, for instance, break down according to gender. Although 90 per cent of all tweens play video games, YTV's survey found that 20 per cent of boys spend their allowance on such games, compared with three per cent of girls. The Japanese video game Pokémon, introduced

$2\frac{1}{2}$ years ago, has sold 11 million copies worldwide and Pokémon products and spinoffs have earned $6 billion in sales. It is a role-playing game in which kids train and collect Pokémon characters and then pit them against each other. Ron Bertram, spokesman for Vancouver-based Nintendo of Canada Ltd., likens Pokémon to hockey-card trading. "It's social, " Bertram says. "To complete the game, you hook up your game to a friend's and trade Pokémons back and forth."

Female tweeners spend more on CDs and bestow their adulation on pop bands. These teeny-boppers made the Spice Girls a global phenomenon and devour one teen idol after another. The Backstreet Boys drew an audience of 1.3 million in Canada when they appeared on the 1997 YTV Achievement Awards; now, though, they are old cheese. Replacing them are such new groups as 98 Degrees, British Columbian foursome The Moffatts, and Take 5, a quintet formed in 1997 by Orlando, Fla.–based Trans Continental Records, the same outfit that created the Backstreet Boys and 'N Sync. Take 5's CD debuted in February and the teens have accrued a legion of die-hard fans. Sixteen-year-old singer Tilky Jones recalls being at a video arcade, and when they left, "this girl ran up and licked the seat."

The teeniest bopper of them all is Aaron Carter, an 11-year-old who squeaks out pop ditties like *Crazy Little Party Girl*. The brother of a Backstreet Boy, the mop-topped Carter played Toronto in February, drawing a seething mass of tweenage music lovers laden with cash. How devoted are his fans? Well, Georgia Pournaras, an 11-year-old Torontonian, has wallpapered her bedroom with 40 Aaron Carter posters, including one placed on the ceiling above her bed. She often sports a Carter T-shirt and talks about him "every day." Jennifer Sparacino, a 15-year-old from Oshawa, Ont., to date claims to have spent $5,000 on Backstreet Boys and Carter merchandise. She was teary-eyed after his recent concert, but said: "I saw him and I saw his mom. I am so happy."

In the 1970s and 1980, adolescents could pretty much be divided into jocks, rockers and preps. Now, says Environics' Saraq, there are at least a dozen teen "tribes" defined by their fashion, music and magazines. "Ravers," for example, listen to techno groups (Fatboy Slim, Portishead), read magazines such as *Vice* and *Tribe*, wear plastic pants, beads and neon shirts with such labels as Snug and Fiction. "Boarders," by contrast, tune into Offspring and Korn, wear punk-band T-shirts and Vans sneakers, and read the magazine *Transworld*. The result is a teen culture without a single overriding identity. As

Chris Staples, creative director of the Vancouver-based advertising firm Palmer Jarvis DDB, puts it: "The Pepsi Generation has splintered into 100 subsets.

"One of the most significant traits tweens and teens share is their multiculturalism. They are, by far, the most racially diverse generation in Canada's history. And they are getting more so: a 1996 Statistics Canada survey found that 45,000 of the 200,000 immigrants who enter the country each year are school-age children and teens. Kids are constantly balancing parental pressure with the mores of their Canadian peer group. "My parents are always trying to get me to hang out with friends in my own religion," says Nazim Berjee, 18, who lives in North Vancouver but is originally from Kenya. "I don't see the difference. I have friends that are Muslim and friends that aren't. I judge people not because of their skin colour or religion but on whether they are good people." Berjee spends his money on food, movies, CDs and track suits—and is about to buy a dress suit he can wear for a Muslim holiday and his high-school graduation.

If baby boomers were the TV generation, then their children are the Web generation who commune by the light of their computer monitors. Echo kids are accustomed to gathering information and communicating online—and tweens are even more wired than their teen elders. They grew up with the Web, and they have more time to spend online. "The teens that have Web access want to go out—why sit in front of a computer?" says Youth Culture's Butler. "Tweens have curfews. They're not old enough to go out late, so they surf."

Stores are trying to cut through the entrenched wariness of teens with ad campaigns that focus less on the product than on the lifestyle of the target market. In 1998, Montreal-based chain Le Château introduced Le Château Junior Girl, a tween clothing line, and opened youth-oriented Chateauworks stores in Toronto and Montreal. Quebec teens favour European styles and turn to Québécois magazines such as *Adorable* for tips. "They take their cues from Quebec pop stars and media," says Franco Rocchi, Le Château's vice-president of sales. "A Quebec teen will wear a grey blazer, where a teen from Edmonton is more likely to wear L.A.-inspired fashions like cargo pants."

Nationwide, Eaton's has launched a teen-oriented clothing department called Diversity that sells popular brands (Mud and Roxy among them). The departments are exuberantly decorated, and the TV ads are understated and built around the ubiquitous expression "Whatever." Each spot shows a teen recounting a personal anecdote, sometimes in a foreign language with no translation, and there is no mention of the store until the very end. The commercials are designed to stand as pieces of pop art. "There is so much opportunity for teens to avoid your message," says Andrew Macaulay of Roche Macaulay and Partners, which created the spots. "You have to reward them with something. The Diversity ads offer a teen talking honestly to you and you're hearing something interesting." Whatever.

In any case, independent stores without big marketing budgets pursue teens in other ways—including personal service. "They're like their parents, they like independent shops," says 26-year-old Shafin Devji, who, along with his father and two brothers, owns Soular, a teen store in the West Edmonton Mall. "If I see a kid come in three or four times, I'll say, 'I'm going to knock the tax off.'" Soular sells a range of suitably wild styles, everything from rave label Porn Star to Fubu—a New York–based company that sold $304 million worth of hip-hop gear in 1998. Customers pay $85 for a Fubu T-shirt. Devji says the new line of Fubu suits will cost up to $1,000 and he expects they will pay it—"they have to have it to fit in."

Lunatic Fringe in Toronto, where the target shopper is 15 and female, is located near five high schools. Teens are encouraged to hang out after school, and each weekday at 4:30 p.m., owner Allison Liss holds a basketball competition on the store's indoor mini-court. The winner gets a free pair of jeans. And instead of seasonal sales, Liss holds "parties" complete with pizza and prizes. Liss says teens want specific, hot labels such as Roxy, a California line of surf clothing. "It's almost like selling fish—it has to be fresh," she says. Her customers can be fickle. "These kids will drop you in a second."

That said, it is difficult to find a teen anywhere in North America who is not wearing a label of some kind. Even those who choose second-hand clothes are quick to point it out—they, too, are trying to make a statement. "They are trying to be different just like everyone else," Saraq says. And when they laugh at consumerism and advertising, says Sarah Crawford, director of media education for CHUM Television in Toronto, teens are, in effect, poking fun at themselves. "Some say, 'I know I'm a shallow consumer, but so what,'" she says.

Ironically, teens' cynicism may be the most direct route to their wallets. Case in point: The Offspring, an Orange County, Calif.–based pop/punk group whose single "Pretty Fly (For a White Guy)" and accompanying video satirizes affluent white teens who mimic inner-city black culture. (Hip-hop fashions are a $7.6-billion-a-year business in North America—and they are selling not just in inner cities but also in suburban malls.) The video shows a geeky kid sporting gold chains, baggy pants and a powder-blue Fubu football jersey. The lyrics rhyme off a series of caustic observations: "So if you don't rate, just over-compensate / at least you'll know you can always go on Ricki Lake / The world needs wanna-bes." And the wanna-bes are buying: according to an Environics survey, the song was No. 1 with 14- to 19-year-olds in Canada in recent weeks, and the album has sold more than four million copies in North America.

Once sown, the seeds of consumerism will continue to flourish. Rich, informed and populous, the current generation of teens and tweens will wield economic clout even as it grows older. Still, experts say that, at some point, there will be a backlash against wanton mate-rialism. "There is not a well-expressed oppositional culture among today's youth," says Saraq. "But anti-consumerism is growing and it will find a voice." If so, then Echo kids may follow in the footsteps of their parents, the baby boomers who in the late-1960s and early '70s loudly questioned conventional morality, materialism, government and, closer to home, their parents. Foot says intergenerational conflict may arise again as the years pass. "You'll have the 52-year-old parent who wants to relax at the cottage," he says, "and the 23-year-old son or daughter who wants to shoot around the lake on a Jet Ski."

The kids themselves predict a backlash, if for no other reason than they are suffering from advertising fatigue. They are being pitched 24 hours a day, seven days a week, and most say they are vehemently opposed to the increasing corporate presence in schools. Back at the focus group, the majority is against schoolyard basketball courts spon-sored by a shoe company if it means their classrooms will then be fes-tooned with logos. "I don't want my life to revolve around buying and selling," Grainger says emphatically. "There should be some safe haven from advertising. You have to sometimes see the sky between the billboards."

Clarifications

Gen Y: An article published in Business Week Online on February 5, 1999, defines Generation Y as: "Born during a baby bulge that demog-raphers locate between 1979 and 1994, they are as young as five and as old as 20, with the largest slice still a decade away from adolescence. And at 60 million strong, more than three times the size of Generation X, they're the biggest thing to hit the American scene since the 72 mil-lion baby boomers."

Slackers: Originally, a slacker was someone who avoided work or who was lazy. In recent years the word has been applied to GenXers. Sarah Dunn's book *The Slacker Handbook,* written in the early nineties, details the lifestyle of the slacker. Most reviewers of the title on on-line bookstore Amazon.com seem to boast about shoplifting the book (which is now out of print).

David Foot: Canadian author and professor David Foot has written on demographic trends in his books *Boom, Bust and Echo* and *Boom, Bust and Echo 2000.*

Focus group: A small sample group selected to elicit opinions or emotional responses to a particular subject.

Talking Points

Do you buy according to brand names, or is there a backlash against brand names? Do you and your peers consider any brands unacceptable?

The article mentions that kids sometimes help parents make family purchases, such as buying a computer. In 2001 a series of ads for Dell with the catchphrase "Dude, you're getting a Dell" became popular and apparently helped Dell's bottom line considerably. The thrust of the ads was that the lead character, Steve, would influence his peers to persuade parents to buy a Dell. Steve was a character much like the ingratiating Eddie Haskell of the old sitcom *Leave It to Beaver.* The ads were supposed to appeal to kids, but I felt they actually appealed to parents, particularly mothers. If you know about this series of ads, discuss. Did "Steve" have an influence on you?

Web Research

One of Canada's most interesting opinion pollsters is Environics, which has a Web site at *www.environics.com.*

Youthculture is a research company that researches media issues related to young people. The Web site is at *www.youthculture.com.*

The Canadian Council of Social Development is at *www.ccsd.ca.*

Writing That Works

Expert opinion/classification: "In the 1970s and 1980, adolescents could pretty much be divided into jocks, rockers and preps. Now, says Environics' Saraq, there are at least a dozen teen 'tribes' defined by their fashion, music and magazines. 'Ravers,' for example, listen to techno groups (Fatboy Slim, Portishead), read magazines such as *Vice* and *Tribe*, wear plastic pants, beads and neon shirts with such labels as Snug and Fiction. 'Boarders,' by contrast, tune into Offspring and Korn, wear punk-band T-shirts and Vans sneakers, and read the magazine *Transworld*."

Studies and statistics: "One of the most significant traits tweens and teens share is their multiculturalism. They are, by far, the most racially diverse generation in Canada's history. And they are getting more so: a 1996 Statistics Canada survey found that 45,000 of the 200,000 immigrants who enter the country each year are school-age children and teens."

Examples: "Ironically, teens' cynicism may be the most direct route to their wallets. Case in point: The Offspring, an Orange County, Calif.–based pop/punk group whose single "Pretty Fly (For a White Guy)" and accompanying video satirizes affluent white teens who mimic inner-city black culture." Notice how this particular example dates this article.

Metaphor: "Once sown, the seeds of consumerism will continue to flourish."

Arch Enemy

by Konrad Yakabuski

ROB Magazine, August 31, 2001

Every family has its values. The "McFamily," the 1.5 million mostly teenaged people who work under the Golden Arches around the world, are reminded of their employer's values from their first moments on the job. The McDonald's code of conduct is embodied in a series of pithy quotes attributed to founder Ray Kroc, many of which are tacked to staff bulletin boards and routinely repeated by managers at the fast-food behemoth's almost 29,000 worldwide outlets. One Krocism stands out: "None of us is as good as all of us."

Taken on its own, the expression seems a straightforward appeal to team spirit. But for the hundreds of ex-McFamily members who, in the past decade, have fought to unionize at least a dozen McDonald's restaurants in Canada, it has come to symbolize the chain's zero-tolerance attitude toward dissent. Many of those who led the union drives in Quebec, Ontario and British Columbia say they were made to feel selfish, like spoilers ruining a good thing for other, more obedient employees. They recall being passed over for raises and promotions, excluded from all-expenses-paid outings and reduced to fewer and fewer hours, more often than not during the dreaded closing shift. In short, they were made to feel they were no longer wanted or valued. They became the family's black sheep.

Pascal McDuff and Maxime Cromp did not intend to become the latest McCasualties when they launched an attempt to unionize their McDonald's outlet on Montreal's bustling Peel Street in the summer of 2000. The duo, now both 19, were undaunted by the failure of those who had gone before them. They took on a mission to establish better working conditions for themselves and their 40-odd co-workers—to improve on the low pay and paltry raises, the arbitrary schedule changes, the favouritism displayed by managers toward some employees, the harsh discipline and harassment experienced by others. More than anything, they sought to empower their generation. "Young people don't have a lot of job options. There's McDonald's, Harvey's, Burger King and maybe a supermarket," says McDuff. "The kids who tried [to unionize] before us were courageous. I felt called to their cause."

The job ladder at a typical McDonald's has seven rungs, from lowly crew worker to store manager. In between are crew trainers, crew chiefs, swing managers, first assistant managers and second assistant managers. Employees at each level exert authority over all ranks below them. McDuff was hired as a part-time crew worker in the spring of 1998. He was two months shy of his 16th birthday and needed extra money to help pay for the studies he would be undertaking at one of Quebec's CÉGEP community colleges. He started at $6.80 an hour, then Quebec's minimum wage. Cromp, also attending CÉGEP, joined the outlet a year later at 16.

Raises were not automatic with seniority, but granted at the discretion of the manager. McDuff learned that firsthand. After his first six months, he'd been limited to a meagre 10-cent raise. After a year on the job, he was earning 20 cents more than the minimum wage—less than the starting salary at a unionized fast-food restaurant nearby.

As much as the low wages, rigid in-store hierarchy and sometimes unpleasant tasks could be vexing, McDuff and Cromp grew to loathe most the climate of their workplace. Like all new McDonald's workers, the two were given the same employee manual when they joined. It's loaded with Krocisms like this one: "Press on. Nothing in the world can take the place of persistence. Talent will not; nothing is more common than unsuccessful men with talent. Genius will not; unrewarded genius is almost a proverb. Education alone will not; the world is full of educated derelicts. Persistence and determination alone are omnipotent." Kroc's folksy advice gives only a hint of his disdain for the educated classes. He had been a high-school dropout and milkshake-mixer salesman before founding the McDonald's chain in 1955. As far as McDuff and Cromp were concerned, Kroc's anti-intellectual bent was alive and well in the modern McDonald's family. Teenage employees often found themselves scheduled to work the closing shift on school nights, even during exams. "Education was never a priority at McDonald's," McDuff says. "We were supposed to have ketchup in our veins."

"I've had a look at what business schools do... They can't teach the kind of instinctual response and reliance on gut feelings that some people are lucky to learn at a young age."—McDonald's Restaurants of Canada senior chairman George Cohon.

McDonald's version of higher learning is practised at the Chicago-based training facility Hamburger University. HU's Canadian affiliate, with "campuses" in Toronto, Montreal and Vancouver, is called the Institute of Hamburgerology. The thousands of managers, executives and franchisees who graduate from HU's two-week course each year are schooled mostly in the McCulture that Kroc proudly begat. It's easy to see why George Cohon and Kroc hit it off. Of his business rivals, Kroc once said: "If they were drowning, I would put a hose in their mouth." Cohon's 1997 memoir, *To Russia with Fries,* echoes the sentiment. "Would I hold back if we had one of our chief competitors on the ropes?" he asks. "Not a chance."

Although a lawyer by training, Cohon, who grew up on Chicago's rough-and-tumble South Side, is also a graduate of the school of hard knocks. A bully's victim in elementary school, he got his revenge years later in high school, by which time Cohon had outgrown his nemesis. Spotting the bully one day sipping water in the hallway, Cohon stepped up and bashed his teeth into the fountain. A few years later, as an army recruit in basic training, Cohon got back at his anti-Semitic drill sergeant by breaking three of his fingers. "Let bygones be bygones?" Cohon asks. "That's not the way things were when I was growing up. That's not the way I am, even today."

Cohon's tough-guy approach worked wonders at McDonald's Canadian arm. Soon after Kroc sold Cohon the exclusive rights to open McDonald's outlets in Eastern Canada in 1968 for $70,000 (U.S.), he offered to buy them back for a cool million, figuring he had underestimated the potential of what he had thought was just frozen wasteland. Cohon held out for a better offer and, in 1971, sold out for several times more than what Kroc had originally offered. Cohon became the company's second-biggest shareholder after Kroc. The latter put Cohon in charge of the entire Canadian operation after buying out Western Canadian franchisee George Tidball the same year. By 1993, years after Cohon had become a Canadian citizen and just before he stepped down as CEO, McDonald's 674 Canadian outlets recorded average sales of $2.3 million, 15% more than the chain's worldwide average and the highest of any major McDonald's national unit. Although McDonald's no longer breaks out the Canadian bottom line separately (Canada is lumped in with the Middle East and Africa), it appears to remain a bright spot, helping to offset the bleeding McDonald's has suffered in Europe thanks to the mad-cow scare. Last year, sales at McDonald's 1,154 Canadian outlets totalled $2.14 billion, up 8% from 1999. For this year, McDonald's first-quarter financial report trumpets "positive comparable sales and expansion for Canada."

As left-leaning young Quebeckers, McDuff and Cromp never quite felt at home in the McFamily. McDuff is the son of a postal worker and his stay-at-home wife. Cromp's parents are both social workers in Montreal's poverty-stricken Pointe Saint-Charles neighbourhood. Both teenagers are political activists—Cromp, as a card-carrying member of the Parti Québécois's radical wing, McDuff as a sympathizer of the anti-globalization movement.

To Cromp and McDuff, the Krocisms seemed disingenuous. Instead of fostering teamwork, they felt managers often pitted employees against one another. They felt it was not the best workers who were promoted, but rather the most obedient. The latter, the two say, were encouraged to blow the whistle on co-workers who criticized managers.

The two young men thought things went from bad to worse at the Peel Street outlet after franchisee Michel Marchand brought in a new manager, Ismael Mejnaoui, in early 2000. "He laid down the law," McDuff says. "So we were forced to rush even more." By the summer of 2000, the minimum wage had risen to $7. McDuff was making $7.60 after two years on the job and had climbed only a single rung to crew trainer. Cromp, too, had moved up just a notch and was earning $7.75. One evening, while waiting on a subway platform after work, Cromp asked McDuff what he thought about forming a union. Recalls McDuff: "We realized we had nothing to lose."

In June, 2000, Cromp and McDuff sent an e-mail to the Confédération des syndicats nationaux (CSN), Quebec's second-largest trade-union central and its most staunchly social democratic. Days later, the two met with CSN organizers Henri van Meerbeck and Kevin Schwankner. Both knew the fast-food industry well. Van Meerbeck, 50, had successfully organized dozens of restaurants, including several Kentucky Fried Chickens and a McDonald's outlet in Saint-Hubert, Que.—which would have been a singular achievement, but for the fact that the restaurant closed shortly afterward. Schwankner, 36, joined the CSN after working 12 years at a Harvey's in the Montreal suburb of Brossard. During his stint there, the outlet was organized by the United Food and Commercial Workers Union. Working conditions improved dramatically. The union won the adoption of a formal pay scale (with a starting salary pegged 35 cents above the minimum wage), with regular raises and promotions based on seniority. Labour relations and health and workplace safety committees were set up with employee and management representatives. Employees won the right to be accompanied by a union representative in all their disciplinary dealings with management, and a formal process for investigating grievances was established. Managers were prohibited from cutting employee hours without giving sufficient notice. Employees working after 8 p.m. won an extra 30 cents an hour.

(It's not surprising that it is in Quebec that unions have been most active in attempting to organize the fast-food industry. The province remains Canada's most union-friendly: 39.9% of Quebec workers belong to unions, compared to a national average of 32%, and the province has some of the farthest-reaching workforce regulations on the continent.)

McDuff and Cromp liked what they heard and began talking to their co-workers—quietly, having been warned by their CSN mentors of what could happen if McDonald's management got wind of their scheme. McDonald's had become legendary for dispatching a "flying squad" of experienced officials to any restaurant where a union incursion loomed. The task of these officials was to warn employees of the pitfalls of unionization and the benefits of keeping the McFamily united. Literally hundreds of unionization attempts at outlets in North America had been pre-empted this way in the past. "At first, we knew not to mention the word 'union,'" remembers McDuff. "Our first goal was simply to make employees conscious of their working conditions."

On July 31, 2000, Cromp and McDuff were confident a strong majority of employees felt as they did, and proceeded to launch the critical sign-up drive. Time was of the essence; they feared a failure to sign up a majority of employees quickly would doom their initiative as McDonald's swept in with its flying squad. Cromp and McDuff worked feverishly over a 36-hour period to meet individually with each employee. In the end, about three-quarters signed union cards. "I knew we were asking for trouble," says Patrick Bibeau, now 19, a crew worker at the Peel outlet. "But I was for it."

"Unions are inimical to what we stand for and how we operate." —former McDonald's Corp. labour relations chief John Cooke

"If every single member of a crew in a particular restaurant joined a union, (McDonald's) would still not negotiate with the union." —McDonald's U.K. vice-president Sidney Nicholson

With $40 billion (U.S.) in worldwide sales, McDonald's remains the globe's dominant restaurant chain and the world's most recognized brand. More than 45 million people—including three million Canadians—eat at McDonald's on any given day. Last year, it served 16.5 billion (including repeat) customers. The company, headquartered in Oak Brook, Ill., is the world's largest owner of real estate (it typically makes most of its profits as a landlord to its franchisees), the largest U.S. purchaser of beef, pork and potatoes, the globe's biggest operator of playgrounds. It employs 75,000 Canadians, half a million Americans. North American teens depend on McDonald's more than any other single organization for their first job.

McDonald's did not become so ubiquitous by being a pushover. Kroc, who died in 1984, has often been depicted as a despot. He forbade restaurants from hiring women until a labour shortage forced him to relent in 1968. Even then, Kroc insisted that female employees be "kind of flat-chested" and devoid of distracting accoutrements such as eye shadow or nail polish.

Kroc's successors, including current CEO Jack Greenberg, have continued the tradition of central control through the fastidious store inspections the company uses to enforce operating disciplines, which are mind-bogglingly extensive. The operations manual provided to franchisees runs to more than 700 pages. The company's mantra, QSC & V (a Krocism that stands for quality, service, cleanliness and value) should have a "U" tacked on for "uniformity." While some local menu items are tolerated, franchisees undertake to ensure that customers are treated to exactly the same experience—from the look, taste and "mouthfeel" of the food to the speed with which it is served—whether they are in Montreal or Moscow, Boston or Bahrain.

Providing such uniform service leaves little leeway for flexible working conditions. Were unions to significantly infiltrate McDonald's operations, the company's ability to dictate the conditions under which its restaurants operate would be greatly reduced. Hence, McDonald's, or at least its franchisees, have consistently fought to keep unions out of their operations the world over. In North America, they have a perfect track record of rebuffing organized labour. Unions have made inroads in continental Europe and Mexico. Even where unions exist, the absence of closed-shop labour laws means that usually only a minority of employees are covered. In Russia, where Cohon opened the first McDonald's in 1990 and where McDonald's of Canada continues to jointly oversee operations, only 17 of 450 workers belong to the union at McComplex, the food-processing facility in Moscow. A committee of the State Duma, citing alleged intimidation tactics used by McDonald's, recently concluded it "violated the rights of citizens to establish a labour union."

The company's antipathy toward organized labour came under the microscope at London's so-called McLibel trial in the mid-1990s. The company had sued Helen Steel and Dave Morris, two Greenpeace activists, for their part in distributing a pamphlet that delineated a litany of alleged transgressions by McDonald's—from animal and environmental abuse to selling unhealthy food.

While the trial produced some startling revelations—McDonald's, it was learned, had infiltrated London Greenpeace with paid informers in 1989—labour issues provided perhaps the most sparks. The trial revealed that, after an employee was fatally electrocuted by a fat-filtering machine in 1992, a U.K. Health and Safety Executive report concluded: "The application of McDonald's hustle policy (i.e., getting staff to work at speed) in many restaurants was, in fact, putting the service of the customer before the safety of employees." McDonald's U.K. acknowledged having been convicted of 73 offences in relation to the employment of young people in the early 1980s. McDonald's officials were questioned about John Cooke, the company's U.S. labour relations head in the 1970s, whose job it was to keep unions out. Cooke's tactics, which had defeated some 400 unionization attempts in the United States, included using flying squads, "rap sessions" with employees and "stroking." Company officials also admitted that in 1973, employees in San Francisco had been asked to take polygraph tests during a bitter union drive.

Judge Rodger Bell issued an 800-page ruling in February, 1996. Although he ordered Steel and Morris to pay McDonald's £60,000 in damages (later reduced to £40,000), the duo came out looking like victors. McDonald's said it had no intention of collecting the money and would no longer try to quash the pamphlet. But the bad publicity from the trial had taken its toll on the company's image. And Judge Bell's ruling didn't help. Although Steel and Morris failed to prove that McDonald's had a formal policy of thwarting unionization, the judge found, "as a fact," that McDonald's is "strongly antipathetic to any idea of unionization of crew in their restaurants."

"A union at McDonald's would answer no need and would only complicate things. It would be a fifth wheel .... And in an organization such as ours, if something is unnecessary it's not a neutral presence. It's counterproductive."—McDonald's of Canada senior chairman George Cohon

In Canada, McDonald's has denied any direct involvement in fighting unionization, insisting such matters are strictly between employees and their franchisee. "McDonald's is not anti-union. McDonald's is pro-employee," one official told *The Globe and Mail* in 1997. (McDonald's Restaurants of Canada officials refused to be interviewed for this article and, in recent years, have consistently spurned all media requests for comments on the union matter.)

Once a unionization effort is under way, time is the union's greatest enemy. The longer a McDonald's franchisee can prolong labour board hearings on an accreditation request, the greater the odds the union drive will fail. Workers grow weary, legal bills pile up for the union, and annual employee turnover—typically 75% or more in the fast food industry—dilutes the ranks of union sympathizers.

The high turnover rate is attributable to a single factor: More than two-thirds of fast food workers are under 20. As Eric Schlosser notes in his recent book *Fast Food Nation,* "Fast food kitchens often seem like a scene from *Bugsy Malone,* a film in which all the actors are children pretending to be adults.... There's nothing about the work in a fast food kitchen that requires young employees. Instead of relying on a small, stable, well-paid and well-trained workforce, the fast food industry seeks out part-time, unskilled workers who are willing to accept low pay. Teenagers have been the perfect candidates for these jobs, not only because they are less expensive to hire than adults, but also because their youthful inexperience makes them easier to control."

About a dozen unionization attempts have been launched at McDonald's outlets in Canada in the past decade. None has been a success in the long run. In recent years, unions have organized a dozen Starbucks and 50 KFC outlets in British Columbia, and dozens more Harvey's, Tim Hortons, KFC and St-Hubert BBQ Chicken restaurants in Quebec. McDonald's remains the union movement's toughest nut. Franchisees have made remarkably similar responses to ensure it remains that way:

In 1993, the Service Employees International Union signed up 67 of 102 employees at a McDonald's in Orangeville, Ont. A week before the certification application was filed, a McDonald's human relations specialist showed up at the restaurant to "chat" with employees. McDonald's said this was a coincidence. The franchisee, Cam Ballantyne, fought the union bid during months of hearings at the Ontario Labour Relations Board. Formerly pro-union employees suddenly came forward to withdraw their signatures; lawyers for others cited the Age of Majority Act to claim they were too young to unionize. The change-of-heart group, mostly minimum-wage earners, did not say who paid their lawyer. Meanwhile, Ballantyne treated anti-union employees to a tobogganing party. He posted a notice on the staff bulletin board, claiming wages at unionized fast food restaurants were lower. After months of wrangling, the union agreed to a new vote. It lost 77 to 19.

In 1997, the International Brotherhood of Teamsters signed up 51 of 62 employees at a McDonald's outlet in St-Hubert, Que. The franchisees, Tom and Mike Capelli, hired lawyers from Fasken Martineau Dumoulin, a major national corporate law firm. New managers were recruited from McDonald's of Canada to run the restaurant. The

Capellis' lawyers challenged the accreditation request before a Quebec labour commissioner, claiming the union needed to sign up a majority of workers at all six of the brothers' McDonald's franchises. After hearings held over several weeks, the commissioner rejected the claim. Then, six anti-union employees hired their own lawyer (they didn't say who paid him) to challenge the impartiality of the commissioner. Quebec's Court of Appeal rejected their claim. In early March, 1998, the labour commissioner issued a final ruling certifying the union. It was too late. Two weeks earlier, the Capellis had suddenly closed down their restaurant.

Also in 1997, the Teamsters signed up 41 of 54 employees at a McDonald's outlet in Montreal's Plateau Mont-Royal neighbourhood. The franchisee, Laurent Vignola, also argued—unsuccessfully—that the union needed to sign up a majority of employees at all of his franchises. Then, he hired about 40 new part-time employees, arguing before the labour commission that the union no longer had a majority of the outlet's employees behind it. He lost on that point too. The hearings, however, hit an impasse after weeks of arguments. Ultimately, the Teamsters agreed to a new vote in early 1999, but by then only 12 of the outlet's original 54 employees remained. The union lost.

In 1998, the Canadian Auto Workers signed up a majority of the 85 employees at a McDonald's restaurant in Squamish, B.C. The franchisee, Paul Savage, hired 28 new employees and went before the B.C. Labour Relations Board to argue, unsuccessfully, that the new group should be included in the vote. Then, a group of dissident employees hired their own lawyer, and went before the board, claiming that under the Infant Act they were ineligible for union membership. They lost. The union was recognized and sought to negotiate a first contract, but no progress was made. Under B.C. law, an employer can ask for a new vote if no contract has been signed within 10 months. Savage sought a new vote in 1999. This time, the batch of employees Savage hired the year before were included, while many of the original pro-union employees had left. Employees voted 45 to 26 to decertify.

"People are our one true thing. We succeed or fail every day, in every restaurant, because of our people."—McDonald's Corp. CEO Jack Greenberg, April, 2000

"Simply put, we aspire to be the best employer in each community around the world"—McDonald's Corp. 2000 Annual Report

Patrick Bibeau worked the closing shift at the Peel Street McDonald's on Aug. 2, 2000. The atmosphere was tense. Earlier in the day, the union's request for certification had been filed with the Quebec's Bureau du Commissaire-général du Travail (labour relations office). Bibeau and his pro-union cohorts knew their bold gesture would not go unanswered by franchisee Michel Marchand. But little did they anticipate how swiftly and broadly their challenge would be met.

Just after 8 p.m., Marchand arrived at the outlet with a new manager in tow. Anna Mancuso, who had earlier managed Laurent Vignola's Plateau Mont-Royal restaurant during its union bid, came to Peel Street directly from McDonald's of Canada's regional headquarters—even though franchisees are expressly forbidden from hiring corporate employees. Marchand would later tell labour commissioner Michel Denis that an "emergency" forced him to bring in Mancuso. The latter, according to labour board transcripts, was accompanied by an "adviser" from McDonald's regional head office. Shortly after their arrival, two dozen teenagers—hired that very day—were brought by bus to the restaurant for their orientation. Most would later tell the labour board that they were contacted, interviewed and hired within minutes by Marchand. None ended up working more than a few hours a week. But their hiring boosted the payroll at Peel Street to 69 non-management employees.

Within days, Marchand had hired new lawyers, led by Benoît Turmel, the same Fasken Martineau solicitor who had represented both the Capelli brothers and Laurent Vignola in their battles against the Teamsters in St-Hubert and Plateau Mont-Royal. Turmel sought to raise the bar. He asked commissioner Denis to include the 24 newly-hired employees in the tally for the union vote and to deem all four of Marchand's McDonald's franchises as part of the bargaining unit. A positive verdict on either motion would have put the pro-union employees in the minority and doomed the certification bid.

While his lawyers led the legal battle, Marchand was busy on other fronts. In September, he suspended McDuff for a week for having "publicly tarnished" the restaurant's image during a pro-union rally. During the rally, McDuff denounced the "abuse" employees had undergone since the union bid was tabled—including the suggestion that union dues would reach 40% of workers' salaries instead of the typical 2.5%. After the rally, Marchand posted a letter on the staff bulletin board: "I take these accusations personally and they hurt.... The [pro-union] rally disappoints me. Acts like that perturb our ability to serve our customers and work as a team." Marchand warned employees not to become pawns in "a bigger agenda for the CSN," and he ended by thanking them for their support "in these difficult times." McDuff and Cromp dismissed Marchand's appeal. But other employees took it more seriously, especially since Marchand, who had rarely visited the restaurant before the union bid was tabled, seemed to be always at the outlet now, gamefully chatting up employees. He also began treating them to frequent outings. Cromp learned of one trip to a local water park only after the group left without him. It didn't matter; he, along with the other union leaders, had been scheduled to work that day.

In November, barely a week before Denis was to table a final ruling, lawyer Philippe Garceau and his associates intervened to claim they had just been hired by a group of five Peel Street employees to challenge the union bid. He asked Denis to delay a ruling until he could prepare a case. He refused to name the anti-union employees or to disclose who paid his fees. In his Nov. 24 final ruling, Denis dismissed Garceau's attempt to intervene as yet another "stalling tactic."

Denis was even more scathing toward Marchand. The sudden hiring of 24 new employees—a number representing more than half of the restaurant's workers before Aug. 2—"was a scheme to improperly inflate the number of workers and thus deprive the [union] of its representative character," Denis concluded. Denis noted that in the month following the union's tabling of its certification request, Marchand had hired a total of 32 new employees at the Peel Street outlet but only seven new workers at all three of his other franchises. He noted too that one of the 24 employees hired on Aug. 2 had only accompanied a friend and had not even filled out a job application. "Either [Marchand] is remarkably effective at rapidly recruiting personnel," Denis observed dryly, "or he acted precipitously to counter the union organization." He ended his ruling with these words: "The labour commissioner hereby certifies le Syndicat des travailleuses et travailleurs du McDo—CSN [the McDo Workers' Union—CSN]."

Overnight, McDuff, Cromp and their cohorts became heroes in Quebec—painted in the media as teenage Davids triumphing over a corporate Goliath. The Peel Street outlet became the only unionized McDonald's in North America. Within days, however, Garceau appealed to Quebec's Tribunal du Travail (an appellate tribunal in labour relations cases) to have the certification set aside on behalf of the dissident employees. He argued that Denis was not impartial, had insulted him and had failed to consider his clients' claim that they had not paid a nominal $2 fee when signing their union cards, a violation of Quebec's labour law. Almost six months later, Judge Louis Morin rejected Garceau's complaints, noting that Denis and his agents had led an "exceptional" investigation to authenticate the representative nature of the union. Judge Morin found "quite normal, given the circumstances, that [Denis] question the seriousness of [Garceau's] intervention." Rather than insulting Garceau, Denis was simply expressing his "exasperation" at Garceau's refusal to name his clients and to appear in person before Denis (he sent an articling student). "If I had been in the commissioner's place," Judge Morin concluded, "I wouldn't have been so patient."

Morin's decision, coming in May, was merely a moral victory for the union. In late April, Marchand had suddenly announced he would close the Peel Street outlet by the end of the summer. His reason: a three-fold rent increase. The union challenged Marchand's explanation, noting that the Peel Street building's commercial value had been recently reduced on city rolls to $1.6 million from $2.3 million in 1995, a change apt to make rent go down rather than up. Besides, the union argued, the outlet was in the heart of downtown Montreal's busiest office and shopping district—the Sainte-Catherine Street strip—where business is the briskest it's been in years. Nevertheless, on June 22, on the eve of Quebec's St-Jean-Baptiste Day celebrations, Marchand told employees the Peel Street outlet would close that evening. With only a few hours notice, they were out of a job. By the next morning, the golden arches and other McDonald's signage that had adorned the building for 25 years had been taken down.

"It seems as though McDonald's is becoming more sophisticated with every organizing attempt," sighs Sarah Inglis, who led the union bid in Orangeville eight years ago and now works as an organizer for the Hotel Employees & Restaurant Employees International Union in Toronto. "It would be unusual to see the same type of tactics used by several individual franchisees in different parts of the country unless the umbrella body, McDonald's of Canada, was giving them a helping hand." Roger Crowther, the CAW national representative who organized the Squamish McDonald's in 1998, agrees. While attempting to negotiate a first contract, Crowther sat across from two lawyers—a rarity, he says, in his 25-year union career. "Here's this franchisee who's telling me he can't pay more than the minimum wage but who has not one, but two, full-time lawyers." Adds Edward Kravitz, the CSN lawyer who led the Peel union's case before the labour board: "If it walks like a duck, has web feet and quacks, it's probably a duck." But even Kravitz concedes it's almost impossible to prove McDonald's unbroken success in beating back unions in North America is a formal company policy, orchestrated and bankrolled by head office.

The thing about McDonald's and unions, though, is that for every organization bid that fails, another is born. In April this year, workers at the McDonald's outlet in Rawdon, Que., a resort town of about 9,000 northeast of Montreal, were granted union certification after the franchisee suddenly sold his restaurant. The new owner agreed to talk to the union. But the CSN is not holding its breath. McDonald's franchisees have a track record as tough negotiators. Under Quebec labour law, the Rawdon franchisee, Sylvain Vincent, can seek a decertification vote next spring if no contract has been signed. That is, if the outlet is still open by then. CSN negotiator Jean Archambault worries Vincent might simply shut the place once the tourist season is over.

If the outlet does close, it, like the Peel Street restaurant, will be an anomaly. In 1999 and 2000, McDonald's says, "less than 1% of existing restaurant locations closed" in Canada. What's more, it plans to open 300 new Canadian outlets within three years, buttressing this country's status as McDonald's biggest market after the United States and Japan.

As for McDuff and Cromp, they, like all the teenage veterans of the union war, have moved on. McDuff will study political science at the Université de Montréal this fall, while working part-time at a community radio station. He wants to become a journalist one day. Cromp, meanwhile, has loftier ambitions. When not training at the track—his personal best is 10.8 seconds in the 100 metres—he dreams of eventually becoming premier of Quebec. As Ray Kroc would have said, press on, boys, press on.

Clarifications

Behemoth: A huge animal mentioned in the Bible. Although the Bible does not clearly identify the animal, it is usually believed to be a hippopotamus, although there are some votes for elephant and even dinosaur. The discussion comes from the fact that while a behemoth "eats grass like an ox" and has bones that are "strong pieces of brass," it also "moves its tail like a cedar" and apparently has a navel (quotes taken from Job 40: 15–18). It is also described as lounging around in the shade and the river, which sounds like a rhinoceros to me. The actual animal notwithstanding, its name just means "very big."

The black sheep of the family: This expression is used to refer to the member of the family who has gone astray. Apparently the origin referred to selling wool at the market, where black wool got a lower price than white wool. One Web site speculates that the price was lower because it was harder to dye black wool.

Disingenuous: Insincere, with unclear or hidden motives.

Blow the whistle: To speak out or raise concerns about a company. In 2002, an employee "blew the whistle" on the accounting practices of the U.S. energy company Enron. The movie *The Insider,* starring Russell Crowe, is about an employee in a tobacco company who blew the whistle on the firm.

Flying squad: A police group organized for rapid deployment. Such a group would usually be sent in where there was a problem, which is why the McDonald's group is referred to as a flying squad. The CAW also has a grassroots movement using this name. Its Web site is at *www.flyingsquad.iwarp.com.*

Talking Points

The McDonald's brand has been so successful that it has infiltrated the English language as a prefix: *Mc.* The writer talks about McCasualties, McCulture and the McLibel trial. Many of us use the term *McJobs.* From these examples you can see that *Mc* is often used in a derogatory way. Does this mean that the McDonald's brand is in some ways unsuccessful? Or have the anti-McDonald's forces been successful in using the company's own brand against it? McDonald's has used the *Mc* reference itself. Its Web site has a link to McSports—if the link still exists, look at the red hockey mask with the golden arches, which is a way of co–branding sports and fast food.

Do you agree with the statement, "None of us is as good as all of us"?

Is the article balanced? Are both sides of the issue presented equally? Could more of the McDonald's point of view have been presented?

"Youthful inexperience makes them easier to control." From your own work experience, would you agree or disagree with this statement?

If you check the McDonald's corporate web site at *www.mcdonalds.com*, you will see that the issue of corporate social responsibility is addressed right on the front page. In fact, my unscientific opinion is that the more a company is challenged by its customers, the more likely it is to have a CSR policy. Create a list of companies with public relations problems and check their Web sites for CSR policies. For starters, check the Nike, Talisman and Starbucks sites.

You may have noticed that quotes from McDonald's executives are interspersed throughout the article, although not always well integrated with the text. One reads, "'A union at McDonald's would answer no need and would only complicate things. It would be a fifth wheel.... And in an organization such as ours, if something is unnecessary it's not a neutral presence. It's counterproductive.'— McDonald's of Canada senior chairman George Cohon." The next paragraph goes on to say, "In Canada, McDonald's has denied any direct involvement in fighting unionization, insisting such matters are strictly between employees and their franchisee." How does the use of quotes from management work in this article? What points might the writer be trying to make by using this technique?

Web Research

You can read more about Ray Kroc on the Time 100 Most Important People of the Twentieth Century page at *www.time.com/time/time100*. You'll hear him talking as well, sounding like your grandfather on a rant.

The Ontario Ministry of Labour Web site at *www.gov.on.ca/lab* includes the Ontario Labour Relations Board.

The International Brotherhood of Teamsters has a Web site at *www.teamster.org*.

You can read about the McLibel trial at the appropriately named McSpotlight Web site: *www.mcspotlight.org*.

Writing That Works

Analogy: "Teenage Davids triumphing over a corporate Goliath." This is a reference to the biblical story of David and Goliath, in which a young David slew the giant Goliath armed only with a slingshot.

List: "Rap sessions with employees, stroking and flying squads."

Introduction and conclusion frame: The article is framed with quotes from Ray Kroc. It opens talking about his pithy sayings, and closes with one of them, used somewhat ironically. What is the effect of this framing? Is it in fact a kind of arch, or a kind of containment?

Today's Lesson Brought to You By...

by Fran Fearnley

Today's Parent, October 1, 2000

A grade-six class settles down to a math lesson on simplifying fractions. Students open their textbooks and read: "The best-selling packaged cookie in the world is the Oreo cookie. The diameter of an Oreo cookie is 1.75 inches. Express the diameter of the Oreo cookie as a fraction in simplest form."

Here's a group of grade fours learning about energy. A local utility company, with the clearly stated objective "to increase public support for nuclear power development," has supplied the attractive teaching kit—complete with film strips, booklets and a board game on energy issues.

A principal is reading an upbeat memo from a school official about the board's contract with Coca-Cola. The cheque for the school's cut is now available for pick-up ($3,000 for elementary; $25,000 for high schools), but there's also some "not-so-good news," the official writes. "We must sell 70,000 cases of product (including juices, sodas, waters, etc.) at least once during the first three years of the contract." Then the memo suggests ways of achieving this, including putting vending machines in common areas and allowing students to buy and consume Coke products throughout the day ("If sodas are not allowed in classes, consider allowing juices, teas and waters."). The board official signs off as The Coke Dude.

Far-fetched? Paranoid? No. These are actual examples of what's happening in the United States. High schools in particular have become prime marketing venues, but elementary schools are fast catching up. From hair-care surveys and Clairol shampoo samples on school premises, to Prozac representatives giving presentations on National Depression Screening Day, anything seems possible. Indeed, when Vancouver's *Adbusters* magazine ran an article, complete with photos, about students in the US sporting tattooed logos for Nike, Pepsi and Guess as a school fundraiser, many readers didn't realize the Tattoo You Too! program was a spoof.

There's plenty of evidence to suggest that Canada is not far behind. With education funding on the decline, teachers, administrators and parents are accepting, and in some cases initiating, a diverse range of school–business partnerships. Meanwhile, many teacher federations warn that corporate support comes with strings attached.

Purists like Heather-Jane Robertson, author of *No More Teachers, No More Books: The Commercialization of Canada's Schools,* argue that the term "partnership" is a misnomer. "When you talk about partners it implies that both parties have an equal say. That's simply not the case here," she says. "Corporations have the power and the money, and schools are dependent because they are cash-strapped." Robertson, who has been researching this topic for over a decade, is adamant that schools be off limits to all corporate exposure, however well intentioned it may appear. "Corporations are not in the business of educating a responsible citizenship," she says. "They are there to promote and market themselves. That doesn't make them evil. That's simply what they do."

Are corporations really taking advantage of a young and captive audience? It's not that simple. Many mentoring and work-placement partnerships are enthusiastically received by all concerned. And we should remember that, historically, schools courted business for help with a range of initiatives. Not surprisingly, companies view their role in a positive light. The Conference Board of Canada's 1999 *Business and Education Best Practices Ideabook* lists many lofty goals for its members, including "better awareness of schools' needs" and "opportunity to mentor youth." The closest anyone gets to acknowledging a self-serving motive is with phrases like "enhanced public image in the community" and "public recognition." What's wrong with that?

It depends on who you talk to. Jacqueline Latter, spokesperson for the Ontario Education Alliance, believes that public recognition is a euphemism for "creating marketing loyalty in very young consumers." An example is the Campbell Soup Company's Labels for Education project. Launched in Canada in 1998 (it's been running in the US since 1973), it was billed by Campbell's as a "fantastic opportunity for schools to further learning during times of tight budgets."

Debbie McCarthy at Campbell's says all K–8 schools across the country were "targeted" with a mailing that promised a 1,000-label credit to get the school started. About 3,600 schools have chosen to participate. "They just collect labels from a selection of healthy soups and then use the labels to get free educational products," McCarthy explains. "There's a catalogue for them to choose from, with every-thing from multimedia suites to science equipment." Asked why Campbell's runs the program McCarthy responds, "We are the top company in Canada in terms of soup consumption, and we wanted to do a good job as a corporate citizen."

Robert Gendron, principal of Beaver Lodge Elementary School in Winnipeg, which won Campbell's Race to the Finish Line competition last year, says, "I love the Labels for Education campaign. There was no pressure on us to advertise. Our community grasped it with great enthusiasm." There was some negative press about the program, he explains, from people who felt that only schools in more affluent neighbourhoods could participate successfully. Gendron doesn't buy that, but he does agree that schools must evaluate fundraising schemes carefully. The parent council discussed whether this program was "nutritionally and ethically sound" before it was accepted unani-mously.

In contrast, mother of two Janice Harvey of Waweig, New Brunswick thinks "Campbell Soup–type promotions are sleaze phi-lanthropy." In her opinion, all incentive programs that involve a product purchase should be out of bounds in schools. Campbell's position is that they are not selling anything but simply having partic-ipants remove labels from products that are on their shelves anyway.

Wal-Mart's Adopt-a-School Program also has its supporters and detractors. Each store chooses a school in its community to support, with activities such as in-store fundraising, and employees making donations and volunteering in the school. Wal-Mart's head office matches funds raised up to $2,000. Director of public affairs Andrew Pelletier says no school has ever rejected an "adoption" and that it's a "grassroots, community-based initiative with no strings attached." He says that Adopt-a-School has generated a lot of good publicity for

Wal-Mart, but that's simply because it works. "Good deeds should generate goodwill. We are earning our place in the community."

At Stephenville Primary in Newfoundland, principal David Warr is as enthusiastic as Pelletier. "Wal-Mart employees donated money to our breakfast program and some of them volunteered to serve breakfast for a day to the students," he says. "And Wal-Mart matched dollar-for-dollar the money raised by the playground committee." He says there was no request to use the logo in the school or promote the company in any way. The media had photo opportunities when Wal-Mart employees served breakfast and when the donation cheque arrived, but Warr doesn't take issue with that.

Lisa Widdifield, a parent activist in London, Ontario, doesn't have such a sanguine attitude. "It's a strategic marketing plan. It's great advertising for Wal-Mart. Adopting a school—please. Are we orphans?" Indeed, businesses talk about educational sponsorships as being "strategic philanthropy," which is, in fact, an oxymoron.

"Schools have become a charity," laments Erika Shaker, a senior researcher with the Canadian Centre for Policy Alternatives, an Ottawa-based think tank. "They have been forced to look for outside funding and that's further contributing to inequities in individual schools. The only way to be fair is to fix it from a tax base." Corporations want to support this "charity," continues Shaker, "because the school is the most powerful environment in which to reach kids."

There are all kinds of ways to get into the classroom but no consensus as to what's OK and what isn't, and teachers themselves have mixed feelings. A recent survey by the Alberta Teachers' Association showed that there was 56 percent support for school–business partnerships and 40 percent support for accepting donations in exchange for public recognition. But only 16.5 percent supported exclusive sponsorship agreements. And a resounding 82.3 percent opposed advertising in schools. One respondent wrote, "This prostitutes our children's minds for bucks."

The most active watchdogs—people like Shaker and Robertson— say the biggest temptations are related to our society's love affair with technology. If a partnership involves schools receiving computers, televisions and satellite dishes, then school boards are eager to say yes. The most controversial example is the Youth News Network (YNN), which works like this: Schools get about $200,000 worth of technology in exchange for a contract that requires students to watch ten minutes

TOPIC 8: Young Consumers and Workers

of YNN's current affairs programming and $2\frac{1}{2}$ minutes of commercials. At the moment it's only being offered to secondary schools but rumours (impossible to substantiate) are rife that they plan to reach younger children.

Despite initial concerns about the commercialism of the venture—and there is still an active lobby against them—YNN is now making real headway. As one Calgary principal puts it, the drawbacks were ultimately viewed "through the lens of financial realism." It always comes back to cash.

Controversy is not what companies are looking for when they align themselves with a good cause, and for that reason some have chosen to put their dollars to work through a broker who understands both public sensitivities and educators' needs. Some, such as Toronto-based Classroom Connections, operate on a not-for-profit basis, claiming to match corporate clients with responsible, ethical, educationally valid projects. Often they create sponsored educational materials (SEMs), which are distributed free or at low cost to schools. The range of SEMs includes the good, the bad and the ugly, but even the idea makes Janice Harvey bristle. "Curriculum involvement is the most insidious of all."

Classroom Connections' unit on literacy, designed for parents of young children and paid for by UPS, gets top marks for being a hands-off sponsorship. The unit on money and banking gets a lower grade, since the Royal Bank's logo makes its way into the video in several places, and the expectation—made explicit in the teacher guide—is that students will visit not just any bank, but a Royal branch. And a unit on responsible pet care, sponsored by Ralston Purina Canada, clearly crosses the fine line parents and educators talk about constantly. Under the guise of a media project, students review promotional material from the company (which includes product coupons), are directed to its Web site, and design a responsible pet care ad that could earn the school a digital camera. A savvy teacher could include competitors' material and review the way Ralston Purina projects a warm, fuzzy image, but Classroom Connections has not written the curriculum from that perspective. It's all a bit too cozy.

The most problematic SEMs are those created by and about the companies themselves. This is particularly popular in industries facing a PR challenge, such as mining, nuclear energy and forestry. Canfor Corporation's Tree School primary lesson plans are full of value-laden statements: "In British Columbia our working forests provide jobs, products and many economic benefits. Stumpage fees and taxes help support our health care and education systems." Their description of forestry management is so gung-ho, children might actually believe that the industry's first priority is to provide a perfectly balanced ecosystem for future generations, rather than logging.

No discussion about school–business partnerships is complete without a look at the cola wars. Once upon a time schools had water fountains. Then some introduced vending machines, and in 1994 the former Toronto Board of Education entered into the first board-wide beverage contract in Canada, with Pepsi winning the tender. "It was a major issue when it first came up," says Brian Lenglet, comptroller of board services. "People were very concerned about nutritional issues, caffeine and the whole question of monopolies."

When several school boards in the Greater Toronto Area amalgamated in 1998, the vending machine issue came up again. But this time there was little debate about whether it was a good idea, only about how to negotiate the best deal. Lenglet says public opinion was muted—there were only three presentations made in opposition. (Schools can opt out of having a vending machine, and elementary schools can only sell juice and water unless the parent council approves soft drinks.) Coca-Cola won the day and board revenue rose from half a million to $1.8 million a year, which is divided between participating schools and system-wide initiatives, including the board's breakfast programs.

Lisa Widdifield understands why the pop machine protests have declined (many major urban boards have now succumbed). She's been active in persuading her own school board, Thames Valley District, to resist the temptation, but it's hard work and she's not convinced they'll hold off in the long run. "Parents are battling changes that are coming too fast. We have become reactionary because we don't have time to be proactive. It's impossible to keep up."

Perhaps for the same reason, public opinion seems to be shifting, too. A 1997 Environics survey reported a 74 percent disapproval rate for advertising in classrooms. But in 1999 Angus Reid asked a long, convoluted question about allowing advertising in classrooms in exchange for donations, and found 53 percent approval. Although likely answered by many who had insufficient information, it nevertheless demonstrates an increased willingness by Canadians to accept a Faustian bargain.

Last week there was a knock on my door. I live up a long country lane and don't get many unexpected visitors. I answered the door to my neighbour's ten-year-old son, Logan, complete with bike, helmet, a knapsack and rosy cheeks. He was selling chocolate bars for $2 to raise money for his school playground. I bought one immediately. A few years ago I might have said, "No thanks, Logan," but with everything I now know it seemed like such an uncomplicated way to support my local school.

Where Do We Draw the Line?

While many school boards do have policies to deal with corporate involvement, many are not explicit, or they have no teeth. The Toronto District School Board, for example, has a policy that reads: "Schools should not partner with business that are engaged in activities, provide services or manufacture products that are deemed inappropriate for student consumption or use." Arguably, the board's Coca-Cola contract violates that policy.

"It's not easy to have one policy that fits all eventualities," says Calgary's Joyce Eynon, past president of the Canadian Home and School Federation. "If there's a marketing idea out there it will make its way into the school eventually. We must recognize, too, that parents come to the table with different values and beliefs." Despite these challenges, everyone agrees that school boards need to decide where to draw the line.

The following suggestions have been gleaned from parents, advocacy groups, school councils, school boards and teacher federations, and from partnerships, like the Conference Board of Canada and the Learning Partnership.

• School boards must develop clear policies to manage partnerships and sponsorships after thorough discussion and input from parents and educators.

• It is not sufficient to talk about "appropriate recognition" or "promotional considerations" for corporate involvement. Policies must spell out what is and isn't acceptable.

• There is a difference between a logo that acknowledges the role of a sponsor and commercial advertising, but one can lead to the other very quickly, so definitions are advisable.

• Provincial ministries and local politicians should be kept in the loop so they don't contradict or undermine school board policies.

- Each partnership must be confirmed in writing with all details and expectations clearly spelled out.
- Corporations should not be able to cherry-pick schools in affluent areas to sponsor or provide with equipment.
- Control of the curriculum must rest with educators.
- All partnerships must improve the life of the school and either directly or indirectly enhance children's learning.
- There should be no exploitation of staff, students, or parents. (YNN, which requires students to watch commercials during instructional time, would clearly violate this principle.)
- Product sampling on school premises should be prohibited.
- Partnerships should provide additional educational benefits to students and not replace provincial funding.
- No program should ever become totally dependent on funding from an external source.
- School boards should require sponsored educational materials (SEMs) to meet the same standards as standard curriculum materials. They should be subject to rigorous evaluation to ensure they're unbiased and devoid of stereotyping.
- In order to guide corporate partners, boards should build on good examples, rather than highlighting problems.
- Schools must offer a diversity of views. The non-profit sector should also have opportunities to partner with schools.
- Schools should teach media literacy from an early age so that students learn to evaluate marketing ploys, advertising and propaganda.
- All partnerships and policies must be regularly evaluated to ensure that they are still relevant and reflect community standards.

Clarifications

Sanguine: Cheerful and optimistic. However, the word is often misused to mean calm, and it is not clear from the context which meaning the writer intended. The word originates in the medieval idea of the four "humours," in which the relative proportion of bodily fluids (blood, bile, phlegm and black bile) determined one's temperament. Too much blood—indicated by a ruddy complexion—meant you were courageous, hopeful and ready to fall in love.

Oxymoron: Words used together that mean the opposite of each other. E.g., jumbo shrimp.

Insidious: Something that is spread subtly and stealthily, but harmfully.

Faustian bargain: Goethe's character Faust gained power and wealth by selling his soul to the Devil. Many writers have used this archetype, including the writers of the TV show *The Simpsons*.

Talking Points

Should fundraising in schools be tied to product purchase? Is it acceptable in some cases? If so, what cases are those? For example, does it make a difference if the product is nutritionally superior?

Divide the class into two types of groups: product groups and school board groups. The product groups should create a product and try to sell it to the school board, while the school board groups should come up with a list of requirements.

While some businesses seem to operate in an underhanded way to influence children, many can be considered philanthropists. For example, Microsoft head Bill Gates donates millions of dollars worth of computers to libraries every year. But there seems to be a thin line between philanthropy and self-interest. Research the history of philanthropy in Canada. A starting point is Charity Village at *www.charityvillage.com*, Canada's "supersite for the non-profit sector." This site has huge resources.

How did your high school raise money? Did you sell chocolate bars, fruit from Florida, pizzas? Did you have a bingo night? Is bingo, with its gambling and smoking connections, a more acceptable means of raising money than a deal with a pop company?

Web Research

The Conference Board of Canada's 1999 Business and Education Best Practices Ideabook is available in pdf format at *www.conference-board.ca/education/pdf/Awards/idea99e.pdf*.

Find the Environics Research Group's Web site at *www.environics.net.*

To read about Wal-Mart's "Good Works," investigate the Wal-Mart Foundation's Web site at *www.walmartfoundation.org*.

Writing That Works

Introductions—examples: The article starts with several examples of corporate sponsorship in schools in the United States. The examples can also be seen as shocking statements. The examples are not yet true of Canada, but the reader might believe they are until he or she reaches the fourth paragraph.

Suggestions: Like a good report, the article presents the problems and then suggests how the problem can be dealt with.

Question and answer: "Where do we draw the line? While many school boards…."

Statistics: "A 1997 Environics survey reported a 74% disapproval rate for advertising in classrooms." However, in the same paragraph, the writer also notes how statistics can be tweaked: "But in 1999 Angus Reid asked a long, convoluted question about allowing advertising in classrooms in exchange for donations, and found 53 percent approval."

TOPIC *9*

FUNNY BUSINESS

INTRODUCTION

According to Statistics Canada, the crime rate decreased steadily through the nineteen-nineties (with the exception of a few crimes such as stalking, which increased slightly), perhaps because of an increase in awareness and reporting. In spite of the statistics, however, there is a general feeling that all crime has increased and that we are living in difficult times. Try telling your parents or your grandparents that they are living in a world that is safer than the one they grew up in, and no doubt most of them will disagree.

Business crime, often called white-collar crime, includes a huge range of crimes that are mostly categorized as "crimes of property." They include embezzlement, bribery, tax evasion, fraud, identity theft, postal crimes, and computer crime. In recent years, of course, computer crime has increased because of the growth of the Internet. Killer viruses arrive on our home and business computers regularly, and our e-mail is loaded with shady offers to get rich quick, such as the one that asks you to allow your bank account to be used by the Nigerian Central Bank to, in effect, launder money (read more at *www. scambusters.org*).

In 2001, the focus on white-collar crime turned to money laundering, because of the relationship of that crime to terrorism. "Disaster fraud" also took the spotlight. Because of the large number of people affected by the collapse of the World Trade Center towers and the huge sums of money collected by various organizations, many people saw September 11 as an opportunity to make money. According to an article on the National White Collar Crime Center Web site, the U.S. National Insurance Crime Bureau expected to be contacted about many fraudulent insurance claims as a result of the WTC catastrophe, including claims for false business receipts, damaged or destroyed cars that weren't actually at the scene, and false bills submitted by contractors, cleaners and the like for work that had not been done.

In Canada, meanwhile, attention has focused on organized crime, particularly the kind perpetrated by biker gangs. Although many biker crimes are not involved with white collar crime, groups such as the Hells Angels and the Rock Machine have become big business entities.

The Royal Canadian Mounted Police (*http://www.rcmp-grc. gc.ca/scams/ecbweb.htm*) notes that its "Economic Crime Prevention Objective" is:

> *To reduce, control and prevent business-related or white-collar crimes such as fraud and false pretences, theft, breach of trust, secret commissions, offences against the Government of Canada, the corruption of public officials, offences relating to property rights, crimes involving computers, the insolvency process, securities fraud, and counterfeiting on an interprovincial, national, and international scale.*

Follow the Money

by Katherine Macklem and John Intini

Maclean's, October 22, 2001

$17 billion in Canada alone; $2 trillion worldwide. International authorities believe these vast sums are laundered annually through banks and businesses, masking ill-gotten gains with the lustre of clean capital. Before Sept. 11, the money was considered to be the proceeds of organized crime. Now, with attention intently focused on Osama bin Laden and his Al-Qaeda network of terrorist cells, the world is beginning to understand that those billions of criminal dollars are interlaced with money that funds terrorist activities. "Extremist organizations," says Supt. Dave Beer, who heads the RCMP's proceeds of crime branch, "are by definition criminal organizations: they walk the same path, they work in the same shadows."

Even in Canada—a notorious laggard in the international effort against money laundering—there's been a massive shift in attitude. An anti-laundering law, which had been languishing for 15 months under attacks from the legal and banking communities, was kicked on to the fast track on Sept. 12. In the first week of October, Finance Minister Paul Martin froze the assets of known terrorists and terrorist organizations. This week, as part of Ottawa's raft of major anti-terrorism measures, the justice department is expected to introduce new legislation that will further beef up the anti-laundering law. "Suddenly, the world has awakened to this," says Brian Butler, a senior investigator at the Ontario Securities Commission. "The attacks have galvanized the world."

The ties are close between terrorist groups and organized crime, even though their objectives differ—one, driven by political or religious motives; the other, by greed. They use similar methods to hide money, move money, even raise money. According to an international task force devoted to combating money laundering, terrorist groups finance their operations using the same nasty businesses that organized crime is into: extortion, robbery, fraud, gambling, and the trafficking of drugs and counterfeit goods. Terrorists also have their own distinct sources of funds, such as state sponsorships and charities that operate as fronts.

"When you're talking about the financing of terrorism, there is a traditional element, which is the money-drugs-arms-money circle," says Jeffrey Robinson, author of *The Laundrymen* and other books about organized crime. The Taliban, he says, is one of the biggest drug pushers in the world and accounts for 80 per cent of the heroin distributed in Europe, even—thanks to stockpiles—after a putative ban on opium poppy growing. He suspects much of the Taliban drug money goes directly to support bin Laden's Al-Qaeda network. Whatever the source of the money, great effort is put into concealing its trail.

The toughest step in money laundering is the first—converting cold cash into a financial instrument. Often the money earned from an illegal activity is commingled with cash income earned from a legitimate business—say a casino or restaurant or video-rental shop. Once the money is deposited in a bank, says one banker, it's washed. The next step is to hide its trail, and this—thanks to bank secrecy, lawyer-client confidentiality, and offshore accounts—is easy: money skips in and out of bank accounts, numbered companies and offshore institutions. It is wired internationally between individuals using numbered accounts and a multitude of assumed names. It's likely to make a quick stop in Panama, one country that still permits bearer notes. With this financial instrument, ownership of the accompanying asset—company bonds, perhaps, or even an investment certificate in a firm whose owner is difficult to trace—is conveyed to whoever is holding the paper.

The money may also have travelled around the globe through a centuries-old system known as hawala, which originated in South Asia and is common among émigrés who send money home privately to relatives. A hawala—illegal in many parts of the world—is a network of independent merchants who operate an underground banking system, often across borders, that is based on trust, where records are kept to a minimum and are often in code. Money, in the form of cash or sometimes gold, is left with one merchant who phones or faxes a fellow hawaladar, who passes on the sums, again in the form of currency or gold, to the recipient. Later, the second merchant will recoup his outlay, minus a small commission, when money needs to go the other way. In the early 1990s, Scotland Yard busted six merchants who moved $180 million a year between Britain and India. "The hawala works because people do not violate the trust," says author Robinson. "If they do, they get killed."

U.S. officials believe the Sept. 11 attacks cost as little as $500,000 (U.S.), or roughly $26,000 per hijacker—not a huge sum of money. After all, the main weapons—the airplanes—were stolen, and box cutters are cheap. Still, the 19 hijackers needed money to cover their rent and living expenses, to pay for airplane tickets and pilot school. Investigators around the world are now searching for the money trail they left. So far, its traces have been well concealed. But it's known that on the eve of the attacks, $15,000 was wired by three of the hijackers to the United Arab Emirates. The sum is thought to be "surplus" funds, left over from the money that financed the hijackings. It was sent in three separate wire transfers to a man, called a "paymaster" by one source, holding a Saudi passport who'd entered the U.A.E. in June and left on Sept. 11 for Karachi, Pakistan. It's also known that 11 of the hijackers stopped in London on their way to the United States. It's suspected the stopover was to pick up money. The hawala between London and Karachi is one of the biggest, Robinson says.

Unlike most bin Laden cells, which finance their own activities, these operatives appear to have been given significant financial support. "Think of bin Laden as the chairman of the board of a holding company with lots of semi-autonomous subsidiaries," says Robinson, a speaker this week at a major annual conference in Montreal on money laundering. "He seeds them and says, 'Go do it.' He has enough of them out there, you know. It's a percentage game." Ahmed Ressam, the Montreal-based militant who entered the U.S. with a trunkful of bomb-making material on the eve of the millennium, is an example of the more traditional bin Laden method. Ressam, who will be sentenced in February, was linked to groups in Canada and the U.S. involved in credit-card fraud and counterfeiting passports.

With its proximity to the States, plus sophisticated capital markets, a welcoming immigration policy and lax anti-money-laundering laws, Canada has long been viewed as the perfect locale for washing dirty cash. Chris Mathers, now president of KPMG Corporate Intelligence Inc. in Toronto, worked for 20 years as an undercover RCMP officer. For 10 years, he operated a bogus money-laundering operation. When it came time for meetings with the "bad guys," he recalls, he'd propose Amsterdam or Panama. "I like to go to exotic places," he says. "They'd say, 'Vancouver's nice.'" The reason? "You take a hit for money laundering or drug trafficking in this country and it's almost unheard-of for you to get serious jail time." Canada's reputation among its friends internationally is similarly loose. "Canada is home to virtually every ethnic organized crime group in the world," the U.S. state department lamented in early 2000, in a country report that began: "Canada remains vulnerable to money laundering."

At the time of the state department report, Ottawa was pushing through Parliament new anti-laundering legislation that brings Canada closer to its international peers. The law was passed in June, 2000, and was expected to go into effect last spring. It calls for mandatory reporting of suspicious transactions by banks and a wide range of other players, including real estate brokers and lawyers. Cash transactions inside Canada—or transfers out of the country—of more than $10,000 must be reported. The measure establishes a new federal government agency, the Financial Transactions and Reports Analysis Centre, or FinTRAC, which will track suspicious deals and act as a centralized financial intelligence unit. But resistance from the banking industry and legal circles has delayed the law's accompanying regulations. The banks were opposed to the legislation because they didn't want to be gatekeepers or take on what a Bay Street law firm, Osler, Hoskin & Harcourt, deemed "potentially onerous, costly and in many ways problematic obligations." A veteran Canadian securities regulator retorts that the new law could cost some banks part of their business. "In the industry we regulate, everything deals with making or losing money," he says. "These are the people who think greed is good."

The banking industry's concern, says Denise Harrington, spokeswoman for the Canadian Bankers Association, is that the new legislation will create "extra work and volume that won't necessarily get at the problem." The banks, which have voluntarily reported suspicious transactions for the past 10 years, have a "long history of co-operating with law enforcement," she says.

The Federation of Law Societies of Canada, a national umbrella organization, is taking a tougher stance than the bankers. The law undermines the principle of client confidentiality, says federation president Maurice Laprairie—and once the regulations take effect, the federation intends to launch a constitutional challenge. "For the first time," says Laprairie, "lawyers will have to report to a federal agency what their clients are doing and not tell their clients."

On Sept. 12, some of the controversial regulations were put into the official Gazette, making them active. Still, it won't be until Nov. 8 that mandatory reporting of suspicious transactions—a rule that has been common around the world for years—begins in Canada. And other key elements—reporting of cash and cross-border transactions of more than $10,000—may not be brought into effect before the end of 2002.

Some critics are dismayed not only by the delays in the law, but also by its content. Unlike its U.S. counterpart, the Financial Crimes Enforcement Network, FinTRAC does not have law enforcement powers. In fact, police will need to seek a court order before they can get from FinTRAC a detailed disclosure of a suspicious transaction. By comparison, any U.S. law enforcement agency can access the FinCEN database—no search warrant required. "FinTRAC: it's simply a way to employ people and pretend Canada's doing something," says Robinson, who is based in London. "Shame on Canada."

To the RCMP's Beer, however, Canada has made impressive strides in the past two years, from the creation of FinTRAC and the coming mandatory reporting of suspicious transactions to the withdrawal from circulation of $1,000 bills, which were popular among carriers of cash. "At this point, we have the laws and regulations in place to provide a good foundation to shed that reputation of Canada being a money-laundering haven," Beer says. And the attacks on the U.S. have had a major impact: "The level of co-operation has just skyrocketed."

That co-operation will be essential. The Canadian financial services industry is so closely intertwined with the U.S. industry that the two have really become one. Now, with the global links between terrorism and money laundering becoming abundantly clear, Canada just may find the will to intertwine its laws on the movement of money a little more tightly with the rest of the world.

Clarifications

Bearer notes: A bank note that is cashable by the person holding it—the bearer—without proof of identity.

Scotland Yard: The original address of the headquarters of the Metropolitan Police in London, England. Scotland Yard is a short street that used to be the home of a palace where visiting Scottish kings stayed when in London. *Scotland Yard* is often used to indicate the CID or Criminal Investigation Department. The police have now moved from this address, but the new site acknowledges the original address through its name: New Scotland Yard.

Bay Street: Like *Scotland Yard, Bay Street* is used as a description of the activity that takes place there. As many financial institutions have their homes on Bay Street in Toronto, the address is used to indicate financial connections.

Greed is good: A Canadian securities regulator is quoted as saying: "These are the people who think greed is good." This expression (and the sentiment) is taken from a defining movie of the eighties: *Wall Street,* starring Michael Douglas as financier Gordon Gekko.

Talking Points

A report from the U.S. State Department notes that "Canada remains vulnerable to money-laundering." After September 11, 2001, Canada's refugee policy came under attack. In April 2002, the CBS television show *60 Minutes* quoted an expert who claimed that there are at least fifty terrorist organizations in Canada. Assuming these claims to be true, what should Canada do?

The last sentence of the article notes that Canada will intertwine its laws with those of the rest of the world in response to the attacks of September 11, 2001. Is this an overreaction, or is it something that should have happened much earlier? Should Canada allow itself to be pressured by the U.S., or is retaining our sovereignty more important?

Web Research

The Financial Action Task Force on Money Laundering at *www1.oecd.org/fatf* gives an excellent overview of money laundering. It was established by the G7 (Group of Seven nations, which includes Canada) meeting in Paris in 1989. It is particularly interesting and relevant on the subject of money laundering by terrorist groups.

Check out the RCMP Web site. Apart from money laundering information, you can view Canada's ten most wanted criminals, the latest scams, and the schedule for the Musical Ride at *www.rcmp-grc.gc.ca*.

If seeing Canada's ten most wanted isn't enough, go to the FBI's Web site at *www.fbi.gov/mostwant/terrorists/fugitives.htm* and view the most wanted terrorists.

A fascinating site is the Criminal Intelligence Service of Canada at *www.cisc.gc.ca*. Click through to the most recent intelligence report on organized crime. The 2001 report included a section on motorcycle gangs, Asian gangs and "traditional organized crime"—which is, apparently, "Italian-based" crime.

The International Money Laundering Network (or IMoLIN), at *www.imolin.org*, is also a good source for research.

Writing That Works

Introduction—startling fact or statistic: "$17 billion in Canada alone; $2 trillion worldwide. International authorities believe these vast sums are laundered annually through banks and businesses, masking ill-gotten gains with the lustre of clean capital."

Quotations from authorities: "'Suddenly, the world has awakened to this,' says Brian Butler, a senior investigator at the Ontario Securities Commission. 'The attacks have galvanized the world.'"

Parallel structure: "They use similar methods to hide money, move money, even raise money"; "Some critics are dismayed not only by the delays in the law, but also by its content."

Definition: "A hawala—illegal in many parts of the world—is a network of independent merchants who operate an underground banking system, often across borders, that is based on trust, where records are kept to a minimum and are often in code."

Metaphor: "…the perfect locale for washing dirty cash."

Quotations introduced—name and position: "The banking industry's concern, says Denise Harrington, spokeswoman for the Canadian Bankers Association, is that the new legislation will create 'extra work and volume that won't necessarily get at the problem.'"

Will Cybercriminals Run the World?

by Bruce Sterling

Time Canada, June 19, 2000

Picture this scene from the near future: organized crime gets hold of encryption technology so powerful even IRS supercomputers can't crack it. An underground electronic economy emerges, invisible to U.S. tax code. The Federal Government, unable to replenish its coffers, let alone fund a standing army, shrinks until it wields about as much power as a local zoning board. Militias and gangs take over, setting up checkpoints at state borders and demanding tribute of all who pass.

This scenario, in which crypto-wielding cybercriminals take over the world, has become a standard plot device in turn-of-the-century science fiction. I've even used it once or twice. But there is good news on this front. Running the world turns out to be surprisingly challenging. It isn't something an evil mastermind can do just by hitting return on his keyboard.

Encryption algorithms—the mathematical rules by which secret codes are made and broken—have been at the center of a simmering spy-vs.-nerd war since the early 1990s. The anti-encryption forces, which control the technology through laws originally passed to regulate munitions, are led by a handful of spooky U.S. government agencies (such as the FBI and the National Security Agency) with support from the White House that rises and falls from one election cycle to the next—more on that faction later.

The pro-encryption forces are the nerds; with a nod to the cyberpunk school of science-fiction writers, they call themselves "cypherpunks." Though their numbers have always been small, cypherpunks are brave, bold and highly motivated. And they have some programming talent.

Being nerds, however, they are rather unworldly. They are similar in dress, zip code, outlook and philosophy to the Berkeley free-speech activists of the early 1960s, except that the cypherpunks have a bigger megaphone: the Internet. They can encrypt free speech and software as well, so various uptight authority figures cannot stop their heroic data.

The cypherpunks, like the hippies, love to tilt against windmills. Their most glamorous imaginary weapon is not free speech or free software or even free music. It is free money, anonymous electronic cash and untraceable digital funds, free of all government oversight and laundered over the Internet. Dotcom stocks have turned out to be surprisingly close to this utopian vision. They are rather destabilizing.

Luckily for taxmen worldwide, however, money isn't "money" just because some hacker says it is. We don't secretly print our own personal currency on pink paper at Kinko's—not because it's impossible but because nobody would want it. If Alan Greenspan were a masked Kleagle in a big white crypto hood, nobody would use dollars either.

Offshore "data havens" are another piece of classic cypherpunk vaporware. Here's the pitch: just subvert one little Internet-hooked island country, say Tuvalu (.tv) or Tonga (.to), let it pass a bunch of pirate-friendly laws, and you can store anything there that American computer cops disapprove of. This might yet become a real business opportunity if the Internet gets better policed.

But piracy only looks like the free-and-easy island life. It's actually hard work, because it lacks efficient economies of scale. Once you start seriously churning out the product, you quickly become very visible: warehouses, trucks, employee payrolls—it all adds up. The sweet charm of piracy is free, daring little "us" vs. big nasty "them." But any "us" that gets large enough is automatically a "them." Bill Gates was once a hippie programmer, a college dropout from Seattle. But a hippie with a billion dollars is no longer a hippie; he's a billionaire. A hippie with $50 billion is considered a trust.

It's not that a cybercriminal world of conspiratorial smugglers, scofflaws, crooked banks and tax evaders is impossible. Such countries already exist. It's just that they're not anyone's idea of high-tech paradise. They are places like Bulgaria.

It's amazing how clunky and unproductive an economy becomes once its people despise and subvert all its big institutions. Members of the Russian mafia don't shoot people because they like to. They shoot them because in Russia these days a bullet is the quickest way to get things accomplished. In such places, industrial consumerism just curls up and vanishes. Black markets take its place; there are no more fast-food chains, so everybody eats lunch out of the trunk of a car.

If everything on the Net was encrypted and belonged to small groups of with-it hipsters, you would never find a bargain there. You would never find much of anything. You'd have to wait till some hacker in the know was willing to give you the power handshake and turn you on to the cool stuff. That might not cost very much, but it doesn't feel very free.

It has taken some anxious years of real-world experience for people to figure out that crypto turned loose in cyberspace will not make the world blow up. Crypto's more or less around and available now, and no, it's not an explosive munition. The threats were overblown, much like Y2K. The rhetoric of all sides has been crazily provocative.

One expects that of fringe people in Berkeley. The U.S. government, on the other hand, should have been fairer and more honest. The crypto issue, which is still smouldering and poisoning the atmosphere, could have been settled sensibly long ago. We would have found out that some small forms of crypto were useful and practical and that most of the visionary stuff was utter hogwash. It would have shaken out in a welter of disillusionment, just as Flower Power did. But we never got to that point, thanks mostly to the obstreperous attitudes of the anti-crypto forces, who are basically spies.

The FBI does most of the upfront P.R. in the anti-crypto effort. The FBI doesn't like the prospect of losing some wiretaps. That's just the FBI; it would say the same thing about telepathy if it had it. The true secret mavens of crypto are at the NSA. Spy-code breakers such as Alan Turing invented electronic computers in the first place, so the NSA has a long-held hegemony here. The NSA sets the U.S. government's agenda on crypto, and it will not fairly or openly debate this subject, ever.

The NSA would rather die than come in from the cold. Frankly, for the NSA, coming clean probably means a swift death. Heaven only knows what vast, embarrassing skullduggery the agency is up to under Fort Meade with its 40,000 mathematicians, but whatever it is, the NSA certainly doesn't want to stop just because computers belong to everybody now. So the U.S. government has never been honest about crypto and what it means to people in real life. The whole issue is densely shrouded in billowing dry ice and grotesque X-Files hooey. And that's why crypto is still very scary.

Clarifications

Berkeley free-speech activists of the early 1960s: The student Free Speech Movement began at the University of California at Berkeley in 1964. Read more about it at the Berkeley library Web site at *www.lib.berkeley.edu/MRC/FSM.html.*

Vaporware: Vaporware (or, in the Canadian spelling, vapourware) is software that hasn't been written yet. In other words, it's a way to sell something before you put the work into making it.

Scofflaws: As it sounds, it means people who scoff at the law.

Alan Turing: A British mathematician and computer theorist. His Turing Machine was the theoretical prototype of the computer. Unfortunately, Turing died in 1954 and so did not live to see the world his theories led to.

Tilt at windmills: A reference to the novel *Don Quixote,* by Miguel de Cervantes. Don Quixote spent his time jousting with windmills—a fruitless activity—and the expression has come to refer to doing something pointless, particularly in regard to changing the world.

Alan Greenspan as a masked Kleagle in a big white crypto hood: So much to explain in this reference! Alan Greenspan is the Chairman of the United States Federal Reserve Board, or "Fed," which is responsible for setting interest rates in the U.S.; while a Kleagle or a Grand Kleagle is a leader in the Ku Klux Klan, which explains the reference to the big white hood. As for a "crypto" hood, *crypto-* is a prefix meaning hidden or secret. However, in this context it refers to cryptography, or code making.

Talking Points

Bruce Sterling has a sophisticated vocabulary. Judging from the context, what do the following words mean: *hegemony; mavens; welter; obstreperous; subvert?*

Web Research

Read about Bruce Sterling at *http://lonestar.texas.net/~dub/ sterling.html.* He's not Canadian but has written a book (the "steampunk" novel *A Difference Engine*) with William Gibson, who *is* Canadian.

Writing That Works

Introduction—scenario: "Picture this scene from the near future: organized crime gets hold of encryption technology so powerful even IRS supercomputers can't crack it. An underground electronic economy emerges, invisible to U.S. tax code."

Humour—self-deprecation: This type of humour has a speaker putting himself or herself down in a friendly way: "…a standard plot device in turn-of-the-century science fiction. I've even used it once or twice."

Humour—absurdity: "We don't secretly print our own personal currency on pink paper at Kinko's—not because it's impossible but because nobody would want it. If Alan Greenspan were a masked Kleagle in a big white crypto hood, nobody would use dollars either."

Humour—referential: "You'd have to wait till some hacker in the know was willing to give you the power handshake and turn you on to the cool stuff."

Comparison: "They are similar in dress, zip code, outlook and philosophy to the Berkeley free-speech activists of the early 1960s, except that the cypherpunks have a bigger megaphone: the Internet. They can encrypt free speech and software as well, so various uptight authority figures cannot stop their heroic data."

Parallel structure: "Their most glamorous imaginary weapon is not free speech or free software or even free music. It is free money."

Argument: Note how Sterling uses humour, especially mockery, to develop his thesis that there is nothing much to worry about.

He Likes to Watch
by Raizel Robin

Canadian Business, September 3, 2001

On a sunny morning last May, a senior partner in a large construction firm left his office in the suburbs of Toronto. The partner—let's call him John—got into his car, fired up the engine and headed out on some errands. At first, he did nothing out of the ordinary—an appointment with an insurance company, a couple of meetings with clients. Business as usual.

Then John took a detour and went downtown. Way downtown, ending up in the gritty, concrete wasteland where Dundas and Sherbourne streets meet. There, he spotted a woman (later described by a witness as a "crack whore") hanging around on the corner. John flagged her down, and she got into his car. The two of them then drove to a secluded industrial park near Toronto's lakeshore, where she serviced him in the comfort of his car.

Scenes like that are, no doubt, common. But this one was unusual because the whole tawdry event was caught on videotape. Stranger still, the witness was no run-of-the-mill voyeur: he was an investigator with the Toronto-based private investigation firm King-Reed & Associates Ltd. And it wasn't a suspicious wife who hired the surveillance crew; it was the head of the construction company, who had long suspected that John was skimming company clients for a sideline business. The investigator dug up evidence to prove that, too.

The videotape sits among the hundreds of other surveillance tapes that King-Reed has made in the past year alone. "Executive monitoring," as it is euphemistically known at the company, is a service many PI firms across Canada offer, and it generally consists of doing background checks through court documents, performing media searches, occasionally rooting through people's garbage and, sometimes, just asking around. In certain cases, it even means tailing prospective hires, all in the name of preemployment screening. Though clients who request such services still make up a relatively small amount of King-Reed's total business—about 10%—the firm's director, Brian King, says the number has grown significantly in the past decade. Why the paranoia? To avoid a load of embarrassment, not to mention costly lawyers' fees.

Consider the case of Florida-based Sunbeam Corp. When Albert Dunlap, a.k.a. "Chainsaw Al," was appointed CEO in 1996, he was a Wall Street superhero known for his tough-love economics, which he detailed in his bestselling memoir, *Mean Business: How I Save Bad Companies and Make Good Companies Great.* Unfortunately, this time around, the Chainsaw made a poorly performing company even worse. In 1998, board-appointed auditors discovered that Sunbeam's profits were the stuff of fiction, and they alleged that Dunlap had, among other things, declared revenue on products that were still in inventory. After firing him, Sunbeam filed for bankruptcy protection, brought in new management and launched a lawsuit against Dunlap, alleging fraud. The US Securities and Exchange Commission agreed with Sunbeam, finding that, among other things, at least US$62 million of Sunbeam's reported income of US$189 million in 1997 came from accounting fraud. The SEC has launched a lawsuit against Dunlap for an undisclosed sum; the matter has yet to go to court.

The news got even worse—and more embarrassing—for management. This summer, a reporter called the board to inform them that Dunlap had faced similar allegations 20 years earlier. The fact that no one had bothered to look past Dunlap's résumé both stunned and appalled the company's new CEO. "I find it most unusual," Jerry Levin told *The New York Times* this past July, "that anyone could be hired as a chief executive of a major company without having their background thoroughly checked."

But just how thorough is too thorough? Do you really want your prospective employer to know about your family, your university hijinks, perhaps even your lunch-hour sex habits? The high-profile Sunbeam case was a wake-up call for corporate North America, and it set human resources experts and executive search teams atwitter over how far they can go when looking into the backgrounds of potential hires. And here's the scary part: it's further than you'd think.

Brian King, director of King-Reed & Associates, is settled in an over-stuffed leather swivel chair behind his desk, the midday sun filtering through the open blinds of his corner office. His attire is crisp and immaculate, his hair cropped short, but there are hints of private-eye slickness about him—the tiny flash of a gold stud in his ear, the George Hamilton tan, the big, Chiclet-white smile. About the only rough spot on the shiny veneer is his eyes. Puffy, bloodshot and irritated, they make him look tired, drained, as though he's seen too many cheats, liars, criminals and broken hearts over the years. Or maybe it's just his workday, which keeps him holed up in his office from 7 a.m. to 9 p.m. These days, there's more work coming through the door than his firm can keep up with.

Despite his busy schedule, King is a tireless self-promoter, thrice pointing out the framed newspaper articles that mention his firm and drawing attention to his interviewing skills, his black belt in Tae Kwan Do and his ability to tan quickly. He even talks about his skill in spotting liars, and how you can box them in, get them to tell you the truth if you ask the right questions. You can tell a liar just by his body language, he explains—little things like brushing the nose with a finger or not making eye contact.

All these things presumably help private eyes discern which execs are the good guys and which are the bad. And this is the kind of service that increasing numbers of Canadian corporations are using as they attempt to make their screening processes as thorough as possible. Where do clients come from? Companies in the pharmaceutical, sales, banking, insurance and telecommunications industries, mostly. Companies with lots of cash. While a basic public-records search service costs about $300, a growing number of clients are asking for more of everything—from criminal records checks to in-depth interviews—and will even spend $10,000 or more to fund a week of surveillance.

It might be a little early to call the use of private eyes by corporations a full-blown trend, but as Michael Stern, director of the Toronto-based executive search firm Michael Stern Associates Inc., puts it, "There's more of a focus overall on due diligence and making sure—particularly at the senior level—that the person you bring onboard has been checked out as thoroughly as possible." Stern says he's never used an investigator in his background checks on executives, but adds: "You have no one to blame but yourself if it turns out that there were certain questions you should have asked, but didn't."

If you're an exec in a Canadian organization looking to hire someone—and unless you live in Quebec, where the privacy laws are different—your province's human rights legislation states something like Ontario's: you cannot discriminate on the basis of "a record of offenses." Although it sounds pretty straightforward, the wording is actually somewhat deceiving, as it doesn't refer to a criminal record. Rather, it refers to provincial offenses only, such as hunting without a licence or dumping waste illegally. So in order to find out if the person you're considering hiring as chief financial officer has, for example, defrauded a past employer, it's legal for you to ask her to agree to a criminal records search for that specific information. How much you need to know can become a question of ethics, and it depends on the job. "If you're hiring someone to pave roads for you, it probably doesn't matter that they have a record for theft," says Chris Mathers, president of KPMG Corporate Intelligence Inc., a unit formed three years ago in response to client demand. "If you're hiring them to work on the cash register, then it does."

Seems like a no-brainer. The trouble is that getting access to that kind of information can be tricky. Crooks and cheats tend to lie, so they're not likely to cough up the fact that they might have puffed profits somewhere else. Corporations, then, are stuck with the burden of digging the dirt up themselves or hiring someone to do it for them, and there's more dirt than you might think. Mathers, who once worked undercover for the RCMP running a business that laundered money for drug traffickers, cites the example of a former client of his who was acquiring a company. Mathers had the senior executives of the target company fill out personal history forms, which he would then pass to his client. On the form was a box the execs had to check off to authorize a criminal records search. "Almost immediately, one of the very senior people came to us and said, 'Look, I've had a little problem,'" Mathers says. It turned out the executive had been arrested for a sex offense eight years earlier and knew he'd be discovered if he signed the form. His explanation: it was a simple misunderstanding. "When we did the inquiry," Mathers continues, "we found that the 'misunderstanding' was that he didn't understand he wasn't allowed to try to have sex with children."

There's a reason for background checks, says the CEO of a Toronto-based investment firm who wished to remain anonymous for fear that future business partners would know he was using private eyes to check up on them. "And they don't happen often enough," he continues. After retaining King-Reed's services to look into a potential business partner's background on a multimillion-dollar real estate deal, the CEO pulled out. The reason? The guy had a record—for money laundering. What if it's a lesser offense, though? Say you got caught smoking a joint in university. Would that affect your ability to do your job today? Not likely, though it might be enough for management to pass you over. Although Canada's privacy legislation makes it illegal to access health or income tax information, you can get it on the black market of personal information if you want it badly enough. "We have to protect the privacy of individuals," says Mathers, "but not so that people with a criminal past can make use of that privacy legislation to shield their past activities from legitimate citizens."

Canada's privacy commissioner, George Radwanski, did not return phone calls to comment on the legal niceties of privacy and hiring. (Perhaps not surprisingly, his office wouldn't disclose his reason for being unavailable.) New privacy legislation contained in Bill C-6—the Personal Information Protection and Electronic Documents Act—states that you can't collect, use or disclose personal information (name, address, telephone number, etc.) without a person's consent unless it's for journalistic, artistic or literary use. That might make it more difficult to do background inquiries.

"It's probably true that private investigators will have to jump through more hoops to obtain personal information about someone," says Toronto-based privacy lawyer Ara Arzumanian. Companies who go as far as using a private eye don't want the subject to know they're being investigated. If you're looking into someone for a merger or an acquisition, it could jeopardize your business with them if they know you're nosing around. Still, it's not uncommon for large companies, especially those based in the US, to use investigators when considering a merger or acquisition target in Canada—and to keep it quiet when they do.

Typically, they're looking for two things. First, there's the obvious background check to ensure the chief executives at the target company haven't done anything illegal and aren't incompetent. (A prime example was Bre-X, whom King-Reed investigated for a client who was considering doing business with the mining company two years before allegations of fraud hit the media and Bre-X stock self-destructed on the TSE. Based on King-Reed's report, the client decided against it.) The second reason is a little fuzzier. Often, the company just wants to know that the person "has the right fit," as King explains it.

How does a PI make that determination? It's actually not terribly difficult; it just requires some legwork. Criminal records are public information, but they are kept in a repository that only the police can access—and at the courthouse if a trial took place. If you go through the cops, you have to pay a fee in most places and get the person's consent to authorize a search. What if you don't want the CEO of your acquisition target to know you're looking? You can comb through news clippings to find any mention of the person's name in connection with a court case. Once you know the name of the case and where it went to trial, you can go to that courthouse and access the records immediately. To establish someone's reputation, you have several avenues. You can ask around in the community, or phone their colleagues. Want more? Go through their garbage—as long as it's on the curb, it's perfectly legal to sift through it. (Careful about recycling, though. If you take someone's bottles and cans, it's theft.) And then there's always family court and litigation records, also available at the courthouse. "In many cases, you can tell a lot about these executives by looking at divorce records," says King, referring to the wealth of personal information you can find in the pleadings between parties—anything from alleged affairs to a person's net worth.

If all else fails, get creative. King recalls a time he was hired to do due diligence on a small Ontario-based chocolate manufacturer that a big US company wanted to acquire. The American firm was run by executives who were "very religious Baptists," says King, and they wanted to ensure that the people who ran the target company had the same sort of moral rectitude—or, as King says jokingly, "They wanted to make sure they would be hiring people whose every second word wasn't the F-word." King hired local people to go in undercover as customers, buy chocolates and get to know the owners. They did a litigation search and criminal record check, then talked to people in the community who knew the owners of the company. "Within a week, we had a good understanding of what the people were about. They fit—they were OK."

No one's hurt, no laws broken, so what's the harm? It comes down to a question of ethics. Stern tells of a client he recently met with who is currently the CEO of a US company. Stern asked the CEO what he would do if he was up for a bigger job and the company said he had the skills and experience, but it just wanted a private eye to check into his personal life. "He said he would ask: 'What areas would you want to look into, and are you sure that there is some relevance to the job?'" Stern explains. "'If I'm a subscriber to 12 gambling sites, and that's how I like to spend my evenings, and it doesn't affect my job, then no.'"

It's a scorcher of an August day in Toronto, and Terry Brook, an investigator with King-Reed, is on the tail of a trader. Brook is a baby-faced 29-year-old with observant eyes of the most intense blue. Patting his stomach, he complains that his six-foot-three frame could be leaner. Today, as is often the case, he doesn't know exactly why he's following the trader—corporate clients often supply information on a need-to-know basis. "Maybe he's about to leave for a competitor," muses Brook. "Or maybe he's doing some insider trading. Who knows?"

Brook knows all he needs right now, however, and it's enough to make any paranoid's skin crawl. He knows the name of the trader, where he works, his age and birth date, his car's make and model, his home and work address, his marital status, and that he's supposed to watch what the trader does for the afternoon.

After clearing some baseball equipment out of the back seat of his nondescript SUV, turning his alt-rock radio station down a notch and setting up a small Canadian Tire fan, Brook pulls out a notepad, his handheld video camera and some binoculars. He keeps an eye on the trader's driveway, waiting to see where he goes—if he leaves the house at all. Fifteen minutes later, the vehicle is like a sauna. It has to look empty, with the engine off and the windows sealed. There is no air conditioning, no fresh air. Despite the thrash-metal song on the radio and the constant humming from the fan, several couples walk by without even a glance in the SUV's direction.

Forty minutes into the stakeout, the trader makes a move. He comes out of the house, opens the door of his minivan, rearranges a few things, then gets behind the wheel. Brook follows him around town for the afternoon as the trader does his errands and has a meeting or two—that's about as exciting as it gets. Brook gets out of the SUV and follows him into several buildings, at one point getting into an elevator with him. The whole time, the trader is oblivious, never glancing at the SUV or at Brook. He goes about his business without even a hint of the fact that right behind him—at times right beside him—there is someone watching his every move.

Clarifications

The George Hamilton tan, the big, Chiclet-white smile: In case this description means nothing to you, the actor George Hamilton is known for having a full-body tan, even, so rumour has it, sunbathing with his toes separated by toothpicks. Chiclets are a brand of small rectangular gum about the size of teeth.

Bre-X: In 1997, Bre-X, a Canadian gold mining and exploration company, was exposed as having given false reports about the gold it had found in Indonesia. The reports had led to a huge surge in the company's stock price, which fell to almost nothing once the scandal was uncovered.

Due diligence: A legal term referring to the amount of care exercised by a reasonably prudent person. In the case of one company buying another, it means the purchasing company must be careful to check that the other company is not doing anything illegal or nasty.

Insider trading: Illegal insider trading occurs when executives of a company sell or buy shares when they have inside knowledge about an event that will affect the price of the share. For example, in 2002, family members of the CEO of ImClone sold shares in the company days before the U.S. Food and Drug Administration rejected a license for a cancer drug the company produced. Many Web sites offer to help you with so-called "insider trading" tips; one is *www.quicken.ca*. However, these kinds of tips are not illegal as they do not actually come from inside the companies in question.

Talking Points

The author of the article asks, "But just how thorough is too thorough? Do you really want your prospective employer to know about your family, your university hi-jinks, perhaps even your lunch-hour sex habits?" What are the limits here? Does an employer have the right to look into these types of activities?

What business crimes are currently in the news that might have been stopped if companies had used the services described in the article?

Web Research

Find the complete Privacy Act on the Department of Justice Web site at *http://laws.justice.gc.ca/en/P-21/*.

The University of Ottawa has a Human Rights Research and Education Centre site at *www.cdp-hrc.uottawa.ca/links/sitescan_e. html.*

The KPMG Corporate Intelligence Web page, with articles and links to other forensic accounting sites, is at *www.kpmg.ca/english/services/ fas/fornsic/corporate_intelligence.html.*

When Pros Become Cons
by Robert Reguly

Canadian Business, October 1992

It's the annual open house at Beaver Creek penitentiary, just outside the Northern Ontario resort town of Gravenhurst, and a couple of dozen townspeople are being shown there is nothing to fear from the 122 inmates, about a half-dozen of them white-collar crooks, on their escorted shopping expeditions to town for treats like pizza and ice cream. All the inmates have transformed themselves into pussycats, according to the federal classification system, and are serving out their terms in this minimum security institution with no walls and no menacing guard towers. There aren't even cells. Instead, most prisoners have private rooms where they can install their own television or compact disc player—as most do—or even a computer.

No wonder many call it Club Fed. Beaver Creek and the 12 other minimum security prisons like it across Canada are where the federal penal system puts those prisoners it considers to be non-violent. That includes the most tractable of the system's murderers, rapists and drug dealers, who come here after serving time in much harsher medium or maximum security prisons. It also includes most of the system's white-collar criminals. Defraud your employer or dip into a client's trust fund, and Beaver Creek or a similar prison is where you will likely wind up. In theory, a stay at Club Fed is the deterrent that keeps business people on the straight and narrow. In practice, life here doesn't seem so different from life outside.

On this rainy Saturday, the mini-putt golf course is deserted. In the cafeteria, a group is sitting at one of the tables for four, smoking and drinking coffee while waiting for lunch. Today, it's hamburgers. The system allots $3.85 per prisoner per day for food, wholesale, so macaroni and meat loaf are staples. It's the prisoners' weekend off from their five-day workweek chores of making coffee tables and end tables for government offices, microfilming documents under contract to municipalities, picking up roadside trash in cottage country or shovelling snow. At this moment, one lucky prisoner is in a home-style unit with his legal or common-law wife for three days of uninhibited bonding in private. The demand is so great that a second unit has been approved.

The prison's sparkling gymnasium has been transformed for the open house into a display room of the crafts made by prisoners—kids' toys, water-color paintings, nature scenes etched into elaborately framed glass mirrors. In the exercise room at one side of the gym a bunch of prisoners are pumping iron. The music room, opposite the gym, contains a variety of instruments, including saxes, clarinets, a set of drums and a Yamaha electronic keyboard, which prisoner Julius Melnitzer has reserved to play for two and a half hours every Wednesday night.

Melnitzer, a lawyer from London, Ont., and one of the more notorious white-collar criminals in recent years, pleaded guilty last winter of defrauding Canadian banks and financial institutions of $67 million. He conned five banks by printing up $100 million in forged blue-chip stock certificates as collateral for loans. He blew his borrowings on manorial houses, exotic vacations, fast cars and beautiful women The court in a forlorn gesture, ordered him to pay back $20 million in unrecovered money, although any hope of seeing that money is remote. Melnitzer was given a nine-year sentence and, since he was considered non-violent, was shipped to Beaver Creek to atone.

Melnitzer, who declined to be interviewed, had a rough introduction to prison. He began as a kitchen helper, but his mouthing off at finding the work demeaning earned him a five-day stretch of cleaning toilets. Today he spends his time teaching other prisoners and, of course, playing the keyboard. He was even given a 72-hour pass, plus travel time, to go home for his daughter's graduation.

His case demonstrates that the wages of sin can be very good indeed. A federal prisoner—that is, anyone sentenced to two years or more—has to serve only one-sixth of a sentence before being eligible for day parole or release to a halfway house. That's virtually automatic for a crook who steals at penpoint. After serving another one-sixth of his sentence out in the community, which requires only a nightly sleepover, the criminal is eligible for a full parole on completing one-third of his sentence.

Melnitzer, unless he does something stupid to alienate the authorities, will be outside after serving 18 months. That works out to $122,000 a day in time served for the amount he admitted to defrauding from the banks and others. Not bad money for playing the keyboard.

A sentence at Club Fed is not exactly a week at a tropical resort. But for those sent here, durance vile is more than tolerable. Other countries and other cultures may consider lopping off a limb or hard labor as the only fit response to crime. For Canada's penal system, the philosophy is a bit different. It's to reform prisoners through work, study, recreation—and even a bit of golf.

At the Bath, Ont., minimum security prison, just outside Kingston, hitting a few balls on the driving range is only one after-work activity prisoners can indulge in. They can also cook up steaks brought by their families on barbeques around the visitor reception centre; play tennis or shuffleboard; or pursue their hobbies in the crafts centre.

None of this may sound like the dire fate that you imagined lying in wait for those who have transgressed the law. But, then, punishment isn't the goal of the system. Correctional Service of Canada, the operator of the prisons, says its overriding concern in deciding who gets sent to a minimum security facility is to protect the public from criminals who may be violent. White-collar crooks usually are nonthreatening, at least in the physical sense.

"We look at whether an inmate presents a risk to the public or to the local community," says Les Judson, the warden at Beaver Creek. "Lawyers, white-collar people, [break and enter] artists, don't have violence in their backgrounds. There is a perception by the public that white-collar crimes get some kind of different treatment. That's emphatically not true." But he allows: "Some require psychological counseling because of their propensity to take advantage of people."

Instead of punishment, the goal of incarceration at Club Fed is to ease prisoners safely back into society, this time as legally productive citizens. The latest plan is to help inmates, many of whom are functionally illiterate, gain basic living skills by accommodating them in row houses grouped in clusters to form a mock neighborhood. Each of the eight inmates in a two-story house will have his own bedroom but share a living room, laundry room and kitchen. Each prisoner will be responsible for making his own meals with food selected from a central depot on a $4-per-person daily allowance.

If nothing else, Club Fed does save the taxpayer money. Judson points out that it costs $33,000 a year to keep a prisoner at the Beaver Creek minimum security prison, compared with $67,000 in maximum security prisons and $44,000 in medium security institutions.

The biggest problem that many white-collar inmates face when they arrive at Club Fed is the enormous cultural gap that separates them from the other inmates. No longer can they depend on a silver tongue to get them out of trouble. "The white collars are quite shocked by these people," says Michael Quirt, a Beaver Creek psychological consultant. "A lot of white-collar inmates' trappings and control attitudes don't work inside. They have to learn to shut up more and be careful what they say and how they say it. You don't talk to your friendly neighborhood drug addict the way you talk to your board of directors."

Still, after an initial period of denial, most white-collar inmates settle down to their fate—and some actually enjoy prison life. Quirt says that away from their former pressure-cooker lifestyles, they take up broader reading and sports—"not to win"—and find time to smell the roses. For the first time in their hyperactive lives, they have time to talk to their children.

It's a life that a discerning inmate might well be reluctant to leave. The parole board at the Bath prison recently had to turn thumbs down on a request from an inmate, a disbarred lawyer, who declared that for the first time in his life he had found a purpose for his existence— teaching literacy skills to unschooled fellow prisoners. Forget his parole, he told the board. He wanted to stay.

Clarifications

White-collar criminals: White-collar crime is defined by the *Columbia Encyclopedia* as crime of property "committed by people of relatively high social status in the course of their professional or business careers."

Durance vile: The Scottish poet Robert Burns (1759–1796) first used the term "durance vile" in his poem *Epistle from Esopus to Maria*. The poem's narrator was supposedly in the workhouse, which is where people were sent in Britain when they were unable to survive any other way. The phrase was picked up by the American comic W. C. Fields, who used it in many of his monologues to mean *in jail*. Here is a verse from Burns's poem:

> *A Workhouse! ah, that sound awakes my woes,*
> *And pillows on the thorn my rack'd repose!*
> *In durance vile here must I wake and weep,*
> *And all my frowsy couch in sorrow steep;*
> *That straw where many a rogue has lain of yore,*
> *And vermin'd gipsies litter'd heretofore.*

Club Fed: The reference here is to Club Med, a chain of resorts.

Talking Points

The implication of this article's title, "Club Fed," is that the prisons are more like resorts than prisons. Do you agree that white collar prisoners are treated too well? Should all prisoners be treated equally, or should the fact that some committed what are sometimes called "victimless crimes" play a part in sentencing? Are white-collar crimes in fact victimless?

At the other end of the price spectrum, it costs the government over $3,000 a day to keep Quebec Hells Angels leader Maurice "Mom" Boucher in prison. A hundred million dollars has been spent fighting the Hells Angels in Quebec, including the construction of a new, specially fortified courthouse. Sixty million was needed for a special anti-biker police squad, named the Carcajou squad. (Facts taken from an article published in the *Globe and Mail* on January 13, 2002). Is this expense justified?

Web Research

Read the laws of Canada on the Department of Justice Web site at: *http://canada.justice.gc.ca*.

Take a closer look at the Beaver Creek facility (mentioned in the article as the then-current home of Julius Melnitzer) at the Correctional Service of Canada site: *www.csc-scc.gc.ca*.

Writing That Works

Introduction—anecdote: The story of the townspeople being shown what sounds like a resort, rather than a prison, sets the tone for the rest of the article.

Description: "The prison's sparkling gymnasium has been transformed for the open house into a display room of the crafts made by prisoners—kids' toys, water-color paintings, nature scenes etched into elaborately framed glass mirrors. In the exercise room at one side of the gym a bunch of prisoners are pumping iron. The music room, opposite the gym, contains a variety of instruments, including saxes, clarinets, a set of drums and a Yamaha electronic keyboard, which prisoner Julius Melnitzer has reserved to play for two and a half hours every Wednesday night." Note that the description here is used as an emotional device. The prison actually sounds like a pleasant place to live.

Analogy: "A sentence at Club Fed is not exactly a week at a tropical resort." This analogy, or non-analogy, comes after descriptions of the prison that make it sound as if it is a tropical resort. This particular analogy relates to the title: "Club Fed."

TOPIC *10*

THE WORKABLE FUTURE

INTRODUCTION

Predicting the future has always been a tricky thing. For every pre-
scient Jules Verne novel or Star Trek episode, there is someone who
predicted that man would never fly, that there would be nuclear war
by 1980, and that the Y2K bug would have planes dropping out of the
sky as the century turned. Bad predictions leave the predictors looking
foolish for years. Imagine having predicted, as a movie company executive did in the actor's early years, that Clint Eastwood would never
become a movie star, or that the Rolling Stones would be more successful if they dropped the singer with the big lips.

In business and technology, the list of failed predictions is large
and amusing. Here is a selection:
- "That's an amazing invention, but who would ever want to use
one of them?" President Rutherford B. Hayes to Alexander
Graham Bell, 1876.

- "It doesn't matter what he does, he will never amount to anything." Albert Einstein's teacher to his father, 1895.

- "I have anticipated [radio's] complete disappearance—confident that the unfortunate people, who must now subdue themselves to 'listening-in' will soon find a better pastime for their
leisure." H. G. Wells, *The Way the World Is Going*, 1925.

- "The problem with television is that the people must sit and
keep their eyes glued on a screen; the average American family
hasn't time for it." The *New York Times*, after a prototype televi-

sion was demonstrated at the 1939 World's Fair.

• "The Japanese don't make anything the people in the U.S. would want." Secretary of State John Foster Dulles, 1954.

• "In all likelihood, world inflation is over." Managing director of the International Monetary Fund, 1959.

• "The concept is interesting and well-formed, but in order to earn better than a 'C,' the idea must be feasible." A Yale University management professor in response to student Fred Smith's paper proposing reliable overnight delivery service. Smith went on to found Federal Express.

• "By the turn of this century, we will live in a paperless society." Roger Smith, chairman of General Motors, 1986.

The predictions in the following chapter sound more plausible. Read them with the quotations above in mind.

Robot Renaissance
by Danylo Hawaleshka

Maclean's, August 21, 2000

Takeo Kanade is fun to be with. Pleasant, bright—very bright, in fact—Kanade speaks with a playful enthusiasm, smiling or chuckling often when making a particularly fantastic point about his work in robotics, and the future. A self-described optimist, Kanade is the internationally respected director of The Robotics Institute at Carnegie Mellon University in Pittsburgh. And like many in his field, Kanade is convinced that rapid advances in computing power mean today's children will live to see machines that are smarter than they are.

Such a machine may be a humanoid robot, or it may take on a form more suited to its task. Kanade is confident that, whatever it looks like, scientists' creations will in effect outdo human evolution within a generation. "Why not?" he asks, pointing out that computers evolve much faster than humans because of their ability to copy data. "A child born today has to start almost from zero," says Kanade, "but machines can download—copy. And copying is one of the most powerful forms of learning."

The idea of building a thinking robot in our own image to do our bidding is not new, but it is becoming increasingly tangible, especially as computing power vastly expands. The Honda Motor Co. in 1996 unveiled the P2, the first bipedal robot able to walk untethered to a power source or command centre. It was the result of a 12-year research effort costing an estimated $150 million. In 1997, Honda revealed the P3, smaller and with longer battery life than its predecessor. Research to improve the closely guarded secrets of the P3 design continues; Kanade is collaborating on a new vision system.

But many scientists, Kanade among them, question whether we really need to build a humanoid. They say it makes more sense to design a robot's body to suit its task. That logic doesn't do much for Robert J. Sawyer, Canada's award-winning author of science fiction set in the near future, who thinks smart robots will almost certainly look like us. "The contemporary roboticist saying with disdain, 'Well, why does it have to look like a human?' is kind of like a contemporary chef saying, 'Well, why does it have to be palatable to our taste buds when I make a meal?' The answer," says Sawyer, "is because that is what we want."

It also seems quite likely what we will get. Hans Moravec, principal research scientist at The Robotics Institute, believes that at least some of the machines we build will come in human proportions and, certainly, think like us. But more to the point, super-smart mechanical devices are, barring cataclysms, a near-term inevitability, says Moravec, an Austrian-born Canadian who grew up in Montreal. In his 1998 book *Robot: Mere Machine to Transcendent Mind,* Moravec sees robots soon performing better than humanly possible. He calls these intelligent machines our "mind children" and writes that "it behooves us to give them every advantage, and to bow out when we can no longer contribute." In an interview with *Maclean's,* Moravec argued that humans, designed for the Stone Age, have changed the world, and now they, too, must change. "I want robots to succeed us," he said. "Trying to prevent that is almost obscene in my mind."

The prospect is no doubt frightening to many. Michael Greenspan, a research officer at the National Research Council's Institute for Information Technology in Ottawa, has followed both sides of the emerging debate. "Often, when people think of advanced applications of artificial intelligence, they think of some dark Orwellian world where these systems impinge on our freedoms," says Greenspan. "But the reality is there are a lot of cases where you can have extreme improvement in health care and quality of life." For his part, Kanade sees no ethical quandary in creating a physically and mentally superior robot, and dismisses the suggestion that such a device be considered a life-form. "It's not a life-form; it's an intellectual entity," Kanade says. "And frankly I don't see any problem in teaching a 'student' who is far smarter than any other student. What's wrong with that?"

Without doubt, both the dream and the nightmare have a long history. "Robot" comes from the Czech word *robota,* meaning "forced labour." Its use today derives from a Czech play written in 1920 depicting society as dependent on mechanical slaves for physical and mental work. Since then, robots have permeated popular culture, and are usually portrayed as either loyal servants or diabolical threats. On the charming side, there was the loveable tin tub known as Robot in the 1960s TV series *Lost in Space,* the bumbling but earnest android C3PO in 1977's *Star Wars* and the brilliant but emotionless Data in TV's *Star Trek: The Next Generation.* More frightening, of course, was the mainframe-like HAL 9000 in 1968's *2001: A Space Odyssey,* which set out to kill the human astronauts aboard the space ship they shared. It should come as no surprise, says Sawyer, that robots are normally thought of as servants, given mankind's long history with slavery. "The idea of having somebody who is like you but forced to be subservient to you," says Sawyer, "seems to be deeply ingrained in our psyche."

So far, it's true, the robots around us are completely service oriented—and demand for them has become intense. Orders for industrial robots in North America skyrocketed 60 per cent last year, totalling $2.1 billion, according to the Robotic Industries Association, a trade group in Ann Arbor, Mich. The biggest gains came from robots that weld, handle materials and assemble products, especially in the auto industry, but robots are increasingly being used to load pallets with beer or toilet paper, put together cell phones and computers—even decorate cakes. "There are lots of manufacturers who have got to do a lot of something in a hurry," says Jeff Burnstein, the association's director of marketing, "and robots have the flexibility to help them do that."

Robots are also beginning to make their mark outside of factories. San Diego-based Pyxis Corp. makes the HelpMate, a robotic courier for hospitals used to transport pharmaceuticals, lab samples and medical records between wards. HelpMate resembles a trash can with signal lights, much like *Star Wars'* other famous robot, R2D2. Sonar keeps it from bumping into things as it rolls along a little slower than a person walks. Don Chase, a product manager at Pyxis, says HelpMate's acceptance is remarkable, with people who use them frequently naming their robots, dressing them up for Christmas parties and giving them photo ID just like human staff.

Yet for all their practical applications, such robots lack the jaw-dropping star appeal of Honda's P3 humanoid. There is something uncanny about seeing the P3 stride eerily across a room on two legs that move like a gawky teenager's. With a battery pack good for 25 minutes, the P3 negotiates stairs and uneven terrain as easily as it crosses a level floor. Its eyes are digital camera lenses, it has two arms and hands (but no fingers), and it can push a cart, flip a switch, close valves, bow, wave, shake hands.

Not everyone is impressed. Paul Johnston, who is a vice-president with Ottawa-based PRECARN Associates Inc., a consortium of Canadian organizations and companies dedicated to building intelligent and robotic systems, concedes that Honda's motivation for P3—besides publicity—included development of legitimate technologies related to balance and control. "Nobody diminishes the achievement in it," he says, "but the skeptics would say, 'And what use is that robot?'" For its part, Honda says successors to the P3 could one day aid hospital patients, act as a security guard or work in a nuclear power plant.

There is still a long way to go towards a truly human-like machine, legged or not. Building a thinking android requires major advances in sensors and reasoning. Moravec at Carnegie Mellon notes the human brain has some 100 billion neurons, each with thousands of connections. Even with digital processor speeds doubling almost annually, Moravec estimates it will take 20 to 30 years before machines can approach what the brain is capable of. "We still don't have the computer power," says Moravec. "We'd like to build a 747, but we only have a rubber band to power it."

Still, major progress has been made. In the past decade, computers have composed sophisticated music that passed for human creations, IBM's Big Blue defeated world chess champion Garry Kasparov, while researchers at Carnegie Mellon built a robot equipped with a sophisticated vision system that drove a van across the breadth of North America. Each year, the machines get a little smarter, a little more independent. "In 30 years," says Kanade, "humans will probably not be the best at doing most of the things we do today." To the nightmare scenarists, it won't be long after that before the machines start to think hard about turning the tables. "If you're more intelligent than the masters," says Sawyer, "I can't see any reason whatsoever why you would say, 'This strikes me as an eminently equitable relationship. I will be more powerful and more intelligent, but I'll take all the orders from that little weak sack of flesh over there and be happy about it.'" Perhaps. But that, of course, will require a robot that understands what happiness is.

Robo-helpers

Mention robots and someone is bound to ask whether one exists to vacuum the house. It does, but getting mechanical maids to market has proved tricky. They tend to be expensive, for one thing, and several manufacturers are still trying to perfect their prototypes' crucial obstacle sensors. Undaunted, Pittsburgh-based Probotics Inc. makes Cye, a wheeled robot that pulls a wagon and can vacuum when fitted with an accessory. The vacuum version, retailing for $1,160, navigates using radio waves and a personal computer. British vacuum manufacturer Dyson Inc., meanwhile, is testing the DC06, which is packed with over 50 sensors and three microprocessors. No release date has been set for what is seen by some as the Rolls-Royce of robo-vacs, with a price to match: $5,200. Likewise, the Eureka Company of Bloomington, Ill., has produced a prototype using sonar that is expected to retail for $1,500, but it too still needs work. There is also the matter of training service people to fix them. "Add a microprocessor and sonar technology to your vacuum cleaner," says Eureka spokeswoman Kathy Luedke, "and you've got a whole different critter."

Clarifications

Humanoid: The *-oid* part of the word comes from the Greek *oeids*, meaning shape or form. A humanoid, therefore, is something that has human shape or form but is not human.

Cataclysm: A violent, devastating event such as an earthquake or volcanic eruption. When the word describes a non-physical event, it is being used metaphorically to mean something that shatters us mentally, rather than physically.

It behooves us: It is suitable or morally necessary for us.

Stone Age: The period in human development when humans used stone tools. The Stone Age began about two million years ago and encompassed the Paleolithic, Mesolithic and Neolithic ages. The end of the Stone Age came at different times in different parts of the world, but generally it was over around four thousand years ago. Contrary to what you might see on *The Flintstones,* Stone Age humans did not coexist with dinosaurs.

Some dark Orwellian world: A reference to writer George Orwell's vision of the future, as described in his novel *Nineteen Eighty-four.*

Prototype: The original example or model.

Talking Points

Should robots look human, as Robert J. Sawyer contends? I recently heard a commentator on the CBC remark that the reason we hate rats is that they don't look like our children; in other words, they have long narrow faces rather than the chubby round faces we associate with infants. What types of human features should a robot have in order to appeal to us?

How do you imagine humanity using robots of the future? What kind of work would you like to give to robots?

How has Hollywood affected how we think about robots? Two contrasting visions that come to mind are the *Terminator* movies and *A.I.* Will these preconceived notions influence the way we eventually use robots?

Web Research

Visit the Web site of the Robotics Institute of Carnegie Mellon University at *www.ri.cmu.edu.*

The Honda P3 is a fascinating humanoid. Take a look at it in a QuickTime movie on the Honda Humanoid Robots Web site at *www.honda-p3.com.*

The National Research Council's Institute for Information Technology Web site has many links for researching Artificial Intelligence at *www.iit.nrc.ca/ai_point.html.*

Writing That Works

Definition: "'Robot' comes from the Czech word *robota,* meaning 'forced labour.' Its use today derives from a Czech play written in 1920 depicting society as dependent on mechanical slaves for physical and mental work."

Examples: "On the charming side, there was the loveable tin tub known as Robot in the 1960s TV series *Lost in Space,* the bumbling but earnest android C3PO in 1977's *Star Wars* and the brilliant but emotionless Data in TV's *Star Trek: The Next Generation.* More frightening, of course, was the mainframe-like HAL 9000 in 1968's *2001: A Space Odyssey,* which set out to kill the human astronauts aboard the space ship they shared."

Examples: "Still, major progress has been made. In the past decade, computers have composed sophisticated music that passed for human creations, IBM's Big Blue defeated world chess champion Garry Kasparov, while researchers at Carnegie Mellon built a robot equipped with a sophisticated vision system that drove a van across the breadth of North America."

Expert opinion: "Paul Johnston, who is a vice-president with Ottawa-based PRECARN Associates Inc., a consortium of Canadian organizations and companies dedicated to building intelligent and robotic systems, concedes that Honda's motivation for P3—besides publicity—included development of legitimate technologies related to balance and control. 'Nobody diminishes the achievement in it,' he says, 'but the skeptics would say, "And what use is that robot?"'"

Tomorrow's Body Shop
by Michael Smith

ROB Magazine, February 26, 1999

"What you're looking at here is a human femur," says John Davies, tossing a bone onto the only clear spot on his crowded University of Toronto desk. The femur has been sawed through lengthwise to expose its interior, a complicated three-dimensional lacework called trabecular bone. It's that 3-D filigree of bone—or more precisely, the ability to re-create it in the lab—that biomaterials and dentistry professor

Davies hopes will turn his brand-new company, BoneTec Corp., into a moneymaker.

In another U of T building a few hundred metres west, biomedical engineering professor Michael Sefton talks about lessening the need for heart donors by growing hearts in the lab. In Quebec City, Laval University surgery professor François Auger is making living skin, blood vessels and, most recently corneas. Mississauga, Ont.'s GenSci Regeneration Sciences Inc. already has a human-bone product on the market and hopes to turn its first profit this year. In the United States, dozens of companies are promising—and some are delivering—living tissue off the shelf.

Welcome to the new world of tissue engineering, where the goal is to repair humans in the same way that we fix cars, by removing the worn or damaged parts and popping in new ones straight from the factory. It's a glorious dream and one sustained by the fact that some simple tissues are already available. For example, a doctor trying to heal ulcerated skin can now reach into a cupboard and pull out living lab-grown patches.

Predictably, however, the hype is outrunning the help. If you go by the U.S. magazine *Business Week,* opportunity for profit is enormous. Last July, the magazine devoted a cover story to the industry, opining that dozens of start-up companies are about to "perfect living organs grown in the lab." Reconstructive surgeon Peter Johnson, former president of the Pittsburgh Tissue Engineering Initiative, says tissue engineering is a medical paradigm shift that will revolutionize the pharmaceutical industry, eventually creating an $80-billion (U.S.) market. "It's so promising," says Johnson, who recently left the non-profit Pittsburgh research consortium for a job at TissueInformatics.Inc. Alan Tuck, chief strategic officer of Organogenesis Inc., one of the U.S.'s leading tissue-engineering companies, says simply: "We're building the future."

But the future is not here yet, and even a tissue-engineering booster like Johnson, who bought into the promise early, acknowledges that there are enormous hurdles to be overcome. No one really knows yet how to make cells grow into functional organs, and solving the technical problems will require a co-ordinated array of skills and knowledge. And like pure biotechnology, tissue-engineering products usually take 10 years to win marketing approval. (Biotechnologists deal mostly in proteins, which are really just specialized kinds of chemicals with useful effects on the body. Tissue engineers, on the other hand, seek to grow actual tissues in the lab—ranging from skin cells to organs.)

Above all, the hurdles are financial. Getting over the scientific, organizational and regulatory hurdles for any given product is estimated to cost about $200 million. The field, warns Canadian venture-capitalist Calvin Stiller, is littered with "white coats with stars in their eyes and, on the other side, slick dudes with PowerPoint"—that is, on one side, impractical scientists obsessed with a dream and, on the other, shark entrepreneurs overselling that dream. No wonder, as he puts it, "it's a nuclear winter" when it comes to finding money for speculative medical start-ups. "That said," adds Stiller, CEO of the $250-million Canadian Medical Discoveries Fund, "we're putting money in there."

Putting money in doesn't guarantee getting money out, of course. Stiller, whose life-sciences venture-capital fund is based in London, Ont., likes to compare both biotechnology and tissue engineering with diamond mining. When you find diamonds, he says, you just dig them up and sell them. But finding a scientific gem is just the first step: "If you find a diamond in biotech, it just takes more money," Stiller says. The same is true for tissue engineering.

Translation: Everything is a long way off and will cost a lot. John Davies says that his BoneTec Corp. is five years away from having a product to sell. BoneTec had its start in the academic labs of Davies and fellow U of T professor Molly Shoichet, where then-doctoral student Chantal Holy found a way to spin a common polymer used in surgical sutures into a complicated, bonelike foam. It was, Davies says, the first time that scientists had been able to duplicate the internal structure of bone. Seeded with bone cells from the patient and bathed in a growth medium, the biodegradable foam is intended to be the scaffold on which real human bone could grow in the lab. And that could make bone grafts—difficult and painful procedures—much easier.

Now, to obtain bone for a graft, surgeons cut into the patient's hipbone and "hack some out with a hammer and chisel," says Davies, not without a certain relish at the gruesome image. With BoneTec's foam, that initial surgery—fraught with its own pain, cost and risk of complications—could be replaced by a syringe that would extract bone marrow cells. These cells would be seeded onto the foam and grown into bone, which would then be used for the graft. So, last March, with support from an angel investor, the three researchers formed BoneTec to commercialize the process. Within six months, they had obtained three offers from venture capitalists for seed money to keep the research going.

In attracting swift investor interest, BoneTec is unusual. But that may be because BoneTec has carefully chosen its territory in order to shorten the regulatory process and therefore the length of time before the company can start to sell product. The biodegradable polymer it uses has already been approved for use in humans. The bone cells themselves aren't subject to regulation, since they come from the patient. The only possible question regulators could ask, Davies says, is whether the process of storing the cells can be made completely free from contamination. He still has to show that the foam works as well as conventional bone grafts, and that will take expensive human trials. But a version of the product may be tested on a small scale in periodontal surgery this year, he says. If results are as good as he hopes, sales could start within five years. Within this industry, that would be a remarkably short time frame.

When BoneTec does hit the market, it's going to face at least two established bone makers—GenSci, and Osteotech Inc. of Eatontown, N.J. Both make products using processed, demineralized human bone from cadavers that can be used in grafts instead of bone chips carved from a patient's hip, although these products fall short of creating actual bone in the lab.

But the rewards are enticing. The size of the potential market is "anybody's guess," says Louis Plourde, GenSci's director of investor relations. If every surgeon in the United States and Canada gave up on the hack-and-chisel method, an industry report estimates there would be a market worth more than $500 million (U.S.) a year for tissue-engineered alternatives, Plourde says.

Still, there's the issue of cash. One reason venture capital is scarce for tissue engineering is that investors learned a few things from biotechnology. Not that biotech is a bad investment, necessarily, but count on waiting a minimum of a decade for any returns. The same is true for tissue engineering, says Martin Godbout, formerly with the Montreal biotech investment firm BioCapital Investments, LP: "Biotech is the most regulated industry in the world, and tissue engineers will face the same difficulties. As long as you're playing with human bodies, you face these hurdles."

So far, Canada's big biotech success is Montreal's BioChem Pharma Inc., which went public in 1986. Nine years later, its main product, the anti-HIV drug 3TC, was approved for sale. BioChem Pharma had $347.4 million in sales in 1998, with net income of $114.8 million.

So far, there is no comparable success story in Canadian tissue engineering, although bone-maker GenSci is making a bid for the role. GenSci got its start more than a decade ago, when a Vancouver doctor, James Trotman, learned about a severely underfunded Seattle company that had some interesting ideas about bone regeneration. He invested in the company, moved it to Vancouver and took it public in 1992 as BioColl Medical Corp. The company went through another metamorphosis in 1997 when it merged with Osteopharm Ltd., changed its name to GenSci and started trading on the Toronto Stock Exchange. It formed some important strategic and marketing alliances, and hopes to turn its first profit in 1999. If Plourde's estimate of the market is correct and if GenSci can compete aggressively, who knows? It could have a shot at being the next BioChem Pharma in a few years.

It's not a game for the faint of heart, however. Take the U.S. star player Organogenesis. The Canton, Mass., company's Apligraf lab-grown skin made from human skin cells cultured into discs of living tissue has been on the market for nearly two years, and revenues for the third quarter of 1998 were about $350,000 (U.S.) To get to that heady position took the company more than a decade and left it with an accumulated deficit of $96 million (U.S.).

On the plus side, says Organogenesis's Alan Tuck, Apligraf's revenues are low so far because the product, used to treat hard-to-heal skin ulcers associated with poor blood circulation, is still winning acceptance. In the long run, Organogenesis is hoping for the lion's share of a market it estimates at between $10 billion and $20 billion (U.S.) a year, as is rival Advanced Tissue Sciences of La Jolla, Calif., which has a similar product grown in its labs. Is the market really that big? Only time will tell. But investment manager David MacNaughtan of Royal Bank Capital Corp. says dryly: "I've never yet seen a business plan that didn't say [the company] was going after a $1-billion product."

Despite its low revenues thus far, Organogenesis is considered a success story. But it's successful at least partly because what it's doing is relatively simple. Skin cells, it has been known for decades, will spontaneously form themselves into layers and start to grow if given the right environment and growth factors. But there are only a few tissues—bone is another—that have a similar ability to self-organize.

Growing a full-fledged human organ in an incubator is another story several orders of magnitude more difficult, and yet that's where the glamour (and the hope of megaprofits) lies. Imagine the number of people who would line up for organ transplants if the supply weren't limited by availability. That's one reason U of T's Sefton is leading an international group of tissue engineers in an ambitious 10-year push to make a human heart in the lab. The challenges are enormous—learning how to grow heart muscle cells, shape them into a heart, make them develop blood vessels, make them strong enough, and learning how to prevent deadly immune responses when they're implanted. But none of those difficulties, Sefton says, is a show-stopper.

But the money might be. "We are talking about raising $5 billion (U.S.) over 10 years," Sefton says. Cash on that scale doesn't come from venture capitalists; it comes from governments. Sefton's goal is to persuade the U.S. Congress that, like the Human Genome Project before it, the drive to build hearts will be profitable, both scientifically and economically. He and his collaborators, who include tissue-engineering pioneers Robert Langer of MIT and Joseph Vacanti of Massachusetts General Hospital, are putting together a financing proposal that could go to Congress within the next six months. The National Institute of Health, which administers most of the medical-science funding in the U.S., has recently started encouraging grant requests from tissue engineers after years of routinely refusing them.

Sefton looks back at the flood of companies that flowed out of the biotech boom, driven by new discoveries from the Human Genome Project, and sees the same thing happening with his so-called LIFE initiative. "Even without the LIFE initiative," Sefton says, "tissue engineering has already spawned many start-up companies." One of them is Sefton's own Rimon Therapeutics Ltd., which aims to commercialize a polymer that causes blood vessels to form and, in the long run, to create a lab-grown pancreas that would eliminate the need for diabetics to have insulin injections.

François Auger's Quebec City start-up, Altertek/Bio Inc., faces yet another problem. The Laval University professor has been "ringing the bells" for tissue engineering for more than a decade and has only in the past year started to see venture-capital interest. Altertek has the technology to grow some living blood vessels, which could eventually be used to replace small heart arteries. Auger's lab also has just succeeded in creating living corneas. He estimates that hundreds of thousands of North Americans each year are cornea-transplant candidates. You'd think these projects would bring the money pouring in. Venture capitalists are uniformly wowed, but reluctant to lay down the cash. "We have good science," says Auger. "What is more difficult is getting good management, and that we're working on."

Auger's work does have support from The Medical Research Council of Canada, and it is the only tissue-engineering work in Canada to get government money, an MRC spokesperson says. The Quebec government has also supported him. He expects to have venture-capital backing and a strategic alliance with a Maryland company in place this year. But putting lab-grown arteries into patients is still "three to five years and a lot of money away," he says.

Some heartening characteristics exist in the field, though. Too many biotech pioneers were academic scientists from so-called pure-science fields such as biology, genetics and mathematics. Many were not successful in making the transition from the lab to the boardroom. At a Montreal biotech meeting in September, James Tobin, former CEO of the U.S. biotech firm Biogen Inc., warned that too many biotechs are really only interested in using investors' money to pursue knowledge. "If you can't produce a real product to help a real patient ... then you probably ought to quit now and get out of the way," Tobin said. "You should be pruned."

Since biotech became a commercial reality, roughly two decades ago, Tobin says the industry has spent more than $70 billion (U.S.) on research and development. There are currently only 19 big winners—products that sell more than $100 million (U.S.) a year. Biogen's only product, beta-interferon, used to treat multiple sclerosis, is one of those winners, after 20 years of research and development and nearly $1 billion in total expenses. "And we're considered a success," Tobin says. "What's wrong with this picture?"

Tissue engineers contend that they have the industrial know-how that the pure scientists lack. "In biomaterials, you can't help having exposure to industrial problems," says BoneTec's Davies. "It's not the same in pure science."

In the BoneTec lab, in U of T's high-ceilinged Mining Building, John Davies and Chantal Holy are examining a small dish containing a dozen white lozenges, each about the size of the first joint of a human thumb. They are part of Holy's latest product run—she, Molly Shoichet and Davies are still refining the way they make their biodegradable foams, aiming for more complete control over the complex internal structure. "These are a bit larger than we'd want for clinical use," Davies says, "but the structure is pretty good." The question for investors, of course, remains "Is bioengineering where your money should go?" Not unless you can afford to take big risks and are ready to wait—perhaps for a very long time.

Clarifications

Calvin Stiller: Cal Stiller was a professor, surgeon and medical transplant pioneer before becoming the CEO of the Canadian Medical Discoveries Fund.

Angel investor: An angel investor is one who is willing to invest in a risky company in hopes of a high return. The term comes from the practice of early–twentieth century businessmen investing in Broadway plays. An angel helps finance the earlier stages of development of a business or product, before the venture capitalist gets involved.

Venture capitalists: Venture capitalists fund start-up businesses. You can find extensive information about venture capitalists and angels at *www.about.com.* Also, a search of *www.oingo.com* will allow you to limit your search to the specific meaning "speculator" and find out about, among other things, Canadian venture capitalists.

Metamorphosis: Literally, a biological change in shape or form. It can also be used metaphorically to indicate a non-physical change.

A market it estimates at between $10 billion and $20 billion (U.S.) a year: As a comparison, Microsoft had sales of just under $27 billion in 2001.

The Human Genome Project: A fifteen-year project that was started in 1990, the Human Genome Project is expected to conclude in 2003, earlier than originally planned. Read more about this gene-mapping project at *www.ornl.gov/TechResources/Human_Genome/home.html.*

Talking Points

Pharmaceutical, drug and medical research companies often have interesting and descriptive names. Using information from the article "The Game of the Name" (page 32), see whether you think the companies mentioned in this article have appropriate names.

The article talks about growing human hearts. At the moment the trend seems to be breeding a special kind of pig for the purposes of transplantation. What are the ethical issues involved in the different forms of heart transplant? Would you have any qualms about having a pig heart?

Web Research

The Pittsburgh Tissue Engineering Initiative has a Web site at *www.pittsburgh-tissue.net*.

The National Research Council (NRC) is Canada's leading organization for scientific and technical research. Search its Web site at *www.nrc.ca* to find biotech regulations in force in Canada.

LIFE Initiative: Living Implants from Engineering, Dr. Michael Sefton's Web site at the University of Toronto, is at *www.utoronto.ca/IBBME*.

If you have a business plan you can search for an angel investor of your own at *www.vfinance.com*.

Writing That Works

Definition: "Biotechnologists deal mostly in proteins, which are really just specialized kinds of chemicals with useful effects on the body. Tissue engineers, on the other hand, seek to grow actual tissues in the lab—ranging from skin cells to organs."

Short topic sentences: This writer has a tendency towards writing short, pithy topic or introductory sentences. The technique is effective: "Still, there's the issue of cash."; "It's not a game for the faint of heart, however."; "But the money might be."

Expert opinion: "Tissue engineers contend that they have the industrial know-how that the pure scientists lack. 'In biomaterials, you can't help having exposure to industrial problems,' says BoneTec's Davies. 'It's not the same in pure science.'"

Expert opinion: "At a Montreal biotech meeting in September, James Tobin, former CEO of the U.S. biotech firm Biogen Inc., warned that too many biotechs are really only interested in using investors' money to pursue knowledge. 'If you can't produce a real product to help a real patient ... then you probably ought to quit now and get out of the way,' Tobin said. 'You should be pruned.'"

The Next Big Thing: Nothing
by Paul Kedrosky

National Post, November 28, 2001

With the economy trundling along at the tail end of the recession, tirelessly future-focused technologists only want to talk about what is coming next. Here is the answer: Nothing. And it is about time.

No, it is not that nothing is coming for the economy. Most technologists are magnificently naive about macroeconomics, but few if any are anything but blissfully optimistic for the super-bounce coming in the impending recovery.

Instead when technologists fret about what is coming next, they are worrying about which new technology will set the world afire, the way the Web browser did in the 1990s or perhaps the way computers, spreadsheets and the word processor did in the 1980s.

And what do technologists point to? There is a cacophony, but they point to next-generation cellular phones or perhaps some iteration of personal digital assistants like the Palm. Or better yet, maybe wireless networking.

Not the much-maligned Bluetooth variety, of course, but the better-faster-stronger 802.11b standard. And in the background lurks a witch's brew of science projects, from nanotechnology, to the fruits of proteomics and genomics.

All of these horses for courses have punters placing bets that they'll be the Next Big Thing. These innovations have the requisite characteristics, techies argue. They make older technologies obsolete; they change the way people behave; they are premised, in part, on new companies that can upset the existing order. These are all part of an implicit orthodoxy, a founding myth of chained logic in the world of technology. Things Change Fast. The Small and Nimble Will Unseat the Large and Slow. New Technologies are Wildly Profitable for the Winners.

But here is a secret: the founding myth, that chain of logic, is a lie. To the extent that there have ever been killer applications—and that is a debatable point—they have been unpredictable, generally unprofitable for the first-mover and only identifiable in retrospect through a heroic exercise in revisionism.

It doesn't matter whether you look at the personal computer market where Altair beat the PC clone-makers by years with the first personal computer, only to vanish; or the spreadsheet market where Visicalc and a range of others beat current incumbents by ages, only to disappear in a sea of red ink. Or, more recently, the giggling mess that was Netscape Communications, a supposed purveyor of killer applications that was going to unseat bad, sad, slow Microsoft.

All of these companies, these vendors of killer applications, the poster-children for the Killer App Orthodoxy, failed. And failed quickly. And unprofitably, many without generating a penny of profit. As far as market magnets go, these killer apps seem more like twinned Scylla and Charybdis than a useful target.

So why does no one in an industry badly in need of some perspective concede this to be true? Why does no one, even sotto voce, concede that one of their founding myths, that of the killer application that will give order to all that came before, is blatantly false?

It is, of course, for the same reason any failing religion refuses to change. Because it can't. It is so intimately tied up in the mosaic of myths that got it to where it is, it wouldn't know where to begin if it were to change. To insiders, the killer-application tenet is no more questionable than faith in Jimmy Jones, belief in the addled musings of Reverend Sun Myung Moon or, better yet, in faith the Flat Earth Society's ideas will one day be borne out.

Those beliefs, however flawed, are what make these people what they are.

Technologists are staunchly forward-looking people who motivate themselves, and a legion of parrots in the popular and trade media, by talking endlessly about the future. "We speak not of this world, but of the world that is to come!" they say, in a spooky parody of the New Testament, making the religious underpinnings explicit.

But what happens when the myths fall apart? Because the collapse of the Internet as the Next Big Thing put a little fear into the blue-eyed believers, as did the corresponding collapse of the startup factories pumping out dime-a-dozen Standard Industrial Classification-code-killer startups in every e-commerce category. But it has left most believers more than a little confused, frantic in their search for the next thing that will change the world.

The trouble is, while the flow of useful new products is unceasing, few new technologies can have the impact old ones did. We are like a market iceberg, with more and more technology fused beneath the waterline. It isn't as easy as it once was to run around disrupting things with killer applications—there is too much invested in what went before. More and more, prior killer applications looked like youthful flings had by a young technology market, not some pre-ordained paroxysm that unseats the existing order.

And consumers and corporate buyers bear that out. They are putting their feet down, doing a kind of buyer's boycott, saying they don't really care what gets flogged next, because they're still trying to make money off the last round of goods they were sold.

With all these false gods falling by the roadside, markets are nervous. But that is okay. As Nietzsche might have argued, it is the death of a religion, of a false god; it forces a kind of low-rent market existentialism, with people finally taking responsibility for setting their own market actions.

It is about time.

Clarifications

Bluetooth: A short-range wireless technology that will allow us, among other things, to have our homes networked wirelessly. We will be able to network several computers, a printer, PDAs (Palm Pilots, etc.), and probably the television and the microwave, networked without wires. The name comes from King Harald Bluetooth, a Danish king who lived from 910 to 940 AD. He did not, as you might expect, have blue teeth. In fact the word means dark-haired or dark-complexioned, an unusual appearance for a Dane. He was known as a good king who united Denmark and Norway, which is why Danish mobile phone maker Ericsson Mobile Communications chose the name for its technology.

Nanotechnology: Science and technology on a small scale, particularly building circuits and devices from single atoms and molecules.

Orthodoxy: A generally accepted set of beliefs or practices. The term originally referred to religious practice, but is often used in broader contexts.

Jimmy Jones: The head of an American cult that set itself up in Jonestown, Guyana. In 1978, after a member of the U.S. Congress who had been sent to investigate was ambushed and killed by Jones' followers, Jones orchestrated a mass suicide of more than 900 men, women and children using cyanide-laced Kool-Aid. He himself was one of the suicide victims.

Reverend Sun Myung Moon: Moon is the head of a cult known as the Unification Church. He is particularly known in North America for his mass weddings, where hundreds of couples are married at the same time.

Talking Points

The author draws parallels between religion and mythology and the fervour for the "Next Big Thing." Discuss this idea.

Web Research

This article does not lend itself to research; however, you can look up terminology such as *killer app* at the Net Lingo Web site: *www.netlingo.com.*

Writing That Works

Literary allusion: Scylla and Charybdis: These two "monsters" are found in Homer's *Odyssey,* an ancient Greek saga. They are believed to be geographical, one a rock resembling a women, the other a whirlpool—the literary equivalent of "out of the frying pan into the fire," since if you avoid one you fall into the other. As Shakespeare wrote in *The Merchant of Venice:* "When I shun Scylla your father, I fall into Charybdis your mother."

Introduction—startling statement: As with many startling statements, this one is combined with a sort of question. What is the next big thing? Nothing.

Examples: Big things that were first on the market and then more or less disappeared: Altair, Visicalc, Netscape.

Question and answer: "So why does no one in an industry badly in need of some perspective concede this to be true?" "But what happens when the myths fall apart?" Notice that the writer does not answer these questions immediately, but takes a sentence or two to explain what he means, and *then* answers the questions.

The Lonely Planet
by John Ibbitson

The Globe and Mail, March 2, 2002

Imagine a world of lonely children. They are lonely because there are so few of them. They long for brothers or sisters, cousins, classmates, friends. They share the world with old, tired people, who are dying slowly, selfishly.

The old people are lonely too, and they are poor. Because there are so few young people, pension funds are drying up, jobs are going begging for want of workers, knowledge is stagnating for want of innovative young minds, economies are shrinking for want of consumers.

Is this a sad world? In many ways, no. Hunger has largely disappeared. The environment is rebounding. Europe, though rapidly growing empty, has never looked more quaint. Best of all, much of the developing world has been developed.

Unless things go badly. Maybe Europe struggles with race riots. Maybe Japan is bankrupt. Maybe China has started to gobble up eastern Russia. Maybe the Hispanic president of the United States has decreed Spanish as America's second language. Maybe the French language in Canada is about to disappear.

Why imagine any of this? Because what is perhaps the most common assumption of modern times, that the world's population is exploding, is no longer true.

We all know that women in the West long ago stopped producing the 2.1 babies apiece that are needed to maintain population stability. This month, Statistics Canada will release the first hard data culled from the 2001 census on the state of the nation's inhabitants. It will portray Canadians, especially those born here, as a people who are growing ever older and bearing too few children to sustain their numbers.

Now, the developing world is embracing the trend. Sasigarn Eampornchai, a 30-year-old diplomatic staff worker in Bangkok, says her mother had four children, but "I am not going to have any." She is single, and has decided that, even if she marries, "it is too difficult to bring up a child" in today's troubled economic climate.

This in teeming Thailand, whose population has tripled from 19 million to 60 million in the past 50 years? But for years the government has plastered the countryside with propaganda advocating smaller families. "It used to be normal to have lots of children," Eampornchai says. "Now, it is normal not to."

According to the latest data from the United Nations Population Division, the birth rate in many countries we still think are baby-booming has fallen very near, if not below, the replacement level. China. Brazil. Practically the entire Caribbean.

Elsewhere, former population factories such as India, Indonesia and even Bangladesh are plummeting toward population stability. Only in sub-Saharan Africa and the Islamic Middle East are birth rates still high, and even here they are starting to drop, even plunge.

In as little as 40 years, growth could halt and the planet's population start to decline. Like all trends, that decline will be long-term and, at least for a while, inexorable. The world will be gripped by depopulation.

The aging and shrinking of humanity "will become the transcendent political and economic issue of the 21st century," says Peter G. Peterson, chairman of the Council on Foreign Relations and the Institute for International Economics.

"This is not a crisis as speculative as, say, global warming, which we have spent a lot of time talking about," adds Peterson, who served as U.S. secretary of commerce under Richard Nixon. After all, he says, "the people have already been born."

In some places, the shrinking has begun. The number of Russians is already in steep decline. After the fall of the Soviet Union, the fertility rate plunged, from 1.9 in 1975 to 1.1 now. At the same time, the health infrastructure deteriorated and the Russian male's notorious fondness for cigarettes and vodka lowered his life expectancy to 60.

From 1992 to last year, the population slipped from 148 million to 145 million, and is expected to decline by 12 million more in the next 15 years. At this rate, Russia estimates it will have only 85 million people by 2055. More drastic estimates put it at 55 million. And next door to that vast, empty land will be 1.2 billion Chinese.

"The fact of population decline will colour all sorts of social, political and economic aspects of life in ways that will be both subtle and direct," says Nicholas Eberstadt, a political economist at Harvard University and a consultant to the World Bank and U.S. State Department. "It will be the overarching context to everything in life."

It is already the overarching context of life in Japan, which never had a baby boom, because of the ravages of the Second World War, and whose fertility rate is now a mere 1.3 children per woman.

As a result, the Japanese population will start to decline by 2007. Unless Japanese women start having more babies—many, many more babies—the country will lose 30 per cent of its population by 2050. By 2100, it will have declined by half. To extrapolate to the ridiculous: If current population trends in Japan continue unabated, according to one estimate, by 3000 a mere 500 Japanese will remain.

The solution, of course, is immigration. But Japanese obsession with racial purity is deeply rooted; it is difficult to emigrate there and almost impossible to obtain citizenship. And to sustain its population, Japan would need to open the floodgates. By 2040, the Japanese will be losing 800,000 people a year.

Japan is not alone. German researchers predicted last year that, unless immigration limits were lifted, their population would decline from 82 million to 60 million by 2050. By then, the number of Italians will have fallen from 57.5 million to 43 million, and Bulgaria's population from 7.7 to 4.5 million.

Fine, but there are two worlds: a developed world, where the birth rate is low, and much, much larger developing world, where the birth rate remains high. Right?

Nope.

Throughout the developing world, fertility rates are dropping rapidly. Some of the world's most populous countries are at, or below, the magic replacement rate of 2.1 children per woman needed to keep a population from going into decline. China (because of Draconian family-planning policies): 1.8; Thailand (because of more enlightened family planning): 2.0 and dropping fast; Brazil (for reasons no one can quite fathom): 2.2.

Nat Eampornchai says years of government campaigning paid off and even Thai couples keen to have kids got the message. "The concept of having two children for each family was very popular."

Now, populations are being brought under control in many parts of Asia. Birth rates in prosperous southern India are declining so rapidly that, by 2015, the national figure is expected to be comparable to Europe's today. Indonesia will reach replacement rate by around 2005; the Philippines by around 2015. Taiwan is already at 1.8.

The same is happening in Latin America. In the past quarter-century, the fertility rate in Mexico has gone from 5.3 to 2.5, in Colombia from 4.3 to 2.6, in Guyana from 4.0 to 2.3. Even in regions where fertility rates remain high—the Islamic Middle East and sub-Saharan Africa—there are marked signs of a slowdown. Syria's birth rate has declined in 20 years from 7.4 to 3.7. Algeria's has gone from 7.2 to 2.8. Kenya, once considered out of control, has gone to 4.2 from 7.9. As well, Africa faces an especially sorrowful form of population control: the scourge of HIV-AIDS.

The drop is such that demographers are now debating when the worldwide population will plateau, and when we may actually start to see global population decline.

The UN's official projection sees the global figure, now 6 billion, expanding rapidly until 2040, when it will hit 9 billion, and then growing much more slowly until it stabilizes at 11 billion in 2100.

That scenario is called the "medium variant," but the UN also has a more extreme "low variant" that assumes birth rates continue to decline rapidly. It sees the global population topping out at only 8 billion, around 2040, and then starting to shrink.

This is by no means an academic debate. The United Nations, the World Bank and hundreds of governmental and non-governmental agencies spend billions on family-planning assistance to developing countries, predicated in part on the assumption that global overpopulation is a real and pressing issue. But if in fact the population is stabilizing, is all that aid necessary?

That such questions should even be asked deeply worries Stan Bernstein, senior resident adviser to the UN Population Fund. First off, he doesn't buy the low-variant projections. Yes, only last week a delegation informed the UN that Iran had officially reached replacement fertility rate. But other countries, such as Nigeria and parts of Latin America, are not having great success.

Obsessing on fertility rates, Bernstein says, ignores the larger issue. It is not simply how many babies a woman has, but the quality of care she receives in planning for and raising her family.

Regardless of what happens by 2050, he says, before then "we are talking about adding three billion people more than we have now." And "just focusing on a number doesn't tell the story. It doesn't capture its diversity, and it forgets the fact that, of the 6.1 billion people we have now, half of them are living at under $2 a day."

In some ways, of course, depopulation will be a boon. In over-crowded Japan, "low population density means more space—more available land, greenery, and housing," Makoto Atoh, deputy director-general of the National Institute of Population and Social Security Research, noted recently. "These benefits might even create a spiritu-ally affluent society."

But not a materially affluent one. Japan's economy has been stag-nant or in recession for a decade. "I can't help but wonder whether Japan's industries and the economy can take" losing 800,000 people a year, Atoh worries. "Economic management would be hard, economic growth would plummet, and living standards would worsen."

It's no secret why the world's population exploded in the 20th century. Women kept having babies at the same rate they had always had babies. But vastly improved nutrition, sanitation and medical care both lowered the infant-mortality rate and extended life spans.

The reasons for the impending depopulation are more complex. The ongoing rural-to-urban migration has something to do with it. (Children are a help on the farm, a hindrance in town.) Improving economies and literacy rates around the world make parents aware of the cost of large families and the birth-control techniques for avoiding them.

But the biggest cause must surely be the growing empowerment of women. As women become better educated, as they are able to make choices about how much emphasis to put on career and how much on family, they invariably decide to marry later and to have fewer children. From Tijuana to Taipei, the most reliable sign of a maturing economy is a decreasing birth rate, which also means that women in that society are gaining control over their bodies and their lives.

"It is a combination of economy and society," concludes Nat Eampornchai in Bangkok. Many of her friends, she adds, are childless and most plan to limit themselves to families of one or two. There is just no time. "We go to school more and we work more, and by the time we're ready for a child, we're already 30."

Even in places where economic and social development lag, repro-duction is falling off. Bangladesh is one of the world's poorer nations, but the fertility rate has dropped from 5.7 in 1975 to 3.5 today, en route to an expected 2.1 in 2025.

"I have argued," says Eberstadt, the Harvard economist, "that the people who would best explain this change are not social scientists but novelists, because novelists are much more in touch with the Zeitgeist, with the spirit of the times, with individual motivations."

But Valerie De Fillipo, director of the international arm of the Planned Parenthood Federation of America, sees the declining fertility rates as "a success story," proving that international efforts to provide couples with reproductive choices are bearing fruit. "Individual choice on a global scale contributes to a better environment for all of us. But it doesn't in any way inspire complacency," she says. "It is just another statement that access to family planning is a key and critical issue in sustainable development."

Among developed countries, the United States has the healthiest fertility rate, steady at about 2.1. Afro-Americans' family sizes have dropped greatly over the past decade, because of increasing black affluence as well as campaigns to discourage teenaged pregnancy. Latino birth rates, however, remain high, pushing Hispanics past blacks as the largest non-European population in the country.

In Canada, however, deaths will outnumber births by 2025. By then, thanks to our open-door immigration policies, the population will have grown from 30.7 million to 36 million. But that growth will be concentrated in Ontario, Alberta and British Columbia. Other areas are expected to remain stagnant or decline, like Saskatchewan, Newfoundland and perhaps New Brunswick.

Quebec is in particular trouble. It accounts for about one-fifth of Canada's population, but receives only 12 per cent of its immigrants. It also has a very low birth rate, and expects an absolute decline in population by 2018.

What will it be like to live in a world that is losing people every day? Ever the extremist, Pat Buchanan predicts the end is near for Western civilization.

Back in 1960, observes the perennial presidential candidate and conservative gadfly in his new bestseller, *The Death of the West,* people of European origin represented one-quarter of the world's population. Today, it's one-sixth, and will slip to one-10th by 2050. "Western women are terminating their pregnancies at a rate that represents autogenocide for peoples of European ancestry," he declares. His solution: ban non-European immigrants from European-based nations, and promote a spiritual revival that will increase fecundity.

It is to laugh. But Europe, Russia and Japan have some difficult choices ahead. They can either try to run their countries with dramatically shrunken populations, or they can embrace immigration—something that doesn't sit well with many Europeans. The issue colours elections and gives life to extreme right-wing parties.

News item: Spain was gripped last month by the death of an Ecuadorean immigrant—he drowned after being thrown into Barcelona's harbour by a bouncer who refused to let him enter a bar. The number of immigrants in Spain has doubled in the past six years to one million, leading to much social tension.

News item: Two Oslo youths described as neo-Nazis were convicted last month in the slaying of Benjamin Hermansen, a 15-year-old Norwegian of Ghanaian descent who was killed because he was black.

Friction like this will only increase, as the need to bring in newcomers to bolster sagging populations clashes with Europeans' ancient sense of civilization and identity.

The immigrants may not wait for the Europeans to make up their minds. "Around 1900, Africa's population was a third that of Europe's," observes Thomas Homer Dixon, director of the Centre for the Study of Peace and Conflict at the University of Toronto. "Today, they're roughly equivalent. By 2050, Africa's population is projected to be three times that of Europe."

Even though fertility rates are coming under control, populations in Third World countries will continue to swell as the burgeoning generation of the young enters its reproductive years. Resources will dwindle, and the temptation to move to increasingly empty Europe, invited or not, will become irresistible.

"We're seeing riots outside the Chunnel in France. We're seeing dead bodies wash up on Spanish shores. Lots of people are already trying to get in, and that's only the beginning of what we're going to see, which for these societies will be very destabilizing," Homer Dixon predicts.

The United States also struggles with racial tensions. Increasing Hispanic immigration has prompted some whites to demand a constitutional amendment declaring that English is the only official language in the United States. Prompted by groups such as English First, Pro-English and U.S. English, 24 states have laws requiring that government business be conducted in English.

Nonetheless, U.S. society is robust, as is its birth rate. And a high tolerance for immigrants—perhaps the single greatest asset of a developed country in an era of depopulation—should ensure that neither the American nor Canadian population ever goes into decline.

Does that mean that we are immune to the demographic scourge being inflicted on Japan, Russia and Europe? Hardly. Our populations may be stable, but their makeup is undergoing a revolution of its own: aging.

Over the next 10 years, the number of workers under 30 will decline by 25 per cent. By 2030, people over 65 will have gone from one in seven to one in four. Immigration can mitigate, but can never reverse, the twin effects of lower fertility rates and increased longevity—what some now call "the perfect demographic storm."

"Starting from now, right now, the working population will never again be as large," says Paul Hewitt, director of global aging at Washington's Center for Strategic and International Studies. "This means that sometime during this decade, all of the major industrial countries are going to make a historic shift, an epochal transformation, from an era when the primary source of social crisis was unemployment to one in which the primary source of social crisis is labour shortage."

No Western country is ready to deal with the issues that depopulation and aging raise. None has a pension system that's fully prepared to go from a large work force and a small retired population to the exact opposite. No country really has contemplated the economic impact of a steady decline in the number of people who buy homes, and a steady increase in the number of people living in nursing homes.

A shrinking consumer base will certainly shake the Canadian and American economies. Hewitt argues that it will send Europe and Japan into a permanent economic decline—in fact, he thinks it's already contributing to the weakness of the euro.

Ironically, this could be good news for the world. Capital flows to where markets expand. As markets shrink in developed countries, as workers become scarcer and scarcer and consumers fewer and fewer, corporations will seek new markets, new places to invest.

Provided that Third World nations take steps to lessen the risk to investors, by introducing reliable and impartial legal systems and educating their citizens, the 21st century could witness an unprecedented shift of capital to the developing world. It would raise living standards and finally attack the roots of poverty.

But even the developing world is not immune to depopulation's down side. As Third World countries tame their birth rates and improved health care increases people's life spans, *their* populations are starting to go grey. Ten years ago, India had 56 million people who were over 60; by 2021, the number is expected to almost triple to 137 million. Who will look after them?

Finally, there are the more ephemeral questions. What will a world with fewer children be like? Will they be cosseted and protected, or will they find themselves pushed relentlessly to produce, produce, produce, to pay the doctors' bill for their parents, their grandparents and their great-grandparents?

Will creativity and invention wither, with fewer young minds available to create and invent? And will the young rebel by having lots and lots of children? Will they say: "I'll never forgive my parents for making me an only child—it was so lonely. My children are going to have brothers and sisters. We're going to be a real family."

Global trend lines do not change easily or swiftly, but they do change. A generation or two down the road, parents may start having babies again, perhaps for reasons we cannot yet fathom.

It won't be easy. From his vantage point at Harvard, Nicholas Eberstadt speculates that reversing the tide "will require something on the order of a religious revival, a change in ideology—a maybe not-terribly-pretty nationalism or ethnocentrism.

"It would have to be in the order of a mass movement. Nothing less would do it."

But that is a destination far distant. For this century, the story is the baby bust. It is a story full of unanswerable questions and uncertain hopes. Many of us won't live to watch its fruition. But some will, and for them, every year the world will have more empty space.

Clarifications

The fall of the Soviet Union: The Union of Soviet Socialist Republics (USSR) was established in 1922 and dissolved in 1991. In the early nineties, the economy was shrinking, various states were demanding independence, and on August 19, 1991, military leaders staged a coup, detaining then-Premier Gorbachev at his dacha—the Russian equivalent of a Canadian cottage. The coup collapsed, but power passed to Boris Yeltsin. In September the Congress of People's Deputies voted for dissolution of the USSR.

Draconian policies: Draco was an Athenian politician around the year 621 BC who created a code of law. His laws were considered very harsh, and were said to be written in blood because so many crimes were punished with the death penalty. His laws were replaced within a quarter of a century by Solon, the founder of Greek democracy. We still call harsh laws "draconian."

Third World: According to the on-line *Columbia Encyclopedia,* "The term *Third World* was originally intended to distinguish the non-aligned nations that gained independence from colonial rule beginning after World War II from the Western nations and from those that formed the former Eastern bloc, and sometimes more specifically from the United States and from the former Soviet Union (the first and second worlds, respectively)." The term now is generally used to describe developing countries.

Chunnel: The tunnel underneath the English Channel, between France and England, has been nicknamed the Chunnel, a combination of *channel* and *tunnel.*

Ephemeral: Fleeting or passing quickly.

Talking Points

How many siblings do you have, and how many children do you expect to have? Looking back a generation or two, how many children did your grandparents and great-grandparents have?

Web Research

Read The State of World Population on the UN Population Fund Web site at *www.unfpa.org/swp/swpmain.htm.*

Statistics Canada has information on population growth at *www.statcan.ca/english/Pgdb/People/popula.htm.*

Watch the population of the world grow at the World Population Awareness Web site at *www.overpopulation.org.* The counter there seems to be moving very quickly, faster than a Millennium countdown sign.

Writing That Works

Introduction—scenario: The opening scenario describes a world with a shrinking population—a worst-case scenario.

Question and answer: "Why imagine any of this? Because what is perhaps the most common assumption of modern times, that the world's population is exploding, is no longer true."

Question and answer: "Is this a sad world? In many ways, no. Hunger has largely disappeared. The environment is rebounding. Europe, though rapidly growing empty, has never looked more quaint. Best of all, much of the developing world has been developed."

Question and answer: "Fine, but there are two worlds: a developed world, where the birth rate is low, and much, much larger developing world, where the birth rate remains high. Right? Nope." Notice how this question is followed not so much by an explanation as by a correction. The author states our common misconception. He then goes on to explain the true situation.

Rhetorical question: "This in teeming Thailand, whose population has tripled from 19 million to 60 million in the past 50 years?"

Expert opinion: "The aging and shrinking of humanity 'will become the transcendent political and economic issue of the 21st century,' says Peter G. Peterson, chairman of the Council on Foreign Relations and the Institute for International Economics."

Cause and effect: The article explains that the population of the world will drop in this century, then goes on to look at what effect that will have.

Part Three: Research and Documentation

You may prefer to start your search for information on the Internet, or you may prefer to use the library first. At some point, however, you should probably visit both. The best resource for library research is the librarian. Many college and university libraries have wonderful Web pages as well. One excellent guide to library research can be found on the Duke University Web site at *www.lib.duke.edu/libguide/home.htm*.

ELECTRONIC RESEARCH

Electronic research is research done either on a library database or on the Internet.

Library Databases

Most college and university libraries subscribe to databases that students can access from their library Web site. The best known of the sites you might find at your library are EBSCO and Electric Library. The Canadian version of the Electric Library site is especially good for magazine and newspaper articles from this country. If it is not readily available through your school, you can sign up individually for a free thirty-day trial at *www.elibrary.ca*.

Subscription or Pay-per-Article Databases

Most students will not want to pay for information if it is possible to get it for nothing. However, here are a few places you might consider if you are desperate.

InfoGlobe–Dow Jones Interactive

InfoGlobe–Dow Jones Interactive (*www.globeinteractive.com/products/igdji.html*) is the Canadian version of the Dow Jones business news and research site. You can subscribe or buy articles one at a time. Chances are that if you ever work for a company where you need to do business research, this is where you will go to do it.

Northern Light

Northern Light (*www.northernlight.com*) is a combination of an on-line search engine and a library database. It searches a list of 7,100 full-text publications and sorts the results into folders. If you like the look of an article that the search returns, you can buy it for a dollar or two.

A tip for both of these pay-per-article databases: once you have found an article title that looks interesting, type the title into a Google Advanced Search. You may find the article somewhere else on the Web for free.

World Wide Web Searches

The easiest way to find information is on the Internet. However, the problem with the Internet is that there is so much of it. Google, for example, currently searches over two billion Web pages. How can you find the needle you are looking for in that haystack?

Here are three excellent sites that simplify your Internet search.

Google

The best search engine is Google (*www.google.com*). With its simple user interface and its ability to retrieve the best sources, it easily out-classes the opposition. Dig below the minimalist surface and you will find endless resources. A favourite resource of teachers is the Advanced Search feature, which allows us to detect plagiarism of articles from on-line sources.

To use Google most effectively, take advantage of methods that allow you to limit your search:

• Use quotation marks around phrases, so the words are looked for as a phrase, not just individually.

• Use the plus (+) and minus (–) symbols to ensure that words are either included or excluded.

Vivisimo

Founded in June 2000 by computer scientists from Carnegie Mellon University, Vivisimo (*www.vivisimo.com*) is a leader in document clustering software. Searches return results clustered into subject folders that look similar to the folders you find in Windows Explorer on a PC computer. With Vivisimo it's easy to know what to ignore in the list you retrieve.

Oingo

Oingo (*www.oingo.com*) is a meaning-based search engine. A team of editors has compiled lists of the various meanings of every word and the connections between words. Once the initial search is complete, you can select a limiting word from a drop-down menu to narrow the search further.

ACCEPTABLE INTERNET SOURCES

Much of the Internet is unregulated, and it is not always clear who is posting material. It is up to you to make sure that sources you quote are acceptable and appropriate. Here are some types of sites that may be suitable.

- Professional associations—but watch out for associations with an agenda to push.
- Government sites—especially Canadian government sites.
- Newspapers or journals with reputable print versions—to some extent you can judge acceptability by the appearance of the Web site. If the Internet version looks like the *National Enquirer,* don't use it as a source.
- On-line journals or newspapers associated with known organizations.
- Databases associated with professional organizations.
- Library databases such as EBSCO or Electric Library.
- On-line dictionaries and encyclopedias with paper equivalents.
- Companies large enough to be listed on a stock exchange such as the TSE or NYSE. Note, however, that company sites should be evaluated for bias. Look for news articles published elsewhere, white papers (authoritative reports on major issues) and factual information that can be substantiated elsewhere (stock prices, for example).

• Universities and colleges (but don't use personal student pages posted on university Web sites).

Questions To Ask Yourself About Internet Sources

Use these questions to help you evaluate Web sites.

1. What is the purpose of the Web site? Is it mainly to provide information? What kind of information does it provide? Is the information extensive, or just short snippets? If the information lacks depth, why is it there?

2. If the main purpose of the Web site appears to be informative, is it also selling something? For example, does it have a link to Amazon.com to sell books? Does the site have advertising, such as banners, or those frequent, annoying pop-up ads? In other words, is the information provided as a marketing tool? My rule of thumb is: more than one pop-up ad and the site is off my list. And that one pop-up ad must be site-related, such as a subscription solicitation.

3. Is the information appropriate to the type of site?

4. Has the site been reviewed? A "Web award" doesn't count, as it will probably be only for appearance. In fact, a Web award is probably a reason to avoid a site, as it indicates a certain level of amateurism.

5. Who operates the Web site? Is it an authoritative, well-known organization or business? Does the site contain statements of authority or, conversely, statements that lack authority or deny responsibility? Might the operators have a bias? Will the bias matter?

6. Is the site up to date? Is it maintained regularly? Do all the links work?

7. Does the site appear to be permanent? What is the creator's relationship to the server? (For example, a student at a university likely to move on after a few years would not bode well.)

8. Does the site offer good service as regards navigation, searching, help and a qualified content manager? Added features? Links to other sites? (Links should be limited to only the best sites, and they should work. A huge list of links is probably not helpful and indicates a lack of primary research).

9. Is the appearance appealing? Are links clear? Is the information you seek where you think it should be? Or is important content buried within the site and difficult to find?

10. Is the site on a first-level domain? In other words, does the first section of the address apply to the entire site on some level. The section you are looking at could be a department, such as a computer studies department in a university, or an area on a government Web site, but it has a relationship to the primary domain. However, a site that begins with *homestead, geocities* or *members* may seem very useful, but it will be a personal site and therefore possibly biased.

Another checklist to help you evaluate Web sites can be found on the Virtual Chase site at *www.virtualchase.com/quality.*

DOCUMENTING SOURCES

MLA-Style Documentation

For a complete list of examples that illustrate documentation of sources in the MLA (Modern Language Association) style, consult the *MLA Handbook for Writers of Research Papers* by Joseph Gibaldi. The MLA Web site at *www.mla.org* also has some good advice. The examples here are for basic types of citations used in business writing and for electronic sources.

Essays and reports using MLA-style documentation use in-text references and a list of works cited. In-text references usually include the author's name and the page number from which you have quoted. It is often a good idea to acknowledge the source in the actual text, and not just in parentheses after a quotation. For suggestions on how to do this, see "Acknowledging Sources Within the Text," in Part One.

The "works cited" list is placed on a separate page at the end of the document. The list is double-spaced and in alphabetical order by author's last name. The second and subsequent lines of each entry are indented half an inch (1.27 cm) from the first line—a "hanging indent." Make your life easier by using the hanging indent function of your word processor rather than trying to guess half an inch with the space bar. Another tip to make your life easier is to learn how to sort entries alphabetically with your word processing software. That way you don't have to worry about the order as you create the works cited list.

The *MLA Handbook* provides extensive examples for documenting all kinds of print and non-print media. However, it is still somewhat lacking in how to document electronic sources. The problem is that many of the Web sites business students use fall into the "personal and professional" category. MLA gives only three examples of such sites, at least one of which is no longer accessible (see section 4.9.3 of the *MLA Handbook*).

A second common source of information for business students is the library database. The best way to document this type of research is as a work from an on-line service (see section 4.9.7). This means that your school has to be included in the entry, as shown below.

Sample documentation styles for various kinds of print and electronic sources are shown below.

MLA: Print Sources

BOOKS

Author's name. *Title of the Book*. Place of publication: Publisher, year of publication.

Examples

Cooper, Sherry. *Ride the Wave: Take Control in the Acceleration Age*. London: Prentice Hall, 2001.

Tapscott, Don. *Growing up Digital: The Rise of the Net Generation*. New York: McGraw Hill, 1998.

If a book has more than one author, the second and subsequent names are in first name–last name order. Titles may be either italicized or underlined. Ask your teacher which style he or she prefers.

ARTICLES IN WEEKLY OR BIWEEKLY MAGAZINES

Include the following information when citing a weekly or biweekly magazine:

Author's name. "Title of Article." *Magazine Title*. Date [day month year]: page numbers.

Examples

Reguly, Eric. "A Trend You Can't Buck." *Time Canada*. 18 Feb. 2002: 21.

Freed, Les. "No More Letter Bombs." *PC Magazine.* 12 June 2001: 148–155.

Note that volume numbers are not included in this type of citation, even if known. Months other than May, June and July are abbreviated.

ARTICLES IN MONTHLY MAGAZINES
Include the following information when citing a monthly magazine:

Author's name. "Title of Article." *Magazine Title.* Date [month year]: page numbers.

Examples
Scott, Sarah. "The Accidental Moguls." *ROB Magazine.* Dec. 2000: 56–64.

Fearley, Fran. "Today's Lesson Brought to You By…" *Today's Parent.* Oct. 2000: 124–132.

As with weekly and biweekly publications, volume numbers are not included and longer month names are abbreviated.

ARTICLES IN NEWSPAPERS
Author's name. "Title of Article." *Newspaper Name.* Date [day month year]: page number including section.

Examples
Moses, Barbara. "Bad Bosses and How to Handle Them." *Globe and Mail.* 6 May 2002: C1.

De Bono, Norman. "Student Rush Boosts Real Estate." *London Free Press.* 8 May 2002: B1.

Omit volume numbers and abbreviate longer month names, as above. Editions (late edition, early edition, etc.) are included between the date and the page number.

MLA: Electronic Sources
Electronic sources follow the same basic format as print sources, with the addition of a URL (that is, a web address). However, electronic sources are often more difficult to cite than are paper sources. Below

are some main types of electronic sources, as identified in the *MLA Handbook*, and some examples of each type.

PERSONAL WEB SITES

Personal Web sites can range from simple one- or two-page home pages to fairly professionally produced sites. What makes a site personal rather than professional is that it does not belong to a business or organization. However, personal Web sites are sometimes available on institutional sites such as university sites. Citations should follow this order:

> Name of the person who created the Web site. *Title of the Site,* or Home Page. Date of last update, if given. Name of organization associated with the site, if applicable, which is rarely the case with personal pages. Date of access <URL>.

Examples

Rowat, Mitch. Home Page. 1 April 2002
<http://gs.fanshawec.ca/mrowat>.

Wellman, Michael. Home Page. 4 Jan. 2002. 1 Apr. 2002
<http://ai.eecs.umich.edu/people/wellman>.

Dunlop-Addley, Joseph. *Joseph's Website of Film Information.*
1 Apr. 2002 <http://gs.fanshawec.on.ca/Jda>.

Kartye, Travis. Home Page. 1 Apr. 2002.
<http://www.kartye.com>.

Note that the words *Home Page* are not italicized or underlined in the citation. The prefix *http://* is always included in the address; note that this is different from the style we have used in this book. Here, to save space, we have included *http://* only to designate addresses that do not contain *www*.

PROFESSIONAL WEB PAGES

Professional Web pages include those belonging to businesses, organizations, and institutions. The *MLA Handbook* suggests that professional sites be documented in the same way as personal sites; however, given the large size of many professional sites, the information required is not always enough to identify the precise location of the relevant page. Also, some professional sites keep the same basic URL wherever you go on the site, while others show search strings that would be difficult to copy. My rule is that the URL should be either the basic domain name (*www.domain.com*) or the domain name plus one more level (*www.domain.com/nextlevel/*) Other than that, there should be enough information for the reader to find the site. I also like to see one or two levels of title included in the entry.

> Author or group. *Title of Primary Web Page: Title of Secondary Web Page.* Date of last update, if given. Name of organization associated with the site. Date of access <URL>.

Examples

> Air and Waste Management Association. Air and Waste Management Association: Education Centre. Air and Waste Management Association. 1 April 2002 <http://www.awma. org/resources/education/>.

When citing an article on a professional page, add the title after the author's name:

> Author or group. "Title of Article." *Title of Primary Web Page: Title of Secondary Web Page.* Date of last update, if given. Name of organization associated with the site. Date of access <URL>.

Examples

> "Annual Reports." *Corporate Information: Investor Relations.* JDS Uniphase. 1 April 2002 <http://www.jdsu.com>.

> Meulbroek, Lisa K. "Restoring the Link Between Pay and Performance: Evaluating the Costs of Relative-Performance-Based (Indexed) Options." *Harvard Business School: Division of Research Working Papers.* Harvard Business School. 2001–2002. 1 April 2002 <http://www.hbs.edu/dor/>.

> "Ace Beverage." *Corporate News and Info.: Success Stories.* Sierra Wireless. 1 April 2002 <http://www.sierrawireless. com/Solutions/>.

Include the following information when documenting on-line periodicals:

> Author's Name. "Title." *Name of Periodical.* Volume or issue number. Date of publication. Number of pages or paragraphs, if known. Date of access <URL>.

Examples

> Foss, Krista. "Freedom Far off, Retirement Study Finds." *Globe and Mail.* 15 December 2001. 6 para. 1 April 2002 <http://www.globeandmail.com>.

> Falciglia, Ronny. "I Lied About Making $800,000 Working from Home ... And So Can You." 1 May 2002. 10 May 2002 <http://www.theonion.com/onion3816/working_from_home.html>.

> Ketcham, Christopher. "The Israeli 'Art Student' Mystery." *Salon.com.* 7 May 2002. 10 May 2002 <http://www.salon.com/news/feature/2002/05/07/students/index_np.html>.

> Tham, Irene. "Gadget Converts Woofs into Words." *Cnet News.com.* 10 May 2002. 10 May 2002 <http://news.com.com>.

The "Gadget" example is taken from a newswire (a service that sends up-to-the-minute news to the media), and yes, there *are* supposed to be two "dot coms" in the URL.

ARTICLES IN DATABASES

Articles in databases often need to be retrieved through a search. When including the URL in the citation, take the reader to the search site of the database, or as close as you can. Don't include a search string (something that looks like this: *search?q=search+movie&hl=en&meta*) in the citation because it is almost impossible to type accurately—even if the search is still valid, which it frequently is not. If the URL displayed when you find the article is *not* a search string, then include it in the address.

Author or group. "Article Title." Publication date, if given. Name
of database. Version number of database, if applicable [this
may be a year]. Date of access <URL>.

Examples

Advanced Education and Labour. "Technology and Literacy
Report." July 1996. National Adult Literacy Database. 1 April,
2002 <http://www.nald.ca/fulltext/fullttext.htm>.

"Olympic Games." *The Canadian Encyclopedia.* 2000. Historica. 1
April 2002 <http://www.histori.ca/historica/eng_site/
index.html>.

Note how it was necessary to break the URL in the second entry above.
The *MLA Handbook* suggests that you insert a space to break the URL,
so the full URL does not move to the next line. I suggest, as well, that
you always break a URL after a slash.

ARTICLES RETRIEVED THROUGH SUBSCRIPTION SERVICES OR LIBRARY DATABASES

Subscription services fall into two categories: 1. databases such as
Electric Library, ProQuest and EBSCO, available through school and
public libraries, that allow you to retrieve previously published articles; and 2. services such as America Online (AOL) and CompuServe,
from which you can retrieve information and articles not published in
magazines or newspapers. Encyclopedias may also be considered in
this latter category, depending on whether or not they are accessed by
subscription. The on-line version of *Encyclopædia Britannica*
(*www.britannica.com*), for example, recently changed to a subscription
service. The *MLA Handbook* suggests that if the URL of the service is
not known, and the article is retrieved by using a keyword, the keyword should be included in the citation.

For a database of previously published articles, cite in this format:

Author's name, if known. "Title of Article." *Title of Journal.* Name
of subscription service. Version number or year of service.
Organization or library where service was found. Date of
access <URL of database>.

Scrivener, Leslie. "Take This Job and Love It." *Toronto Star*. Electric Library. London Public Library, London, Ontario. 1 April 2002 <http://www.elibrary.com>.

ARTICLES FROM ONLINE GOVERNMENT PUBLICATIONS

Electronic government publications are documented in the same as the paper versions, with the addition of the URL:

Author or government agency that issued the document. "Title of Article." Title of Publication. Place of publication: Publisher, date of publication <URL>.

Example

Canadian Heritage. "Patriotic Songs." *Canadian Symbols*. Ottawa: Canadian Heritage, 10 May 2002 <http://www.pch.gc.ca/ceremonial-symb/english/emb_songs.html>.

MLA: In-Text Citations

In MLA style, when quoting from a secondary source you must place parenthetical documentation immediately after the quotation (whether direct or indirect), and then list details of the source in a list of works cited. The references in the text must match the works cited list, and vice versa.

The parenthetical reference usually consists of the author's last name and the page number where the information can be found. However, if the author's name is mentioned in the text, only the page number is placed in parentheses. If two works by the same author have been mentioned in an essay, or if no author is given, then the title of the article or book should be placed in parentheses with the page number. Longer titles may be abbreviated. The parenthetical reference should be as close to the quotation as possible without interrupting the flow of the writing.

The examples below cite a quotation from page 44 of Sherry Cooper's book *Ride the Wave: Take Control in the Acceleration Age*, published in 2001 by Prentice Hall.

In her book Ride the Wave: Take Control in the Acceleration Age, Sherry Cooper notes that "[i]ncreasingly, financial institutions are expected to be at the cutting edge of technology, while at the same time providing unmatched customer service" (44).

or

Sherry Cooper, Global Economic Strategist for the Bank of Montreal, believes that banks "are expected to be at the cutting edge of technology" (Ride the Wave 44) and yet still maintain good customer service.

(Note: This example assumes you have used more than one work by Cooper.)

or

An economist for the Bank of Montreal believes that financial institutions "are expected to be at the cutting edge of technology, while at the same time providing unmatched customer service" (Cooper 44).

When the source referenced is electronic, the format is the same as for print. The author's name is used, and if no author is available, the title of the article or Web page is given. Some on-line journals number paragraphs, in which case the parenthetical reference can include the paragraph number. Chapter or section number may used in the parenthetical documentation if available. Most business journals or professional Web sites do not follow the practice of numbering paragraphs. The best way to reference electronic sources is probably by including details in the text. Do *not* use URLs in parenthetical documentation. Use whatever comes first in the works cited listing.

The examples below cite an article from the Nua Web site (*www.nua.com*), an on-line source for Internet demographics and trends. The Web site has a free e-mail newsletter and a database of short pieces, taken from other sites, about various trends. The newsletter article cited has an author, but the short article from the database does not. Subsequently, in the database article a short version of the title is given in parentheses.

An article on Nua, an on-line Internet demographics Web site, quotes a January 29, 2002 report from IDC Research: "As mobile billing and payment becomes more sophisticated after 2003, consumers will also use their phone to pay bills, buy tickets for entertainment, and to pay parking meters and vending machines" ("Travel to Lead...").

or

IDC Research reports that mobile phone users will find new uses for their phones in the next two years ("Travel to Lead...").

If you have any difficulty with referencing Internet sources, the easiest solution is to mention the site in your text.

APA-Style Documentation

The American Psychological Association (APA) style of documentation is similar to the MLA style. A list of all sources used in the report or essay is placed at the end of the document on a separate page, and is entitled "References." Each source appearing in the essay or report must appear in the reference list. A list that includes works not used in the text is called a bibliography.

The reference list is double-spaced. The first line of each entry is placed flush to the left margin, and all subsequent lines of the entry indented "a few spaces" to the right—a hanging indent (most word processing packages default to a half-inch hanging indent). Book and journal titles are italicized. Only the first word of book titles is capitalized, although periodical (journal, magazine and newspaper) names are all capitalized.

The reference list is alphabetized according to the author's last name, which comes before the initial. If several authors are named in one entry, all the authors' last names are followed by the initials and the entry is placed alphabetically by the first author's last name.

APA: Print Sources

BOOKS

Author's name. (Year of Publication). *Book title.* Place of publication: Publisher.

Examples

Cooper, S. (2001). *Ride the wave: Take control in the acceleration age.* London: Prentice Hall.

Tapscott, D. (1998). *Growing up digital: The rise of the net generation.* New York: McGraw Hill.

ARTICLES IN JOURNALS AND MAGAZINES

Author's name. (Year, plus month and day of publication for weekly, biweekly, or monthly publications). Title of article. *Title of Magazine, volume number,* pages.

Note that when a volume number is included, the pages are given as numbers only, but when volume number is absent, the page numbers are preceded by *pp.*

Examples

Scott, S. (December, 2000). The accidental moguls. *ROB Magazine,* pp. 56–64.

Reguly, E. (2002, Feb. 18). A trend you can't buck. *Time Canada, 27,* 21.

Freed, L. (2001, June 12). No more letter bombs. *PC Magazine, 20,* 148–155.

Note that both the periodical title and the volume number are italicized and that the word *volume* or *vol* is not used, just the number.

ARTICLES IN NEWSPAPERS

Author's name. (Year, month and day of publication). Title of article. *Title of Newspaper, volume number,* pages.

Examples

Harris, M. (2001, Jan. 13). On the trail of the mother of all biker gangs. *Ottawa Citizen,* p. A4.

Arrison, S. (1999, May 24). Trying to package a unique Canadian identity. *Toronto Star,* pp. C4, C8.

APA: Electronic Sources

Generally, APA format is easier than MLA style to use with electronic sources.

The APA Web site (*www.apastyle.org*) gives two important principles for documenting electronic resources:

1. Direct readers as closely as possible to the information being cited; whenever possible, reference specific documents rather than home or menu pages.
2. Provide addresses that work.

ARTICLE IN AN INTERNET-ONLY JOURNAL

As yet, there are not many journals or magazines that exist only on the Internet. However, this is likely to change. Here is how to document them in APA style. Note that web addresses do not take a period at the end (this is to avoid the possibility of someone thinking a period is part of the actual URL).

> Author, A. A., & Author, B. B. (Date of publication). Title of article. *Title of Journal, volume number.* Retrieved month day, year, from http://web address

Examples

> Appelbaum, A. (1990, March 1). Beyond the bottom line. *Salon: Salon Ivory Tower.* Retrieved April 1, 2002, from http://www.salon.com/it/feature/1999/03/01feature2.html

INTERNET ARTICLES BASED ON A PRINT SOURCE

If you view an article electronically that is also available in print form, the reference should follow this format:

> Author, A. A., & Author, B. B. (Date). Article title [Electronic version]. *Journal or Newspaper Title, volume number,* page numbers if given.

Examples

> Robin, R. (2001, September 3). He likes to watch [Electronic version]. *Canadian Business,* pp. 23–24.

> Foss, K. (2001, December 15). Freedom far off, retirement study finds [Electronic version]. *Globe and Mail,* p. A3.

APA suggests that you include retrieval details and the URL only if you have reason to believe that the electronic version is different from the paper version.

NONPERIODICAL INTERNET DOCUMENT

Nonperiodical on-line documents might include a Web page or a report, and should be referenced as follows:

> Author, A. A., & Author, B. B. (Date of publication). *Title of article.* Retrieved month day, year, from http://web address

Example

> Chiriac, J. (n.d.). *Sigmund Freud's self-analysis.* (n.d.) Retrieved May 12, 2002, from http://www.freudfile.org/self-analysis.html

When an Internet document consists of more than one Web page, provide a URL that links to the home page or entry page for the document. If no date is available for the document, as in the example above, use the abbreviation *n.d.*

PART OF NONPERIODICAL INTERNET DOCUMENT

> Author, A. A., & Author, B. B. (Date of publication). Title of article. In *Title of book or larger document* (chapter or section number). Retrieved from http://web address

If the author of a document is not identified, begin the reference with the title of the document.

Example

> Bonus/leave options finalized. (May 7, 2002). In *Human resources and payroll: Announcements, site updates and additions.* Retrieved from http://hr.gmu.edu/announcements/

ELECTRONIC ARTICLE RETRIEVED FROM DATABASE

When referencing material from a database, follow the format appropriate to the work retrieved and add a retrieval statement that gives the date of retrieval and the proper name of the database.

Example

> Brown, M. P., Helford, M. B., & White, L. D. (2001). Role of early supervisory experience in supervisor performance. *Social Psychology, 64,* 44–49. Retrieved June 22, 2002, from PsycARTICLES database.

APA: In-Text Citations

APA uses in-text citations consisting of author's name with the date in parentheses. For a direct quotation, the page number is added. When citing more than one author, as is common in the social sciences, list all the references separated by semicolons. The author can also be referred to in the text, in which case only the year need be placed in parentheses.

When citing an entire work, cite the name and year of publication.

Example

Population growth has slowed and may in fact begin to decrease in the next fifty years (Ibbitson, 2002).

Use the initial only if you are citing authors with the same last name. When you name the author in the text, cite only the year.

Example

According to John Ibbitson (2002), world population growth has slowed and may in fact begin to decrease in the next fifty years.

Specific citations of pages or chapters follow the year.

Example

According to the latest data from the United Nations Population Division, the birth rate in many countries we still think are baby-booming has fallen very near, if not below, the replacement level (Ibbitson, 2002, p. F1).

Personal letters, telephone calls and interviews that cannot be retrieved are not given in the reference list but are cited in the text.

Example

John Bryant (telephone conversation, May 9, 2002) confirmed that the population....

Parenthetical references may mention more than one work, particularly when ideas have been summarized after drawing from several sources.

Finally, according to the APA Web site: "When citing an entire Web site, it is sufficient to give the address of the site in just the text (and *not* in the reference list). For example, 'Kidspsych is a wonderful interactive web site for children (http://www.kidspsych.org).'"

THE PICK OF THE SITES

Many excellent Canadian Web sites are mentioned in this reader. Here are some of the best.

Government

The Bank of Canada: *www.bankofcanada.ca*

The Canada Foundation for Innovation: *www.innovation.ca*

Canadian Government's National Crime Prevention Centre: *www.crime-prevention.org*

Conference Board of Canada: *www.conferenceboard.ca*

Canadian Museum of Civilization: *www.civilization.ca*

Department of Foreign Affairs and International Trade: *www.dfait-maeci.gc.ca*

Foreign Affairs and International Trade Sustainable Development home page: *www.dfait-maeci.gc.ca/sustain*

Finance Canada: *www.fin.gc.ca*

Financial Action Task Force on Money Laundering: *www1.oecd.org/fatf*

Government of Canada's Canadian Identity links: *www.gc.ca/* (click on "Non-Canadians" and "Canadian Identity")

Human Resources Development Canada: *www.hrdc-drhc.gc.ca*

Industry Canada's NUANS (Newly Upgraded Automated Name Search) site: *www.nuans.com*

Justice Canada: *http://canada.justice.gc.ca*

National Research Council of Canada's Institute for Information Technology: *www.nrc.ca*

Natural Resources Canada: *www.nrcan-rncan.gc.ca/inter*

Statistics Canada: *www.statcan.ca*

StatsCan's Business Gateway: *www.businessgateway.gc.ca*

Strategis, Industry Canada's business research Web site: *http://strategis.ic.gc.ca*

Strategis' Canadian Intellectual Property Office: *http://strategis.gc.ca/sc_mrksv/cipo*

Team Canada Web site: *www.tcm-mec.gc.ca*

On-line Business Magazines and Newspapers

Canada Newswire's archive: *www.newswire.ca*

Canadian Business magazine, with a searchable database of articles: *www.canadianbusiness.com*

Canoe's financial Web site: *www.webfin.com*

Globe and Mail's ROB Magazine (Report on Business), with complete full-text articles: *www.robmagazine.com*

Marketing Magazine: www.marketingmag.ca

National Post's Financial Post, with articles dating back sixty days: *www.canada.com*

Ottawa Business Journal: www.ottawabusinessjournal. com

Profit magazine's Profit Guide: *www.profitguide.com*

Strategy, a Canadian marketing magazine: *www. strategymag.com*

Opinion Pollsters

Angus Reid Marketing Research and Public Opinion site: *www.angusreid.com*

Environics Research Web site: *http://erg.environics.net*

Pollara (includes polls on "What Canada Thinks"): *www.pollara.ca*

Workplace.ca has a huge database of surveys on work: *www.workplace.ca/survey/survey_archive.html*

Non-Government Research

Jantzi Social Index: *www.mjra-jsi.com*

Royal Bank's Workplace Research and Surveys: *www.royalbank.com/careers/workressurv/*

The Blue Book of Canadian Businesses, a database of about 6,000 companies: *www.bluebook.ca*

Canadian Policy Research Networks: *www.cprn.com/cprn.html*

Business Ethics (a Canadian resource with articles, case studies, and news): *www.businessethics.ca*

Canadian Business for Corporate Responsibility: *www.cbsr.bc.ca*

Canadian Centre for Ethics and Corporate Policy: *www.ethicscentre.com*

Canadian Institute of Stress: *www.stresscanada.org*

Catalyst, a New York- and Toronto-based organization concerned with women in business: *www.catalystwomen.org*

Watson Wyatt's Human Capital Index: *www.watsonwyatt.com*

Marketing, Branding, Naming and Trademarks

Adbusters (culture jamming, ad-busting, protesting): *www.adbusters.org*

A Hundred Monkeys, a naming and branding consultants (a very good site, not Canadian but can't be left off the list): *www.ahundredmonkeys.com*

Branding Canada Page, a personal site with links to all the best branding sites on the Web: *www.storm.ca/~dclarke/branding.html*

Interbrand (an on-line exchange and discussion forum): *www.brandchannel.com*

Metaphor Name Consultants (includes case studies and information about naming companies): *www.metaphorname.com*

Internet Evaluation

Evaluating the Quality of Information on the Internet: *www.virtualchase.com/quality/checklist.html*

CREDITS

Abramson, Ruth & Collison, M., Eggertson, L.,Guttormson, K., Williams, L. "Skills that Go to Waste" appeared in *Time Canada*, May 7, 2001. Reprinted by permission of *Time Canada*.

Arrison, Sonia. "Trying to Package a Unique Canadian Identity" appeared in the *Toronto Star*, May 24, 1999. Reprinted by permission of Sonia Arrison, Director, Center for Technology Studies (CTS), Pacific Research Institute.

Baillie, Susanne. "Steps to Global Success" as appears with "Why Canadians Can't Market". Reprinted by permission of the author.

Brethour, Patrick. "Web Spawn: The Keystroke Kids" appeared in *The Globe and Mail*, December 17, 2001. Reprinted by permission of *The Globe and Mail*.

Came, Barry. "Diamonds and Blood" appeared in *Maclean's*, July 31, 2000. Reprinted by permission of *Maclean's*.

Cernetig, Milo. "Canada Isn't Working" appeared in ROB Magazine, April 27, 2001. Reprinted by permission of *The Globe and Mail*.

Chu, Showwei. "Welcome to Canada, Please Buy Something" appeared in *Canadian Business*, April 30, 2001. Reprinted by permission of *Canadian Business*.

Clark, Andrew & Deziel, S., McClelland, S., Oh, S. "How Teens Got the Power" appeared in *Maclean's* April 22, 1999. Reprinted by permission of *Maclean's*.

Cobb, Chris, *The Ottawa Citizen*. "The Coffee Crunch" appeared in *The Ottawa Citizen*, November 25, 2001. Reprinted by permission of *The Ottawa Citizen*.

Cooper, Sherry. "Face Off" appeared in *Canadian Business*, April 30, 2001. Reprinted by permission of the author.

Davidson, Hilary. "Samaritan Inc." appeared in *Profit* May 1, 2000. Reprinted by permission of the author.

Davidson, Hilary. "Why Canadians Can't Market" appeared in *Profit*, April 1, 2001. Reprinted by permission of the author.

Doe, Peggy. "Creating a Resilient Organization" appeared in the *Canadian Business Review*, June 22, 1994. Reprinted by permission of the author. Peggy Doe is a Principal with Mercer Delta Consulting Ltd. and works with CEOs and executives in leading organizational change.

Dumayne, Brian. "Distilled Wisdom" appeared in *Fortune*, May 15, 1995. Reprinted by permission of *Fortune* and author. © 1995 Time Inc. All rights reserved.

Fearley, Fran. "Today's Lesson Brought To You By…" appeared in *Today's Parent*, October 1, 2000. Reprinted by permission of the author.

Grace, Kevin Michael. "One Nation Under Molson" appeared in *Alberta Report*, Volume 27, Issue 2. Reprinted with permission of *Alberta Report*.

Hawaleshka, Danylo. "Robot Renaissance" appeared in *Maclean's*, August 21, 2000. Reprinted by permission of *Maclean's*.

Holloway, Andy. "How the Game is Played" appeared in *Canadian Business*, April 2, 2001. Reprinted by permission of *Canadian Business*.

Ibbitson, John. "The Lonely Planet" appeared in *The Globe and Mail*, March 2, 2002. Reprinted by permission of *The Globe and Mail*.

Jones, Deborah. "The Work-Family Crunch" appeared in *Chatelaine*, April 1, 1996. Courtesy of *Chatelaine* © Rogers Media Ltd. and the author.

Kedrosky, Paul. "The Next Big Thing: Nothing" appeared in the National Post Online, November 28, 2001. Reprinted by permission of the author.

Klein, Naomi. "The Tyranny of the Brands" appeared in *The New Statesman*, February 24, 2000. Reprinted by permission of Klein Lewis Productions Ltd. Naomi Klein is an award-winning journalist and author of the international bestseller *No Logo: Taking Aim at the Brand Bullies*.

Macklem, Katherine & Intini, J. "Follow the Money" appeared in *Maclean's*, October 22, 2001. Reprinted by permission of *Maclean's*.

MacQueen, Ken. "Feeling the Pain" appeared in *Maclean's*, December 3, 2001. Reprinted by permission of *Maclean's*.

McQuaig, Linda. "Face Off" appeared in *Canadian Business*, April 30, 2001. Reprinted by permission of the author.

Moses, Barbara. "Bad Bosses." Reprinted by permission of the author.

Newman, Jennifer & Grigg, D. "Labour Researchers Define Job Satisfaction." Republished by permission of Newman & Grigg Psychological and Consulting Services. Dr. Jennifer Newman and Dr. Darryl Grigg are registered psychologists and directors of Newman & Grigg Psychological and Consulting Services, a Vancouver-based corporate training and development partnership.

Newman, Peter C. "A Land of Excellence" appeared in *Maclean's*, January 7, 2000. Reprinted by permission of *Maclean's*.

Nikiforuk, Andrew. "When Water Kills" appeared in *Maclean's*, December 6, 2000. Reprinted by permission of Andrew Niforuk, a Calgary-based freelance journalist.

"Opening Our Eyes to Immigration" appeared in *Time Canada*, May 7, 2001. Reprinted by permission of *Time Canada*.

Pearson, Kali. "Teacher's Pets" as appears with "Why Canadians Can't Market." Reprinted by permission of the author.

Reguly, Robert "When Pros Become Cons" appeared in *Canadian Business*, October 1992. Reprinted by permission of the author.

Renzetti, Elizabeth. "The Game of the Name" appeared in *ROB Magazine*, August 31, 2000. Reprinted by permission of the author. Elizabeth Renzetti is a journalist in Toronto.

Robin, Raizel. "The Big Bet" appeared in *Canadian Business*, June 25, 2001. Reprinted by permission of *Canadian Business*.

Robin, Raizel. "He Likes to Watch" appeared in *Canadian Business*, March 9, 2001. Reprinted by permission of *Canadian Business*.

Schachter, Harvey. "Battle Wary" appeared in *Chatelaine* July 1, 1997. Courtesy of *Chatelaine* © Rogers Media Ltd. and author.

Scott, Sarah. "The Accidental Moguls" appeared in *ROB Magazine*, November 24, 2000. Reprinted by permission of the author. Sarah Scott is a Toronto magazine writer.

Seymour, Rhea. "Ms versus Mr." appeared in *Profit*, December 1, 2000. Reprinted by permission of the author.

Smith, Michael. "Food Fright" appeared in *ROB Magazine*, October 29, 1999. Reprinted by permission of the author.

Smith, Michael. "Tomorrow's Body Shop" appeared in *ROB Magazine*, December 29, 2000. Reprinted by permission of the author.

Sterling, Bruce. "Will Cybercriminals Run the World?" appeared in *Time Canada*, June 19, 2000. Reprinted by permission of *Time Canada*.

Taylor, Christine. "Building a Business Case for Diversity" appeared in *Canadian Business Review*, March 22, 1995. Reprinted by permission of the Conference Board of Canada.

Thompson, Clive. "Hey Wassup? Nothin'" appeared in *ROB Magazine*, December 29, 2000. Reprinted by permission of Featurewell.com.

Yakabuski, Konrad. "Arch Enemy" appeared in *ROB Magazine*, August 31, 2001. Reprinted by permission of *The Globe and Mail*.

Vlessides, Michael. "Licence to Whale" appeared in *Canadian Geographic*, January 11, 1998. Reprinted by permission of the author. Freelance journalist Michael Vlessides currently lives in Canmore, Alberta.

INDEX OF AUTHORS